The Calligraphic State

Comparative Studies on Muslim Societies
General Editor, Barbara D. Metcalf

The Calligraphic State

Textual Domination and History in a Muslim Society

Brinkley Messick

UNIVERSITY OF CALIFORNIA PRESS
Berkeley   Los Angeles   London

This book is a print-on-demand volume. It is manufactured using toner in place of ink. Type and images may be less sharp than the same material seen in traditionally printed University of California Press editions.

University of California Press
Berkeley and Los Angeles, California

University of California Press, Ltd.
London, England

Copyright © 1993 by
The Regents of the University of California

First Paperback Printing 1996

Library of Congress Cataloging-in-Publication Data
Messick, Brinkley Morris.
    The calligraphic state: textual domination and history in a
Muslim society / Brinkley Messick.
        p.   cm.—(Comparative studies on Muslim societies; 16)
    Includes bibliographical references and index.
    ISBN 0-520-20515-4 (pbk : alk. paper)
    1. Islam—Yemen.   2. Manuscripts, Arabic—Yemen—Public opinion.
3. Islamic law—Yemen.   4. Yemen—Civilization—20th century.
5. Diplomatics, Arabic—Yemen—History.   6. Public opinion—Yemen.
I. Title.   II. Series.
BP63.Y45M47   1992
297′.1975—dc20   91-44118
                                                                       CIP

Printed in the United States of America

The paper used in this publication meets the minimum requirements of
ANSI/NISO Z39.48-1992 (R 1997) (Permanence of Paper). ∞

*To My Mother and the
Memory of My Father*

CONTENTS

CONTENTS

ILLUSTRATIONS

ACKNOWLEDGMENTS

Funding for two periods of research in Yemen was provided by a Foreign Area Fellowship (September 1974 to March 1976) and a post-doctoral grant (January to June 1980), both from the Joint Committee on the Near and Middle East of the Social Science Research Council and the American Council of Learned Societies.

Of the numerous officials and friends who made research in Yemen possible I would especially like to thank former Prime Minister 'Abd al-'Aziz 'Abd al-Ghani and former Director of Antiquities Isma'il al-Akwa'; former Ibb Governor Hamud Baydr; Ibb judges Ahmad Muhammad al-Haddad, Muhammad al-Wahhabi, and Yahya al-'Ansi; scholars Muhammad b. 'Ali al-Akwa', Ahmad al-Basir, Qasim Shuja' al-Din, Muhammad Yahya al-Haddad, Muhammad 'Ali al-Ghurbani, and Ahmad 'Ali al-Rashdi; and 'Ali Isma'il Basalama, Ahmad 'Ali Sabahi, 'Abd al-Karim al-Akwa', Ahmad 'Abd al-Karim al-Akwa', Qasim al-Mansub, Hajj 'Ali 'Aziz, 'Azzi Fahmi Sabahi, Muhammad b. Muhammad al-Ghurbani, Muhammad Zain al-'Awdi, Naji al-'Ubahi, Muhammad 'Abduh Mus'id, Muhammad 'Abd al-Jalil Sabahi, Isma'il 'Abd al-Qadir Basalama, Muhammad Lutf Sabahi, Hamud al-'Awadi, and 'Abd al-Baqi al-Mansub.

Among the many other individuals who helped me along the way, I want to mention my teachers, Schuyler Cammann, L. Carl Brown, Avram Udovitch, and especially Hildred Geertz; Lawrence Rosen and Dale Eickelman; fellow scholars concerned with Yemen, John Kennedy, Etienne Renaud, Paul Dresch, Martha Mundy, Jon Mandaville, Daniel Varisco, Najwa Adra, Shelagh Weir, Robert Burrowes, Tomas Gerholm, Jon Swanson, Jeffery Meissner, and Lucine

Taminian; Amherst Law Seminar colleagues John Brigham, Patricia Ewick, Christine Harrington, Sally Merry, Ron Pipkin, Austin Sarat, Susan Silbey, Adelaide Villmoare, and Barbara Yngvesson; two very helpful readers for the University of California Press; and anthropology students and faculty at the University of Massachusetts (Amherst) and Brandeis University.

Special debts are owed to Margaretta Sander, who accompanied me on both trips to Yemen, and to Robert Tyler Sander-Messick, who made the second trip at six months of age. From the inception of this book, and as her own work on Morocco evolved, Stefania Pandolfo provided invaluable intellectual support. Parts of the work date to a period, in 1983–84, of regular interchanges with Timothy Mitchell, who had begun his own important work on related issues in Egypt. At a late stage, historian of Islamic law David Powers generously read and suggested revisions for the entire manuscript. Reading and rereading difficult passages over many months, Karen Seeley has patiently helped me bring the work to completion.

None of these individuals is responsible for any of the remaining deficiencies.

Parts of Chapters 7, 8, and 11 have appeared previously in Messick 1986, 1988, 1989, 1990.

I am grateful to Robin Page of Jenkins and Page, New York, for preparing the map of Yemen and the diagram of the spiral text.

Introduction

This book examines the changing relation between writing and authority in a Muslim society. Its backdrop is the end of an era of reed pens and personal seals, of handwritten books and professional copyists, of lesson circles in mosques and knowledge recited from memory, of court judgments on lengthy scrolls and scribes toiling behind slant-topped desks. As understood here, the calligraphic state was both a political entity and a discursive condition. My aims are to reconstruct one such textual polity and detail its gradual transformation in recent times. In highland Yemen, located in the southwestern corner of the Arabian Peninsula, the initial inroads of the printing press, new-method schools, and novel conceptions about the state and its texts date to the late nineteenth century, but many aspects of the venerable local manuscript culture persisted well into the twentieth.

Textual domination, in this analysis, entails the interlocking of a polity, a social order, and a discursive formation. I focus attention on a number of discursive features, particularly modes of authoritative expression, that are shared by several categories of texts and built into the practices of a number of important institutions. I trace connections between the literary processes behind the constitution of authority *in* texts and the social and political processes involved in articulating the authority *of* texts. For all its complexity, however, textual domination is a partial phenomenon, one that intersects in each historical instance with other dimensions of authority and with the relations of a specific mode of production. In the case at hand, neither the patrimonial-bureaucratic aspects of state authority nor the agrarian context of the associated production system are given the full treatment they deserve.

While it is perhaps well understood that complex Asiatic states, from the hydraulic (Wittfogel 1957) to the theatric (Geertz 1980), have derived legitimacy and exercised control by means of various types of written texts, precisely how they have done so in particular settings is not. From the formal interpretation of sacred scriptures to the mundane recording of administrative acts, textual relations have underpinned diverse polities. To investigate the role of texts in a specific state, however, requires a view of writing that stresses its cultural and historical variability rather than its universal characteristics, and its implication in relations of domination rather than its neutrality or transparency as a medium.

This inquiry differs from a standard political history with respect to its categories, chronologies, and choices of significant institutional sites. As is indicated by the compounds (textual authority, textual domination) I use to qualify Max Weber's familiar terminology, this is partly the consequence of narrowing a project that he elaborated. Other differences derive from extending a type of analysis developed by Michel Foucault (1970; 1977) to a non-Western setting. While Foucault's studies of shifts in "epistemological space" in the West must be adapted to the currents of a different history, his detailed investigations of the "small acts" and the "micro-physics" of disciplinary power assimilate readily to ethnographic method. Both Foucault and Benedict Anderson (1983) suggest new ways anthropologists and historians can read texts for their changing "rules of formation." I have drawn on Anderson's path-breaking analysis of the print foundations of that relatively recent type of "imagined community," the nation-state. My efforts to depict the calligraphic state are, in part, a response to his call to understand nationalism in relation to the "cultural systems that preceded it, out of which—as well as against which—it came into being" (1983:19).

Writing at the time of his collaboration in the 1950s with the Islamicist Gustave Von Grunebaum, Robert Redfield predicted that the then existing division of scholarly labor in research on the literate "world civilizations" would eventually yield to a convergence. He wrote that "the contextual studies of anthropologists will go forward to meet the textual studies made by historians and humanists of that same civilization" (1967 [1955]:30). For the Middle East the anticipated convergence has spawned divergent outcomes, which have been assessed by Talal Asad. At the conclusion of his review, Asad advocates a redoubling of *textual* efforts: "If one wants to write an anthropology of Islam, one should begin, as Muslims do, from the concept of a discursive tradition that includes and relates itself to the founding texts" (1986:14).

Two research activities, local-level ethnography in a provincial town and textual analysis of works of Islamic jurisprudence, have been brought together here. A distinctive feature of the resulting presentation is the juxtaposition of circumstantial detail concerning recent highland history and practice with the arguments and rationales of formal Muslim scholarship. Such juxtapositions raise several questions. While the principal texts referred to have been important in the highlands for centuries, they are with one exception neither indigenous nor specific to Yemen, having enjoyed equivalent esteem in places as different from the highlands as Egypt and Indonesia. Such texts have thus figured centrally in the processes of unity and diversity in interregional thought in Islam. While the book is intended to contribute to the specific history of Yemen, it also addresses textual concerns of broader civilizational and comparative relevance.

Another question concerns the nature of the formal textual thought. The specific types of text involved are basic manuals of *shari'a* jurisprudence and their commentaries. Containing concise summaries of principles intended for memorization by advanced students and for reference by practicing scholars, manuals were the representative and authoritative works of the several schools of shari'a thought. Although legal phenomena are a major concern of the following chapters, caution must be attached to the conventional gloss for the shari'a as "Islamic law." The shari'a is better characterized, to adapt a phrase from Marcel Mauss (1967:1), as a type of "total" discourse, wherein "all kinds of institutions find simultaneous expression: religious, legal, moral and economic." "Political" should be added to this list, for the shari'a also provided the basic idiom of prenationalist political expression. For the social mainstream, the shari'a represented the core of Islamic knowledge, while the basic shari'a manuals were the standards of formal instruction. This total discourse was first modified and displaced, creating something approximating the form and separate status of Western law, as part of the larger processes that brought about the rise of nation-states. Given its former discursive range, the codifications and other, often radical changes worked upon the shari'a were fundamental to the creation of these new states, in far more than the narrow legal sense.

In treating the shari'a as the centerpiece of a societal discourse, I place emphasis on the appropriation of its idioms, the flexibility and interpretability of its constructs, and the open structure of its texts. In this manner I have moved away from an understanding framed in terms of the Western standard for law, which has obscured the shari'a's different range of social importance and its distinctive modes of interpretive dynamism. While suggesting that the discourse was considerably less ideal and rigid than has frequently been claimed, I recognize that the practical status of the shari'a has varied widely according to place and time in the Muslim world. In Yemen, the level of shari'a applicability has been comparatively high. In the twentieth-century imamate in particular, shari'a constructs provided the principal language of statecraft, shari'a manuals were studied by all advanced students, exclusive-jurisdiction shari'a courts handled both civil and criminal cases, and the shari'a tithe on agrarian production was the main source of government revenue. In addition, a spectrum of jurisprudence-anchored transactions, dispositions, and other types of relations structured undertakings ranging from commercial dealings and agrarian leases to the transmission of family estates. Not to be underestimated, however, are such important local limitations to the scope of the shari'a as the predominance of tribal custom beyond the sphere of the state and the roles of administrative and commercial custom within it.

A question remains concerning the relation of shari'a text to social practice. I devote considerable attention to fine points of doctrine in works that are in some cases many centuries old and in others, mainly contemporary shari'a-based legislation, too recent to have been fully implemented. The simple justifications for such attention are that the old manuals were considered actively authoritative by local scholars until recent decades and that the new legislation had become the law of the land. Recognizing, nevertheless, the often substantial remove of such law "on the books" from many aspects of ordinary experience, I have also examined several types of what might be termed intermediate texts. An important example is the collection of interpretive guidelines on specific doctrinal matters established for court application by ruling Yemeni imams, including those of this century. Still closer to local realities are documents and writings that pertain directly to practice. The corpus I have utilized dates mainly from the last century and a half and was obtained from private individuals and official sources in the provincial capital Ibb. These texts include complaints, nonbinding opinions, and court judgments; deeds of sale and other contracts; estate papers of several types; and various sorts of bureaucratic records. Although purely local in address, most represent documentary genres known to other Muslim societies. Such writings formed the basis for a specialized ethnography of texts, an inquiry into practice and its written representation, resulting in a genre-by-genre view of structure and change in textual authority.

Historical writing provides another perspective on the relationship between formal doctrine and local practice. I have made use of the works of a long series of distinguished Yemeni historians, beginning with Ibn Samura of the twelfth century A.D. and continuing down to such transitional figures as Zabara, al-Wasiʿi, and al-Jirafi, from the first part of the twentieth, and such contemporary scholars as Muhammad and Ismaʿil al-Akwaʿ. All these historians shared a common intellectual formation in the texts of shariʿa jurisprudence. As is true also of the shariʿa manuals and the other types of texts I have used, the histories are both sources for and objects of analysis. In particular, the important genre of biographical histories is vital for tracing the lives of individual carriers of shariʿa knowledge and for examining manifestations of the genealogical theory of intellectual transmission. In older annalistic works, I looked for structural assumptions and methods rather than dynastic chronologies, while in the first printed works, by the quasi-official historians of the present century, I read for evidences of a discursive rupture.

My approach to the on-the-ground reality of textual domination is thus twofold. In taking account of formal shariʿa doctrine and such mediating texts as imamic opinions, local documents, and highland histories, I have endeavored to balance colloquial understandings with the viewpoints of a body of knowledge not constituted as an "informant's discourse" (Bourdieu 1977:18). The unusual extent of my emphasis on the doctrinal is necessitated also by the fact that we have not yet properly understood the rationales contained: the appropriate sources, notably the shariʿa manuals and commentaries I focus on, have not been given the contextual attention they deserve. Within the doctrinal corpus, reasonings and assumptions have not been understood systemically, in terms of their widely ramifying interconnections. Far from being unmindful of the ideological nature of the intellectual world presented by the jurists and historians I have read, I maintain that the requisite first steps in understanding the power implications of a discourse are to know its constructs and arguments, to analyze its linkages across domains, and to identify its modes of situating, appropriating, and silencing the world of the dominated. If the manuals and other texts cannot be taken as unproblematic sources for the derivation of practice, they at least offer important clues to the construction of the terrain.

While in a structural sense such domains of activity as authoring, instruction, opinion giving, and notarial writing seemed to persist, in Marx's phrase, "untouched by the storm-clouds of the political sky," in another sense discursive reproduction was as decisively shaped by the presences (and absences) of states as it was by the movements of intellectual history. Reconstructing from highland history, my broad intentions are to indicate what an account of a textual polity might generally consist of while also identifying the predispositions particular to such a phenomenon in a Muslim society. As presented here, then, a textual polity entails both a conception of an authoritative text, involving structures of authorship, a method of instructional transmission, institutions of interpretation, and modes of documentary inscription, and a pattern of textual authority, which figures in state legitimacy, the communication of cultural capital, relations of social hierarchy, and the control of productive resources.

Historical materials are differently mobilized in two distinct sets of chapters. Mainly in the first set (chapters 1, 2, 4, 7, 8, 9, 11), evidence from various periods and of several categories is used to create a composite view of the calligraphic polity and discursive condition. Although based in large part on historical evidence, the picture created is nevertheless relatively timeless, as emphasis is placed on elucidating structural consistencies across the several domains of the textual polity. Interspersed in this presentation, the second set of chapters (3, 5, 6, 10, 12) is primarily devoted to a specific course of historical change in highland Yemen over the past hundred years. These two historical motives overlap, however, inasmuch as the reconstruction is close to the facts of earlier periods of Yemeni history and the specific history of recent change makes use of analytic constructs.

Chapter 1 introduces the culture of the authoritative text, taking the manuals of one school of shari'a thought as a specific instance. With the Quran as paradigm, the genealogies of textual transmission were anchored in recitation, a leitmotif of this "written law" tradition. Coupled with a distinctive emphasis on the efficacy of human presences, recitational methods recurred throughout key domains of textual practice, as is demonstrated in later chapters on instruction, court witnessing, the conduct of state affairs, and the creation of property instruments. In contrast to the theoretically self-sufficient legal codes that would eventually replace them, shari'a manuals were "open" texts, built of contending viewpoints and always necessitating interpretive elucidation. Chapter 2 extends the discussion of manuals to a second major highland school of shariʿa thought, that of the former ruling imams. An ideal imam was a commander capable of wielding the pen as well as the sword. In this century, the shariʿa politics of the imams was initially turned against the occupying Ottoman Turks and was later challenged by the emergent discourse of the nation-state.

Chapter 4, on instruction, presents the methods and rationales of transmission in Quranic schools and in advanced lesson circles. In this complex "culture of the book," the recitational reproduction of authoritative texts relied on the backgrounded services of writing, while in a coexisting textual sphere reading and writing techniques were standard. Chapter 7 concerns the division of interpretive labor between two categories of worldly interpreters. An appreciation of the activity of interpreters called *muftis* is central to an understanding of the continuing vitality of the shariʿa. Chapter 8 examines the relation between interpretation and social hierarchy as defined by the dominant shariʿa image of society. Together with various legitimations, the contradictions of shariʿa doctrine reinforced its hegemonic efficacy. Chapter 9, on the judgeship, further develops the ideal of presence as it relates to shariʿa court processes and to governmental practice under the imams. Chapter 11 investigates the use of ordinary legal documents such as contracts and deeds, and considers why their value as evidence was questioned.

While this first set of chapters reconstructs the textual polity, the second set concerns the course of recent changes. Introducing themes relevant to the analysis of discontinuities discussed throughout the book, chapter 3 examines the transformation of authoritative shariʿa texts through the process of codification. It begins with the pioneering nineteenth-century Ottoman code, considers the colonial-period contexts for such discursive shifts, and concludes with a brief account of shariʿa legislation by the Yemen Arab Republic in the late 1970s. Chapter 5, on instructional changes, opens with a contemporary Yemeni skit that looks back at the old Quranic school. It then traces the late-nineteenth-century appearance and later imamic hybridization of "new method" schools. Chapter 6, on the local advent of print culture, examines twentieth-century textual initiatives in state publishing, library reform, and official-history writing. Chapter 10 analyzes the history of court reform and concludes with another recent skit, this one critical of former judicial practices. Chapter 12 departs from a discussion (at the end of chapter 11) of how notarial practice has been changed by the intervention of the state and goes on to develop a summarizing spatial analysis. Shifts in the design of writing in genres such as letters and legal documents are related first to parallel developments in bureaucratic record keeping and in official seals, and then, by extension, to alterations in physical space and changes in the "space of knowledge."

YEMEN

The corner of Arabia bordering on the Red Sea and the Indian Ocean entered the colonial age in 1839 with the British seizure of the old port of Aden; the highlands to the north were incorporated in the Ottoman Empire in 1872. At the turn of the twentieth century, the region found itself on the periphery of two great world empires: the British, with imperial interests focused on India, and the Ottoman, with its center of gravity in the eastern Mediterranean. British control in the south would not be lifted until 1967 (with the creation of the People's Democratic Republic of Yemen), but that of the Ottomans in the north ended in 1918 with the collapse of the empire at the close of World War I. At that time, the highlands passed into the hands of the Hamid al-Din line of Zaidi imams, who ruled until the Revolution of 1962, which gave birth to the Yemen Arab Republic. Political artifacts of the colonial era, the two Yemens were finally unified on May 22, 1990, as the Republic of Yemen (map 1).

The recent political history of the highlands involves entities as different as a bureaucratic empire, a patrimonial imamate, and a nation-state republic, while a colonial enclave was active immediately to the south. Unlike the countries of North Africa and the Arab successor states to the Ottoman Empire in the central Middle East, all of which came under some form of European control, the highland portion of Yemen was independent from 1919, avoiding a direct experience of colonial rule by a Western power. Imamic rule in the years 1919–1962 meant relative isolation from the rest of the world as the inaccessible mountain topography complemented an explicit policy of keeping Yemen closed to all but the most necessary outside influences. The clear and dramatic impacts of foreign rule in much of the "Third World"—colonial architecture, colon populations, appropriations of land, foreign-owned enterprises, extensive missionary activity, impositions of Western law, colonial languages, and so forth—did not occur

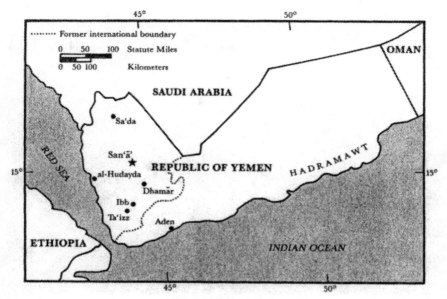

Map 1. The Republic of Yemen.

in highland Yemen. Prior to 1962 the main Western influences were mediated through Ottoman-introduced institutions or filtered northward along the trade routes from colonial Aden.

A challenge posed by this history is to understand a course of change that occurred amidst determined internal constraints and at an unusual remove from Western contacts. Despite its relative isolation, however, twentieth-century imamic Yemen was neither a medieval kingdom nor a cultural fossil "virtually unchanged," as one observer put it, "from the pre-Islamic or early Islamic period." According to now standard political histories (al-Shamahi 1972; Wenner 1967; Salim 1971; Stookey 1978; ʿAfif 1982; Peterson 1982; Douglas 1987), the traditionalism of highland society was disturbed first by the rise of a nationalist opposition, starting in the 1930s, and then later and more decisively by the actions of former military cadets trained and radicalized by foreign advisors. Without detracting from the significance of these events, this study begins by assessing earlier restructurings under Ottoman rule at the turn of the twentieth century.

Ibb town (see fig. 1), where I resided for a total of two years in the mid-1970s and at the beginning of the 1980s (Messick 1978), is located

Figure 1. Ibb ca. 1950.

in the southern highland region known as Lower Yemen (*al-yaman al-asfal*). Upper Yemen begins with the higher elevations beyond the Sumara Pass north of town. The north–south road linking the principal highland towns runs from the capital, San'a', south to Dhamar, descends into Lower Yemen at Sumara, and arrives at Ibb before continuing on to Ta'izz, the capital during the 1950s. With Dhamar, also a provincial capital, Ibb shared the rank of fourth largest urban center in the Yemen Arab Republic with a population that has grown from 17,494 at the time of the first census in 1975 to 48,806 in 1986. At one point or another in Yemeni history most of the major highland towns and some of the coastal Tihama towns served as capitals for ruling groups, but Ibb has been perennially provincial.

At 6,700 feet above sea level, the town sits on a spur of the towering Jabal Ba'dan massif and looks out over a seasonally verdant mountain valley. Stone villages dot the landscape, and here and there a few trees

Figure 2. Terraced agriculture near Ibb.

edge the cultivation, but there are no forests to soften the rugged scenery. Until recent decades, producing terraces came up to the town walls. During the dry winter months, stone retaining walls of fallow terraces mark off the undulating valley floor and step up the mountainsides like curved contour lines on a map (see fig. 2). In the wet summer, these contours are obscured as sorghum, first a brillant green and later a ripening yellow, blankets the countryside (Tutwiler and Carapico 1981; Varisco 1985). In the higher elevations of Ba'dan to the east, wheat is more common, while the lower slopes and wadi bottoms of al-'Udayn to the west specialize in two important cash crops, coffee and qat. Yemeni coffee acquired international commercial renown in the sixteenth century, but qat, the tender, alkaloid-containing leaves of which are consumed by many Yemenis on a daily basis, has retained a purely regional significance (Schopen 1978; Weir 1985; Varisco 1986; Kennedy 1987). Although there is some spring-fed irrigated cultivation, most of the local agricultural abundance is made possible by regular rains (nearly 1,500 mm mean annual). Pumped northward by the Indian Ocean monsoon system, moisture-bearing clouds begin to form over the valley about midday during the late spring and summer, providing spectacular afternoon storms.

Stored grain was the foundation of the old agrarian polity. During the fall harvest and for weeks thereafter, long lines of donkeys laden with grain earmarked as state tithes, endowment revenues, and landlords' shares still make their way up the old stone roads to Ibb. Carefully measured out and recorded, the grain is stored in numerous underground grain-storage pits located beneath houses and other buildings, and later disbursed as in-kind salaries, distributed as official charity, sold to grain traders, and directly consumed. Together with this redistributive flow of grain, long-distance trade, to which the region contributed agricultural and pastoral products, is as old as the town itself. Before the late 1950s, when the more dynamic members of the local merchant community began to move out to larger stores in a new commercial district fanning out below the main gate, Ibb's small shops, warehouses, and merchant hostels were strung along the two narrow thoroughfares that fork just inside the main gate and meet again before reaching the Great Mosque on the other side of town.

In former times (and to about 1960) Ibb was astride a major camel caravan route through the mountains, which linked the port of Aden with San'a', the principal northern highland town. Ibb was also a stopping place on an old pilgrimage route to Mecca. Foreign travelers of several centuries admired the cut stone steps with which the old road traverses the mountain passes at either end of the Ibb valley. Paved in 1975, the new main road reduced a six-day trip from Ibb to San'a' to three hours.

The capital since 1946 of a province bearing its name, Ibb was referred to as a town (*madina*) as early as the tenth century A.D., although in the immediately following centuries it was also described as a village and as a fortress. Under the rule of local dynasties in the thirteenth through the fifteenth century, the town was securely walled and endowed with such important facilities as an aqueduct, a public bath, and a number of mosques and schools. An eighteenth-century Danish traveler (Niebuhr 1792, 1:351) estimated there were eight hundred houses in the town. Closely clustered, multistoried buildings permitted a relatively large population to reside in a relatively small, walled-in space. Everything in the town, buildings, paved streets, walls, and bastions, was of locally quarried grey stone, creating an effect relieved only by the curves of whitewashed domes and the occasional tree in an intersection of alleys or in the market square. Until the 1950s, when expansion outside the walls began, the caretaker of the old main gate would call out for stragglers before locking up for the night.

PART I

Authority

CHAPTER 1

Genealogies of the Text

The theoretical descent of Roman jurisprudence from a Code, the theoretical ascription of English law to an immemorial unwritten tradition, were the chief reasons why the development of their system differed from the development of ours. Neither theory corresponded exactly with the facts, but each produced consequences of the utmost importance.

SIR HENRY MAINE

Viewed in detail, the development of the *shari'a* across the Muslim lands was a phenomenon involving specific men and specific texts. We know something about the particulars of this history because of the existence of accounts arranged in the form of biographical entries. Created by early Muslim historians, these biographical works played a crucial role in tracking the transmission of Islamic knowledge across regions and through successive generations. One such work, composed in twelfth-century Yemen, covers the early generations of Yemeni shari'a scholars. It also traces the arrival in the highlands of authoritative shari'a texts of the era, describing the specific teacher-to-student connections by which they were introduced and then diffused. A local node in one reported line of transmission was a man by the name of Faqih al-Nahi, until his death in 1171 a resident of the town of Ibb.[1] The text in question was a famous one, authored by an eminent shari'a jurist of the preceding century named al-Shirazi who lived and taught in Baghdad, an international center of Islamic learning.[2]

"Between me and the author are two men," al-Nahi of Ibb used to say to his colleagues. In this shorthand manner al-Nahi expressed the particular legitimacy of his stature as a scholar and teacher. It was a remark worthy of citation in an intellectual world in which the texts of knowledge were literally embodied, their conveyance reckoned in terms of known relayers. Authority of this sort relied upon the specification of human links between intellectual generations. Al-Nahi could explain that he had learned the text from his teacher, who had received it from an individual who had acquired it directly from al-Shirazi, in the author's Baghdad lesson circle. Then, as now, Yemeni scholars were travelers, circulating in search of teachers and knowledge not only throughout their native highlands but also northward to Mecca and beyond to Cairo, Damascus, and Baghdad. Completing his studies with al-Shirazi, the traveling scholar in question returned to reside in Yemen, where he taught the text to his own students, including a man who would later teach it to a third generation, which included al-Nahi of Ibb. Each of the two intervening scholars identified in al-Nahi's personal line of reception is the subject of a separate entry in the same biographical history.

Authoritative texts are as fundamental to the history of shari'a scholarship as they are to the history of the other intellectual disciplines. Such a text was "relied upon" in a place and time:[3] the knowledgeable consulted it, specialists based findings upon it, scholars elaborated its points in commentaries, teachers clarified its subtleties, students committed its passages to heart. Authority in a text depended on a combination of attributes both ascribed and achieved: there were the built-in features of textual ancestry and authorship as well as an acquired reputation and record of dissemination. The fates of such texts were diverse, ranging from an enduring general prominence or more limited respect among the cognoscenti to a purely ephemeral authority and the all-but-forgotten status of the superseded. Since this authority would change radically in the course of the late nineteenth and the early twentieth century, its modalities must be examined in some detail.

A primary sort of textual authority was derived:[4] it followed from the existence and importance of an original, genuine, and ultimately reliable text, which refers back to the position and identity of the Quran. "In the genealogy of texts," Edward Said writes (1983:46), "there is a first text, a sacred prototype, a scripture, which readers always approach through the text before them." A genealogy of authoritative texts in Islam must begin with a consideration of the Quran as the authoritative original. The paradigmatic, Urtext qualities of the Quran concern both content and textual form. Substantively, the Quran and the Sunna, the practice of the Prophet, constituted the two fundamental "sources" (*usul*, sing. *asl*) for the elaboration of shari'a jurisprudence. Discursively, the Quran represents both the end and the beginning of the *kitab* (text, scripture, writing, book). Just as Muhammad was the last, the "seal," of the Prophets, and also the first Muslim, the Quran was the definitive and final *kitab*, whose particular authority would initiate and delimit a discursive tradition.

A central problem in Muslim thought concerns the difficult transition from the unity and authenticity of the Text of God to the multiplicity and inherently disputed quality of the texts of men. A concurrent underlying tension was generated in shari'a scholarship where an unresolvable gulf opened between divinely constituted truth and humanly constituted versions of that truth. Purists of all eras, including many contemporary "fundamentalists," have made a distinction between the divine shari'a, defined as God's comprehensive and perfect design for His community, and a humanly produced shari'a, or, more precisely, the corpus of knowledge known as *fiqh* (usually translated "jurisprudence"), a necessarily flawed attempt to understand and implement that design. In this gap between divine plan and human understanding lay the perennially fertile space of critique, the locus of an entire politics articulated in the idiom of the shari'a.

If the transition from the divine plan to its human versions was difficult, it was also necessary, for the truth of Revelation could only be implemented through the medium of human understanding. With the death of the Prophet Muhammad in 632, the Muslim community found itself cut off both from further Quranic Revelations and from the Prophet's own practice, that is, from further elaborations of the two "sources" of secure knowledge. Thereafter, the community confronted the problems of developing a more detailed corpus of rules and procedures while continually adjusting to new social realities.

The growth of the fiqh as a body of knowledge, resulting from the work of jurists in the early centuries of Islam, brought with it the inevitable disagreements associated with purely human creativity. Authoritative fiqh works endeavored to further define the already definitive. Their derivitiveness was both necessary to their nature and the crux of their problematic: they were texts in the world of the Text. Participating with self-assurance in an authentic tradition, such texts had their recognized antecedent sources and their means of establishing legitimacy. At the same time, they pertained to history rather than to the eternal; to societies of rifts and hierarchies rather than to the ideal communitas of the *umma*; to difference rather than to certainty.

Condensed and practical fiqh manuals, known as the *mutun* (sing. *matn*, lit. "text"), were a distinct category of authoritative text. At first glance, such manuals seem to have little to recommend their consideration. Since they contain neither the elaborations of material nor the refinements of method that characterize the field as a whole, the *mutun* might be thought the least impressive works of the jurisprudence literature, their bare-bones presentations being notable mainly for feats of compression. But these handbooks took on a significance that went far beyond their modest literary qualities, and they eventually became the most widely disseminated of all shari'a texts. As instructional standards, they were influential gateways to the central academic discipline, representing for many the sum total of advanced (that is, post-Quranic-school) instruction. Particular manuals came to be symbols of the separate "schools" of shari'a thought, which in the Sunni tradition were one and the same as its principal subdivisions. Containing simple but authoritative statements of position on the range of substantive issues, manuals were studied by all educated adherents of a school at the outset of advanced instruction, and they were later referred to by scholars in their various interpretive activities. In addition, these compact works were among the typical source texts upon which the expansive commentary literatures of the fiqh were based.

Manuals appeared on the intellectual scene at a relatively late date, however. These were not the earliest works, handed down from the formative centuries of Islam, but were instead the products of a more mature, developed, and institutionally established later thought.[5] In contrast to the discourse-setting sort of originality of the foundational fiqh works, by jurists such as Malik, Abu Hanifa, al-Shafi'i, and Ibn Hanbal, for whom the four standard "schools" are named, the manuals were determinedly derivative. They offered creative synopses, in which a body of doctrinal views pertaining to a particular school was sifted, selected, and summarized. While most of the earlier classics were in the category of exhaustive (literally "long") works, manuals were examples of an "abridgment" genre that became common across the intellectual disciplines.

Manuals were similar to the long jurisprudence works in overall topic coverage but differed radically in depth of presentation. They included sections on ritual matters, such as ablutions, prayer, fasting, tithe and alms-giving, and the pilgrimage; the numerous types of contracts, transactions, and dispositions covering agrarian production, commerce, and the family; rules concerning evidence, court procedure, and punishments; and a variety of miscellaneous matters, such as hunting and dietary rules. Principles connected with the leadership of the Muslim community were covered in sections concerning the conduct of war, certain types of crimes, taxation, and the administration of justice.

The great Ibn Khaldun, who died in 1406, viewed with disapproval the routine use of such abridgments in his era.[6] They have a "corrupting influence on the process of instruction," he wrote, because they "confuse the beginner by presenting the final results of a discipline to him before he is prepared." Ibn Khaldun's general pedagogic concern was with the acquisition of a properly developed intellectual *habitus*.[7] While he believed that the "crowded" meanings of the abridgments were an obstacle to this acquisition, he deemed contact with the "repetition and lengthiness" of the long works "useful." Regardless of Ibn Khaldun's opposition, however, some manuals went on to become classics in their own right, remaining basic to the intellectual landscape for centuries, until the moment of modern changes in the nature of schooling, knowledge, and the law.

SHAFI'I TEXTS

One of four standard schools of Sunni legal interpretation, the Shafi'is take their name from the early jurist Muhammad b. Idris al-Shafi'i (died 820).[8] The word *madhhab*, conventionally translated as "school," literally means a "path," and in technical scholarly contexts the reference is to those jurists who claim intellectual descent from an eponymous jurist, in this case al-Shafi'i. In a broader, nontechnical sense, madhhab identities were a means of expressing geopolitical loyalties. In Yemen the Shafi'i school is associated with Lower Yemen, where Ibb is located, and with regions further South and East—the territory, until the unification of 1990, of the People's Democratic Republic of Yemen (South Yemen).

Prior to the tenth century, the Maliki and Hanafi schools, both developed earlier than the Shafi'i, represented the main currents of Yemeni legal thought. Although al-Shafi'i held a brief appointment (and is said to have engaged in political intrigue) in Yemen, the main centers of his teaching and later influence were Cairo and Baghdad. Ibn Samura, the historian who reported on the biography of Faqih al-Nahi, documented the advent and initial spread of Shafi'i thought in the highlands. In succeeding centuries, al-Shafi'i's intellectual descendants rose to predominance in instruction and judgeships throughout the central Middle East. With the sixteenth-century spread of the Ottoman Empire, however, the Shafi'i school was officially (but not always popularly) supplanted in most of these areas by the Hanafi school, which was favored by the Ottomans. Nevertheless, the Shafi'i school today probably has more adherents than any other in the Muslim world, its main centers other than southern Arabia being Egypt, East Africa, and populous Southeast Asia.

For many centuries now, Ibb has supported an active community of Shafi'i scholars. Despite their seemingly remote mountain valley location, town jurists were far from parochial. In terms of texts studied, theirs was not an unconventional local version of the shari'a. Beginning with Ibn Samura and continuing to the present century, biographical histories provide views of the changing scholarly community in Ibb. A recently published work (Zabara 1979) devoted to noted individuals of the just-completed (fourteenth) Hegira century contains an entry on a distinguished Ibb scholar and prominent political figure who lived from 1876 to 1922, some seven and a half centuries after Faqih al-Nahi. Like al-Nahi, 'Abd al-Rahman al-Haddad was an adherent of the Shafi'i school of shari'a jurisprudence. Both men were connected to the school through their relations with particular teachers and specific texts. In al-Haddad's case the teacher was his father, and the key text was a celebrated old manual known as *Al-Minhaj*. His biographical entry opens as follows:

> The learned scholar and man of letters, the bright and sagacious 'Abd al-Rahman, son of 'Ali, son of Naji, al-Haddad, the Shafi'i, the Yemeni, the Ibbi, was born in the town of Ibb in the year 1293 [1876] and received instruction from his father, in Shafi'i jurisprudence [beginning with] *Al-Minhaj*.[9]

Ibb scholars such as 'Abd al-Rahman al-Haddad and, in the next generation, men such as his nephew and son-in-law, Ahmad b. Muhammad al-Haddad, whom I knew in the 1970s as an old man and a practicing court judge, commenced their higher studies with two standard Shafi'i texts, the just-mentioned *Al-Minhaj* by Muhyi al-Din al-Nawawi, a Syrian who died in A.D. 1277,[10] and a still more radically concise manual, known as *Al-Mukhtasar* ("the abridgment") or simply as the *matn*, the "text," of Abu Shuja', a resident of Basra active in the twelfth century.[11]

Both were classics of the Shafi'i school widely studied beyond the boundaries of Yemen. Al-Nawawi's and Abu Shuja''s manuals are to the Shafi'i school what Khalil's well-known *Abridgment*, for example, is to the Maliki school predominant in North and West Africa. In nineteenth-century Cairo, students of Shafi'i jurisprudence at the famous al-Azhar mosque-university began with the shorter work by Abu Shuja', while *Al-Minhaj* was a principal intermediate text in the typical sequence of study.[12] At the same time, at the eastern end of the Muslim world, in Malaya and Java where the Shafi'i school was predominant, the same two texts were fundamental in both instruction and Islamic court rulings. Both were translated from Arabic into French, *Al-Mukhtasar* just after mid-century and *Al-Minhaj* two decades later. For use in British-administered colonies, including the nearby Indian Ocean port of Aden, an English translation of the French edition of *Al-Minhaj* was available by 1914.[13]

In the following two sections, I examine the recitational and open identities of the fiqh-manual genre as a means of introducing some of the main features of the core discursive tradition. I elaborate upon the paradigmatic qualities of the Quran and make comparisons with the texts of the collateral science of hadith.

RECITATION

Writing is the outlining and shaping of letters to indicate audible words which, in turn, indicate what is in the soul. It comes second after oral expression.
IBN KHALDUN

Concise fiqh manuals were explicitly designed to be memorized. The extreme brevity of Abu Shuja''s text was intended, as the author notes, to "facilitate its study for the educated and simplify its memorization for the beginning student." Referring to a larger work summarized in his manual, al-Nawawi says, "Due to its great size, many contemporaries, except for the most dedicated, are unable to memorize it, and I therefore undertook to shorten it to about half that size to simplify its memorization."

Recitation and memorization were at the foundation of Muslim pedagogy, in both literal and general methodological senses. In neighborhood Quranic schools in Ibb, as elsewhere in the Muslim world for many centuries, young children began their instructional lives by acquiring the sacred text by rote. The goal was recitation from memory, and the basic method was oral repetition, which was supported by the technology of the pupil's individual lesson-board. The passage to be learned was written on the board, and once it was memorized the writing was washed off, to be replaced by the next passage to be acquired. A similar pattern was repeated at the higher academic level, in training in the shari'a, the principal subject matter of advanced instruction. At this level Ibb students worked to memorize basic manuals, such as Abu Shuja''s *Al-Mukhtasar* and al-Nawawi's *Al-Minhaj*.

Pedagogical activity, in primary instruction as in advanced work, proceeded ideally from an initial oral recitation (or dictation) by the teacher to the listening student. The student later repeated the text segment on his own, often until memorization was achieved. Finally, returning to the teacher, the student endeavored to accurately reproduce the original recitation. Writing intervened in these procedures in facilitating the work of repetition; its role was decisive but understated. Manuscript copies were often made by advanced students in the course of study, but these were considered by-products of the learning process. Students eventually received licenses to teach, which entailed permission for *riwaya*, the "oral transmission" of a particular text or texts through recitation.

The paradigm for this was the Quran. Received orally by a Prophet who, according to doctrine, could neither read nor write,[14] the revelations contained in the Quran are considered the spoken Word of God. The textual character of the Quran is quite different from that of the Bible, or at least the Gospels, which are considered humanly authored and which constitute a "book" in a sense closer to the contemporary Western meaning. The Quran, by contrast, is a recitation-text. The Prophet was instructed by the Archangel Gabriel to "recite," and the Quran, an extended "recitation," was received by him and then orally reconveyed in this way to his companions. As the Quran circulated in the world, recitations were repeated and memorized, the text was preserved in human hearts, and, in the event, a discursive style was set in place. The Quran's written form, the physical text located "between the two covers," would always be backgrounded in relation to its emphasized recitational identity. A century ago, Snouck Hurgronje urged Western scholars "to give up the erroneous translations of Quran by 'reading,' and [the root verb] *qara'a* by 'to read.'"[15] By attending to the revealed Word and recitational (versus read) qualities of the Quran, recent scholarship has begun to revise earlier assumptions about the identity of this sacred text as a book or scripture in the conventional Western sense.[16]

If the links of recitational reproduction were crucial to the authoritative character of both teacher and transmission, they were essential as well beyond the lesson circle. Recitation (*qira'a*)[17] is the mode in which the Quran figures in ritual life, and a recitational style also structures the articulation of basic shari'a principles in legal practice. Trained jurists such as shari'a court judges did not have to refer to written versions of authoritative legal manuals any more than professional Quran reciters (or ordinary individuals in prayer) had to "read" the Quran: both recalled the text directly from memory. Memorization of at least a small portion of the Quran is essential to the performing of daily prayers, a hallmark of membership in the Muslim community. Although memorization of the whole Quran was highly valued, the minimum necessary for prayer is the brief first section known as the *fatiha*, or "opening." Unlike the restricted scholarly lineages associated with the authoritative texts of the intellectual disciplines, the "descent group" of the paradigmatic authoritative text comprised all those who identified themselves as Muslims. In contrast to this community-defining status, shariʿa scholarship passed down narrow channels, through such men as Faqih al-Nahi of Ibb.

Elements of the recitational complex were set in place early on, in dialogue with a reciprocally constituted form of "writing." A parallel to the patterned receipt and transmission of shariʿa scholarship existed in the separate but closely associated scholarly discipline of *hadith* studies. The most significant hadiths report on the words or actions of the Prophet Muhammad and are, therefore, crucial in ascertaining his *sunna*, the statements and acts that represent his authoritative practice. Like the memorized and recited Quran, the once only orally trans-mitted hadith reports were also set down in written recensions, but this occurred despite specific Prophetic orders (also in the form of hadiths) to the contrary. Those who would undertake the recording of such reports had to contend with contradictory dictums (e.g., "Abu Saʿid al-Khudri said: 'I asked the Prophet permission to write the hadith down but he refused it'"; "Do not write down anything from me except the Quran. He who has noted down anything from me apart from the Quran must erase it"; but, on the contrary, "ʿAbd Allah b. ʿAmr asked the Prophet permission to write the report down. It was granted"; and, generally, "Commit knowledge to writing").[18] Some early scholars held it was forbidden to place hadith reports in writing; others advocated memorization and cautioned about the unreliability of writing. One warned: "Strive eagerly to obtain hadiths and get them from the men themselves, not from written records, lest they be affected by the disease of corruption of the text."[19] The recording process went forward, but only after a century during which such reports were transmitted by exclusively oral means. As had occurred when the Quran was set down in a definitive written text,[20] the human interventions to preserve such reports in writing were fraught with intracommunity conflict. Collec-tions of reports of established authenticity became the foundational works in the field of hadith studies.

In Ibb such studies were integral to scholarly activity. For example,

another of the town's twelfth-century cohort of scholars was a renowned specialist in hadith, nicknamed Sayf al-Sunna ("Sword of the
Sunna").[21] In the year 1184, he traveled from Ibb to Mecca to hear the
recitation of one of the most authoritative of all hadith collections, a
work known as the *Sahih*, by Muslim b. Hajjaj (d. 875).[22] Returning
to Ibb, Sayf al-Sunna taught this text in the same recitational way he
had received it, licensing in his turn a number of regional scholars to
transmit it to their own students.

As the field of hadith scholarship developed, the essential critical
activity was to sift authentic from fabricated reports. Methodological
emphasis in this discipline was placed on the close scrutiny of the individual transmitters. Since reports were initially handed down orally,
attention was focused on the character and circumstances of the human
links in the "chain" (*isnad*) of transmission. It was said that "knowing
hadith reports means knowing the men." The reliability of a handed-
down oral report of what the Prophet had said or done depended on
the existence of an unbroken and unimpeachable series of reputable
and reliable word-of-mouth transmitters. A "science of men" (*'ilm
al-rijal*), as it was called, grew up at the center of hadith studies,
influencing also the early development of biographical histories. The
parallel orientation in the discipline of shari'a scholarship is indicated
by Faqih al-Nahi's previously cited statement that "between me and
the author are two men." In later centuries, the great length of intellectual genealogies as well as breaks in their links would contribute to local
crises of textual authority.

Both a whole fiqh manual and the one or more sentences of the
typical hadith report were referred to as a *matn*, "basic text." Manuals
and individual reports shared a kind of textuality in which writing, or
the text in its written form, was considered secondary and supplementary. The privileging of the recited word over the written text and an
associated concern with the specific connections of oral-aural transmission marked both genres of authoritative text. Paradoxically, these
distinctive attitudes grew up within the context of an encompassing
literate tradition and a thoroughgoing social reliance on writing.
Walter Ong (1982:26) has written that Muslim cultures "never fully
interiorized" writing. Both Ong and Jack Goody (1968:14) refer to
such privileging of recitational forms as "oral residues," features indicative of a "still" partly oral society. But this recitational emphasis is
perhaps better understood as a complex motif of a fully realized type of
civilizational literacy. Muslim societies elaborated diverse, historically

specific textual worlds, central elements of which were their particular understandings, and relative valuings, of the recited and the written. It is only with the application of Western-modeled yardsticks for complex forms of literacy and for universal (evolutionary) routes of oral-to-written shifts that cases such as the Muslim one can be made to appear incomplete, marked by residuals, or stalled in development.

One version of the divine-to-human transition was in the specific relation, and movement, of recited word to written text. Although there are major differences in structure and history, the associated Muslim attitude toward writing may be initially compared to one Derrida (1974) has detected in the Western tradition, beginning with Plato and continuing down to such figures as Rousseau and Saussure. According to Derrida, concrete writing has been consistently denigrated while a metaphorical writing, a kind of natural or divine inscription associated with the spirit, the voice, and speech has been extolled. In relation to this primacy of the spoken word, concrete writing was considered exterior instead of interior, human instead of divine, and artificial rather than natural. Consonant with the central Western metaphysical concern for "presence," speech was deemed the valued locus of truth, the means of direct voicing of the spirit, and, for Saussure, the proper focus of scientific linguistics. Writing—secondary, representational, supplementary—was frequently condemned as evil or contaminating. As such philosophical, theological, and theoretical positions were taken, however, it was concrete or "fallen writing" that was the consistent medium of intellectual discourse.

In Muslim societies, a culturally specific logocentrism, as Derrida terms this privileging of the spoken word, has had widespread institutional implications, many of which are connected to the recitational cast of the basic texts. In its varied forms, recitation purported to convey an authoritative genuineness of expression by replicating an originally voiced presence. Recitational logocentrism went hand in hand with a concern about the problem of authorial absence in certain written texts. While recitation was thought to maintain a reliable constancy of meaning, the secondary medium of writing was seen as harboring a prospect of misinterpretation. "Once a thing is put into writing," as Plato has Socrates say in the *Phaedrus* (1952:158), "the composition, whatever it may be, drifts all over the place." Extending the authority-giving presence of an original author to other places and times would be the work not only of recitational devices but also of writing. In written form, however, the general misreadability of the medium was dangerously extended by the open potentiality of the texts themselves. An author's voice, and thus his presence and his truth, could be securely recovered only through the technique of recitation.

All this was especially crucial in connection with the sacred text and similarly treated authoritative texts, including fiqh manuals and hadith reports, which partook of the privileged quality of the recited word. When textual authority, involving the restoration of an original voiced presence, was at stake, recourse was had to the faithful recitational reproduction, directly from memory or, secondarily, by reading the *matn* in question aloud. According to al-Shafi'i, an authoritative relayer of hadith should be "capable of transmitting the hadith letter for letter [*bi-hurufihi*] as he heard it." Relaying a report in the form of its gist or paraphrased meaning was unacceptable and dangerous: "If he transmits only the meaning and is unaware of what might alter its sense, he might unknowingly transmute the lawful into the unlawful and vice-versa." Al-Shafi'i concludes that if a relayer "transmits letter for letter there remains no ground for fearing a change of the meaning."[23]

Recitational mechanics began at the alphabetic level. Much has been made of the supposed consequences of alphabet differences, especially the contrast between the "absence" of vowels in the Semitic languages and their presence, in the form of alphabetic letters, in languages such as the Greek. A tendency to focus on comparative civilizational advantage has obscured contextual consideration of how particular non-Western alphabets related to the systems of which they were a part.[24] As it usually appears on the page, Arabic script consists of strings of unvoweled consonants. The act of voweling, whether by marking in the vowel signs over and under the consonantal string or by voicing them in recitation, is an interpretive act, lending the script a particular significance in the process. This is important because written texts often allow alternative vowelings.[25] While script preserves a string of consonants, recitation unites consonants and vowels, enabling the production and reproduction of a whole. Given the nature of its script conventions, there is an identifiable physical loss in "reducing" something in Arabic to writing. In comparison with a fully vocalized "word," a written text can be considered an incomplete consonantal fragment. Preserved in its voweled-consonant recitational form, by contrast, a memorized text is one that has been embodied complete.

Versification was often mobilized to enhance the mnemonic accessibility of basic texts. Further accentuating an already predominant recitational design, repetitions of what Jakobson called a "figure of sound" facilitated the task of memorization while evoking the much admired oral declamations of the poets. The versification of scholarly texts presented the compositional challenge of compactly presenting complex matters, complicated by adherence to a set rhyme scheme. Many authoritative texts in jurisprudence and in other fields were composed and studied in verse form. Two of the basic texts used in turn-of-the-century Ibb, for example, one in hadith and the other in grammar, were compositions of a thousand verses each, and were thus known, with their respective author's names, as "al-Suyuti's Thousand" and "Ibn Malik's Thousand."[26] Earlier on, Shafi'i scholars in Ibb had relied on a verse-text jurisprudential manual by Ibn al-Wardi.[27] In several formal genre categories,[28] verse has long represented a principal channel for the assertion of scholarly views and rebuttal, as well as for the display of erudition and ingenuity.[29] Since they intimately and succinctly convey character and personal attitudes, verse excerpts also abound in biographical dictionary entries.

Composition could also be recitational, although this was typical only for the taught subset of the literary corpus. Al-Shafi'i's own works, including his famous *Risala*, are an example. Such works were constituted in the teaching circle. As al-Shafi'i dictated his leading pupils took down his spoken words in writing. He would later correct the text when it was read aloud in his presence.[30] An origin in recitation confirmed an authorial presence and thereby enhanced the authority of the work. Additionally, the *Risala* takes the form of a discussion, with questions by an anonymous interlocutor and answers given by al-Shafi'i. In this respect, the *Risala* resembles nothing so much as the Platonic dialogues. This dialogic, question-and-answer format occurs in many treatises constructed either in the form of a scholarly disputation or as queries posed to an authoritative interpreter.

A Yemeni example of recitational composition is a work by a former ruling imam who was deposed and in prison. This work, the basic jurisprudence manual of the shortly to be discussed Zaidi school, was, like *Al-Mukhtasar* and *Al-Minhaj* of the Shafi'is, designed for memorization. The imam taught it orally to a fellow prisoner who, upon release, had a written text prepared.[31] In terms of its framing, however, the imam's manual is different from al-Shafi'i's *Risala*. Like other manual texts, it was explicitly intended for oral instruction and memorization, but rather than presenting a quasi-modeling of direct speech, it is condensed and formulaic. In the Zaidi manual, the author's intention is preserved, not by a compositional format recalling an original interchange, but by a determined concision that facilitates the memorized acquisition of the fullness of his words.

This authoring in the lesson medium seems comparable to the situation in medieval England where "dictating was the usual form of literary composition" and where the individual activity of composition could be experienced as dictating to oneself (Clanchy 1979:219). But the comparison is deceptive, for the English case is one taken from the cusp of a particular historical transition to what Ong (1982:95) calls "high literacy," in which an author "puts his or her words together on paper." The Middle Eastern examples, however, pertain to another history, governed by specific cultural assumptions about the inscribing of authorial presence in recitational media. They also concern only one segment of a literate system that, in other sectors, already exhibited the compositional features of "high literacy."

A prominent feature of the intellectual and institutional landscape of Islam, the recitational complex was, at the same time, far from comprehensive. Recitational emphases mainly concerned certain core subjects, such as shariʿa jurisprudence and supporting fields, which were also the instructional mainstays of the old curriculum; within these subjects, recitational structuring was especially relevant at the level of the fundamental texts. Beyond these core subjects, there were important recitational influences, but there were also intellectual fields (medicine, history, philosophy, etc.) and other domains of activity where reading and writing predominated relatively unfettered by recitational concerns.[32] Qualification must also extend, however, to the place of recitation within its principal strongholds, the core subjects and the authoritative texts. There, a foregrounded recitational construction of the transmission processes, an ideological emphasis on recitation, audition, and memorization, must be weighed against the evidently important, but consistently underplayed roles of the techniques of reading and writing.[33]

A sectoral supervaluation of recited texts also did not rule out a comfortable general relation with written texts. The coexistence of recitational forms and their written versions was taken for granted. An early exemplification of this is found in further comments by al-Shafiʿi concerning his inclusion of numerous hadiths in his famous *Risala*: "I did not want to cite reports that I had not fully memorized, and I have lost some of my books, but I have verified the accuracy of what I memorized by checking it with the knowledge of scholars."[34] In another passage he establishes basic principles regarding memorization and written sources. An authoritative relayer "should have learned the report by heart, if he relates it from memory, and should have memorized the written text if he relates it from its written form."[35] As the importance of memorized retention is repeatedly stressed, an interdependence with writings is consistently recognized.

In Yemen, as elsewhere in the Muslim world, there was a flourishing culture of the book, expressed in such activities as library keeping, the calligraphic arts, bookbinding and selling, and manuscript copying.[36] Some scholars made a personal practice or profession of copying books. One such Ibb copyist, who "copied in his own hand numerous books and . . . wrote lines of his own poetry on each of them,"[37] had studied calligraphy (*khatt*), among other subjects, with the town's noted early hadith specialist Sayf al-Sunna. Another is said to have wanted to make a copy of a well-known book by al-Ghazzali, but lacked gallnuts, the standard ingredient in one type of ink. He used instead the wood of a locally abundant tree and composed lines of poetry to the effect that in the Ibb region, because of the availability of that particular species, one's work need never be interrupted by the lack of conventional ink (Ibn Samura 1957:193).

While authoring was a phenomenon of the *qawl*, an individual's "word" or "voiced opinion," copying was one of the *yad*, the "hand" or "handwritten script." Manuscript copies conclude with appended statements, "in the hand of so-and-so," which identify the copyist. The relation of *qawl* to *yad*, of voiced word to handwritten script, is another variant of the basic relation of original to supplement. Within the sphere of the written supplement, however, there were conventions to establish the relative authority of the versions. A familiar patterning was reproduced: copies had their own sort of genealogy. Most authoritative, as might be expected, was the autograph, a manuscript copied out in the hand of the author. In such cases *qawl* and *yad* came as close to convergence as possible. Otherwise, in the ordinary activity of manuscript copying, there was an important distinction between the written "original" (*asl*) and the written "copy" (*nuskha*). This relation of original and copy, internal to the written realm of manuscripts, suggests a replication there of the wider opposition of basic text to supplement. When a copy was completed it could be vested with authority through careful comparison with the original (a collation procedure referred to as *muqabala bil-asl*, "comparison/encounter with the original"). This was the work of two men, present to each other, involving an activity exactly parallel to the recitation (dictation) and audition of the teacher-student lesson interchange.[38] In this manner the copy could take on the authority of the original and become, in turn, an *asl* (a source text) with respect to copies made from it. That authoritative copy making closely followed the structural pattern of authoritative knowledge transmission illustrates the reach of recitational models beyond the sphere of the core pedagogy.

OPEN TEXTS

> *There can be no commentary unless, below the language one is reading and deciphering, there runs the sovereignty of an original Text. And it is this text which, by providing the foundation for the commentary, offers its ultimate revelation as the promised reward of commentary. The necessary proliferation of the exegesis is therefore measured, ideally limited, and yet ceaselessly animated, by this silent dominion.*
>
> M. FOUCAULT, *THE ORDER OF THINGS*

An additional set of attitudes surrounding authoritative texts may also be introduced with reference to instructional methods. As a second and integral part of the standard lesson, an initial recitation by the teacher of a segment of a *matn*, or basic text, was followed and complemented by his elucidating commentary, his *sharh*. This *matn/sharh*, text/commentary relationship was a fundamental one. In the pedagogical format, the relation of basic text to expansive commentary was also one of recitation meant for memorization to supplementary interpretation meant for nonmemorized understanding. While students would endeavor to acquire the *matn* by heart, this technique would not be applied to the *sharh*. The *sharh* served the subordinate role of informing a student's comprehension of the principal focus of instruction, which was the *matn*. The text/commentary relationship was crucial also to the format of books. The written literature of shari'a jurisprudence, for example, developed largely by means of interpretive elaborations on basic texts.

Radically compact expression in *matns* both facilitated the memorization of essential formulae and absolutely required interpretive commentary to clarify the "crowded" meanings. Standing alone, abbreviated *matns* are often only barely comprehensible, since they are composed in a kind of stripped-down, subconventional prose in which many of the connecting words and phrases of ordinary discourse are elided. A minimal accomplishment of a *sharh*, in the oral lesson as in written composition, was the filling in of such rudimentary connections.

In written works, the resulting expanded text, that is, the *matn* plus *sharh*, typically represented a much closer approximation of normally comprehensible prose. This transformation was made possible by a very important and immediately obvious fact about the text/commentary relationship: its physical aspect. While the *matn* is a textual "body," *sharh* means to "open up" (another referent is to surgery). The commentary, ranging from trivial linking words to lengthy and important doctrinal elaborations, is inserted in spaces opened up in the original text. Although they remain distinct, the two are not physically isolated from each other, as are either footnotes located on another part of the page or entirely separate volumes. With the commentary embedded directly in the original text, grafted into spaces opened up in its body, the two alternate in a jointly constituted, *matn*-and-*sharh* text: a segment of *matn* is followed by a segment of *sharh*, which is followed by another segment of the *matn*, and so on. A range of markers, from different ink colors (see fig. 3) and a type of overlining to conventional wording shifts ("he said"/"I say") were used to signify the transitions back and forth between the two.[39] In such a situation, reading involved traversing already familiar or even previously memorized segments of *matn* (as well as citations of Quran or hadiths) embedded in the larger commentary text.

In a work of *sharh*, interpretations literally become part of the text interpreted. If it consisted only of its insertions, a work of commentary would be merely a collection of disconnected and unviable fragments. Instead, a *sharh* work is actually taken to be the sum of the *matn* and the added comments, involving a complex notion of full quotation. Encompassed by the larger *sharh*, the *matn* appears in continually interrupted bits and pieces, but the quotation is faithful, word for word, and eventually complete. Interpretive in intent, the commentary genre joins two insufficiencies. It is the destiny of a *matn* to be interpretively expanded by *sharh* and that of a *sharh* to depart from a global invocation of a *matn*. A related sort of embedded, in extenso quotation of *matn* is also basic to hadith works. In synopses, the quotational process worked in reverse: as interpretive reductions rather than expansions, the distillations depended on preexisting full texts. At issue in both expansive and retractive genres are distinctive conceptions of originality and authorship.

Fundamental to both the pedagogy and the organization of books, the text/commentary relationship had further structural resonances. On a microlevel, the relationship is comparable to that of consonants and vowels in Arabic. A relation of insertion similar to that between

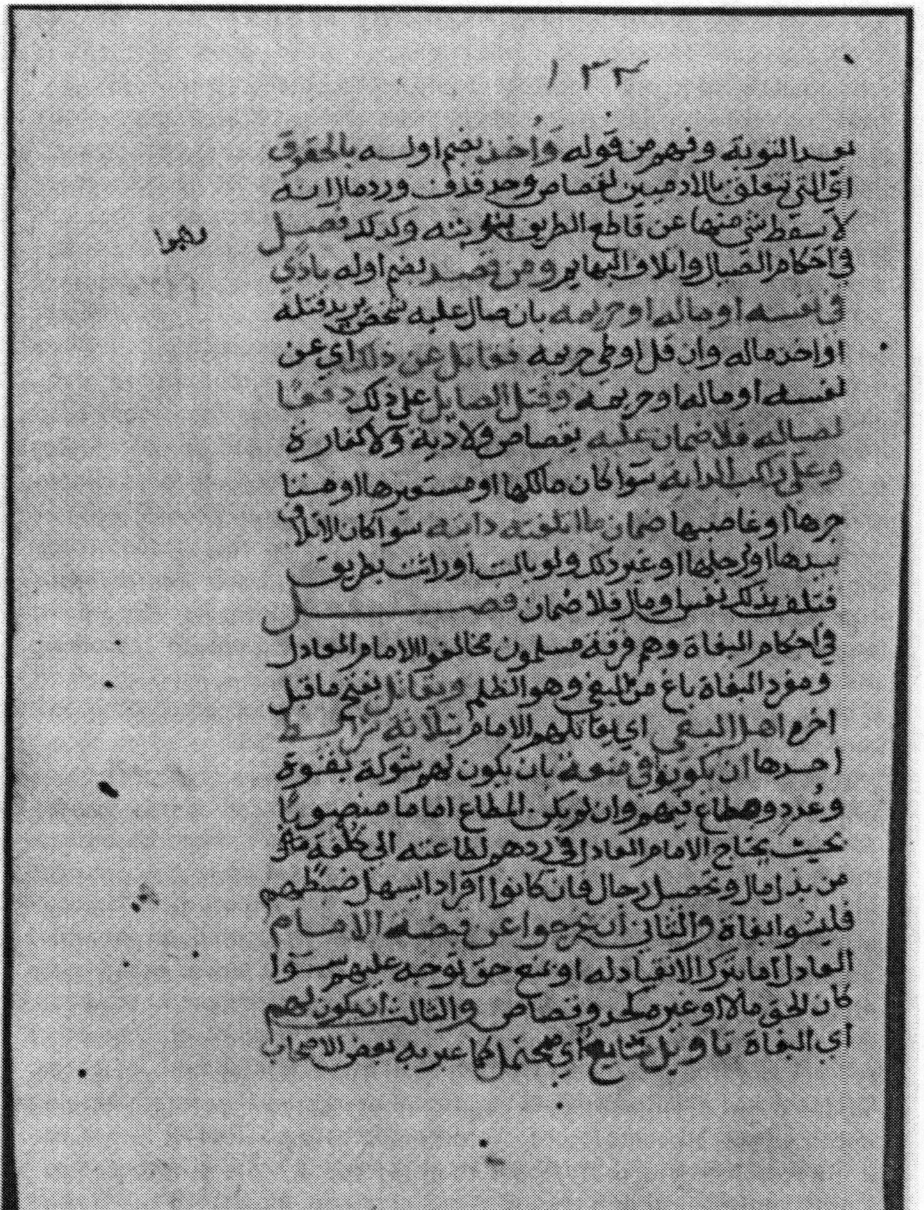

نعم التوبة وفهم من قوله وأخذ نعم أوله بالحقوق
اقتلى تتعلق بالادميين لنصاص وحد قذف ورد مال انه
لا يسقط شئ منها عن قاطع الطريق بتوبته وكذكذ فصل
في أحكام الصيال والاصلاء والبهائر ومن قصد نعم أوله بادى
في نفسه أو ماله أو حريمه بأن صال عليه تخير ريد قتله
أو أخذ ماله وان قل أو طح حريمه فجائل عن ذلك أى عن
نفسه أو ماله أو حريمه وحد قتل الصائل على كذ فمن
لصاله فلا ضمان عليه تنصاص ولا دية ولا كفارة
وعلى ركب الدابة سواء كان مالكها أو مستعيرها أو منا
جرها وغاصبها ضمان ما تلفته دابته سواء كان الاتلاف
بيدها أو رجلها أو عذركك ولو بات أو راث بطريق
فتله بذلك بنفسه ومال فلا ضمان فصل
في أحكام البغاة وهم فرقة مسلمون مخالفون للامام العادل
ومؤرد البغاة باغ مرتليغ وهو النظم ومسائل ينغ مائل
أخرى اهل البغى أى بما تكهم للامام ثلاثة شرطـ
احدها أن يكونوا في منعة بأن يكون لهم شوكة بقوة
وعدد وصطاع نعمهم وإن لو يكن للبغاء اماما صنصوبا
نحيث يحتاج الامام العادل في ردهم لطاعته الى كلفة متى
من بذل مال وحصار رجال فان كانوا أفرادا ايسها بضطيهم
فلنوا بغاة والثاني أن تخرجوا على حصة الامام
العادل إما بتركـ الانقياد له أو منع حق نوجه عليه سواء
كان للحق مالا أو غيره حكم ونصاص والثالث أن تكون لهم
أى البغاة تأويل تنابع أى يحتمل كما عبر به بعض الاصحاب

Figure 3. Commentary by al-Ghazzi, in black ink, on text by Abu Shuja', in red ink, shown here in gray. Late-seventeenth-century copy, Arabic ms. 4350. By permission of the Houghton Library, Harvard University.

consonants and vowels obtained between *matn* and *sharh*. Like an un-voweled consonantal string, a *matn* can and frequently does stand alone; by contrast, neither vowels nor commentary insertions are independently viable. But both consonant strings and *matn*s are open to, and ultimately dependent upon, the interpretive interventions of voweling and textual commentary.

A text and commentary type of relation is also part of a much wider pattern, one that goes to the heart of a general understanding of the growth of the shari'a. An equivalent relationship exists between the Quran, as the paradigmatic text, and the Sunna of the Prophet, with the latter standing as a kind of expansive elaboration, through Muhammad's actions and statements, upon the Revelations contained in the former. Taken together, the Quran and the Sunna, the two "sources," stand in turn in the position of basic "texts" with respect to the body of interpretive elaboration that became shari'a jurisprudence, or *fiqh*. Up to the establishment of the four standard schools of law, this jurisprudence developed through the efforts of the early Muslim jurists, who employed a method of analogically based interpretation (known as *ijtihad*), the refining of which was one of the major contributions of al-Shafi'i. Thereafter, within each of the established schools, the text/commentary relationship was replicated still further, as the authoritative works were themselves subjected to successive commentaries and summaries, some of which became authoritative in their own right. Muslim jurisprudence developed like a branching tree, expanding outward from the single, original, and paradigmatic Quran, complemented by the Sunna, through the foundational early works of the several schools, to the concise manuals and then the outer reaches of proliferating commentaries and glosses.

New contributions stood squarely on the shoulders of earlier works. Both *Al-Minhaj* and *Al-Mukhtasar* are original texts upon which numerous subsequent written commentaries and glosses were based. Each constituted a point of textual departure for a separately branching literary tradition in Shafi'i scholarship.[40] Explicit lines of textual ancestry are traceable. Among the descendants of al-Nawawi's thirteenth-century *Al-Minhaj*, for example, are several sixteenth-century commentaries and synopses, while the same text's ascendant line goes back through a work by al-Rafi'i (d. 1266), which it synopsizes. Al-Rafi'i's text, in turn, was based on two short works by al-Ghazzali (d. 1111), both of which summarized one of the great scholar's own larger works, which was itself based on a work by his teacher al-Juwayni (d. 1086).[41]

The highly implicit and generally "unfinished" qualities of authoritative manuals necessitated and actively invited interventions, from recitational vowelings and the simplest reader emendations to full interpretive commentaries. Such texts were endowed with a dual and contradictory character: their marked stability was anchored in the assumed security of person-to-person instructional linkages and the authenticity of recitational transmission, while their equally fundamental instability derived from an absolute need for elucidation. While the intellectual world that this duality implied was one oriented toward a tension between a settled conservatism and a required, but criticizable, interpretive dynamism, the social world implied was one based on interpretive relations of hierarchy and power (see chapter 8).

Openness in authoritative texts was not only a consequence of concision, however, but equally a matter of internal discursive construction. Although by no means devoid of clear principle, shari'a scholarship was very much an ongoing argument, one characterized as much by recognitions of divergent views as by points of univocal consensus. The open character of such texts was crosscut by a basic positivism, a conviction that truthful positions existed, although particular truths might be known only to God. A polyvocality of competing opinion stood opposed to the notion that authorial presence was the medium of univocal truth. It was acknowledged that individual scholars could differ in their interpretations in the absence of a clear Quranic text or an authentic hadith from the Prophet.[42] Decisive texts, however, especially in the paradigmatic form of individual Quranic passages, were understood to convey truth. A "text" (*nass*) of this type, that is, an individual source-passage within an authoritative text, was defined by scholars as "carrying only one meaning" (al-Juwayni n.d.:46). When, as was often the case, positions were taken but the truth of a matter remained uncertain, this could be represented in manuals and other works by the appended formula "and God knows best."

When divergent views exist on an issue, al-Nawawi is very careful to report this fact. At the beginning of *Al-Minhaj* he establishes terminology to be used throughout the work to identify the status of alternative opinions. He exercises his interpretive preference, but in so doing he does not cover up other voices. "In all instances" he offers an "elucidation and evaluation of opposed opinions, of opposed ways a question can be addressed, and of opposed methods."[43] His terminology allows him both to specify that a particular doctrine appears preferable to him and to indicate whether the doctrine or doctrines rejected are widely accepted or not. Other terms similarly enable him to choose a manner of addressing an issue while also noticing the strength, or weakness, of different approaches. An example of this precision is the usage of the comparative degree—"clearer" and "sounder"—to represent his choices in instances where, as he says, "disagreement is strong." When al-Nawawi simply states his own view, he utilizes the opening expression *qultu*, literally "I said," together with the cautious concluding phrase "and God knows best." The effect of such careful usage is to highlight the essentially disputed quality of many positions advocated. Other terms employed by al-Nawawi include *madhhab*, to indicate the commonly accepted positions of the Shafi'i school, and *nass* ("text"), to indicate the source-text positions of al-Shafi'i himself. Shafi'i's personal doctrine, which sometimes involves "a weak view or a divergent opinion," is further broken down, however, into the often opposed positions he held early and late, that is, during the Iraqi versus Egyptian periods of his career. Al-Nawawi uses the conventional terms "old" and "new" to mark off these different positions held by the school founder.

The overall impression of shari'a jurisprudence as presented in *Al-Minhaj* is of an unstable mix of the settled and the contested. In the text itself al-Nawawi remarks that he "has already begun work on a volume which will take the form of a commentary on the details of this abridgment." Despite the definitiveness *Al-Minhaj* came to represent in the Shafi'i school, it was nevertheless viewed, beginning with its author, as an open site, as a text in need of further clarification. To the extent that an extremely concise manual might be relatively univocal because of the dictates of space, commentaries inevitably opened up points of contention. This is the case with the very brief *matn* by Abu Shuja', the other manual relied upon in Ibb. Nothing beyond a single-view outline was possible in the scope of such a *matn*, but in the hands of al-Ghazzi, his principal commentator, many of Abu Shuja''s points are immediately modified, opened up to alternatives, or even bluntly reversed. As opposed to the Quran (12:1), which identifies itself as the "clear text" (*al-kitab al-mubin*),[44] the discourse of the shari'a literature built up from it appears markedly and openly discordant. Divergences represented by the mere existence of separate schools of shari'a interpretation were further developed within each of the schools. Fiqh manuals served to summarize but could not finally contain the essentially contentious terrain of authoritative shari'a thought.

In many historical settings, schools competed for the intellectual and, the subject of the next chapter, the political terrain. In chapter 2, late-nineteenth- and early-twentieth-century highland history is the backdrop for a discussion of differing shariʿa conceptions of the state. With the Revolution of 1962, however, the Yemeni nation-state required and eventually adopted an entirely new form of law. Chapter 3 examines the transformation of the recitational and open character of authoritative shariʿa texts through processes of codification and legislation.

CHAPTER 2

The Pen and the Sword

Both the pen and the sword are instruments of the ruler to use in his affairs.
IBN KHALDUN

ZAIDI TEXTS

In terms of schools of *shari'a* interpretation, Yemen has a further, quite special, and largely homegrown tradition. This concerns the Zaidi *madhhab*, which takes its name from Zaid b. 'Ali (died 740), a fourth-generation descendant of the Prophet Muhammad. While the Shafi'is, as was noted, are one of four standard schools of the Sunni tradition, the Zaidis are Shi'is. In the local relationship of these two schools, Yemen has experienced its own microcosm version of a dialectic that has structured the Islamic world at large. Whereas the Shafi'i school, which prospered in many locales from the central Middle East to Southeast Asia, has an international identity, the Zaidi school is comparatively unknown, having flourished mainly in Yemen. In both technical ("school" of shari'a interpretation) and popular (geopolitical identity) senses, the two madhhabs have been associated with distinct regions of the country: the Shafi'is mostly concentrated in the southern highland districts of Lower Yemen, the Zaidis mainly in the northern plateau, or Upper Yemen.[1]

In substantive doctrine, regarding everything from ritual matters to contracts, the differences between Shafi'is and Zaidis are minor. Unlike the far more numerous and better-known Shi'is of Iran, the Zaidis prided themselves on being extremely close to many Sunni positions, so much so that they have been considered a virtual "fifth" Sunni school.[2] A fundamental divergence exists, however, between Shafi'is and Zaidis, and this centers on the issue of legitimate rule. While Sunni states were typically ruled by a temporal sultan or a king, the Zaidi state was led by an *imam*. The imamate is an institution of spiritual-temporal rule, although the very "this-worldly" Zaidis differ from other Shi'is in their rejections of the doctrine of imamic infallibility and the concept of a "hidden" imam.[3] Whereas other Shi'i histories were interrupted (e.g., in the seventh or twelfth generations) with the occultation of a last imam recognized as genuine, the Zaidis continued to produce worldly incumbents until the mid-twentieth century. An essential requirement for a Zaidi imam was that he be a *sayyid*, a direct descendant of the Prophet Muhammad through the union of his daughter Fatima and his cousin 'Ali. Early on in Muslim history the Shi'is were a "faction" that resisted the emergent Sunni view of the legitimacy of leaders lacking this strict qualification of descent.

Beyond the descent requirement, according to Zaidi theory,[4] an imam is ideally an individual who, in addition to being of full adult capacity, male, free (not a slave), sound in senses and limbs, and both generous and just, is capable as an administrator, a battlefield commander, and a shari'a interpreter (*mujtahid*). A pious but retiring scholar would not suffice: an imam is meant to be the sort of man who, upon recognizing his own exemplary qualities and perhaps on the urging of his fellows, rises up and makes himself known, actively and even aggressively asserting his call and claim (*da'wa*) to be the imam. As a ruler, as the "commander of the faithful," an imam ought to be outgoing and responsive rather than reclusive, and he had to be willing, as the school's eponym, Zaid b. 'Ali, put it, to "draw the sword."[5] An imam was meant to be a "master," as a twentieth-century Arab visitor said in honoring his host Imam Yahya, "of both the pen and the sword."[6]

Mastery of the pen was taken very seriously: Zaidi imams were the most scholarly of rulers, prolific in a wide spectrum of intellectual genres, most notably in shari'a jurisprudence.[7] As their scholarly achievements demonstrate, many imams were capable of advanced interpretation. The "word"/"opinion" (*qawl*) of such imamic interpreters, especially when reinforced by the consensus of leading jurists, was authoritative among the Zaidis.[8] As had been the practice of some of their predecessors, the ruling imams Yahya and his son Ahmad of the twentieth-century Hamid al-Din line issued collections of personal interpretations, which guided rulings in the courts of their realm. The distinctive form of textual domination in the Zaidi state thus derived from the presence of a qualified interpreter at the pinnacle of authority. Although it was a general phenomenon that the shari'a provided the idiom of authority in premodern Muslim states, the Zaidis were special in their worldly fusion of the roles of interpreter and commander.

Although Sunni states, including several that ruled from capitals in Lower Yemen in the thirteenth through the fifteenth century, were typically led by the temporal authority of a sultan or a king, Sunni schools recognized their own version of the imamate.[9] A Sunni imam differed primarily from a Shiʿi one in not being required to have the specific legitmacy of direct blood descent from the Prophet Muhammad, the issue that preoccupied Shiʿis. There was a descent qualification for a Sunni imam (also known as a *khalifa*, "caliph"), but this pertained to the much more inclusive category of Quraysh, the leading "tribe" of seventh-century Mecca.[10] The other major difference, taking the Shafiʿis and Zaidis now as specific examples, was that the Shafiʿi imamate existed only in theory, in the confines of the *fiqh* manuals, while that of the Zaidis had an existence in both theory and practice. The Shafiʿis nevertheless elaborated formal "requirements for the imam." According to al-Nawawi, he should be "Muslim, of full adult capacity, free (not a slave), male, a Qurayshite, a qualified shariʿa interpreter (*mujtahid*), courageous, of discerning views, and sound in hearing, sight, and speech."[11]

If an ideal Shafiʿi imam was envisioned as scholarly and coura- geous, an interpreter-commander much like that of the Zaidis, in actual Shafiʿi states interpretation and command were decisively separated into an interpretive authority controlled collectively by the scholarly community (the ʿulamaʾ) and a temporal authority held by the sultan or king. Ibn Khaldun remarked upon this division of labor between wielders of the pen and of the sword in Muslim states. In observing that "scholars are, of all people, those least familiar with the ways of politics" and that their intellectual craft was disdained by men in power, Ibn Khaldun was identifying a situation characteristic of Sunni sultanates, not the Zaidi imamate.[12]

Like the Shafiʿis, the Zaidis had their own concise and authoritative manuals of shariʿa jurisprudence, the most important of which is *Kitab al-Azhar* (The Book of Flowers). A chapter devoted to the imamate represents the mainstream Zaidi position on qualifications and activi- ties connected with the position. The *Azhar* text is very similar to the Shafiʿi manuals with respect to arrangement and chapter contents. Its author, Ahmad b. Yahya al-Murtada (d. 1432), was the deposed imam who composed his work while in prison. More than thirty commen- taries and glosses were prepared for this authoritative manual, among them separate multivolume commentaries by the original author and by his sister.[13] *Al-Azhar* was often studied in its composite, commented-

upon form, known as *Sharh al-Azhar*, which was the basic text combined
with its most noted commentary by 'Abd Allah b. Miftah (d. 1472).[14]
A work of enduring importance in the northern highlands, the *Sharh
al-Azhar* came to figure in the intellectual world of Ibb as a result of
conquest.

The first Zaidi imam appeared in the far northern Yemeni town
Sa'da at the end of the ninth century.[15] He was invited by local tribes
to help in settling their disputes. Relations with the powerful northern
tribes would be central to imamic politics of the subsequent centuries,
but, as Paul Dresch notes, "there is something of a paradox involved: the
tribes have always been politically important, and yet tribalism forms
no part of the language of statecraft."[16] Despite wide vicissitudes in the
reach of imamic authority, a long succession of these Zaidi leaders
would be of continuing significance in highland history down to the
mid-twentieth century. Originally confined to a far northern sphere of
influence by strong Sunni states based in the southern highlands, Zaidi
imams eventually managed to assert their control over the districts of
Lower Yemen as well. It was at the conclusion of the first Ottoman
occupation of Yemen, circa 1635, that Ibb and the rest of the southern
highlands fell under extended but gradually weakening Zaidi imamic
rule from the north. This rule continued until a period of nearly complete anarchy at about the middle of the nineteenth century, followed
by the reappearance of the Ottomans in 1872. The second period of
Ottoman rule, which concluded with the dissolution of the old empire
at the close of World War I, was followed by the assumption of independent rule by Zaidi imams of the Hamid al-Din family. These
imams, father, son, grandson, and (briefly) great-grandson, initially
opposed Ottoman authority and then governed the highlands independently until the coming of the 1962 Revolution and the birth of the
Yemen Arab Republic.

In Ibb, dominance was partly played out in the sphere of shari'a
jurisprudence, as a relation between the schools of ruler and ruled.[17]
During earlier, Lower Yemen–based dynasties such as the Rasulids,
the Shafi'i school was the official *madhhab* (al-Akwa' 1980:9), but under
the Zaidi imams it would become subordinate. It was not only in this
period in Yemen that Shafi'is found themselves in such circumstances,
however. Maktari (1971:3–4) suggests that their frequent remove from
state control gave Shafi'i jurists "a measure of intellectual freedom
which uniformity and authority to a great extent denied to the
other schools." As the early Yemeni historian Ibn Samura astutely

observed, "governments have miraculous influence through suppression of knowledge, or in diffusing and publicising it or in swiftly consolidating it."[18] Madhhab politics under imamic rule dictated not only that imamic opinions were applied in the local Ibb courts, but also that scholars trained in the Zaidi tradition were appointed to judgeships and that texts such as the *Sharh al-Azhar* were taught in local schools. There was an impact as well on historical writing: the once prominent Shafi'i voice in biographical histories—including such Lower Yemen–based authors as Ibn Samura, al-Janadi, al-Khazraji, al-Burayhi—was replaced by that of Zaidi historians. From the limelight of historical attention, Lower Yemen passed into the shadows. In these later sources Ibb is regarded as a somewhat remote outpost, and, if they receive mention at all, local scholars are identified by the appended madhhab marker "al-Shafi'i." During the long period of imamic ascendancy and in the absence of such official stimuli as appointments, Shafi'i thought nevertheless persisted in Lower Yemen, its vitality attributable not only to intellectual resistance but also to continuing interchanges with Shafi'i communities elsewhere in Southwest Arabia. To the west, on the coastal Tihama, was the town of Zabid, a great, old center of Sunni scholarship, and there were also important communities of Shafi'i scholars located beyond the reach of Zaidi rule, in sultanates to the south surrounding Aden and especially in the Hadramawt to the east.

Nearly three hundred years of imamic suzerainty, interrupted only by the forty-seven-year interlude of Ottoman rule at the turn of the twentieth century, fostered among Zaidis a sense of their natural role as the overlords of Lower Yemen. In Zaidi eyes, the Shafi'is were a subject population (*ra'iyya*); the inverse of this imaging was the Shafi'i view of the Zaidi imams as tyrants and of their tribal supporters as ignorant and ruthless. A reciprocally hostile sentiment[19] long characterized Zaidi-Shafi'i interaction, although this was recast with the birth of the politics of nationalism in this century. The rigidity of these old stereotypes was in some ways mitigated and in others exacerbated by the substantial southward flow of northerners into the Shafi'i districts during the centuries of Zaidi rule. Governors, administrators, judges, teachers, military personnel, and tribesmen moved into Ibb town and its hinterland. As a consequence, a significant number of the contemporary families of Ibb as well as many powerful rural families trace their arrival in the area to the two-and-a-half-century interval between the early and the late Ottoman occupation.[20] With the exception of some

townsmen who arrived this century and some rural "tribal" families
who retained connections with the North, the descendants of Zaidis
settling in Ibb and elsewhere in Lower Yemen, the scholarly and the
untutored alike, eventually "became Shafiʿis" (*tashaffaʿu*), in either the
narrow juridical or the wider regional identity senses.

Muhammad al-Shawkani

The distinctiveness of the Zaidi school in connection with shariʿa interpretation went beyond the credentials of the imam. For the Shafiʿis and
the other Sunni schools, the right of scholars to engage in interpretation
(*ijtihad*) was eventually placed in question. In the centuries after the
schools themselves had been consolidated, some scholars contended
that the principal issues had been settled and that the requisite levels of
interpretive skill for further fundamental elaboration were no longer to
be found. This position was summarized in a famous assertion, that the
"gate of independent interpretation (*ijtihad*)" was "closed." By contrast, in the Zaidi school, there had been no such debate concerning the
practice of interpretation. For the Zaidis, the "gate of *ijtihad*" had
always been unproblematically open, and the aggressive advocacy and
pursuit of interpretation became a hallmark of their school.

Interpretive issues were at the center of the scholarly project of
Muhammad b. ʿAli al-Shawkani, the towering intellectual figure of
early-nineteenth-century Yemen.[21] A man of multiple talents and
achievements, al-Shawkani was not only an active teacher and a
prolific writer, but also a powerful actor in the Yemeni politics of his
day. In addition to his contributions as a poet and as a historian,
al-Shawkani authored a number of substantial and influential works in
the fields of *hadith* studies, Quran exegesis, and jurisprudence. One of
the leading advocates and practitioners of ijtihad in the entire Muslim
world in his day, he was also the chief judge, the "Judge of Judges"
(*qadi al-qudat*) in the Zaidi imamic state, from his appointment in 1795
until his death in 1834. In his writings, al-Shawkani emerges as a highly
independent thinker, who criticizes, synthesizes, and innovates, both
with respect to the internal debates in the Zaidi school and in mediating
between the Zaidis and the Sunni schools. A Zaidi by ascribed intellectual birthright (and in his political commitment to the imamate), he
strove for an intellectual posture transcending conventional madhhabs.

One of al-Shawkani's works appreciated by Shafiʿi jurists in Ibb
is his commentary on the *Azhar* text. *The Raging Torrent* (*Al-Sayl al-
Jarrar*), as it is known, is a strong, section-by-section critique of the

standard Zaidi manual. In this commentary, as in all his other works, his desire to revitalize the interpretive project of ijtihad comes through clearly. This overriding aim of his scholarship is exemplified by the stated purpose of his biographical history, perhaps his best-known work among the generally educated in Ibb. In the opening pages of this book, *The Rising Moon*, al-Shawkani identifies and then criticizes the Sunni view that interpretive ijtihad pertained only to the early age of Islam.

> The special competence of the early generations of this [Muslim] community with respect to substantial achievements made in the sciences of knowledge has come to be assumed among the uninformed rabble, while at the same time that of the later generations has been ignored. This has proceeded until the notion appeared among adherents of the four [Sunni] schools of the impossibility of there having been a qualified interpreter (*mujtahid*) after the sixth [A.H., twelfth A.D.] century, as some say, or after the seventh century, as others claim. This assertion is indicative of an ignorance that should be obvious to individuals of the lowest level of knowledge, the least perception, the most humble understanding. Because this represents a restriction of divine grace, of the abundance of God, to some of the faithful while excluding the others, to people of some eras while excluding other eras, to individuals of one age excluding other ages. And this without evidence or supporting text. This weak and despicable assertion would deprive the recent era of an upholder of the proofs of God, an interpreter of His Book and the Sunna of His Prophet, and a clarifier of what He established as law for his faithful. This undoubtedly would amount to the loss of the shari'a and the disappearance of religion. God the Most High has, however, undertaken to protect His religion: the intent being not simply to preserve it in the bodies of pages and registers but rather to have actual individuals available to represent it to the people at all times and in every necessity.[22]

Al-Shawkani's purpose in *The Rising Moon* is thus to refute the idea held by some Sunnis that qualified practitioners of ijtihad did not exist after the formative centuries of Islam. He does so by providing biographies of about six hundred men and a few women, Yemenis and non-Yemenis, all of the highest scholarly achievements, who lived in the period from the eighth Hegira century down to his own time. His statement concludes by saying that the shari'a, and Islam generally, survives not so much in concrete writing ("in the bodies of pages and registers") as through embodiment in the lives of individuals, in the living "text" they transmit and interpret. One of al-Shawkani's intellectual endeavors in this connection was to document the specific human links (*isnad*s) by which his own learning had been received. Like al-Shafi'i and others of the earlier generations, al-Shawkani authored a personal genealogical, men and texts, record that established the authoritative transmission of his knowledge.[23] Al-Shawkani's position on ijtihad and his activity as an interpreter have been taken into account in recent reconsiderations of the controversial history of the "closure" of Sunni interpretation (e.g., Hallaq 1984). Such rethinking of the history of ijtihad will influence our understanding of the relative dynamism of the various schools. In the case of Yemen, for example, it cannot be maintained that the Zaidis were unique in their continuing intellectual vigor while the scholarship of the Sunni Shafi'is was "largely frozen in a tenth-century mold."[24]

Al-Shawkani also wrote several treatises on the specialized subject of jurisprudential method. That is, in addition to such works as his commentary on the *Azhar*, which is at the shari'a manual level of applied jurisprudence (*fiqh*) proper, he also wrote in the separate genre of legal studies known as the "sources of jurisprudence" (*usul al-fiqh*). This special, methodological branch of the legal literature, which was launched by al-Shafi'i in his *Risala*, is specifically concerned with interpretation. One way the distinction between the two levels of discourse has been characterized in Yemen is by means of a simple botanical metaphor. In the new Preface to the published text of the *Azhar*, the difference between *usul*, the sources methodology, and *furu'*, the rules of applied law, is explained by means of the manual title, *The Book of Flowers*:

> In the usage of scholars of interpretation in the Islamic community, *fiqh* is said to be composed of *usul* and *furu'*. *Usul* is the science through which shari'a rules are derived from first principles [i.e., Quran and Sunna]. *Furu'* are the applied shari'a rules concerning ritual obligations and worldly undertakings. Such applied shari'a rules are what this book [the *Azhar* manual] contains. The *usul* are like the tree, and the *furu'* are like the branches. On the branches there are leaves and flowers. And the author of this book therefore took flowers (*azhar*) as his title.

Shari'a manuals together with their commentaries and glosses—that is, the *furu'* literature—were the practically oriented product, while the *usul* (commonly known as the "roots") literature contained the methodology. In Ibb, the principal *usul* work studied was the extremely short and memorizable text, known simply as the *Pages* (*Waraqat*) by the famous early Shafi'i jurist al-Juwayni (d. 1086),[25] the teacher of the great al-Ghazzali. Al-Juwayni's text concludes with a concise definition of the intellectual activity of ijtihad and the position of the interpreter, the mujtahid. This discussion is arrived at after a summary treatment of the essential features of several related disciplines, all of which are brought to bear in the exercise of ijtihad. Thus al-Juwayni touches upon key issues of the language sciences, rhetoric, logic, and argumentation; the field of Quranic exegesis (*tafsir*); and the field of *hadith* studies, including the mechanism of oral transmission. The practice of ijtihad is a method predicated on competence in all these fields. The usul, or "roots," of jurisprudence are four: the two foundational "source-texts," the Quran and the Sunna, and two methods, analogy and consensus. An interpreter reasons from the two authoritative "texts" to new applied principles that are not specifically covered in either the Quran or the Sunna, and such individual interpretive acts may become generally accepted through the working of scholarly consensus (see chapter 7).

Nearly a school unto himself, al-Shawkani had numerous students and influenced many colleagues, and as chief judge he was responsible for recommending judicial appointments to the imam. He also visited Lower Yemen where he is said to have taught briefly in the towns of Taʿizz, Jibla, and Ibb.[26] Among his close disciples was his student and son-in-law Salih al-ʿAnsi.[27] As al-ʿAnsi's biographer, al-Shawkani emphasizes his studies in the field of hadith: "He studied under me the two *sahih*s [i.e., the works of al-Bukhari and Muslim] and the *sunan* of Abu Daʾud and some of my own writings." Al-ʿAnsi initially served as a judge in Sanʿaʾ, where he occasionally represented al-Shawkani in the imamic council. Later in his career, al-ʿAnsi was posted to a judgeship in Ibb, where he died in 1875. With this appointment, a local scholarly family of contemporary importance took root in Ibb town society. As eventually occurred in the case of the descendants of other new arrivals from the Zaidi north, the al-ʿAnsi line became Shafiʿi. In this instance it happened that the shift to a Shafiʿi identity occurred in one generation, as Salih's son ʿAli received instruction in Shafiʿi jurisprudence from ʿAli b. Naji al-Haddad (d. 1893), father of ʿAbd al-Rahman al-Haddad, whose biography was quoted earlier. ʿAli b. Naji, the apical ancestor of the Haddad line in Ibb, is memorialized in a poem by his student al-ʿAnsi, who speaks of his mentor's "passion for jurisprudence, which he used to / Dictate to me in the early morning darkness." Al-ʿAnsi goes on to lament the "death of our scholar and the interpreter of our era / Who clarified the ambiguous and the obscure."

Figure 4. ʿAbd al-Rahman al-Haddad, front right, seated next to Saʿid Pasha, ca. 1915.

ʿAbd al-Rahman al-Haddad

Unlike his father, ʿAli b. Naji, al-Shawkani's transplanted student Salih al-ʿAnsi, and others of the previous generations in Ibb, who were witnesses to the dissipated patrimonial authority of the Zaidi imamate, ʿAbd al-Rahman al-Haddad grew up in a district that identified itself as part of the far-flung Ottoman Empire.[28] His dates (1876–1922) nearly coincided with those of the Ottoman Province of Yemen (1872–1918). Trained, as his biography states, on such manuals as al-Nawawi's *Minhaj*, al-Haddad was a distinguished representative of turn-of-the-century Shafiʿi scholarship. By 1904 he had succeeded his father as the Ibb mufti, a judicial post requiring the highest level of scholarly achievement. During the protracted but unsuccessful siege of that year (ensuing from the accession of Yahya Hamid al-Din to the imamate), al-Haddad was a town leader, responding at one point to a Zaidi commander's surrender demand with a well-remembered defiant riposte: an envelope containing five bullets and a satirical poem.

Figure 5. Ibb governor Isma'il Basalama with two sons, after meeting Imam Yahya in San'a', ca. 1920.

Three years later, he was among forty prominent Yemenis sent on a delegation to Istanbul to meet the Ottoman sultan. He was returned to a judgeship and a political position as vice-governor of Ta'izz (which then included the Ibb district). With the outbreak of World War I and the attack on the British near Aden, he headed a Lower Yemen contingent of *mujahidin* attached to the regular Ottoman forces under the overall command of Sa'id Pasha. A photo taken at the time shows al-Haddad, with deep-set eyes and in turban and engulfing robes, seated next to Sa'id in his officer's tunic, high boots, and tarbush. (See fig. 4.) Following the collapse of Ottoman authority in 1918, as Imam Yahya prepared to assume control of the southern highlands, an emissary was sent to reconcile the powerful men of Lower Yemen, including al-Haddad and the governor of Ibb, his father-in-law, Isma'il Basalama (al-Akwa' 1987). This descendant of Hadrami merchants who had settled in Ibb by the early 1800s was also the town's leading merchant in the valuable caravan trade to Aden. (See fig. 5.) Both men and a handful of other regional dignitaries traveled north to offer their allegiance to the imam. Like Basalama, who was reappointed to his post in Ibb, al-Haddad was continued in his political position in Ta'izz and was also made presiding judge of the southern branch of the appeal court.

This Yemeni Shafi'i biography—bullets and a poem, military command and muftiship, political and judicial posts—is one that joins assertive leadership qualities and important state charges with distinguished scholarly credentials. In a manner reminiscent of an ideal Zaidi imam, al-Haddad combined an aptitude for statecraft (*siyasa*) with shari'a knowledge: he "had a great capacity for *siyasa*," his biographer writes, and "when he finished his work issuing juristic opinions and his responsibilities in conducting the administrative affairs of state, he would turn to study the works of al-Suyuti and others like him in the sciences of shari'a interpretation (*ijtihad*)." A more rarely instanced combination of power and knowledge, this alternative Sunni leadership ideal was modeled on the simple modesty of Abu Bakr (the first caliph) rather than, as was the Shi'i ideal, on the charisma of 'Ali (the fourth caliph) and the legitimacy of his issue. "Despite his unusual opportunity," the biographer remarks of al-Haddad, "he accumulated nothing in the way of worldly possessions, not even a house for his children." Al-Haddad was an urbane exemplar of a type of Yemeni "great man" accomplished in both the spoken and the written word. In stories told about him, al-Haddad is said to have expressed himself extemporaneously with audacious self-assurance, whether confronting the Ottoman sultan or the ruling Zaidi imam. In addition to his scholarly and administrative status, he was an *adib*, a man of letters: "Attributed to him are writings and dialogues, in verse and in prose, characterized by the most eloquent style and verbal facility."[29]

Among al-Haddad's last works was a versification of Imam Yahya's recently issued *ikhtiyarat*, his personal shari'a interpretations.[30] This commentary by a leading Shafi'i jurist on the opinions of the pivotal Zaidi interpreter is but one instance of an intellectual dialogue that has gone on in the highlands for many centuries. Aside from those aspects of their schools that set them apart—represented by their respective manuals, such as the *Minhaj* of al-Nawawi, the *Mukhtasar* of Abu Shuja', and the *Azhar* of Imam al-Murtada—in many other respects the Shafi'is and Zaidis of Yemen shared a common intellectual tradition. Beyond a convergence in the Quran itself, highland scholars of both schools held in equivalent esteem a number of fundamental works in such disciplines as hadith, Quran exegesis, grammar, and so on.[31] A revitalizing synthesis of the combined tradition was the great accomplishment of Muhammad al-Shawkani, who is counted as an intellectual ancestor by virtually all Yemeni shariʿa scholars.

SHARIʿA POLITICS

When Ottoman Turkish troops arrived in Ibb in 1872, they found a town adrift in stateless anarchy. Rule by the Qasimi line of Zaidi imams, which in vital early years ended the first Ottoman occupation (circa 1635), had weakened drastically by the beginning of the nineteeth century, and waves of insurrection began to sweep across Lower Yemen.[32] By 1812 a tribal leader of northern ancestry had carved out a domain that was said to extend from the Sumara Pass down to the Red Sea port Mocha; in 1838–41, his son served as the military commander in an uprising led by a local saintly figure named Faqih Saʿid.[33] From mid-century to the arrival of the Ottomans, the breakdown of authority was nearly total. The period is known as the *ayyam al-fasad*, the "time of corruption." Local tribal leaders fought among themselves in the countryside and periodically besieged the towns. In the absence of imamic control, a series of commoner merchants attempted to run the affairs of the capital city, Sanʿaʾ, while in Ibb a town butcher named al-Akhshar, who owned a small cannon, was pressed into service to mount a defense against marauders.[34]

In the scheme of the venerable old empire, the recently acquired province of Yemen was relatively remote, comparatively backward, and intermittently rebellious. Because of the difficult circumstances of Ottoman rule in the highlands, the full array of institutions established in better-integrated and less problematic provinces could not be put in place.[35] In Shafiʿi Lower Yemen, Ottoman rule received a decidedly different sort of reception than it did from the Zaidis of the northern highlands. In Ibb, a district seat,[36] the coming of the Ottomans was significant for eliminating any remaining filaments of Zaidi hegemony. Since the Ottomans were Sunni Muslims (Hanafi school), a further by-product of their rule was a general florescence of local Sunni life. In addition to the stimulus to Shafiʿi scholarship, there was a resurgence in saint-tomb visitation[37] and Sufi brotherhood activity,[38] both of which the Zaidis attempted to suppress. This open flourishing of Sunni diversity in Ibb would be curtailed by the resumption of ever-tightening imamic control, beginning in 1918. It should be noted, however, that some Shafiʿi scholars also disapproved of such forms of piety, as the polemical verses of the senior al-Haddad, a straitlaced shariʿa jurist, demonstrate.[39] Whereas later Zaidi governors in Ibb would merely forbid such activities, as governor of Ta'izz in the 1940s, the future Imam Ahmad ordered the exemplary destruction of the tomb of Ibn 'Alwan, the most important saint of Lower Yemen.[40]

While the fact that the Ottomans were Sunnis offered a formula for compatibility with the Shafi'is, it provided for just the opposite in relations with the Zaidis. In Ibb, the Ottoman administration was considered sound, many Turks were well liked as individuals, and there were marriages into local families. When the town was besieged by Imam Yahya's forces in 1904, town loyalty to the Ottomans was clear.[41] In Upper Yemen, by contrast, the Turks met fairly constant hostility, including two imam-led rebellions, in 1891–92 and 1904. When the imamic historian al-Wasi'i wrote in the mid-1920s about the reasons why the "people of Yemen" (*ahl al-yaman*) had rebelled against the Turks, he was articulating an imamic line, not speaking for the population of Ibb and Lower Yemen.[42] Interviewed by a Syrian traveler in 1927, Ibb governor Basalama said that the differences between Imam Yahya and the Ottomans had concerned "the shari'a." This was not a narrow reference to "legal" differences but a reference to political positions expressed in the shari'a-based discourse of the period. The protracted conflict between the Turks and the imams was fought out as much in the idiom of the shari'a as on the battlefield. The Zaidis were irritated by what they perceived as a Turkish misconception: "Inasmuch as the Turks are foreigners (*'ajam*) they do not understand what 'Zaidi' is—a school (*madhhab*) among the other schools. The founder of this school was the Imam Zaid, son of 'Ali Zain al-'Abdin, whose grandfather was the Prophet Muhammad."[43]

The imams asserted their claim to spiritual and temporal authority in Yemen and attacked the Ottomans for their alleged failure to uphold the shari'a. Zaidi opposition at the turn of the century was framed not in the vocabulary of national aspirations but as a defense of the shari'a. Refusing to allow the imams the discursive high ground, the Ottomans stoutly defended the empire's long-standing commitment to uphold the shari'a[44] and mobilized a locally tailored shari'a politics of their own to counter that of the imams. They argued that the imams represented only the narrow sectarian interest of the Zaidi community, not those of the substantial populations adhering to other *madhhab*s. The Ottomans called for the transcendence of sectarian differences and for solidarity with the Ottoman state to meet the aggressive inroads of the unbelievers, including the British and the Italians, upon the lands of the Muslims.[45]

In the two imamic uprisings, declarations focused on shari'a-framed issues. In a letter to the Ottoman sultan, Imam Mansur (al-Wasi'i 1928:149) claimed he had acted in order to "uphold the shari'a of our grandfather" (i.e., the Prophet). His letter goes on to enumerate a stylized, shari'a-anchored list of wrongs attributed to the Turks, including "forbidden acts," the "consumption of alcohol," "fornication and pederasty," and the nonapplication of the Quran/shari'a-prescribed punishments, the *hudud* (sing. *hadd*).[46] These punishments, the imam pointed out, had been "eliminated by Ottoman law in violation of the sacred shari'a."[47] When Imam Yahya succeeded his father in 1904, there was a similar ideological motif. The new imam "ordered the tribes to lay siege to the towns in which there were Turks, who had brought corruption (*fasad*) to the land, relinquished shari'a precepts, and oppressed the believers."[48] Two years later, following battlefield reverses, Imam Yahya began making overtures toward an eventual coming to terms with the Turks.[49] His initial negotiating position of 1906 stressed a spectrum of interrelated, shari'a-connected issues.[50] The first and second conditions were that court judgments be in accord with the "noble shari'a" and that he be given the power to appoint and remove shari'a court judges. Other conditions demanded a return to shari'a-based state funding structures, including pious endowments (for instruction) and the tithe. Condition six concerned the *hudud*, the shari'a punishments, to be applied to the "perpetrators of crimes among the Muslims and the Israelites, as they were ordered by God Almighty and enacted by His Prophet, [and] which [Ottoman] officials have abolished."

Strict enforcement of the *hudud*, for Zaidi imams as for purists of other periods, was a key summarizing symbol, shari'a shorthand for the existence of legitimate government.[51] If the implementation of a single part of the shari'a could stand for that of the whole, hudud application frequently served this discursive purpose. Ironically, it was these same hudud punishments that were typically singled out both by critical Westerners and by Muslim modernizers—again as the distinctive part representing the whole—to stand for the backwardness of the shari'a. In the shari'a manual of the Zaidi school, the imam's personal responsibility in the "administration of the *hudud*" heads his list of duties, and the same holds, in theory, for a Shafi'i imam.[52] Official imamic historians duly noted their proper enforcement. One way of exemplifying the existence of legitimate authority was by means of reports on otherwise unremarkable instances of punishment.[53] *Hadd* administration notices appeared also in the official imamic newspaper.[54] An account concerning the flogging of an adulteress concluded by saying, "All those attending departed asking God to support our majesty and his perfect state in his efforts to implement the shari'a." A condensed biographical sketch of Imam Yahya that appeared shortly after his death states that "he carried out the hudud established for criminals by God."[55] In this type of shari'a politics, the hudud offered a litmus test of upright rule.

Another integral part of the old shari'a discourse was the classification of the sociopolitical world into *madhhab*s and other equivalent groupings.[56] With the rise of the new political discourse of the nation-state, however, the madhhab construct—technically, a school of jurisprudence and, by extension, a label of regional geopolitical identity—underwent a further shift in meaning. When Isma'il Basalama, the former Ottoman and then imamic governor of Ibb, was asked by his visitor about the issue of Zaidi rule over a Shafi'i district, he responded in a way that both recognized and denied the relevance of madhhab categories. "I am a Shafi'i man," he began,

> and I am free to act and invested with full power in Ibb. I appoint or dismiss whomever I want among the functionaries, and neither His Majesty the imam nor his distinguished government enter into such small matters. He has delegated to me the requisite authority to enable me to govern the people with an Islamic and shari'a government. There is no difference for me between a Zaidi or a Shafi'i, and everything you have heard in the way of foreign propaganda is nothing but lies and slander against Yemen and its people. (al-'Azm 1937:290)

Basalama acknowledges ("I am a Shafi'i man") that a madhhab category fits, but at the same time he asserts that there is no practical difference between Zaidi and Shafi'i, and that the idea of difference is itself the product of outside efforts to divide Yemenis. This interview occurred at exactly the time when the first opposition groups were coalescing in the highlands and in Aden. These groups would frame their opposition to the imams in increasingly nationalist terms, and the government would respond with a quasi-nationalist discourse of its own. The new, "nation" view of Yemen and Yemenis, like the "people of Yemen" usage of the twenties,[57] attempted to override old madhhab distinctions in order to project an image of unified national support for imamic rule. Basic elements of this new discourse, especially its focus on new political wholes ("Yemen and its people") and a reinterpretation of the madhhab notion, already appear as assumptions in Basalama's statement. In its official newspaper, the imamic regime developed the political theme that it was the British who encouraged Zaidi versus Shafi'i sentiment to further the aim of drawing Lower Yemen into their own sphere of colonial influence.[58]

By the Revolution of 1962 madhhab distinctions had come to represent the divisive subversions of national fulfillment and the true shari'a under the old regime. The First Proclamation of the Revolution, issued "in the name of the free and independent Yemeni people (*sha'b*)," states that the first goal of national reform is to "give life to the correct Islamic shari'a, after its death had been caused by tyrannical and wicked rulers." The same provision calls for the "elimination of hatreds and envies, and divisions of descent and of madhhab."[59] Post-Revolution writers would continue to criticize the misuse of the shari'a and the geopolitical divisiveness of madhhab identities. One speaks of the "manipulation of the shari'a" under the imams.[60] "If we look fairly at the two madhhabs, the Zaidi and the Shafi'i," another cultural historian writes,

> and make a detailed study of the subjects of difference between them, we would find them very insignificant ... but the ignorant and the fanatical (*muta'assabin*) made out of them a tool for the destruction of national unity and a means for sowing the seeds of discord among a people tied together by the bonds of unity and brotherly ties for thousands of years. This has had the greatest impact in troubling social life in Yemen and affects its political condition until today.[61]

As a shari'a politics grounded in madhhab affiliations gave way to a nation-state politics anchored in the new notion of a citizenry, so the old manual texts relied upon by Shafi'is and Zaidis would be replaced by a new type of authoritative text, the legislated code. It is to an examination of these specifically textual aspects of discontinuity, illustrated by the ground-breaking nineteenth-century efforts of the Ottomans and (a hundred years later) the legislative work of the Yemen Arab Republic, that the discussion now turns.

CHAPTER 3

Disenchantment

OTTOMAN TEXTS

For the better part of the nineteenth century, the Ottoman Empire had been in the throes of an internal reform movement known as the *tanzimat*, a term derived from the word *nizam*, meaning "order." The reforms occurred in specific response to Russian expansionism and in a larger context of the growing military-technological and commercial-financial strength of the European powers. The Ottomans had felt continual critical pressure from Westerners, one of whose old refrains was "Bring forth your code; let us see it and make it known to our subjects."[1]

In 1869 the Ottoman drafting committee charged with producing the first *shari'a*-derived civil law characterized the old corpus of jurisprudence they had begun to draw upon as "an ocean without shores."[2] Represented in this instance by the standard manuals and commentaries of the official Hanafi school, shari'a jurisprudence had come to be viewed by Ottoman reformers as problematically vast, difficult of access, and generally inappropriate for the times. New understandings of the nature and role of the shari'a would be central to the emergence of new political orders across the Middle East. To the extent that it survived such transitions, the shari'a would be contained in a new type of authoritative textual form, the legislated code.

The key Tanzimat reform concerning the shari'a was the production of the shari'a-derived civil code, known as the *Majalla*. Drafting committee work began in 1869, and the full code was finally promulgated in 1876. Its innovative and contradictory character centered on the fact that it was "Islamic in content, but ... European in form."[3] Distilled in a new, eclectic manner from leading works of the Hanafi school, the

Majalla covered most of the *muʿamalat* (transactions) sections found in the old manuals. This material was equated by the drafters with the "civil law" of the "civilized nations."[4] Included also was a section on judicial procedure, but neither marriage nor inheritance was dealt with. The code was intended for use in the recently created civil (*niẓami*) courts and for convenient consultation in the parallel shariʿa court system. Although the new court structure was not introduced in Yemen, the *Majalla* was applied there in the provincial shariʿa courts. It is remembered in Ibb that two local men received instruction in its provisions.

Among Ottoman reformers, many of whom were astute observers of European society, the shariʿa was considered archaic and unsuited for modern purposes. If "order" was the leitmotif of the reforms advocated, the shariʿa had come to represent precisely the opposite: "disorder." A fundamental criterion of Western law, one that suddenly appeared to be unsatisfied in the shariʿa, was that it be "known." The newly perceived obscurity of the shariʿa was such that the essential task of "finding" the law was considered cumbersome if not altogether impossible. "In works of *fiqh*, general principles are mixed in with specific questions," the *Majalla* committee complained.[5] In addition, the "rules" the committee sought to tease out of the manuals "were scattered throughout the works of various jurists."[6] Drafters of the Ottoman Commercial Code (1850), which was based on French law, stated flatly that the relevant sections in the shariʿa "were not recorded and organized; consequently, they do not meet the needs of present conditions." The authors of the *Majalla*, which was constructed exclusively of shariʿa materials, likewise described these original texts as extremely difficult to work with. Their metaphor, again, was a boundless "ocean" "on whose bottom one has to search, at the price of very great efforts, for the pearls which are hidden there. A person has to possess great experience as well as great learning in order to find in the sacred law the proper solutions for all questions which present themselves."[7]

Painstakingly located in the texts of the oceanlike *fiqh*, the old "pearls" were fixed in the structural grid of numbered code articles, re-presented in an innovative abstract format that rendered the shariʿa into something resembling the familiar form of "law." In the *Majalla* the Ottomans took the significant step of making a portion of the shariʿa manageable and perusable. As the drafting committee wrote, "the need has . . . been felt for a long time for a work which dealt with transactions in general on the basis of the sacred law, containing only the least contested and least controversial opinions and composed in a manner which would be sufficiently clear so that *anyone* could study it easily and act in conformity with it" (emphasis added).[8]

Accessibility in codes required that they be built in an orderly and regular fashion, ideally of conceptual units that could stand alone, equivalent in their logical self-sufficiency and in their independence from any need of interpretive clarification. In selecting "only the least contested and least controversial opinions" from the fiqh manuals, the drafters took an important step toward silencing the open-ended argumentation of shari'a jurisprudence. Once central to a vital intellectual culture, openness was now considered a drawback. As against the purposely unfinished old textuality, the new works were closed by design. In addition, the exercise of interpretive *ijtihad* was specifically disallowed where an article provision already existed.[9] For Muslim reformers elsewhere, ijtihad would be reconceived as an essential tool for the adapting of an invigorated shari'a to the changing necessities of the "modern world." The Egyptian Rashid Rida (d. 1935), for example, drew on the Yemeni jurist al-Shawkani, among others, in his efforts to reassert and define the continuing relevance and importance of interpretation.[10] A new, "free ijtihad" would be a key instrument of early modernist movements.[11] While the gate of this new ijtihad was being opened, that of the old was finally being shut. Codes such as the *Majalla* for the first time brought closure to the "open text" of shari'a jurisprudence.

The idea that this new digest of laws would also be accessible to "anyone" was quite revolutionary, and it directly threatened the exclusive role of the shari'a jurists, specifically the institutional hierarchies of the Ottoman 'ulama', as qualified interpreters. An underlying intention in framing the *Majalla* was to write it "in language comprehensible to every man,"[12] rather than in the esoteric jargon or the highly condensed manual style of the earlier generations. Unlike the basic fiqh works, most of which were in Arabic, the new code was originally written in official Ottoman Turkish. A further aspect of the new accessibility was an explicit policy to disseminate the codified laws through official publication, translation, and distribution. Subversive of the positions of the shari'a jurists and of their entire system of formation in the old system of jurisprudence-centered instruction, this new attitude toward the legal text also foreshadowed the Western notion of the responsibility to the law of the ordinary individual, the citizen.

The positions of the jurists were further undermined by the fact that the *Majalla* was finally promulgated by the Ottoman sultan. The shari'a had theretofore been a "jurist's law," which had been developed and had retained its vitality through exercises of interpretive ijtihad, through commentary and opinion giving. Although the Ottoman Empire had lengthy experience with supplementary administrative law (*qanun*), an essential feature of the shari'a was that it provided no legislative authority to a head of state. Now, however, the production of an entire corpus of shari'a law was taken out of the hands of the jurists and allocated to a new breed of public officials constituted as a drafting committee, with their work to be passed before the sultan for approval and promulgation.

It was general principles and theoretical constructs that the *Majalla* was intended but ultimately failed to provide. Whatever its shortcomings, it was this movement in the direction of abstraction, so characteristic of the constituted form of bourgeois law (Pashukanis 1978:120–21), that the *Majalla* initiated with respect to the shari'a. Abstraction and generalization—the creation of order out of newly perceived "disorder"—would be enduring hallmarks of the transformation of the shari'a into law. In shari'a manuals, for example, key concepts such as "property" were embedded in the chapters, where they figured, not as highlighted terms, but rather as implicit assumptions. In the innovative form given the *Majalla*, by contrast, such concepts were identified and separated out for definition. It has been said that the shari'a was essentially atheoretical, that it lacked the clear statements of general principles that had become requisite in international legal discourse. Despite the paradigmatic position of the contract of sale in relation to other bilateral contracts in the *mu'amalat* sections, for example, it has been repeatedly remarked that in the shari'a there was no "theory of contract."[13] The *Majalla* as a whole opened with a section explicating a "series of fundamental principles," and before each chapter was placed an "introduction containing definitions of all legal terms pertaining to the subject matter of the chapter."[14]

The new authority of codified texts would rest not only on abstraction and generalization, but also on the development of related conceptions of the state and of individuals as responsible legal subjects. An important model was provided by the French Civil Code of 1804. As Weber explains (1978:865), this was the first code to be "completely free from the intrusion of, and intermixture with, nonjuristic elements and all didactic, as well as merely ethical admonitions; casuistry, too, is completely absent." The new type of code "possesses, or at least gives the impression of possessing, an extraordinary measure of lucidity as well as a precise intelligibility in its provisions." These and other characteristics of the French Civil Code were "expressions of a particular kind of rationalism," a "particular method of framing abstract legal propositions," which would be imitated not only elsewhere in Europe but in nation-states born across the Middle East. With the exception of what was to become Turkey, where the shari'a as a whole was summarily abolished in 1926 to be replaced by Swiss law, Western models would be synthesized in various ways with newly formalized shari'a materials.[15] It was with the *Majalla* that this reworking on the shari'a side of the equation began.

The immediately perceived shortcomings of the *Majalla* were several, all resulting from its inclusion of unreconstructed shari'a contents. Critics pressed for more rational codification: its general principles were deemed too few and insufficiently general, and the casuistic approach of the manuals had not been eliminated. It was also considered deficient in its character as a code, since "it was not a complete and exclusive statement of the law as it existed at the time of codification, but rather a nonexclusive digest of existing rules of Islamic law."[16] It was, in short, more of a modernized manual than a fully realized code. Despite explicit recognitions of the contemporary forces of economic change by its drafters,[17] the political economy of the *Majalla* was also not modern enough. Like the shari'a, it seemed not to accept the crucial Western legal notion of "freedom of contract";[18] there was a retention of moral principles rather than a guarantee of free rein for economic action.

COLONIAL SHARI'A

They mingled up religious, civil and merely moral ordinances, without any regard to differences in their essential character; and this is consistent with all we know of early thought from other sources, the severance of law from morality, and of religion from law, belonging very distinctly to the later stages of mental progress.
SIR HENRY MAINE (1861)

In colonial-period reappraisals of the status of the shari'a by scholars, officials, and some Muslim reformers, the particular "rationalism" of the West, including an understanding of the nature of law and its appropriate textual forms, was elevated to the standard for comparison. One aspect of this thought, exemplified by the quotation from Maine, was an evolutionism and a teleology that identified the discursive separations particular to bourgeois societies of the era as the logical end points of normal legal development. Another involved reciprocal negative estimations—as primitive, backward, or traditional—of non-Western discursive formations that did not exhibit such features. As the shari'a was reconceived as a foil for "modern" law, ideas concerning the superiority of Western forms legitimated a variety of colonial-period and early nationalist policies. The same positivism that contributed so fundamentally to the creation of modern Western codes led to significant misunderstandings when serving as the lens for students of "Islamic law."

This type of colonial-period thought was supplemented, however, by a more plural register in which the local importance and regional variations of the shari'a were recognized. While the simple antonymic, point-by-point opposition between the shari'a and Western law was a perspective characteristic of mainstream Orientalist fare designed primarily for home consumption, it coexisted with a specialist literature in which scholars debated scientific issues and addressed the practical problems of colonial administration. While the former was generalizing and essentializing, concerned with "common denominator" Muslims and broad civilizational comparisons that reinforced the uniqueness and the cultural hegemony of the West, the latter was more apt to be contextually sensitive and pragmatic about differences and similarities.

Late in the colonial period, the British chief magistrate in Aden (Yemen) began an article on Islamic family law with a reference to al-Nawawi's *Minhaj*: "A legal handbook, without modification over seven centuries, still regulates much of the domestic life of the people of Aden" (Knox-Mawer 1956:511). Among the colonial-era conceptions that contributed to decentering and bracketing the discursive authority of the shari'a was that it was "immutable." This was in contrast to Western law, which, it was assumed, "responds . . . to the ever changing patterns of social and economic life."[19] The thesis of doctrinal immutability also spawned related understandings, chief among them that the underlying system of instruction was " inflexible."[20] The attribution of an ossified character to Islamic law fit general Western conceptions of non-Western societies as either dormant (simple societies) or stagnant (traditional civilizations) until the enlivening moment of Western contact or colonization. As a consequence, patterns of discursive vitality different from those known in the West would remain unacknowledged.

Following, in part, from the immutability thesis was the conclusion that the shari'a was largely irrelevant. Law that did not adapt to changing societal circumstances must be increasingly out of touch. In addition, there was an attitude exemplified by Maine's opinion of

Hindu law, which he considered an "ideal picture of that which, in the view of the Brahmins, *ought* to be the law."[21] This he contrasted with Roman law, ancestor of the continental systems, which he described as "an enunciation in words of the existing customs of the Roman people." Classification as a "jurists' law" further suggested that the shari'a was largely hypothetical rather than reality oriented, emphasizing, as Weber put it (1978:789), the "uninhibited intellectualism of scholars" rather than the dictates of practice. With manual texts open before them, Western observers could put societies to the test: the lack of fit between rules and practices would be judged as deficiences, either in the legal texts or in the societies in question.

In a double-edged comment, C. Snouck Hurgronje (1857–1936) wrote that Muslims "exhibited an indifference to the sacred law in all its fullness quite equal to the reverence with which they regard it in theory" (1957:290).[22] "Indifference" points to nonapplication and noncompliance. Joseph Schacht (1964:199, 209) would later argue that the "perpetual problem" of Islamic law was the "contrast between theory and practice." Hurgronje's qualifier, "in all its fullness," reveals the yardstick of a textual purist, for whom doctrine and reality are, or ought to be, perfectly matched. In a similar formulation, J. N. D. Anderson (1959:20) states that the shari'a was "never applied *in its purity and entirety* throughout *every* sphere of life" (emphasis added). Seizing exclusively upon the inevitable gaps between texts and practices, observers drew general conclusions about the social importance of the shari'a. Little attention has been given, by contrast, to the obeyed dimensions of the shari'a, or to the extent to which its categories and concerns have influenced behaviors.

The second part of Hurgronje's statement speaks of "reverence . . . in theory." Although the sentiment might appear futile, especially in the case of a purely ideal law, the comment does identify a potent authority adhering in the shari'a. Hurgronje elsewhere remarked upon the puzzling "zeal which thousands of scholars show in studying a law of which only some isolated chapters have retained practical importance" (1957 [1898]:266). Had a context-specific measure of relevance been applied, indications of "reverence" and "zeal" might have been more comprehensible. Had the degree of "practical importance" of the shari'a been considered historically variable, the colonial context in which Hurgronje wrote might have become a relevant issue. Then the question would be this: Is the described combination of nonobservance and reverence characteristic of Muslim societies in all times and places or should it instead be understood in terms of the dislocations and attachments common to situations of colonial domination? Was a problematic specific to the colonial period being read as the timeless nature of the shari'a in Muslim societies?

Another new conception, as significant as it was seemingly simple and unobjectionable, was the labeling of the shari'a as a "religious" or "sacred" law.[23] The counterpoint was "secular" law, and two types of circumstance were modeled: the historical superseding of the traditional (religious) by the modern (secular) and the coexistence of the specialized communitarian (religious) with the generalized public (secular). Designation as a "religious" law relocated the shari'a in a Western-conceived past and future. As a newly specialized and restricted domain of the religious began to be imagined, attempts were made to refashion and reposition parts of the shari'a as its template.

Shari'a materials came to be understood as divisible in a manner that went far beyond the old categories of the *'ibadat* (ritual obligations) and *mu'amalat* (transactions). Thus the *Majalla* report opened by narrowing its focus to the "temporal" (*amr al-dunya*) content of the jurisprudence. In 1926 Dr. 'Abd al-Razzaq al-Sanhuri, the Egyptian jurist who would become the leading drafter of civil codes for new Arab states, wrote that the "point of departure" for this activity must be "a separation of the religious from the temporal portion of Islamic law."[24] While Western scholars acknowledged the comprehensiveness of the shari'a (e.g., as "the whole duty of mankind," as "the totality of Allah's commands that regulate the life of every Muslim in all its aspects," etc.),[25] in practice they restricted coverage to its "legal" aspects. Since the shari'a includes "an enormous amount of material that we in the West would not regard as law at all,"[26] an editing approach was adopted to separate out the "law" from the shari'a. In the influential introduction by Schacht, the systematic sections concern only "those subjects-matters which are legal in the narrow meaning of the term."[27]

A further conception was that, its ritual sections aside, the shari'a had an identifiable "core" or "heart,"[28] located in family, marriage, and inheritance law, in what the French referred to as *statut personnel*. The main support for this view was that these matters were comparatively fully dealt with in the Quran itself. It has been argued that the spheres of ritual and family law were characterized by a uniquely close fit of shari'a theory and practice and that they alone were relatively immune from Western legal "penetrability."[29] A corollary held that the shari'a was purely ideal, deficient or silent in virtually all other key areas of modern legal-legislative life, especially in criminal, constitutional, and commercial law. This legitimated the suppression of large areas of the shari'a while opening new spaces for secular "law," for the "imposition" (Burman and Harrel-Bond 1979) or, more passively put, the "reception" of Western-inspired legal forms. Criminal law was an early focus of Western indignation and intervention. The Dutch, for example, found it necessary to issue a new penal code for their Indian Archipelago colonies, because, as the translator of al-Nawawi and Abu Shuja' put it, it was "clear that no civilized nation can push its respect for indigenous institutions to the extent of sanctioning the application of barbarian punishments, long practiced by virtually all oriental peoples" (Van Den Berg 1882:v; cf. Foucault 1977). Governmental forms were similarly suppressed or incorporated in a variety of colony, protectorate, and mandate formulas while property regimes and commercial regulations were adapted or replaced to fit the requirements of colonial economies.

An implicit contrast was made with the "heart" of Western law, located in forms associated with the market. Prominent in the fiqh, however, are such legal constructs as individually disposable property, a contract of alienation, complex notions of money and capital, and partible inheritance. With particular reference to the commercial sphere, where the shari'a was previously considered a dead letter, Udovitch (1970) has demonstrated the extent to which manual doctrine deeply informed and was informed by practice in premodern times. Descriptions of the shari'a as being viable only with respect to its ritual and *statut personnel* sections diverted attention from the existence of deeper and broader family resemblances to Western law.[30]

In the more pragmatic register, colonial administrators in Algeria, to give one specific illustration, recognized that *milk*, the key shari'a category of individually held property, was both extremely important in the local land regime and very similar to the Western notion of private property. With the different agenda of land appropriation in mind, it was written: "Private property existed and was perpetuated in Algeria on the same basis as among us: it is acquired, transmitted, and held and is recognized by long possession, Moslem testimonials, and regular titles; the laws protect it and the courts assist it."[31]

A last colonial-era conception concerns the mode of thought in shari'a texts. Three-quarters of a century prior to the already cited remarks of the Ottoman drafting committees, British officials in India discovered in Hanafi manuals "a system copious without precision,

indecisive as a criterion (because each author differed from or contradicted another), and too voluminous for the attainment of ordinary
study."[32] For Anderson, a twentieth-century scholar, the old jurisprudence was simply a "hotchpotch."[33] Unlike modern forms of rationality
that emphasized abstract analytical thought, shari'a texts exhibited a
concrete or, in Weber's terms, "substantive" rationality. In contrast to
the Western drive toward the elaboration of concepts and laws, principles in shari'a manuals tended to be developed indirectly, through
particular examples. The result, according to Schacht (1964:205), was
a "literary form" in which "the underlying rule is implied by the
juxtaposition of parallel and particularly of contrasting cases." Given
the theoretical and political exigencies of both code drafting and Orientalist scholarship, such discursive differences would not be neutrally
assessed.

Summarizing the distinctive features of Islamic legal thought Schacht
(1964:5), following Weber, focuses on the "casuistical method," "which
is closely connected with the structure of its legal concepts, and both are
the outcome of an analogical, as opposed to an analytical, way of
thinking." Maine (1972 [1861]:11) wrote that "analogy, the most
valuable of instruments in the maturity of jurisprudence, is the most
dangerous of snares in its infancy." Analogy was especially "dangerous" in league with casuistry. As Weber noted, the elimination of
casuistry was a positive accomplishment of the French Civil Code. For
Westerners, this method of "case" reasoning, in which general moral or
ethical principles are adapted to particular circumstances by means of
analogic extension, had become a despised mode of thought.[34] In the
shari'a, high-level constructs, such as the all-inclusive evaluative scale
known as the "five qualifications" (obligatory, recommended, indiffer-
ent, reprehensible, forbidden), developed not so much through the
analytic refinement of concepts as through the casuistic specification of
applicable phenomena.[35]

Through a feedback pattern such conceptions about the shari'a
circulated among indigenous elites and early nationalists. European-
model schools existed across the region by the late nineteenth century,
Middle Easterners were traveling and studying in Europe, and Western scholarship on Muslim society was available in translation.[36] In
addition to the already cited views of the *Majalla* committee and Dr.
Sanhuri in Egypt, a particularly dramatic example of the interregional
circulation of such ideas is the resounding criticism of the shari'a issued
by the modernizing framers of the Turkish Civil Code of 1926. The

shari'a, represented at this juncture by the *Majalla*, had just been abolished and was being replaced by an adaptation of the Swiss code. These postmortem remarks focused on the link of the *Majalla* (shari'a) with "religion" and with what was understood as a "primitive" evolutionary-developmental stage of society. The memorandum attached to the new code explained that, of the 1,851 articles contained in the *Majalla*, "barely 300 articles satisfy modern needs."

> The rest is nothing but a mass of legal rules which are so primitive that they have no relationship to the needs of our country and are inapplicable. The principles of the *Majalla* are based on religion, whereas human life undergoes fundamental changes every day, even every minute.... States whose law is based on religion become incapable after a short time to satisfy the needs of the country and the nation, because religions express immutable rules. Life, however, marches on and requires rapid changes. As life changes constantly, the religious laws become nothing but empty words without meaning and formalities without value. Immutability is a dogmatic necessity for religion....
>
> The laws inspired by religion fetter the nations in which they are applied to the primitive periods when these laws were first born and they constitute insuperable barriers to progress....
>
> The modern state is distinguished from primitive societies by the fact that there are codified rules applicable to the relationships within the community. During the period of semicivilization, in a nomadic society, the laws are not codified....
>
> It was important therefore that justice in the Turkish Republic emerged from this chaos, this confusion, and the primitive state and adapted itself to the needs of the revolution and of modern civilization through the urgent adoption of a new civil code. This is why the Turkish Civil Code has borrowed the Swiss Civil Code....
>
> There are no essential differences among the needs of the nations which belong to the family of modern civilized societies. The constant economic and social relations have actually made one family out of civilized humanity.[37]

Instructive at the outset, the Turkish case is uniquely extreme in its final resolution concerning the shari'a.[38] Representing a full acceptance of the Western ethos of modernization and an associated desire for world-system assimilation, the memorandum expresses an uncompromising rejection of the shari'a (in the guise of the *Majalla*), which has become a stigmatizing symbol of backwardness.

Where Muslim populations were under direct Western rule, local versions of the shariʿa changed in several characteristic directions. Protracted colonial articulations of the shariʿa with Western law resulted in the emergence of wholly new legal syntheses. In Algeria and Tunisia, colonial French jurists worked out fusions of elements of the shariʿa with aspects of the Roman-law-influenced continental legal tradition, while in British India, a composite of the shariʿa and English law known as Anglo-Muhammadan law appeared. Another type of change, especially in shorter or partial colonial situations, concerned the relation of shariʿa to local custom. From the point of view of the colonizers, custom had to be either standardized or abolished altogether in favor of a unified legal system. Although the shariʿa was considered disorderly relative to Western law, when compared with "custom" it appeared orderly. As a consequence, the interests of colonizers and local elites in seeking to suppress custom and extend the sphere of shariʿa application frequently coincided.

In highland Yemen, in the absence of colonial rule, imams and town-based scholars had long felt an imperative to spread the shariʿa system (instruction, courts, and the state itself) to remote "tribal" districts where ignorance of Islam and pagan custom (*taghut*) were thought to prevail (cf. Dresch 1989). In precolonial Morocco, application of the shariʿa had been confined mainly to the large towns and their immediate hinterlands while custom held sway in the countryside. After the establishment of the French Protectorate in 1912, the sphere of shariʿa court jurisdiction expanded dramatically as the colonial state took control of rural districts (cf. Messick 1989:42). In the circa 1900 British Protectorate over the Fulani Sultanate of Northern Nigeria, where the shariʿa was already predominant, colonial officials promoted a still purer application. According to Schacht, administrators there were "inclined to prefer a formal and explicit doctrine, such as is provided by Islamic law, to changeable and badly defined customs."[39] In the Yemeni sultanates known collectively as the Aden Protectorate, the British were instrumental in the institutionalization of formal shariʿa courts and in the consequent decline of customary law. "Shariʿa law appears in South Arabia largely as the tool of the centralized government, whether indigenous or foreign," Anderson writes (1970 [1955]:11). For the "Protecting Power," he continues, "there is ... a natural tendency to champion the shariʿa, for it is 'tidier' than the vagaries of local custom from the administrative point of view and provides better political propaganda." Promotion of the shariʿa enabled the British to "pose as in some degree the champion of Islam, in partial imitation of the Governments of the Yemen and of Saudi Arabia" (1970:12n).

Translation

British judges in Aden and elsewhere consulted al-Nawawi in E. C. Howard's 1914 English translation of Van Den Berg's earlier rendering in French. Translation, an extremely important part of the general Orientalist project, also had its more pragmatic dimensions. Van Den Berg states in a preface to one of his translations:

> From year to year European control over Moslem populations is extend-ing, so that it is unnecessary to insist on the importance of rendering the two works that form the basis of the legal literature of the School of Shafi'i accessible, not only to a small number of Arabic scholars, but also to magistrates and political agents.[40]

Translations produced under the auspices of colonial administrations were informed by reigning philological methods and understandings about the nature of texts. An initial task was to sift and select among extant manuscripts to identify, or reconstruct, a sound original text. A recognized contribution of many such translations was to publish and, in a new sense, *to create* an authoritative Arabic text. Together with the possible variant readings, the additions, omissions, and alternative for-mulations found in other manuscripts would be relegated to footnotes.[41] However enigmatic or convoluted the original texts appeared to West-erners in argument and style, in translation they could be made to reveal bodies of discrete and objective meanings. Despite the apparent cacophony of its texts, the shari'a could be shown to be "saying some-thing." The resultant raw materials of positive knowledge contributed to the construction of more general notions about the essential nature of Muslim civilization.

In successive translations of the *Minhaj* and of Abu Shuja''s *Mukhtasar* there was a sense of an advancing positive science. Early and partial translations of Abu Shuja''s manual into Latin and Malay were de-scribed by Bousquet, a twentieth-century scholar and translator, as "absolutely barbaric," and the 1859 French translation by Keyzer [Keijzer] was deemed "of very little value."[42] In 1894 Van Den Berg, who had earlier translated al-Nawawi, published his French rendering of the Abu Shuja' text, embedded in the al-Ghazzi commentary. Look-ing back at his predecessor's effort, Van Den Berg notes, "It must not be forgotten that in the thirty-five years which have passed since the publication of the book by Keyzer, science has not stayed stationary and that I have had available to me more powerful means of interpretation than he."[43]

Although, in the estimation of Bousquet, Van Den Berg's effort represented considerable "progress" over that of Keyzer, there remained weaknesses to be rectified. The translation was still of "insufficient rigor." Like Keyzer before him, Van Den Berg had responded to the extreme concision of the text with a "tendency for paraphrase." Bousquet, by contrast, would "proceed systematically in the reverse direction," placing "in parentheses the words and the ideas indispensable for completing the Arabic phrase so as to render it intelligible in French." Bousquet found loose and variable translations of terminology in the earlier translators particularly unsatisfactory. Keyzer's work reminded him of that by Perron of Khalil (the principal Maliki manual), "where the same technical term is rendered by diverse expressions in French," while in the translation of al-Nawawi Van Den Berg had been "satisfied with a vagueness that was the most absolute, the most inexact, and the most exasperating concerning the translation of terms for legal categories." In his own translation, Bousquet adopted a "rigorous terminology," which, he explained, involved "systematically rendering technical expressions by a single term."[44]

As Van Den Berg saw it, his problems in translating al-Nawawi had begun with the "succinct" expression of the original: "Anyone who has studied the Arabic text of a book of jurisprudence and particularly one of the concise style of *Minhaj al-Talibin* will understand the difficulty of explicating all the subtleties, all the double meanings and all the ellipses." A further problem was understood to concern the Arabic language itself: "The construction of phrases in the Semitic languages," he wrote, "is poorly suited for philosophical reasoning," and, as a consequence, the translation of a work such as the *Minhaj* "presents more difficulties than the translation of a code written in a European language." In addition to its crude linguistic ethnocentrism, this is a view that seems to have forgotten the crucial historical role played by Arabic translations and other treatises in preserving and elaborating upon the Greek philosophy so cherished in Western intellectual culture (see Peters 1968).

Van Den Berg mobilized a variety of techniques to tame this unruly text and render it cognizable: in addition to a standard table of contents, a conventional subject index, and an apparatus of clarifying footnotes, he provides a glossary index of key Arabic terms and full

cross-references, via special footnotes and summary tables, to the relevant articles of the several French codes (Civil, General Procedure,
Criminal Procedure, Penal). In addition to these ordering devices,
when a series of points occurs in the Arabic, it is set off in the French
text in a numbered outline format. In the margins throughout the
translation there are topic headings in small print as guides to the
subject matter. In a manner parallel to the efforts of Ottoman and later
code drafters, Van Den Berg endeavored to make his work of translation accessible, orderly, and relevant to international legal concerns.

REPUBLICAN TEXTS

In 1975, a commission of shari'a jurists, composed of men who had
trained either on the Shafi'i manuals of al-Nawawi and Abu Shuja' or
on the *Al-Azhar* text of the Zaidi school, was created to participate in
the drafting work connected with *taqnin*, the legislative restatement of
shari'a materials in the Yemen Arab Republic.[45] Under Ministry of
Justice auspices, this activity was defined as the "legislation of Islamic
shari'a principles in the form (*shakl*) of modern codified laws appropriate to the spirit of the age and its requirements."[46] The republic had
known no impositions or receptions of Western code law, and its legislative efforts were being initiated in a postcolonial era of questionings of
Western values and reassertions of indigenous ones. The Muslim world
climate was one of emergent fundamentalist movements and efforts to
reintroduce the shari'a. As a guiding principle, the 1970 Permanent
Constitution identified the shari'a as "the source of all laws" (Art. 3).[47]

Two varieties of legislation have been produced, one of which is
explicitly shari'a based. The initial fruits of the jurist commission's work
appeared in the fourth volume of republican legislation, covering laws
enacted from 1976 through the first six months of 1977. In his introduction, the Director of the Legal Office observed that it "comprises legislation of tolerant Islamic shari'a principles, a harbinger of learned
efforts in which our honored scholars (*'ulama'*) can take just pride."[48]
What the volume contains, however, is mainly legislation produced by
"government economists and commercial experts" together with administrative regulations divided according to their ministries of origin.
In each of the shari'a-based laws, credit is given to the scholarly commission for a draft version presented to the Ministry of Justice. The
commission's efforts have been associated with the expected substantive
area of *statut personnel*—inheritance, legacies, gifts, endowments, and

marriage[49]—and also with such major pieces of general legislation as the Code of Procedure (1976) and the Civil Code (1979).[50]

This last has a double title, "Civil Code" (*al-qanun al-madani*) and "Shari'a Transactions" (*al-mu'amalat al-shar'iyya*), invoking both the Western model of civil legislation and the fiqh model of the *mu'amalat.* Like the Ottoman *Majalla* (and unlike the Civil Code of the Turkish Republic), this legislation is explicitly shari'a-derived. The first article refers to the law as "taken from (*ma'khudh min*) Islamic shari'a principles." The old notion of the *asl,* "source," is reemployed here, as it is in the Constitution, to identify the new position of the shari'a. Whereas shari'a jurisprudence once drew on "sources," it now has become the "source" drawn upon. In the old tree metaphor, shari'a principles have become the "roots" and legislated laws are the new *furu',* the "branches." The method involved, however, is not that of the *usul al-fiqh,* but rather procedures standard to legislative enactment, as adapted to the Yemeni setting.

The new source-authority of the old jurisprudence is both particular and general. Fiqh is the derivational source for the specific rules contained in the legislation and also the background or reference source for matters not explicitly covered or requiring interpretation. In addition to the "taken from" language, the derivational authority is expressed in Article 13: "Regarding the transactions, their types and particulars, the source is what the shari'a has established." Background authority is stated in Article 1: "If a specific text (*nass*) is not found in this law it is possible to proceed by means of reference to the principles of the Islamic shari'a from which this law is taken." Article 20 specifies that "the authoritative reference for the explication (*tafsir*) of the texts (*nusus*) of shari'a legislation and their application is Islamic jurisprudence (*fiqh*)." As it carefully specifies the influential role of the shari'a as both source and surround, the newly established hierarchy of legal principle nevertheless places "this legislative enactment (*hadha al-qanun*)," the newly derived "law" itself, in the foreground. Writing in English, the director of the Legal Office restates Article 1 to identify the four "sources of Yemeni law" (sources—now in the Western sense). These are law (legislation), principles of shari'a, custom (not contradictory to the shari'a), and principles of justice (in agreement with the shari'a).[51]

Such legislative texts have cleared a new legal space, a privileged enclosure of fixed and orderly rules. Simultaneously, they have relocated the old jurisprudence as an authoritative but distanced backdrop. As in codes enacted elsewhere, the open argument that once

characterized the fiqh is curtailed here: according to Article 2, change
by legislative amendment is envisioned, but interpretive modification
by individual "scholars of religion and carriers of the shari'a" ('ulama'
al-din wa hamalat al-shari'a) is restricted. In its new status as a source,
shari'a jurisprudence is ideally treated by drafters as a "whole corpus,"
in an attempt to hold divisive madhhab concerns at bay.[52] In accord with
the "spirit of the age," there is no explicit critique of the shari'a as too
vast, disorderly, or inadequate, but many of the issues explicitly moti-
vating earlier legislators elsewhere are implicit assumptions here as
well. The new space of law is also explicitly theoretical in construction:
the section heading concerning "the contract in general," for example,
further identifies itself as being concerned with the "theory of contract"
(nazariyyat al-'aqd).[53]

In addressing persons as either natural or legal (i'tibari), the code
moves away from the pronounced individual basis of the fiqh to a more
complex recognition of abstract entities ranging from the state and
cities to official organizations, commercial companies, cooperatives,
and corporations.[54] This integration into the legal requirements of the
world market system is reinforced by numerous specific laws developed
by the Ministry of the Economy, ranging from the new Commercial
Code (1976)[55] to specific legislation concerning such matters as trade-
marks.[56] These laws have been buttressed by the creation of commercial courts in the three largest cities.[57] Representing the first official
alternative to the formerly exclusive shari'a court jurisdiction, the commercial courts are the beginning of a civil court system.

Every piece of legislation opens with the phrase "After perusal of the
Permanent Constitution."[58] As a "constitution," dustur in Arabic, this
new foundational text partakes of a worldwide and also a specifically
Arab-world formula for the authoritative creation of a nation-state
polity. Chapter 1 begins, "Yemen is an Arab Islamic state." The preceding Preamble opens, "We the Yemenis are an Arab and Muslim
people." The document as a whole is headed by five short passages from
the Quran. The first of these, "We set thee on a clear road..." (45:18),
refers to a shari'a (in contrast to the shari'a), invoking the word's general
meaning as a "way," "path," or "road." The second (45:20) refers to
the original authoritative text, the Quran itself: "This is a clear indication for mankind, and a guidance and a mercy for a folk whose faith is
sure." Taking a position developed earlier by some reformers and many
fundamentalists and by Yemeni nationalists, religion is conceived of as
a dynamic force. In striking contrast to rejections of religion as an

immutable block to progressive change, exemplified by the quoted Turkish view from the 1920s, according to the Yemeni Constitution, "Islam, with its instructions, magnanimity, and breadth, is synonymous with development, marches with the times, and does not stand as an obstacle in the path of progress in life."[59]

Three additional opening Quranic verses (3:159, 42:38, 27:32)[60] invoke the idea of consultation, which figures centrally in the conception of the Yemeni state, viz., Article 1: "It is a consultative, parliamentary republic." As was, and is, true among Muslim reformers generally, *shura* (consultation) "represents an indigenous principle of representative or constitutional government in Islam."[61] The legislative body of the Y.A.R. was known as the *majlis al-shura*, Consultative Assembly.[62] Beyond the theoretical design of the state, however, consultation also characterizes the events of a formative moment in Yemeni history, one equivalent in national significance to the deliberations of the Founding Fathers over the Constitution of the United States. The Permanent Constitution was promulgated on December 28, 1970, but before this date an interval occurred during which a draft version was submitted to "all sectors" of the populace for consideration. This is described in the Preamble:

> Three months have elapsed since the publication of the draft constitution on the evening of September 26, 1970, and since then meetings of the various sectors have been held in the capital, towns, and villages in which the constitution was openly debated and opinions and views exchanged about it. The Republican Council has received letters and telegrams on the constitution, has held meetings with Shari'a scholars, the Ulama, Shaykhs, wise and cultured men; it has listened to their views and entered into useful debates with them.

This national discussion, the Preamble concludes, "explicitly proves the Nation's determination to follow the democratic, consultative path by both word and action." A novel sort of popular authority is thus provided for the nation's constitutive document.

This new discourse of nation and people grafts shari'a constructs upon Western legislative and constitutional forms. The singular authorship of the old fiqh texts is replaced by the plural legislative voice; the authoritative manual opinion, by the authoritative code article. Where opinions entered a contentious arena of ongoing argument, the legislated text becomes effective as law from its "date of publication" in the Official Gazette. In Yemen, it has appeared possible, as the Preamble to the Constitution says, to "preserve . . . character, customs, and heritage" while adapting to the standards of the community of "interlocked" nations. In the absence of a colonial rupture with the past, change has seemed to involve critiques of the old regime and systematic installations of new institutions made possible by the Revolution.

PART II

Transmission

CHAPTER 4

Audition

The Quran became the basis of instruction, the foundation for all the habits acquired later on. The reason for this is that the things one is taught in one's youth take root more deeply.

IBN KHALDUN

Going to Quranic school for me, and for all children, was like being taken to the slaughterhouse . . . it had a meaning akin to death.

M. AL-AKWA' (n.d.:33–34)

Prompted from time to time by the deep voice of their teacher or by the rap of his rod, the high-pitched chanting of children reciting their lessons in Quranic schools was a familiar sound in town neighborhoods. In his memoirs, Muhammad al-Akwa' provides a vivid account of his youthful experiences in such a school. Born in 1903, al-Akwa' went on to become an Ibb teacher of advanced students, a political activist jailed in conjunction with the early nationalist stirrings, and, upon release, a judge in a district near Ibb. After the Revolution, he was appointed minister of justice and held other offices while pursuing a career as one of the most distinguished of contemporary Yemeni historians.[1]

It was by playing on his father's "compassion" for an only male child that initially enabled al-Akwa' to delay his entrance into Quranic school. But when all avoidance stratagems had been exhausted, he was forcibly taken to the *mi'lama* in the village where he grew up. To accomplish this task his father sent a close and trusted friend.

> He caught me by surprise, and I yelled and kicked trying to get out of the man's grip, but I couldn't because his hold on me was very firm. I found no way to get free, but I managed to leak on him without his noticing. The urine flowed and he suddenly started and shouted loudly in consternation. He put me down as he tried to avoid getting his clothes soiled, but he didn't let me escape from him or show pity for me. At the same time, we smiled a little, and part of the fear went away. (n.d.:33)

A few years earlier, another young son of a scholarly family had begun attending a similar school in Ibb. Ahmad bin Muhammad al-Haddad, grandson of ʿAli Naji and nephew of ʿAbd al-Rahman al-Haddad, and himself a future mufti and judge in the town, was about eight years old when he entered a miʿlama located in the tiny prayer room of the little Humazi Mosque near his house. With Ahmad at his Quranic school were a group of boys from his quarter, the same ones who stood with him in the regular sundown children's battles.

For generations in Ibb, as the sunset prayer call went out over the town, youths from opposing quarters met in combat under the spreading branches of a large tree in the central market square. As adult shoppers hurriedly dispersed to get out of the way, and merchants closed up their shops, the side alleys would be clogged with boys armed with sorghum stalks waiting to converge on the square. In his day, young Ahmad led the boys from his own and allied quarters. "I used to hit and be hit, but I don't ever remember retreating," he recalled. "In those days I was full of play, and my father tried to correct my behavior with punishments. But they say that when a boy is full of *jinn* (spirits) as a youth he will have great intelligence as an adult."

Pupils addressed their teacher as "Our Master," *Sinna* in colloquial. Sinna's place was a slightly raised dais of cushions while his pupils sat cross-legged on a mat in a semicircle around him. As a child entered in the morning he formally greeted Sinna and kissed him on the hand or knee. Then he retrieved his personal wooden lesson-board, which had been washed and recoated at the end of the previous day with a clay solution that left a grey-white writing surface. Board in hand, he assumed an accustomed place. Thereafter, a pupil could leave only with permission. To be excused to go to the bathroom, for example, a pupil in al-Akwaʿ's school had to rise and say, "May God forgive Our Master," and then make the appropriate indication with his little finger. Permission could be denied to those suspected of faking a call of nature as a subterfuge to go out and play, although then Sinna might have to put up with whining and complaints. Formally excused for the morning meal, or at the end of the morning session just before the noon call to prayer, the children escaped from the miʿlama "like sparrows from a cage."

Though often a humble individual, Sinna was treated with great respect when entertained at meals at pupils' houses. On such occasions he would replace his everyday school clothes with his best attire, including his scholar's turban and multilayered, pure white gowns. In al-Akwaʿ's school there was also a daily institution of bringing blessing upon the teacher and the activities of the school. As they were excused, the children gathered outside the mi'lama, and one pupil led the others in shouting out their blessing at the tops of their young voices.

> "May God forgive Our Master and his parents," cried the leader. "May God forgive Our Master and his parents," responded the others. "And our parents with his parents." "And our parents with his parents," in unison. "And those who study with him and learn from him (lit. "in his hands," *bayna yadayhi*). "And those who study with him and learn in his hands," shouted the class. (n.d.:44)

Sinna had means at his disposal to ensure proper discipline among his unruly pupils. With legal guardians, husbands, and governors, such teachers occupied a social role with a legally recognized capacity for discretionary discipline.[2] The rod was commonly used, and al-Akwa''s teacher had in addition a simple pole-and-strap bastinado device, which restrained the legs of a child so that the soles of his feet could be beaten. In problem cases, Sinna put a pupil in a dark corner where he was not allowed to speak or even gesture to the others. As a still harsher measure, one that al-Akwa' remembers caused feelings of desolation and fear (n.d.:49), Sinna could keep the pupil in the corner when the others had been dismissed for lunch. In a procedure exactly analogous to the political process used to obtain the release of an official detainee, Sinna would entertain the interventions and appeals of some of the pupil's older friends, who would offer their "guarantee" (*kafala*) that the delinquent pupil would not repeat his offense. In cases of grave offenses, Sinna might not accept these mediations, and the pupil would languish in the corner, at which point, just like a prisoner in jail, his lunch would have to be brought from his house.

Corporal and other forms of explicit correction, frequent and fear-inspiring though they might be, constituted only an overt aspect of the broad and subtle disciplining that was an important Quranic-school objective. This was to instill *adab*,[3] a complex of valued intellectual dispositions and appropriate behaviors. A verb from the same root (*addaba*) means to educate, to discipline, and to punish, while *adab* the noun can refer specifically to either literature or manners. In a general sense, *adab* was the primary responsibility of a child's parents. The Quranic school specialized in correct comportment, both among a cohort of pupils and especially in relation to Sinna, and in the memorized acquisition of the Quran, the sacred text.

Quranic-school formation was integral to a later stage of a child's upbringing and development, matters that are elaborated upon in general terms in several law-manual sections.[4] The responsibilites of the mother and the father are differentiated in a section providing for the special circumstance of parental separation. Child rearing (*hadana*) concerns the care of dependent children prior to the age of discernment (*tamyiz*), and in this the mother, or in her absence or refusal, another woman of her family, has the basic right and duty.[5] The responsibilities include such things as proper raising (*tarbiyya*), nursing and later providing food and drink, the cleansing of body and clothes, and care during illness. Specifics for infants, enumerated in a discussion of the hire of nurses, include "washing his head and body and clothes, anointing him with oil, putting kohl in his eyes, swaddling him in the cradle, and rocking him until he sleeps." The mother's child-care responsibility continues until the child is seven, or the point at which the child reaches discernment. At this point, given separated parents, the child must choose which parent to reside with. The implications of a decision to reside with the mother differ for boys and girls: "If a male child chooses her, he resides with her during the night and spends the day with his father, who (should) educate/discipline him [the *addaba* verb], and place him in Quranic school or in a craft apprenticeship;[6] if a female child [chooses her] she resides with her night and day."

In the manual discussions, a child's later development is broken down into the attainments of intellectual and physical maturity. The transition from minority to majority entails the onset of full responsibility in one's actions, including both obligations of the faith such as prayer and fasting and full capacity with respect to one's social undertakings such as contracts. In his or her affairs the minor is under a protective interdiction, which is only lifted with the attainment of this two-part maturity. "Interdiction of the minor," al-Nawawi writes, "is lifted with his physical and intellectual maturity" *bulugh* and *rushd* (1883:16).

> *Bulugh* is marked by reaching fifteen years of age, or by the emission of semen. The earliest moment it is possible is nine years of age. The growth of pubic hair is a decisive indicator of *bulugh* in a non-Muslim but not a Muslim boy, according to a preferred but contested view. [*Bulugh*] in a woman is indicated by menstruation and pregnancy. *Rushd* [in a boy] involves competency in ritual and financial matters, and that he not engage in sinful acts that would invalidate trustworthiness (*'adala*), or be a spendthrift.

It is possible that a youth can mature physically without being mature intellectually, and in such cases the interdiction continues; when a youth matures physically, and he or she is also mature intellectually, the interdiction is lifted. Physical maturity, *bulugh*, is associated implicitly with adult articulateness, with the bodily production of appropriately constituted voicings. From the same b--l--gh root comes the word *baligh*, meaning "eloquent," and also *balagha*, the name of the formal discipline of rhetoric. *Bulugh* thus represents a sexual maturity or puberty that also implies a physical maturation in the capacity to articulate the word. At the onset of a youth's capacity to produce semen, which carries a fertile seed, his word likewise begins to convey a matured intention and is therefore binding when communicated in the social world. Semen and words are the associated ejaculations of potent male maturity.

As an analytically separate issue, intellectual maturity, *rushd*, a prerequisite for adult intentionality, can be examined in a youth, but significantly it is not connected with knowledge that may have been gained in school. The *rushd* indicators are instead those of practical sorts of competency. For boys this examination should take different forms according to the father's occupation; for girls it is undifferentiated.[7] Presumed here is the existence of the sorts of compartmentalized informal knowledges that necessarily attend a complex society and a developed division of labor.

> The *rushd* of a minor can be examined and should differ according to status (*al-maratib*). The son of a merchant is examined about selling and buying and the negotiations involved in them; the son of a cultivator about agriculture and the financial management of those who undertake it; the (son of a) craftsman about that which concerns his craft; and a girl about that which concerns spinning and cotton and the protection of food from the cat, etc.

Set against this backdrop of conceptualization concerning child raising and maturation, the Quranic school was a specialized institution in which most town boys (and some girls) spent at least a few years. It was not by any means limited in its enrollments to the children of scholars or jurists. The result was a wide exposure to an authoritative intellectual world only a few would go on to master. In its later stages the Quranic school amounted to an apprenticeship in the specialized craft of knowledge. Mi'lama training ideally culminated in an individual who had embodied, and was capable of appropriately reproducing, the interrelated forms of both text and behavior. Such training was part of a general process of "inscription," the social construction of what De Certeau terms a "corpus juridique," a legal corpus or body of law. Two complementary processes are involved: humans are entextualized and texts are physically embodied.[8]

Construable in such terms are a series of ritual activities that serve to fix the social identities of children. These are described in manuals and enacted in Ibb. At birth, for example, it is established Sunna to recite the call to prayer in the ears of the newborn. Shouted out five times each day from the minarets, rooftops, or doorways of mosques, the call to prayer is the public summons to the fundamental communal activity of prayer. An infant is by definition unable to engage in prayer, an act that requires the physical capacity for articulation, the memorized Quranic verses, and the conscious formulation of the intent to pray. According to the manuals, at about age seven, or the age of discernment, children should be exhorted to begin praying, and by age ten they should be punished if they fail to pray. In the absence of an ability to pray, the infant can nevertheless be initially imprinted with the heard recitation of the call. The verb for "to call" to prayer is from a root that also gives the word for "ear" and might be more literally translated as "to make hear." Hearing is the paradigmatic opening step in all recitational processes, and what is passively "heard" as the lines are spoken into a newborn's right and left ears is not only a call to community but also the first citation of what will become his or her central recitation, the testimony of the faith, the *shahada*. The call to prayer contains the *shahada* lines "There is no god but God" and "Muhammad is the Prophet of God." This first call, a recited word conveyed in the voice of the parent, is an opening social impression upon a human tabula rasa.

On the infant's seventh day of life there are further recommended ritual undertakings, which are accompanied by animal sacrifice.[9] The manuals specify that two young sheep should be slaughtered for a boy and one for a girl. This is an initial expression of a pattern of gender-based distinctions played out in many other domains of life, including some set forth in manual sections—for example, those concerning relative inheritance shares, blood money payments, and witnessing statuses. In Ibb, rituals surrounding birth include both the activities specified in the manuals and other local elaborations. On the third day after birth, for example, women gather to sing and celebrate with the mother; and on the fortieth day the period of a special food regime for the new mother, visiting by women, and separation of the husband and wife come to a close with a present from the husband.[10]

The gender differentiation in sacrifice is reinforced by the accom-

panying and also manual-mandated act of naming, the fundamental
form of societal, familial, and gender labeling, which also occurs on the
seventh day. In addition to this linguistic form of marking, boys in Ibb
are also circumcised at this time. According to the manuals, male
circumcision is not absolutely required until physical maturity (*bulugh*)
is attained; it is recommended, however, that it occur in conjunction
with the rites of the seventh day. Dramatized and concretized in this
intersection of blood sacrifice, the bestowing of the name, and violent
bodily marking are the broader contours of the general reproduction of
society.

While boys maintained their own separate and unruly activities of
play and combat outside the miʿlama,[11] as pupils under the control of
Sinna they represented the primary liminal group, one temporarily
separated from society in order to be prepared for eventual full adult
participation in society. The Quranic school experience was an extended rite of passage that, for some at least, gradually effected a social
transition from an undisciplined and ignorant child to an *adab*-formed
youth. In the sense that all such passages involve the loss of an old
social identity and the acquisition of a new one, al-Akwaʿ 's association
of going to the miʿlama with the slaughterhouse and death is apt.
Youthful play was eventually silenced.

The pupils' special liminality is demonstrated by the role they
assumed in the vanguard of rites associated with death and burial.
"Among the enjoyable times for pupils," al-Akwaʿ writes (n.d.:53),
"was when someone died and the relatives of the deceased called upon
the school to perform its recitations at the head of the funeral procession." To the relief of the pupils, the school's normal activities were
interrupted so that their youthful voices, repeating the names of God
and the testimony of the faith, could lead the way to the cemetery.[12]

The conclusion of Quranic school studies was marked by a semipublic ceremony known as the *khatam*, which, in Yemen,[13] occurred
when a boy had successfully memorized a portion of the Quran. Guests,
including Sinna as the guest of honor, were invited to a meal at the
pupil's house. His *luha*, his personal writing board, which had been
repeatedly written upon, washed, and recoated over the years of his
memorizing efforts, would now be retired. For the occasion, it was
decorated by Sinna with Quranic verses in painted calligraphy and
hung with herbs and flowers. Khatam ceremonies among the wealthy
and powerful, such as that for the governor's son photographed in
Ibb in the 1950s (see fig. 6), could be extremely lavish events attended

Figure 6. Khatam celebration for Ibb governor al-Sayaghi's son, with local officials as guests, 1950s.

by local dignitaries. For others, the khatam was a far more modest rite to conclude the *mi'lama* passage.

Many pupils simply dropped out earlier without reaching the point of the khatam. Until the time of the Revolution of 1962, the three or four years spent in one of the twelve neighborhood Quranic schools in Ibb would be the extent of many children's (and virtually all girls') exposure to the literate skills. For the sons of governors and of scholars, such as Ahmad al-Haddad and Muhammad al-Akwaʿ, and a small but consistent number of boys of modest and untutored backgrounds, however, the khatam represented the conclusion of only the primary stage of instruction. Already at this level, the characteristic pyramid of traditional instruction had begun to reproduce itself, providing, as always, a modicum of opportunity for upward mobility.

For the scholar-to-be the khatam marked the end of a time of early moral and intellectual formation. When a youth such as Ahmad al-Haddad began to join the *madrasa*, the advanced lesson circles in the prayer room of the Great Mosque, he stopped wearing the simple embroidered headpiece worn by a boy of his status and began to wear the elaborate *ʿimama* turban of a scholar. Instead of the striped gown in

which he led his fellow combatants at dusk he would now wear white.
For special occasions he had white overgarments with long, wide
sleeves, and a sheathed dagger and embroidered dagger belt from his
father to complete his formal attire. People in the community began to
call him "al-Qadi Ahmad," using the appropriate term of address for
a young male from a *qadi* family who had embarked on the path of
knowledge.[14]

Ahmad began to adhere to a more elaborate set of rules of conduct,
for he had become one of the *muhājirin*, the collective name for the
advanced madrasa students. The term derives from the verbal root
hajara, meaning to emigrate, to separate, to dissociate oneself, to aban-
don and relinquish.[15] Devoting themselves to the pursuit of knowledge,
the muhajirin passed their student lives in a kind of seclusion, entailing
a still more developed liminality. The madrasa students were set apart
from the rest of society by their special routines of study, to which they
had initally been adapted by their years in the mi'lama. Ahmad rose
with the dawn call to prayer and made his way from his house through
the dark alleyways to the Great Mosque. Following the prayer and
until sunrise, lessons were held by lamplight; even after sunrise light is
slow in reaching the town because of the high peaks that rise immediately to the east. Following these early lessons, the students returned to
the residence, known as the Hazr, a building located up an alley from
the Great Mosque. Boarding students, such as Ahmad's friend Qasim
Shuja' al-Din, a future teacher and doctor (*tabib*),[16] and some of the
teachers shared rooms in the Hazr. All the students ate their meals
together there, beginning with an early morning "lunch" of sorghum
bread and sorghum porridge. During the day many of the teachers
occupied themselves in such lucrative work as writing contracts and
other documents, while the students worked among themselves on their
lessons until the afternoon prayer, following which they had a "supper"
consisting of the same meal as earlier. They continued to study in the
Hazr residence, pausing to pray at sundown, until the fifth and final
evening prayer, after which they retired.

The muhajirin passed their days between the madrasa of the Great
Mosque and the Hazr. They were expressly forbidden to enter the
nearby marketplace, the center of mundane contact among males going about their daily business. The muhajirin were also not permitted
to smoke tobacco or chew *qat*, the ubiquitous focus of everyday afternoon gatherings for adults. The Hazr was a place of retreat, and the
muhajirin were a community of scholars in training, who studied, took

their meals, and (among the boarders) shared small sleeping cells in communal fashion. They led an existence apart from ordinary society, in a seclusion that was a fundamental part of their lengthy initiation into the world of knowledge.

In demeanor, the students were typically shy and retiring, at least in forays outside their circle of fellow muhajirin. The rude and brash childish behavior that persisted well into Quranic school days was now thoroughly eradicated. Although they were legally mature, and while other youths their age had already embarked upon adult careers in trade and the crafts, the muhajirin retained a distinctive immaturity, a "bashfulness,"[17] when confronted with ordinary social life. It was during his years at the Great Mosque and the Hazr, for example, that Ahmad was engaged to be married to the daughter of his uncle 'Abd al-Rahman al-Haddad. He later described himself as "so shy I could not bring myself to attend the large engagement feast given by my uncle." This shyness associated with the muhajirin identity is as patterned as the stern, often assertive, and even immodest character typical of many scholars who had left their formative years of study behind to become active in public affairs. Yet there were also a few men who seemed to retain that retiring quality, so pronounced among the muhajirin scholars, for their entire lives.

DARASA

In the Great Mosque lesson circles and at the nearby Hazr residence in Ahmad al-Haddad's day teachers and students enaged in a complex of activities known collectively as *darasa*.[18] At its conceptual base, darasa was a pedagogy of recitation, a practice already thoroughly inculcated in youthful rote memorization of the paradigmatic text, the Quran.[19] It was the ability to recite the Word of God that was marked and celebrated in the khatam ceremony. In Quranic school, recitation occurred in its simplest form and in association with the most sacred of texts. The problems of meaning and interpretation, however, remained to be addressed. The classical Arabic of the Quran was itself not immediately clear to the colloquial-speaking pupils who learned to recite it; beyond the Arabic words were complex exegetical issues. In Morocco, where students regularly undertook the considerably more lengthy and challenging effort of committing the entire Quran to memory, they did so without the aid of comprehension. They asked "no questions concerning the meaning of the verses, even among themselves, nor did it occur to them to do so.''[20] In advanced darasa instruction in Ibb, recitation continued to be fundamental, but it was set in combination with interpretive commentaries and elucidating discussions. The essential relation discussed earlier of text and commentary, of recited *matn* and explanatory *sharh*, underpinned darasa pedagogy.

An early suggestion of the key progression from recitation and memorization to understanding and application is found at the Quranic school level. Al-Akwa' writes that when the alphabet was introduced the pupil was initially told to repeat the letters, "alif, ba, ta, tha, jim, etc. . . . until they were memorized" (n.d.: 39). Later, he "went on to the second stage, which involved learning how to place the letters in the written form of script on the writing board." This progression, from instructor recitation, to student repetition leading to memorization, and finally to the supplementation of memory by writing and learned understanding, also characterized the main routine of darasa learning. The relationship of Quranic school to advanced darasa instruction in the madrasa represents more, however, than the simple replication of a structural principle, initially embryonic and later elaborated. The shift from Quranic school to darasa instruction also recapitulates the general movement from the Quran (and the Sunna) to the jurisprudence of the shari'a, a movement from basic text to expansive commentary, from sacred to humanly constituted discourse.

In Ibb the Quran was not much memorized after Quranic school, although there were occasional individuals who went on to earn the title of *hafiz*, one who had learned the whole text by heart.[21] Among them were the blind students in Ibb,[22] who devoted themselves mainly to Quran memorization and the art of recitation (*tajwid*). Their study, in the absence of any capacity for visual reference to a physical text that could be read or otherwise used as a cue, is a pointed reminder of the oral/aural nature of textual transmission and acquisition.

As a pedagogical complex, darasa was concerned with jurisprudence and an array of supporting disciplines, including the language sciences, Quranic exegesis, and the science of hadith. Darasa was broken down into several specialized modalities of learning, although some of the terminology involved is misleading, especially in the light of contemporary usage. Verbs that have come to mean separate activites, such as "to recite" (*tala, tilawa*), "to read" (*qara'a*), and "to study" (*darasa*), were once much closer in their referents. All were used interchangeably, for example, to describe the ritual activity the local muhajirin collectively engaged in on the eves of Friday and Monday, namely, the recited repetition of the Ya Sin chapter of the Quran.

Beyond the Quran, in darasa proper, there were three distinct categories of texts and associated modes of relating to texts. In an autobiographical sketch, al-Shawkani (A.H. 1348, 2:214ff.) provides an unusually detailed example of this tripartite breakdown of textual relations in the scholarly habitus. In his enumeration of the texts he studied in his own formation, al-Shawkani begins with a listing of those he memorized, texts that are referred to as *mahfuzat*, "memorized texts." All were short, abridged works (he also calls them *mukhtasarat*), and a few of them were versified. All are similar in their concision and suitability for rote acquisition to the *matn* of Abu Shuja', which was among the memorized works forming the textual core in the advanced formation of Ahmad al-Haddad and other Shafi'i jurists. First among the texts al-Shawkani mentions in this category is in fact the *matn* of the key Zaidi text, *Al-Azhar*. These texts designed for memorization were closest in structural identity to the Quran and were usually learned in a similar manner.

Such *mahfuzat*, or memorized texts, constituted a first category of post-Quranic textual learning, which al-Shawkani says he began after his Quranic school khatam and before he embarked on his regular course of advanced study. Ahmad al-Haddad likewise recalled that he studied the Abu Shuja' text and the *Minhaj* of al-Nawawi when, as he put it, he was "still young," in his first years at the madrasa of the Great Mosque of Ibb. Al-Shawkani notes, however, that some of his total of eleven *mahfuzat* were accomplished after his formal studies had begun, so that this first category should be considered both an initial stage and a category of basic acquisition coexisting with the other two types of textual relations.

Although he consistently identifies his teachers in connection with the second and third categories of texts, in listing his memorized works al-Shawkani makes no mention of any instructional intervention, indicating that he acquired them directly on his own. As with the Quran, this mode of relating to a text was not concerned with exegetical issues. Unlike the Quranic school process, however, which was guided by Sinna, this memorization usually involved a form of unmediated individual acquisition, designed to build a solid base for later study with teachers focusing on commentaries and interpretive problems. In this instructional absence—from both teachers and their own peers—students labored in the pure presence of the text.

Standard formulas for describing memorization use the verb *hafaza*, which also means to conserve and protect, and to store or place in safekeeping. The two main (and interchangeable) expressions using this verb and referring to memorization are h–f–z *'an zahr al-qalb* (by heart, lit. "on the surface of the heart") and h–f–z *'an zahr al-ghayb*. This usage of *al-ghayb*, a difficult word, which can mean such apparently diverse things as "absence," "concealed," "invisible," and "the supernatural," and as a verb, "to vanish," "to be forgotten," and "to lose consciousness," conveys the paradoxical qualities of memorization as a type of internal inscription. Memorization involves a knowledge Socrates understood to be "written in the soul of the learner"; in the Muslim tradition this knowledge is closest to the true self and yet absented, partaking of the genuine but elusive nature of the divine.

The great majority of al-Shawkani's textual efforts are of a second type, classified as *maqru'at*, from the already mentioned q–r–' root. These are the "recited texts" studied in the pattern of *qara'a 'ala* (or *darasa 'ala*), a verb-plus-preposition formula indicating the standard recitational-commentary lessons guided by a teacher. This format was by far the most typical of darasa instruction. Lessons usually focused on works of commentary; these contained embedded basic texts, which some students had already committed to memory. An example in al-Shawkani's case is the *Sharh al-Azhar*, the important commentary on the basic *Al-Azhar* text. For the al-Haddads of Ibb and other Shafi'is the relevant texts were al-Ghazzi's commentary on Abu Shuja' and Ibn Hajar and al-Ramli on al-Nawawi. While the scale alone of these multivolume works was prohibitive, the essentially disputed nature of commentary as a genre also rendered a memorization approach to them inappropriate. In Ibb some texts of the type memorized by a scholar such as al-Shawkani were learned in the *maqru'at* pattern.

In the typical lesson, oral presentation by the teacher of a section of the work under consideration was followed by his commentary—his lesson *sharh*. Later there was an opportunity for questions from the students. Isma'il al-Akwa' (1980:11) describes the pedagogical technique of the northern highlands as follows:

> Among the Zaidis, the teacher recites (*yaqra'u*) the lesson and then comments upon it to the students. They listen to him and then he asks them during the commentary: has the meaning become clear? If one of them poses a question, he repeats the commentary, clarifying that part of the meaning that had not been clear. The second day, the teacher asks his students for a summary of the previous lesson, and this summary is called *al-dabit*.

Recitation is coupled with attentive listening, whereas commentary is associated with questioning. The situation in Yemen regarding student interventions during or immediately following the commentary portion of the lesson seems to fall midway between what occurred in Morocco, where no questions at all could be asked (Eickelman 1985:95), and Iran, where there were regular questions and extensive formal training in disputation (Fischer 1980; Mottahedeh 1985).[23] It is reported of Sayf al-Sunna, the twelfth-century hadith scholar from Ibb, that he engaged his students in a discussion of the text he was teaching and that he eventually licensed all of them to transmit the text, except for one, who is said to have persisted in a disagreement with him.

The teacher's oral presentation frequently took the form of recited dictation, as is indicated in the already quoted memorial poem referring to the jurisprudence text, "which he used to / Dictate to me in the early morning darkness." This dictation was the beginning of an instructional process the ideal end product of which occurred when a student could return to the teacher to recite back to him (*qara'a 'alayhi*) the learned material. The pattern was established in the Quranic school, where the teacher demanded of the pupil, "Recite your lesson-board" (*iqra' luhaka*). The pupil stood before the teacher, holding the lesson-board with the writing facing the teacher. The request was for the pupil to recite from memory a section of text originally taken as dictation from or written out by the teacher and then committed to memory on his or her own. In advanced study, the equivalent activity involved the accurate, correctly voweled recitational reproduction of the originally dictated work. It was the capacity to accurately reproduce the text that was taken as evidence of a learning achievement. Between the two moments invested with instructional weight—the opening recitation by the teacher and the closing recitation by the student—a great deal went on, but these activities of the interval were rarely remarked upon.

Although the aim of this second and principal type of darasa learning was not memorization, the day-to-day work of repetition of the successive segments of a text could result in an extreme familiarity verging on memorization. In accord with the theory of legitimate textual transmission, the established ideal was to "receive" the text directly from the teacher, but in practice the students frequently did a major portion of their learning independently of the lesson circle. Al-Haddad explained that the procedure in Ibb was to have recourse to teachers only when students could not resolve a question among themselves. "For the most part," he said, "the method of study rested upon independent student efforts prior to formal instruction, with consultation with the teacher only in cases of intractable issues."[24]

"Peer learning," as Eickelman (1985:98) has labeled the key activity of the interval, has been underappreciated in studies of Islamic education "because it is characteristically informal." Vital though it was, peer learning was typically left out of formal accounts of the learning process, including those appearing in biographical dictionaries (cf. Eickelman 1985:42) because authoritative significance in this culture of knowledge was anchored in teacher-to-student nodes of transmission. After the early-morning lessons in the madrasa of the Great Mosque, most of the Ibb student's day, including long hours spent at the Hazr residence, was devoted to study without guidance from teachers. During these same hours, some of the teachers went out to work as part-time notaries preparing legal documents to supplement their incomes. The pattern of separation was similar in Quranic school. After lunch the pupils pursued their lessons alone while Sinna passed the afternoon smoking his water pipe and chewing qat (cf. M. al-Akwaʿ n.d.:44). In Ibb, the importance of peer learning for the acquisition and maintenance of the scholarly habitus was not confined to formal study; often a practice of informal study among learned friends continued in later years.

The theory of legitimate transmission meant not only that significance was attached to emphasized opening and closing moments of the instructional cycle but also that a predominantly oral/recitational character was attributed to the process as a whole. The necessities of theory obscured not only peer learning but also the crucial role of writing. The unmarked activities of the interval were structured by an equally unrecognized reliance upon the activity of the pen. One of the features that distinguishes books by contemporary Yemeni scholars such as the al-Akwaʿ brothers from accounts in the old biographical dictionaries is their attention to formerly unnoticed aspects of the instructional process. Thus Muhammad al-Akwaʿ writes (n.d.: 39) in minute detail about the Quranic school (a subject innovation in and of itself) and mentions that at the outset the pupil was shown how to "hold the pen" and "place the writing board in his hands."

From Ismaʿil al-Akwaʿ's book on Islamic schools in Yemen we learn that a potential artifact of day-to-day study by many of the advanced muhajirin was a written manuscript copy of the text worked on. In a passage very much unlike accounts found in old biographical dictionaries, al-Akwaʿ (1980:269) describes the behind-the-scenes practices of former students in the important Zaidi school in the northern plateau town of Dhamar:

> Most of the students studied without one of them owning a book. They borrowed books from private owners or from their teachers and copied (*yanqulu*) the section for study from them every day. By the time he had finished a book, a student had his own manuscript copy of what he had studied. In a few years he had all of the books of instruction.

Contrary to ideal expectations, it is evident from this description that instructional transmission of the text often involved a mundane physical transfer, a simple borrowing of a book for the purposes of copying and study. Texts were not only carried in the "hearts" of scholars, they were often preserved as well in the form of personal manuscripts. The oral-medium formula of authenticity was quietly buttressed by the services of reading and writing. The existence of such handwritten texts also must be presupposed as a necessary accompaniment to many of the routines of memorization study, just as the "dictation" opening the standard lesson often required a written text as a cue.

Reading and writing figure importantly in the instructional activity of darasa. At the same time, however, their roles were systematically kept in the background while oral dimensions of the same complex of activities were placed in the foreground. This culturally specific devaluation and valuation of the respective roles of written and oral communication was integral to the larger theory of transmission upon which the legitimacy of knowledge hinged. The "dictation" relationship involved both a dictating teacher and note-taking students, but it was the oral recitation-like activity of the teacher and the listening of the students rather than his reading and their writing that were taken to be of consequence. An analytic identification of the important role played by reading and writing in this "recitational" complex should not be overstated, however. There were significant instances of memorization and aspects of transmission that occurred without the aid of a written text, including the mentioned case of the blind students and also the instruction of some teachers, especially those not teaching lengthy commentary works, who "dictated" their lesson texts straight from memory.

In view of the conceptual subordination of reading in the intellectual mainstream, represented by darasa instruction, it might be concluded that there existed no notion of "reading" in a sense equivalent to the Western "silent" and "comprehension" forms. This sort of reading was in fact common and routine, but it flourished without conceptual impediment only outside the instructional core, in subjects and activities relatively marginal or mundane in comparison with those associated with darasa. Such reading was considered an appropriate mode of relating to a number of textual genres, none of which were so rigorously "recitational" in either the character of their authorship or their mode of transmission as the basic darasa texts. In Yemen, the terms for such "reading" tend to be derived from the root ṭ–l–ʿ, as opposed to the several verbs, such as q–r–ʾ, which referred to recitation-reading or dictation. Al-Shawkani, for example, uses words from both sets of roots to set his precocious reading of historical works and literature apart from his formal academic training. Referring to himself in the third person, he writes:

> Before formally commencing his advanced studies he worked hard in the reading (*muṭalaʿa*) of history books and collections of literature, and this was in the days when he was [still] in Quranic school. He read (*ṭalaʿa*) numerous books and many collections, then he commenced formal instruction and studied with/recited to (*qaraʾa ʿala*).[25]

Most of the reading that went on outside the instructional sphere, that is, reading minus the concern for authoritative transmission which is by definition associated with face-to-face encounters and oral-aural connections, was of the ṭ–l–ʿ type. A word from the same root is used, for example, to describe what an administrator does when he is handed a document: he "reads" the document, silently and for comprehension. *Muṭalaʿa* was what one did with most library books.[26]

The issues surrounding the relative importance within darasa of reading and writing skills versus verbal ones are posed more sharply in connection with a third and final category of study. Al-Shawkani concludes his listing of the works he studied with a category that he calls *masmuʿat*, or "heard texts." This comprises a short set of titles (a bit more numerous than his list of "memorized texts"), many but not all of which are the annually recited authoritative collections of hadiths, such as the *Sahih* of al-Bukhari and the *Sahih* of Muslim. The second of these was the work Sayf al-Sunna had traveled from Ibb to Mecca to hear in 1184. During the month of Rajab in many locales in Yemen, regular instruction was customarily interrupted as these hadith collections were recited in the local scholarly community.[27] Many scholarly biographies mention that such texts were "heard."

What is especially interesting about the category of "heard texts" is that it separates out audition alone as a self-sufficient and authoritative

mode of textual acquisition. In fact, of a total of eight distinguishable
methods of receiving knowledge from a teacher, "hearing" and the
recitational study method of the *maqru'at* are considered "the highest
and the best."[28] On the transmitter or teacher's side, adjusted for the
different sort of text being handled, this mode of instruction is similar
to the *maqru'at* style; the terms "dictate" and "recite aloud" (*qara'a*) are
both used in this connection. This instruction always departed from a
written text because the lengthy compilations of hadiths, containing
lists of linked transmitters' names, were not memorized (although,
again, the originally spoken words of the *mutun* or individual hadiths
frequently were).

It is on the student or listener's side that the "hearing" mode is
markedly different. Through oral-recitational means the words of the
author were directly and authoritatively reproduced, as in *maqru'at*; but
with the *masmu'at*, no taking of dictation, no note taking, no writing,
intervened to capture the words. Oral production is matched by aural
reception alone: the great value placed on this sort of communication
finds a model both in the initial transmission of the Quran and in its
subsequent recitational use in ritual. It is in the "heard" texts mode
that instruction most closely approximates the ideals of the legitimate
transmission of knowledge. The fully reproduced presence of an original text—here including the quoted words of each *matn*, the textual
core of the hadith—is associated with an authoritative conveyance, via
the voiced and heard word, across the human linkages between a
teacher and the students assembled in his presence.

LICENSE

There are a number of general formulas applied to what transpires in
the teacher-student instructional exchange. One, concerning a teacher,
is that "a number of scholars benefited from him (*intafa'a bihi*)." This
was a direct response to the fundamental condition placed upon the
acquisition of knowledge—that it be communicated to the benefit of
the community. Since the principal field of knowledge in advanced
darasa was jurisprudence, or *fiqh*, one of the standard ways of stating
that an individual "became educated" was *tafaqqaha*, a verb derived
from the same f–q–h root. Another important general expression for
the reception of knowledge was *akhadha*, meaning "to take." The student "took" some portion of what the teacher had (*ma 'indahu*) in the

way of knowledge. In his autobiography, al-Shawkani says, not immodestly but appropriately in this conception of knowledge transmission, that he "took" all of what his several teachers had, "until there did not remain with any of his teachers anything that he [al-Shawkani] had not acquired."[29] He literally exhausted the text-knowledge of all of his teachers except for one, the very distinguished Zaidi scholar ʿAbd al-Qadir bin ʿAbd Allah,[30] who died before al-Shawkani had completed his studies.

The intense concern for specifying the human links in the transmission of knowledge is expressed through the detailing of precisely which texts were studied, how they were studied, and with whom. Al-Shawkani's seemingly obsessive recounting of a long list of texts, including both his *maqruʾat* and his *masmuʿat*, his "recited" and "heard" texts, with the title of each work followed by the name of the teacher in question, provides a measure of the significance that he attached to the careful demonstration of the particulars of authoritative textual transmission. In addition, he includes the repetition of such key works as the *Sharh al-Azhar* with several different teachers, and he regularly mentions just how much of a book in question was covered. "From the beginning to the end of it" and "all of it" are common in al-Shawkani's lists, but he also frequently notes portions not covered—for example, "except for a missed bit at the end of the middle third"—or that he only worked on "some" of the treatise in question. The same sort of meticulous interest in the minutiae of textual interchange is found some seven hundred years earlier when Ibn Samura (1957: 149) says, concerning a student and a teacher, that "he studied with him some (*baʿd*) of *Al-Tanbih.*" "I asked him about that," Ibn Samura continues, "and he said, 'Up to the chapter on Marriage.'" Elsewhere, Ibn Samura summarizes what occurred as one student received instruction from his teacher as follows: "He took from him and became educated with him with regard to part of his [the teacher's] heard texts and part of his memorized texts" (p. 95).

Equivalent to the *khatam* of Quranic school was the *ijaza* of advanced instruction. Neither should be understood as a diploma delivered at the conclusion of a set curriculum and sequence of academic classes—these were notions that would appear later. Rather, both were "documents," the first an event, the second often a written text, giving evidence of a specific textual transmission, through a specific student-teacher link. Al-Shawkani names the individual with whom his Quranic khatam occurred, just as he names the human mediators of the other texts he learned.

An *ijaza* typically authorized the student to teach in his turn the text that had been learned, using the formula for "oral transmission" (*riwaya*).[31] Such usage represents an important further expression of the oral construction of darasa instruction. In an explicit fashion, ijazas articulate the genealogical manner in which knowledge was handed down through the generations. Ijaza documents could cover all types of texts and modes of learning. Zabara (1956:4–5) quotes an ijaza that gives the student the right to transmit the teacher's *maqru'at* and *masmu'at*, which the teacher says he had likewise received from his own teacher. Ijazas could be either general (*'amma*), or restricted, pertaining to anything from a single text—as in the case of the ijazas Sayf al-Sunna granted to his students for Muslim's *Sahih*—to a delimited discipline.

In provincial Ibb, at least by the turn of this century, the issuing of written ijazas was rare. Oral and biographical history accounts of the last decades of the old darasa system do not refer to a practice of formalized licensing; they mention only the names of teachers, and possibly, but normally separately, the titles of the principal texts studied. In any case, if the older ijaza institution had seemed to offer a marking of the transition from student to teacher, the transition was usually not abrupt. Al-Shawkani describes a period of his academic life during which he simultaneously took lessons from some scholars and gave lessons to others. The historian al-Burayhi describes an individual as "studying with those more learned than he and teaching those less so."[32] Isma'il al-Akwa' (1980:11) points to the practice of charging advanced students to recite the lesson aloud as a distinctive feature of Shafi'i instruction. In Quranic schools, as Muhammad al-Akwa' notes (n.d.: 47), it was customary to have "the older instructing the younger and the ones who understood teaching those who did not."

Just as the ijaza was not a diploma in the contemporary sense, so the "books of study" (*kutub al-talb*) did not represent a conventional curriculum. For the darasa student, the works studied represented at most a specific *madhhab*, they were the standard texts of a particular school of shari'a jurisprudence. The biographical histories give evidence of specialization among some scholars; others dabbled, or in unusual cases such as al-Shawkani, went profoundly into numerous subjects. All, however, began with the key manual texts of their madhhab.

ENDOWMENTS

The teacher may not ask payment.
HADITH

Providing for the expenses of instruction was a venerable charitable and pious activity, one that usually took the form of a special institution known as *awqaf* (sing. *waqf*).[33] These "pious endowments" supported not only students but also the physical plant of instruction, the mosques and residences. The four categories of public endowments in Ibb included separately earmarked funding for the Great Mosque of Ibb (known as *waqf al-kabir*), the town's other mosques (*masajid*),[34] local saint-tomb complexes (*turab*), and advanced instruction (*darasa*). In-kind revenues came from extensive endowment landholdings in the Ibb hinterland, and cash rents were derived from town real estate, including building lots, houses, shops, warehouses, and the public bath.

In the official darasa-endowment register (see fig. 7),[35] document texts refer to *waqf*s "for the darasa of the muhajirin in the Great Mosque of the town of Ibb"; or simply, "endowment for darasa" (*waqf li-l-darasa*). The management of the endowment properties, the collection of the revenue, and the disbursement of food and money to the students was the responsiblity of an official known as the *'aqil 'ala al-darasa*. During Ramadan the normal endowment-supplied fare of sorghum bread and porridge was changed to wheat bread, meat gravy, and clarified butter. For the *'id al-kabir*, the major feast day of the Muslim calendar, two bulls were slaughtered for the students at endowment expense . In Ahmad al-Haddad's day there were more than fifty muhajirin, half boarders, half day students, who were served together with some teachers and a few poor men in groups of four at as many as sixteen tables.[36]

The endowment mandate for its student beneficiaries was to study "the magnificent Quran and the noble knowledge (*'ilm*)," one text reads, "under the supervision of the darasa official, in the assembly mosque of Ibb town." Jurisprudence was to be studied in both its "*usul* and *furu'*," its "roots and branches."[37] As a condition of, and in return for, the support given them, the muhajirin accomplished specially dedicated recitations on Monday and Friday eves. These were in memory of the Prophet and of the local founders: "to the soul (*ruh*) of the Prophet," a typical text says, "and to his [i.e., the founder's] soul, using his name."[38] As such donors accumulated over the years, their names

Figure 7. Opening pages of register (*musawwadat al-darasa*) listing endowment properties for the support of instruction in Ibb. Dated 1896.

were added to a list read out at the conclusion of the recitation by a special Great Mosque functionary. An Ibb testament (*wasiyya*) dated 1904,[39] for example, mentions two agricultural terraces set aside as endowments for "darasat Ibb" and "darasat Jibla [a nearby town]," respectively. These charities are intended, in the founder's words, "to enter me into the recitations (*al-ratib*)"—that is, by the muhajirin at the main mosques of both Ibb and Jibla. Another endowment was to be in memory of the founder's mother, "to enter her into the recitations."

This type of recitation by the muhajirin was actually a specialized public version of a much wider phenomenon. Recitation in memory of a deceased individual's soul could occur as a simple and uncompensated act of devotion. Relevant in this connection is an exchange Muhammad al-Akwaʿ (n.d.:56–57) remembers with his stepmother: "Muhammad," she asked, "when I die will you recite (*tadrus*) to my soul, recite (*taqra*) for me the Fatiha [the opening sura of the Quran], and pray for me?" He answered "Yes" at the time, and as an adult he carried out these recitations . There is, in addition, a separate category of endowments (known as *waqf qira'a*) that pertain to such recitation.[40] Such private endowments were administered directly by the reciter rather than by the Endowments Office. In the Ibb testament of 1904, there are several "recitation waqfs" enumerated, involving designated properties with revenues to be provided the reciters named. Other privately held documents attest to such developments as "stepping down" from reciterships, involving a transfer of both the right to the annual income and the duty of recitation.[41] Some recitational waqfs were intended as small charities provided to nonfamily poor, especially scholars; others were huge family trusts in which the recitational waqf formula shields an important allocation of an estate.[42] That various perils awaited endowments was clearly recognized by their founders: cautions and conditional curses are common in the formation texts.[43]

The several varieties of public and private endowments shared a common legal structure, which is set forth in the chapter on waqf in the jurisprudence manuals. In establishing an endowment an individual undertook a unilateral legal act whereby property was converted from private ownership (*milk*) to endowment (*waqf*) status. There are three distinctive features of this legal transformation. The first is that the transfer to endowment status is an action in perpetuity, valid until Judgment Day, or as the establishing documents read, "until God inherits the earth and all upon it." Second, the property in question is removed (the formulae are *waqafa*, "to stop," and *habasa*, "to restrain") from the circles of worldly transfer. As the documents state, the property may no longer be "sold, inherited, pawned, or given as a gift." The endowment properties are no longer property in the worldly sense that they may be alienated. A third essential feature concerns the intention of the founder. This must be *qurba*, which is "an act pleasing to God," or a "desire to draw near to Him." In theory at least, the legal transfer involved is not understood in terms of the this-worldly intentions associated with ordinary legal undertakings. The support of mosques is one such action pleasing to God; the funding of instruction is another. That the muhajirin were a set-apart group of initiates was thus reinforced by the special qualities of their material support.

CHAPTER 5

The New Method

At an annual awards day ceremony held at the elementary Revolution School in Ibb in 1975, some of the teachers and pupils put on a short skit. A breeze snapped at the Yemen Arab Republic flag bunting that decorated the stage, and an antiquated public address system crackled. Speeches that castigated the old regime, recalled the glorious events of the revolutionary years, and then underlined the importance of education in building the nation's future were made by local dignitaries, including the governor, the provincial military commander, and the director of the Ibb branch office of the Ministry of Education. Poems written for the occasion were also read out, local musicians played some popular tunes, and all joined in the national anthem.

Critical of the past and, somewhat more implicitly, of the present as well, skits are standard fare at the public occasions that have proliferated on the republican calendar. The skit this day was entitled, "Education in the Old Days."[1] In it the teachers who wrote it looked back with a mix of serious and humorous intent typical of such theater at an institution, the Quranic school, which they and many in the audience had attended. For their young pupils, some of whom were the actors, the skit offered a representation of a mode of instruction that was fast disappearing. Unlike most other scripts, this one contains only a few spoken parts and was mainly intended to provide stage directions for a living tableau.

> Initial scene: the curtain rises on a Quranic school room, with a floor covering of reed mats and burlap sacks. Sinna is sitting on the right side leaning against arm cushions. The general situation: the clothes of the poor students are old and some are torn. The clothes of the rich children

indicate wealth. The clothes of Sinna are a gown over a gown, a vest, a scholar's turban, with tooth-cleaning sticks and wooden pens stuck in it, and old-style "white" spectacles attached to the ear by means of two strings. Next to Sinna are a number of rods, inkwells for ink, and a collection of wooden writing boards.

At that moment a group of poor children enters from the left, carrying their writing boards. They go immediately to kiss the hands and knees of the teacher, who receives them in haste and with abuse. This is taken for granted, because they are poor. Sinna addresses them with insults: "Idle ones, sons of idle ones, ones of broken honor, you've come as early as the poor woman to the threshing floor, God curse your fathers. Yesterday, and the day before, and the day before that you didn't bring my food. And two weeks without my Thursday money. Do I work for your fathers instructing you for nothing?"

The students: "Sinna, we asked our fathers and each of them said he will give you all that is owed." Sinna: "You ingrates, each of you will pay nothing less than the full amount"—[aside: "as if their fathers were government functionaries or merchants, like those of Salih and Qasim"]—"all your fathers are worthless destitutes."

At this instant there enters a group of small pupils, whose clothes show wealth. They come to greet Sinna, who raises the chin of each one individually, trying to kiss them. A smile is across his face, and from time to time he praises them and their fathers. Each one of the rich pupils takes out some coins and slips them in Sinna's pocket or in his hand, excusing themselves for the paltriness of the sum. Sinna gathers the money and places it in his gown, while glaring at the poor children and then directing a few blows in their direction.

Sinna turns round to the rich pupils and invites them to sit next to him. He whispers in the ear of one of the students sitting next to him, "Did you tell your mother to send more food, and to provide sorghum stalks too?" He answers, "I told my mother. She's going to."

Sinna calls one of the poor pupils, "Bring me your writing board. Today I've decorated it with verses, and now I'm waiting to see how much your father will give." The boy responds, "Yes, Sinna." The boy takes the decorated board to his father, who after some difficulty manages to borrow a riyal to give to him. The boy returns and gives the riyal to Sinna, who turns it over in his hand a number of times and then puts it in his pocket.

An hour passes, then two, and Sinna does not excuse the children because the sum was too small. The boy tries to ask Sinna to let the children go. Sinna says to him, "Quit your bellyaching, what did you bring me, lowly one, son of a lowly one?" After a long time Sinna excuses the children. The poor boy goes to his house, and he is crying.

THE "NEW METHOD"

Sometime after 1878, the year it was introduced in the capital, San'a',[2] a new educational institution opened its doors in Ibb. Housed in the old Jalaliyya Mosque on the town's Upper Square, the *maktab rushdiyya*, as the school was called (from *rushd*, adolescence), was an advanced primary school of a type legislated into existence by the Ottoman Public School Law of 1869 and instituted thereafter throughout the empire.[3] A new Ministry of Public Instruction, utilizing the public and secular concept of *ma'arif*,[4] was an integral part of the ordering (*nizam*) policies of the Ottoman reformers and modernizers. In the eyes of these reformers, ma'arif, the knowledge imparted in "public instruction," stood in opposition to the old style of knowledge (*'ilm*), with its substantive focus on jurisprudence and its mode of recitational transmission in mosque-school lesson circles. Berkes (1964:160) has aptly characterized the then current concept of ma'arif as "the learning of unfamiliar things." A related conception, focused on the instructional dissemination of "useful knowledge," had been developed for colonial purposes in British India. It too would have an impact on the Yemeni highlands, although indirectly and at a later date, through institutions and ideas in circulation in India-administered Aden.[5]

For diverse political purposes, the new nineteenth-century conceptions of "knowledge" attributed a fundamental vitality and openness to a type of learning, of "unfamiliar things," of "useful knowledge," that seemed to fit consciousnesses of change and advocacies of "modern" goals. The same conceptions also contributed to the rise of an image of old modes of instruction and forms of knowledge as closed, unadaptable, moribund. Educational reforms also had direct implications for the construction of new notions concerning law. The Ottoman system of public instruction was initially created to parallel and compete with the old *madrasas*, just as the new *nizam* courts applying legislated law were instituted as foils (in the central provinces at least) for the old *shari'a* courts. Education reforms further represented an important early salient in the struggle to introduce a comprehensive notion of "public" responsibility, which entailed a thorough reconstitution of the form and scope of the state. This differentiation and elaboration of the "public" sphere, and the constitution of its opposite, the "private," were new to Yemen.

Both in the central Ottoman Empire and in Egypt instructional innovations in the first half of the nineteenth century were destined for the formation of officers and other military specialists, and the methods involved were only later spread to the separately created field of general public education. In Yemen, however, the new *rushdiyya* schools were introduced at the same moment in the late nineteenth century as the first new-style battalions of Yemeni soldiers. As new-method schools acquired the ordered form and discipline of military units, there was a parallel effort toward the "education and training of the minds" of the new soldiers.[6]

While pious endowments supported the instructional activities going on nearby in the Great Mosque of Ibb, the little *maktab rushdiyya* was financed in a novel manner: with budgeted state monies.[7] In the 1916 Ottoman financial summary for the Ibb subdistrict, there appears a separate budgetary subheading for the local Maʿarif section, with a listing of salaries for three individuals, including two grades of Turkish teachers (*muʿallim*) and a locally employed caretaker.[8] Reflecting the competitive split of education in the Ottoman heartlands, and indicating a change already wrought internally to the local "traditional" system, there was another teacher (*mudarris*) on the official payroll. This position, occupied by an Ibb man from the al-ʿAnsi family, is listed among the *ʿilmiyya* officials, who were otherwise the court personnel. As his full-position title indicates, he was a state-paid instructor in what had come to be designated as the "religious sciences" (*ʿulum al-diniyya*).[9]

The *maktab rushdiyya* was the only Ottoman school established in the subdistrict seat of Ibb town, but there were secondary schools, military colleges, technical schools, schools for girls, and schools for orphans opened in the three larger towns of Sanʿaʾ, al-Hudayda, and nearby Taʿizz.[10] As in nineteenth-century Egypt,[11] the new Ottoman schools were adapted from instructional methods developed earlier in the century by the Englishman Joseph Lancaster.[12] Elaborated in a concise guide for the requisite physical layout and associated instructional routines, the Lancaster school design was widely influential. Model schools were established in France, Germany, the United States, and a number of colonial settings. In his study of the birth of new "disciplinary" modes of power in the West, Michel Foucault (1977) examines the Lancaster-method schools as one of the principal sites of a subtle but consequential ordering that quietly invaded and replicated itself in a whole series of institutions, from the prison to the hospital, the factory, and the military barracks. New institutional efficiencies, enabled by new forms of supervision and control, rested upon the differentiation of space and the precise regulation and coordination of time and human activities. As such disciplinary procedures took hold across a spectrum of institutional settings, they were integral to the definition and production of a new type of individual.

Derived ultimately from Western models, educational "order" arrived in the Province of Yemen mediated and adapted by Ottoman planners, legislators, and administrators. According to the legislative model,[13] education was to be given systematic form. Overall, five levels were envisioned, each comprising a set number of years. The four-year program of the *rushdiyya* included, in legislative theory, "elementary religious instruction, Turkish grammar, writing and prose style, Arabic and Persian grammar following the new method, bookkeeping, drawing, elementary geometry, universal history, Ottoman history, geography, physical exercise, and the language of a non-Muslim community in the locality." Students in the empire's commercially active towns could elect to study French in their fourth year. Although there is no indication that French was being used or taught in Ibb,[14] instruction was provided in Ottoman Turkish.

During my residence in Ibb in the 1970s, Ahmad al-Basir, a *maktab rushdiyya* student in his youth, was able to make translations for me from Ottoman Turkish to Arabic. Once a member of a local Sufi order, and later a Quranic schoolmaster, teacher of *muhajirin*, and a prominent Ibb notary, al-Basir had an eclectic educational career, which included years in several of the new Ottoman schools. After Quran instruction in his own neighborhood he attended the Ibb *maktab rushdiyya*. Then he moved to Ta'izz, where he lived with relatives while attending the Ottoman secondary (*i'dadiyya*) school in the mornings and the military college in the afternoons. Later still, however, he studied in the mosque-school *darasa* format in Zabid, where he did advanced work in jurisprudence and related disciplines. Returning to Ibb, he was initially appointed to the Endowments Office as a functionary. Later, under imamic rule, he became one of the teachers in the Great Mosque and began a lucrative parallel career writing legal instruments in the afternoons. In the late 1970s, he was considered one of the last of the town's old-style scholars, which is ironic in view of his extensive exposure to the Ottoman "new method" schools.

While certainly not delivered to Ibb intact, the Ottoman educational program nevertheless marked the local advent of revolutionary new ideas concerning the nature of schooling and appropriate subjects for study. However reduced and adapted, it was a program that stood in sharp contrast to the old sequences of *mi'lama* to darasa lesson circle and of Quran to shari'a manual. If not yet seriously challenged, the *madhhab* approach to knowledge was at least confronted by the existence of the new curriculum approach to "ma'arif." The pursuit of *'ilm* would persist in Yemen for another half century, but its once exclusive field of action was irrevocably altered. Although it initially appeared in Yemen in only embryonic form, the new conception of instruction would eventually displace the old style altogether.

According to the new program, instruction was to be extended in time and have its own space. While *'ilm* was transmitted in the mosque, a multipurpose place, with the Hazr serving as the student residence and the locale of peer learning, the *maktab rushdiyya* and the other Ottoman schools were meant to be schools in the Western sense, ideally utilizing set-apart and specially arranged spaces designed for the newly conceived, daylong activity of instruction. One eventual by-product of this move would be the redefinition of the mosque as the place of exclusively "religious" practices. Furthermore, with teacher-student contact extended to encompass the entire learning day, peer learning, lacking both a space and a time in the new system, would decline.

In Ibb, the Ottomans had to make do with the available room in the Jalaliyya Mosque, but in the minds of the legislators was a different idea.[15] As in Lancaster's conception, the Ottoman schools were to be newly constructed, in conformity to a design set forth in a ministerial plan. This aim of standardization involved the physical differentiation of rationalized seating arrangements and the development of classrooms as separately walled spaces for the instruction of different levels of students. This ordering procedure helped define a student, who was categorized by sex, age, and academic level. In contrast to the Quranic schools and the Great Mosque lesson circles, where students of widely different ages and levels of study intermingled,[16] the new classes were to be composed of groups of children and youths with uniform characteristics.

"Elementary instruction is obligatory in the Empire," wrote the Ottoman legislators of 1869. "Education is a right for all Yemenis," echoed the provisional Yemeni constitution of 1962.[17] Universal education offered a template for a different sort of society, and it carried with it the Western ideology of attainable equality. Replacing the sharply pyramidical pattern of restricted attendance and rapid attrition that appears from the outset of the mosque-school system, and the conception of instruction as but one of many "crafts," the philosophy (at least) behind the Ottoman schools was one of universal access to primary education. Instead of the "ascending individualization" (Foucault 1977:193) of the old social order, with its fundamental distinction between the knowledgeable and the ignorant, with the lives of the "great men" inscribed in biographical histories, a society of educated citizens implementing a form of "descending individualization" was implied. For the first time, schooling was intended to be something appropriate for all boys and girls.[18] Education was in the process of becoming a newly constituted right of the individual, required and guaranteed by the laws of a new form of state. To this end, procedures were elaborated in the central Ottoman districts for keeping local registers of school-age children, and fines were set for parents who did not comply with the law.[19] The advent of *rushdiyya* education for girls entailed not only a modified instructional program that included home economics and needlework but also the radical idea that girls should receive post-Quranic-school instruction outside the home.[20] Most of these ideas would not begin to be implemented in Yemen until after the 1962 Revolution, at the same time that the abstract political notion of the Yemeni "citizen" (*muwatin*) began to take hold.

Important changes in pedagogical technique were part of the nascent transformation of the Ottoman period. Over the longer term, these would entail a shift in elementary instruction from the *luha* writing board of the individual student to the collective blackboard of the contemporary classroom. The *luha* was not merely a highly personal-ized and intimate instrument—each of the boards being a bit different in surface and cut—it also concretely exemplified the fact that students in the same circle worked at diverse paces and levels, with varying capacities applied to different segments of text. By contrast, the black-board, now standard equipment in Yemeni schools, in its distance from the student and in its control by the teacher, entails a comparatively depersonalized and uniform pattern of instruction. A teacher-to-class relationship mediated by the blackboard would replace the numerous Sinna-to-pupil dyads mediated by *luha*s. This change also went to the heart of the old theory of knowledge transmission, which was based on individual teacher-student links, on a student's being formed "in the hands," in the undivided presence, of the teacher. A new sort of teacher, salaried and standardized through professional formation in teacher training institutes, would relate to a new sort of student.

Before the introduction of the classroom blackboard, the initial shift was from *luha*s to slates, which were used in the *rushdiyya* as they were in Lancaster schools. The apparent similarity between the individual

writing board of Quranic instruction and the individual slate of the
new-method schools concealed a fundamental organizational difference, one that accompanied the equally important change in the nature
of the text written down. Instead of routinely centering on dyadic,
"recite your lesson-board" commands from Sinna to individual pupils
taken one at a time, the new method worked upon a collectivity of
concurrently performing individuals who received the same instruction
simultaneously from an orchestrating schoolmaster. In the mornings,
when reciting pupils occupied Sinna's attention one by one, the rest of
the circle were left unattended to pursue their lessons (or not) as they
saw fit. In the afternoons, Sinna turned to his water pipe and qat, and
the pupils were completely on their own. By contrast, in the typically
large Lancaster classrooms, bells and simple semaphores were employed to signal the appropriate numbers of a minutely regimented and
continually engaging instructional program to hundreds of simultaneously attentive pupils, each positioned at a specially designated desk. A
typical writing exercise, for example, followed a sequence of numbered
instructions:

> 9: hands on knees. This command is conveyed by one ring on the bell;
> 10: hands on table, head up; 11: clean slates: everyone cleans his slate
> with a little saliva, or better still with a piece of rag; 12: show slates.[21]

In this manner, it was seen, a school could function efficiently, like a
machine for learning. Each individual was at the same time both
located and occupied; space and time were blocked off, minutely organized, mobilized in the service of a continuing disciplinary hold and
maximum output. Transposed to Yemen, later versions of such pedagogical procedures would eventually result in a class with a single
voice replacing one of many voices, which came to be understood as
representing an undesirable cacophony.

Testing, and the passing and failing associated with it, figures prominently in a system that is based on collective activity and is at the same
time crosscut by the necessity of ranking and marking individual movement through grades. These days, a primary-school student's final
report card, organized by subject matter and according to grades for
class work and written-test scores,[22] concludes by passing the successful
student on to the next level. The old *ijaza*, the granting of transmission
authority by a particular teacher to a particular student for a particular
text, has given way to the diploma (*shahada*), a standardized, state-
issued document of fulfillment, through testing, of abstractly defined

educational goals. This has initiated a system that gives the "same value to all holders of the same certificate, so that any one of them can take the place of any other" (Bourdieu 1977:187).

THE POLITICS OF INSTRUCTION

With the demise of the Ottoman Empire at the close of World War I, Imam Yahya unceremoniously closed the entire Turkish school system.[23] In 1924 the Lebanese visitor Amin al-Rihani recorded a schoolboy's lament: "We had organized schools under the Turks," he said, "where geography and arithmetic were taught. They gave us books, slates, paper, ink, pens, exercise books, and chalk—everything, and all free. Sir, I am sad. Today we have no schools and no teachers except the *faqih* ... and he charges eight riyals per month."[24] The semiofficial imamic historian al-Wasi'i tells a different story, however.[25] "In the days of the Turks," he writes, the educational system was in "total disarray"; it was the imam who "opened the schools and disseminated knowledge (*'ilm*)." In the post-Ottoman period of Yemeni independence educational policy would continue to be a bone of political contention.

It should be noted here that the account I am giving of the relationship of education and social transformation in Yemen is not the familiar one. The standard political history begins with a group of Yemeni students of the mid-1930s sent to study at the Iraqi military academy in Baghdad and continues with those trained later in Yemen by Iraqi military missions of the 1940s and in Yemen and Egypt by Egyptian officers after 1952. Having absorbed revolutionary ideas from their foreign instructors, it was these former cadets who participated in the several attempted coups and eventually launched the successful Revolution of 1962 by a tank assault on the last imam's palace on the night of September 26.[26] By contrast, my account cites another history, emphasizing the far less dramatic, cumulative importance of detailed shifts in organization and techniques. It also dates the formative events in these processes of change to practices instituted in the Ottoman period.

While the imam's abrupt closure of the Ottoman schools might have seemed to imply the elimination of all innovations and a simple return to a unitary "traditional" system of instruction, such was not the case. Imam Yahya was an astute observer of all aspects of the Ottoman system, and his own educational oeuvre, despite its outwardly traditional appearance, was actually very much a hybrid, quietly incorporating·

several of the key features of Ottoman-introduced instructional "order." Some of the schools al-Wasi'i credits the imam with founding, including the Military College, and the School for Orphans, had in fact been established by the Ottomans.[27] As early as 1906, when engaged in preliminary negotiations that would later result in the Treaty of Da''an (1911), Imam Yahya had already demonstrated that he was conversant with the special Ottoman usage of the term *ma'arif*. His fifth demand was for the "transfer of pious endowments to our stewardship so as to revitalize education (*ma'arif*) in the country."[28]

This early idea and others drawn from the Ottoman system were integrated in the foundation of an important new school, *al-madrasa al-'ilmiyya*, opened in San'a' by Imam Yahya in 1926,[29] two years after the al-Rihani visit. Located in the modified, Turkish-style residence of the former Ottoman governor, its carriage garage converted into a mosque, the school had a complete, jurisprudence-centered course of study in the classic style, including set readings in the basic Zaidi text, *Sharh al-Azhar*, and works on *ijtihad* and hadith by al-Shawkani. Over a forty-year period it would graduate many of the country's leading jurists, who assumed judgeships and other posts in the middle and late imamic era and on into the republican period. In its heyday the school had over five hundred boarding students and about one hundred and fifty day students from San'a'.[30]

In structure the *madrasa 'ilmiyya* was quite new: never before in Yemen had *'ilm* been conveyed in a "school" that began to approximate the Western organizational sense of the term. One important element was funding. In the three lines he devotes to describing this school, al-Wasi'i mentions a key fact: that the students' "food and drink are the responsibility of the government."[31] This funding was predicated upon a reorganized system of endowments administration, a move hinted at in negotiations twenty years earlier.[32] Although this sort of funding is still distinct from the purely public mode of financing of the Ottoman system, it was indicative of an emergent attitude toward asserting a new sort of state control over pious endowments. At Imam Yahya's new school the reorganized endowment revenues were put to a use suggested by Ottoman practice: the providing of regular monthly cash salaries for some twenty-four regular staff, including twenty-one teachers and three functionaries. As in the darasa system, students were also provided for.[33]

Other features that distinguished the *madrasa 'ilmiyya* from the earlier 'ilm-transmitting institutions include the division of both the student

body and the curriculum into distinct classes. Al-Wasi'i, who had traveled outside Yemen, observed that "the organization of the school into
grades is like Egyptian schools.[34] In the twelve-year program there were
three levels with four grades to a level. The final year was known as the
"ijtihad class." Venerable *madhhab* texts were converted into a curriculum: subjects of study were identified, and specific books were set up as
a formal program, especially for the higher levels.[35] Progression from
class to class was by means of passing annual examinations. A committee of scholar-examiners, chosen by the minister of Ma'arif, posed questions to the students individually, and rankings by test results on a scale
of one to ten were issued in an annual report. Supervising the overall
operation of the school was a director (*nazir*). These were the rudiments
of an academic form that has become so utterly basic all around the
world that its relatively recent historical emergence is often forgotten.

There were also similarities between the new school and Imam
Yahya's military, where a number of Turkish officers had stayed on.
Both students and soldiers were handled administratively through the
legal mechanism of the bond (*kafala*),[36] which was required for enroll-
ment of either type. As in the case of new military recruits, entering
students had to be accompanied by bondsmen, who undertook to
guarantee "conduct appropriate for students of 'ilm," their obedience
to imamic orders, and financial responsibility for any supplies misap-
propriated. Also like the imam's soldiers, students at the new school
received graded weekly pay[37] and daily allotments of a special type of
government bakery bread. Soldiers, younger students, and government-
supported orphans regularly paraded together on state occasions,
arranged in units and classes.[38]

Instruction was an essential policy area in the imam's shari'a style
of politics in two distinct ways: one concerned *madhhab* control of the
formation of jurists at the highest levels, which the new *madrasa 'ilmiyya*
ensured; another was the perennially felt duty (especially among town
scholars) to push back the frontiers of ignorance by sending teachers out
to rural districts to provide basic instruction.[39] The symbolic importance of this second political objective is indicated by the idealized
summary account of Imam Yahya's first acts upon his triumphant
entrance into the capital in the month of Safar, A.H. 1337 [1918]: "The
imam set the affairs of San'a' in order, forbade officials from oppression
and corruption, and dispatched instructors to all the villages."[40]

The regional version of such instructional policies involved, as in
previous centuries, the movement of Zaidi scholars into Shafi'i districts.

A local example from the early 1920s is the posting of ʿAli b. Husayn al-Akwaʿ (father of Muhammad and Ismaʿil, whose books I have repeatedly cited) to a madrasa in the little village of Maʿain, just outside of Ibb to the northwest. In a few years, he was succeeded in the post by his eldest son, Muhammad, who had just completed his studies in Dhamar and Sanʿaʾ.[41] In his early twenties at the time, Muhammad al-Akwaʿ taught at Maʿain while continuing his own studies with scholars in Ibb.

Like most of his students, al-Akwaʿ resided in Ibb and walked out to the village madrasa every day to hold classes. Conscious both of changes the imam was instituting in Sanʿaʾ and of new ideas percolating northward from British Aden, he organized his students in small groups of four or five according to their level, and he also gave weekly exams. His former students remember that he was fatherly and friendly during the week, even to the extent of joining them in swimming and soccer, but that he became very severe at test time. Maintaining an older practice, the students engaged in regular recitations to the "soul" of the *waqf* founder and received a full sack of grain per month from the waqf revenues, which al-Akwaʿ administered.[42]

It was in such scholarly milieus around the country that nationalist ideas began to be articulated in the 1930s. By 1944, Muhammad al-Akwaʿ's secret political activities against the imamic regime were discovered and he was jailed, which terminated his teaching career. The year before he had been elected head of an Ibb-based group of scholars and rural leaders from nearby Baʿdan known as the Reform Society.[43] Composed of both Shafiʿis and Zaidis of *qadi* families, but no Zaidi sayyids, the Ibb group was one of the earliest nationalist organizations to operate in the country, and it established links both with the Free Yemenis, who had just surfaced in Aden, and with other organizations or groups of individuals in Taʿizz and Sanʿaʾ. Muhammad's younger brother Ismaʿil, also a member of the Ibb group, was responsible for carrying messages and pamphlets printed in Aden, including nationalist poetry and the group's own Reform Program leaflet, north to Dhamar and Sanʿaʾ. It was on such a trip that he too was arrested and jailed.[44]

Whereas the attempts of 1955 and 1961 and the successful Revolution of 1962 would be led by military officers, this first generation of nationalist endeavor, culminating in the abortive coup of 1948, the *dusturiyya* ("Constitutional Movement"), was mainly the work of scholars and intellectuals. They had contacts with Yemenis returned from studies in Cairo and, through merchant connections, with the numerous highlanders resident in Aden. Political activity emerged from the regular intellectual gatherings that were such a prominent part of the scholarly life of the period. In Ibb such men assembled for qat-chewing sessions in the afternoons and for lengthy evening gatherings as well. "The town used to glow at night from the lights of houses where men gathered to study," one participant fondly remembered. Individuals such as Hasan al-Du'ais, a leading Ba'dan shaykh known as "the philosopher," joined rooms of men who took turns reading aloud from and commenting upon such newly available, smuggled works as Jurgi Zaydan's world history. An extension of the youthful activity of peer learning into adult life, such intellectual gatherings occurred in other towns as well, where they took a similar political turn. With other prominent Ibb members of the Reform Society, Muhammad al-Akwa' was initially jailed from 1944 to 1947. After only one year of freedom, however, he was once again brought in and jailed in the aftermath of the 1948 coup, this time until 1955.[45]

Such men turned their jails into virtual academies. Ahmad al-Shami has written an account of the flourishing of Yemeni literature that occurred in the notorious prison in Hajja.[46] He tells how the writers, scholars, and poets among the prisoners eventually overcame their dreadful circumstances: "Lips started to smile again, weariness and fatigue were relieved by literary anecdotes, verses were recalled, and tales and morals drawn from history started to circulate among the prison inmates. . . . Literary sessions took place and discussion circles were convened; jokes, *maqamah*s, poems, and tales were exchanged, and thus the otherwise oppressive and miserable time was killed in a pleasant manner." One of the techniques used by the prisoners recalls their days in Quranic schools. When there were no writing materials, he writes, "we used pieces of wood or flattened tin cans to write on, after blackening them with charcoal or soot. We recorded verses and ideas so that they would not be lost. Then we would commit them to memory, wipe them off, and write others." Among prisoners from the Ibb area, 'Abd al-Rahman al-Iryani and Isma'il al-Akwa' worked on editions of the famous Yemeni poets 'Abd al-Rahman al-Ansi and 'Umarah al-Yamani, while Muhammad al-Akwa' prepared an annotated edition of volumes of the *Iklil* by the early Yemeni historian al-Hamdani.

In this period Aden was both an important refuge and a source of reform ideas for the early nationalist leaders. From the middle of the

previous century, when Aden became a free port, trade volume had
grown steadily, and merchants and laborers were increasingly drawn
to the bustling enclave from the highland Shafiʿi districts around Taʿizz
and Ibb. By 1900 there was regular caravan traffic between Aden and
Ibb: coffee, skins, "bastard saffron" (*wars*), and clarified butter were
sent southward, and the spectrum of Indian Ocean trade goods, including spices, cloth, scents, medicines, and many other items, were
carried northward. Ismaʿil Basalama, who was both an important regional shaykh and the Ottoman governor in the waning days of the
empire, was also the leading merchant of his day.

Educational innovation in Aden dates to an unsuccessful effort to
introduce a new style of school as early as 1856.[47] According to a later
British observer, the "ignorance and apathy of the inhabitants," combined with criticism from India, where colonial educational policy was
then the subject of intense debate, caused the school to be closed after
only two years. A more modest government institution intended to
provide elementary instruction in English was opened under an Indian
headmaster in 1866. By 1877 the Aden Regency School had sixty
students of widely varied backgrounds who studied a Bombay presi-
dency fifth-standard program that included the "elementary histories
of England, India, and Rome; Euclid as far as the first book; geography, arithmetic, and algebra."[48] Instruction in English and bookkeeping (introduced later) proved attractive for Adeni students interested
in conducting trade with foreign firms or obtaining positions in government service. An Arabic Government School was also opened in 1866.
While the sort of education provided by the English-language schools,
employing a "new method" pedagogy applied to a new spectrum of
subjects known as the "Aden syllabus," may have represented the
ultimate local model of "modern" instruction, the Arabic school program was also innovative and was more readily imitated. In the early
years of the Arabic Government School the "medium" of instruction
was the Quran, but "secular reading, writing, and elementary arithmetic" were later introduced. And, unlike local Quranic schools, where
parents paid the teacher, the Arabic Government School was supported
by the colonial government and the Municipal Fund.

In terms of the student population involved, schooling in Aden
remained relatively small in scale until the 1930s and 1940s. At about
the same time that rapid educational expansion was occurring in the
colony, schools inspired in part by Aden models began to appear in the
highlands. One example, connected to the activity of the important

early nationalist leader Ahmad Muhammad Nuʿman, was a school established in a village in al-Hujariyya district (in Taʿizz province close to Aden) in 1934. At this alternative to the regular Quranic schools students studied such subjects as geography, history, arithmetic, and science, and at an associated "club" they could read books, newspapers, and magazines brought back from Aden by workers.

But it was not only the nationalists who were attentive to developments in Aden. In the same year in Ibb, the imamic government under Sayf al-Islam al-Hasan (Imam Yahya's son) opened a new school known simply as the *maktab*, perhaps suggesting descent from the old *maktab rushdiyya*.[49] Like the former Ottoman school, it was a four-year advanced primary school, but it was financed more on the Aden model with support from merchant parents and with the government assuming responsibility only for the teacher's salary and floor coverings. Another educational development in Ibb still more directly reflected the influence of policies in British Aden. A special college in Aden for the sons of hinterland "chiefs" had been founded in 1935–37.[50] By 1940 a similar institution, known as *al-masʿaf*, meaning "to rescue," was established in Ibb. Designed to "rescue" the sons of rural notables from ignorance, the new Ibb institution dovetailed with an ancient Yemeni political device—the hostage system.[51] Holding the sons of rural shaykhs hostage ensured the fathers' good conduct vis-à-vis the state. Several hundred young men from districts radiating around the town thus embarked on a tightly supervised student life (there were soldier chaperons for walks around town), including a mild educational-indoctrination program taught by Zaidi instructors. Among other subjects, they studied the history of the family of the Prophet, touching on the line of descent that produced the Zaidi imams of Yemen. Although the "school" lasted only three years, its brief existence was part of a new awareness of the political potential of instruction as a policy instrument.

After the threatening period of the 1940s, with the initial arrests of nationalists in Ibb and elsewhere and then the abortive "Constitutional" coup attempt (1948), there was also a local reinforcement of the classic strategy in instructional politics. This was to ensure madhhab control in darasa instruction, the idea behind the establishment of the *madrasa ʿilmiyya* in Sanʿaʾ. In connection with his treatment of this institution and other educational programs in the mid-1920s, al-Wasiʿi remarks that in the mosques of Sanʿaʾ, "ʿilm is studied as in the old days." Through the transition to Zaidi rule in Lower Yemen instruction had also continued at the Great Mosque of Ibb. In later years, the San'a' model of the *madrasa 'ilmiyya* was replicated on a smaller scale in other towns, including Sa'da, in the far north,[52] and Ibb and nearby Jibla in Lower Yemen.[53] In Ta'izz, the provincial seat and, after 1948, the national capital of Imam Ahmad, the equivalent new-style 'ilm school was known as the Ahmadiyya. The student body at the Ahmadiyya included a few young men from Ibb, such as Muhammad Yahya al-Haddad, who had been a student with al-Akwa' at Ma'ain, others from Jibla and elsewhere in Lower Yemen, and students from Ta'izz, including young men from the royal family, such as the future imam, Muhammad al-Badr.

The alteration of the Great Mosque program in Ibb was associated with a local reorganization of the endowments system in the late 1940s and 1950s.[54] As the aim of this restructuring and replicating the old practice of supporting study in the madhhab of the ruler, a specially earmarked monthly stipend of half a sack (*qadah*) of grain and two riyals cash was offered as "encouragement" for Ibb darasa students to study the *Azhar*, the Zaidi manual, in both "text and commentary." Those who took up this offer, including the continuing responsibility to recite to the "souls" of the *waqf* founders, were young men with no other means of support, such as an orphan named Muhammad Zain al-'Awdi, who went on to study at the Ahmadiyya and later became an Ibb primary-school director after the Revolution. Al-'Awdi remembers that together the four thick volumes of the *Sharh al-Azhar* served as a perfect armrest for floor-level sitting. At this point before the Revolution, darasa instruction at the Great Mosque had become an intermediate level, situated between the primary instruction offered at the local maktab and the potential for some students to pursue advanced work at the Ahmadiyya in Ta'izz.

CHAPTER 6

Print Culture

Although principally concerned with the administration of schools, Imam Yahya's Ma'arif administration also provided the umbrella for small-scale but significant early departures in state-initiated publishing, library reform, and officially sponsored history writing. The printing equipment in question had been left behind by the departing Turks, and the early imamic usage of it was partly inspired by that of the previous Ottoman administration. Like his school program, the imam's new library was an imaginative hybrid, a recasting of old institutional ideas in newly elaborated forms. The history-writing project, although new to Yemen, bore some resemblance to a far better known scholarly enterprise of the new Turkish Republic.[1] These collateral *ma'arif* efforts were further assertions of a tentative yet determined attitude toward developing the state's identity and extending its authority by means of new textual technologies.

In 1877 the Ottomans brought the first printing press to their province of Yemen.[2] Prior to the establishment of any Muslim-operated presses in the Middle East, European firms had begun publishing books in Arabic, and as Carsten Niebuhr noted in the course of his highland travels in 1763, such printed works were known in Yemen.[3] In the central Ottoman Empire, presses were initially established by and for non-Muslim communities, but printing in the Turkish language was banned until the early eighteenth century.[4] In 1727, when formal legal authorization was obtained, it did not include permission to print the Quran or works on *hadith*, Quranic exegesis, or jurisprudence. An earlier European observer had noted that the Turks refused to allow publication of such texts, "because they think that the Scriptures, that

115

is, their sacred books—would no longer be *scriptures* if they were *printed*" (emphasis in original).[5] In fact, the formal permission granted in 1727 covered only the printing of dictionaries and books in such fields as medicine, astronomy, geography, and history. Permission to print the Quran was not obtained in the Ottoman Empire until 1874.[6] By the end of the nineteenth century Qurans published in both Beirut and Hyderabad were in circulation in the Yemeni highlands.[7]

An Arabic printing press brought by Napoleon to issue proclamations had figured prominently in the shock of the brief French occupation of Egypt in 1798–1801, and by 1822 a Muslim-operated press was turning out textbooks for newly instituted Egyptian schools.[8] Snouck Hurgronje has described the impact of printed texts on lesson circles in Mecca, where books published in Cairo had been available for some years and where a local press was opened in 1883: "All students now bring to lecture printed copies of the text which is being treated, which circumstance has entirely changed the mode of instruction. Formerly the teacher had first to dictate the text, in the margins of which the students then noted down his glosses. Now, on the contrary, the student notes down only a few oral remarks (*taqarir*) of the professor, and often has nothing to write at all (1931:192, 178)." This transformative encounter of printed texts with unreconstructed lesson-circle instruction was not everywhere repeated, however.

In nineteenth-century lesson circles at the Azhar Mosque-University in Cairo, for example, such dramatic changes were forestalled as printed texts were banned.[9] At the Ottoman *rushdiyya* and other higher-level schools in Yemen, textbooks were routinely used, but the program of study was, as I have already noted, totally different from that followed in lesson circles. In the following years, however, in a manner reminiscent of the earlier policy at the Azhar, Imam Yahya at one point explicitly disallowed the use of printed texts in his advanced schools.[10] According to Rossi (1938:579), "the students of the *madrasa 'ilmiyya* ... study texts [that are] nearly all manuscripts and [handwritten] anthologies which they buy or copy for themselves."[11] Former students from Ibb and Jibla report that a rule against printed texts was also in effect later at the Ahmadiyya school in Ta'izz.[12]

How are such restrictions on the use of printed texts to be understood? In the case of the new-style *'ilm* schools, did the policy represent a rearguard effort to maintain an old conception of the appropriate form to be taken by authoritative knowledge? There was no parallel policy to restrict the publication of Yemeni books to subject matters other than works of *fiqh* and related texts of *darasa* instruction. In fact, the *Azhar* manual, the centerpiece of recitation and memorization in Zaidi circles, was published at an early date, but as with most of the other important works of Zaidi jurisprudence, its publication occurred overseas.[13] The main intent of foreign publication may have been to introduce Zaidi-Yemeni thought to a wider Muslim audience, rather than to provide printed materials for instruction in Yemen. Problems of cost and availability concerning such printed texts could also have been a factor in any use in Yemen.

While the texts of Yemeni pedagogy were once exclusively written by hand, under the *ma'arif* system the manual art was decisively supplemented by print technology. In the course of about a century, from Ottoman openings through to the contemporary republican school system, instruction in a manuscript culture would be completely replaced by schooling based on print culture.[14] The old diversity of handwritten texts, including the drafts and autographs of famous scholars, calligraphic exercises, copies made as pious pastimes, artifacts of formal study, products of professional copyists, and so forth, would eventually be reduced, from the point of view of a print-oriented society, to a single basic and increasingly archaic type, the "manuscript," to be collected and curated, kept in library sections that would begin to resemble museums. Texts such as the fiqh manuals pertained to a social, political, and intellectual community articulated in *madhhab*s; printed textbooks, to a curriculum system of public instruction, and the associated sociopolitical, citizen-based universe of nationalism (Anderson 1983).

Manuscripts were still being made well into the present century, however. In 1920, after completing his studies in Ibb, young Ahmad al-Haddad was employed by 'Abd Allah al-Wazir to make a copy of the famous history by al-Kibsi.[15] In the 1930s, a young Zaidi scholar from Yarim, later appointed to an administrative position in Ibb, occupied himself in writing, and then binding in leather, personal copies of both an inheritance treatise and a work of *usul* jurisprudence. "The profession of copyist still flourishes," the visiting Italian Orientalist Ettore Rossi observed in 1938.[16]

Textual commodification is commonly linked to "print capitalism" (Anderson 1983). Although many manuscripts were produced for self-consumption, not all were "subsistence" texts. Copies made in the course of instruction or as a private pious activity did not normally enter into circulation, but many other manuscripts were the scholarly commodities of a different economic order. Most familiar is the work of

professional copyists, who produced handwritten copies for an established fee. Authorship in the manuscript era also had its notions of
drafts and finished products. There was a decisive step in which the text
moved from a tentative draft or a preliminary oral version to a written-
out or dictatable work suitable for circulation. The finished manuscript could circulate either in closed, "genealogical" networks, that is,
through the links of instruction with student or colleague transcribing,
or in open networks of commercial exchange, involving hired copyists.[17]
Although by comparison (with the equivalent print institutions) very
restricted in its implications, there was a version of publishing in the
manuscript era. In Yemen, a verb meaning "to write on white bond"
(*bayyad*) was commonly used to describe the key transition to fair copy.
In listing his own writings, for example, al-Shawkani says of a "published" work such as his famous Hadith study *Nayl al-awtar* that "it was
put on white bond in four large volumes." To indicate that a work
remained "unpublished," that is, it existed only in draft form, he says
"it was not put on white bond."[18]

At the same time as printed works were kept at a distance from advanced schools in twentieth-century imamic Yemen, steps were taken
to promote the new technology in other domains. First among these
was the official Yemeni newspaper *al-Iman* (the Faith), which first
appeared in 1926 as a monthly and later became a daily.[19] Using the
same printing machine, the Ottomans had published a similar official
newspaper (called *San'a'*) in both Arabic and Ottoman Turkish. *Al-
Iman* provides a chronicle of Yemeni political events, major and minor,
internal and in some instances external, from 1926 to 1948, and has
been read by Western observers as a record of "efforts to form a national
consciousness" (Rossi 1938:569) and of "the institutionalization of the
state" (Obermeyer 1981:181).

In his *History of Yemen*, published in Cairo two years after *al-Iman* was
introduced, al-Wasi'i makes an advocacy of newspapers that demonstrates his own awareness of the role then played by the press outside of
Yemen. He first refers to newspapers as among the "essentials of civilization" (*asbab al-'umran*) and then, under a separate section heading,
"newspapers" (which also deals with speeches), he speaks of the press
in lofty and ideal terms: "Newspapers are the great force, the instructive school, the scales for [weighing] the activity of the community
and the indicator of its condition, the vigilant overseer of the government."[20] While, in practice, the imam endeavored to keep the foreign
press of the era out of the country,[21] newspapers were nevertheless a
central figure in al-Wasi'i's ideal portrayal of Yahya's qualities as a

ruler: "The thoroughness of his attention and the excellence of his political administration is [indicated by] the importance he gives to the reading (*iṭlaʿ*) of world news in newspapers and magazines."[22]

In other parts of the Middle East in the era, newspapers were a comparatively developed medium of established or emergent nationalist discourses. As an indicator of rising nationalist thought in the nearby colony of Aden, the first Arabic newspaper to be run as a commercial venture was licensed there by 1940.[23] Soon afterwards, the Free Yemenis in Aden acquired a small press, which was used to print pamphlets (smuggled northward to the Ibb-Taʿizz area and then to plateau towns by men such as Ismaʿil al-Akwaʿ), short tracts such as the "Sacred Charter" of the 1948 coup, some books, and their own opposition newspaper, called *Sawt al-Yaman*, the "Voice of Yemen."[24]

In addition to his official newspaper and a monthly magazine that appeared briefly,[25] Imam Yahya also authorized the printing of a number of books, both at the government press and overseas, especially in Cairo and the Levant. Rossi categorizes the government press output as of 1938 in three groups: editions of venerable old works by Yemeni scholars (a total of six books published and one in press); nine varied contemporary works; and two brief military manuals. Four books appear on the *madrasa al-ʿilmiyya* curriculum list given by al-Akwaʿ (1980). There is also a recognizable emphasis on pedagogical materials of various types. Works of a theoretical nature include a classic treatise on *adab* in darasa instruction; a little book entitled *Risala fi al-tarbiya*, which Rossi describes as a "collection of pedagogical recommendations inspired by modern concepts," authored by the former inspector of elementary schools in Sanʿaʿ; and, finally, the two military manuals, one containing rules of army discipline inherited from the Turks with "few modifications," the other a military pedagogy work by a Syrian officer in the employ of the imam.[26] Many of the remaining publications are short works, including what Rossi describes as a sort of "catechism," and brief treatises on Quran recitation, grammar, and history that appear suitable for use in the lower schools. Rossi states, however, that at the time of his visit in 1937 "neither a textbook nor a syllabary for elementary students has yet been printed in Yemen."[27]

"ONLY FOR READING": LIBRARY REFORM

"Spiders have spun their webs on them," Imam Yahya wrote, referring to the condition of books in the old library collections in a 1925 decree.[28] "Their term [of usefulness] has expired as most are either in torn condition or have been sold or pawned." Library reform was another subfield of activity in the imam's ma'arif oeuvre, one that exemplified and contributed to changes in the identity of texts and the practices of reading. Mosque libraries, housing manuscript book collections designated as pious endowments, were a very old institution in Yemen; like the imam's schools, the new library that opened in the Great Mosque of San'a' in 1925 represented both a rejuvenated continuation of an established tradition and a quietly innovative break with the past. Reform activity, in this domain as in others, was predicated on an initial identification of disorder: the collections were benefiting no one, and the spiders were at work.

The first organizational step was the creation of a specially designated space: a new storey was constructed over arcades along the southern side of the Great Mosque (San'a') courtyard. Access to the library (located "south of the east minaret") was by means of a long flight of steps. There the imam gathered what remained of the old collections together with his own large and newly created endowment. The properly qualified librarian, described in the decree, was to have "comprehensive knowledge of religion and jurisprudence so as to know the relative importance of the books and the disciplines." This librarian —the scholarly brother of the historian al-Wasi'i is named as the first holder of the position[29]—is required to "take a security deposit from each borrower in an amount greater than the value of the book borrowed." "Tens of thousands of endowed books have been lost," the imam wrote, "because of the nontaking of security deposits." With a proper deposit a book could be borrowed for a period of six months. The contractual language of "loan" and "deposit," and the notion that a book may be constituted as an "endowment," come directly from the manuals of jurisprudence. In his initial organizing decree for his new library the imam also appointed a second library official, charged with documenting and indexing the collections.[30] In the same year, the imam dispatched Muhammad Zabara to Ibb and nearby Jibla, where he was ordered to "find out about the endowment books for teachers and students and compile a listing of them in a register."[31]

In subsequent years, developments indicative of a nascent library science occur. An original type of accounting technology (the simple *musawwada* or *daftar* register used for general pious foundation property records, referred to in the original imamic decree) gives way two decades later to a more specialized form of library index (*Fihrist*, n.d.) published by the Ma'arif Ministry press. This embodies a detailed system of classification (*tartib*) that includes categorization according to twenty-six disciplinary and other subject headings and then alphabetical listings by title within each subject. This general classification is supplemented in the index by specification of authors and their dates, indication of a text's handwritten or printed character with the relevant dates, detail concerning volume sizes in centimeters,[32] and, finally, the name of the individual who established the book as an endowment with an associated volume number.

It is not only such things as the holdings of printed books and the use of metric system measures that are indicative of an emergent new order in Imam Yahya's library. Complementing the specially developed classificatory system are an elaboration of detailed rules of "library" conduct, which are set forth in a supplementary imamic order of 1938. In a manner familiar to Western library users, these rules define a library negatively, in terms of inappropriate behaviors: it is forbidden "for some one to enter the library with a book, small or large, in his hand"; "for a reader or borrower to write anything [in a book], even as a correction, except with permission from the librarian"; "for a reader to directly take a book—instead it should be requested from the librarian"; "to take a book [out of the library and] into the mosque itself for reading (*muṭalaʿa*) or recitation (*qiraʾa*) except by [providing] a material security deposit greater in value than that of the book." It is also forbidden to "engage the librarian or anyone else in the library with talk on unnecessary matters, because the library is only for reading (*muṭalaʿa*), not talk." Borrowing privileges are denied to individuals known not to return books or who are "unqualified" with respect to a book requested, while several types of books and a list of specific titles (including a very early Quran and autograph manuscripts by al-Shawkani) are categorized as noncirculating by a decree of 1942.

A library was a place for the activities of *muṭalaʿa*, silent reading or textual consultation, and *naskh*, copying or transcription. Classification systems, rules of conduct, and spatial bounding—the characteristic techniques of introduced order—had made the library a more specialized institution for the activity of relating to texts. But there were still other dimensions of change. Like old Yemeni schools, the original libraries were physically located in mosques and administered by endowment officials. Still linked to the Great Mosque, the imam's new library was somewhat more physically and conceptually distinct (cf. the rules on entering and leaving). While the 1925 organizing decree identifies the director of the internal endowments (*nazir al-waqf al-dakhili*) as responsible for oversight and support of the head librarian, by the 1940s organizational control has passed to the Ministry of Ma'arif. Over the longer term, continual institutional differentiation led from the omnibus authority of the endowments to the more specialized Ma'arif, and recently to a still more specialized organ, the Office of Antiquities and Libraries.[33] While Imam Yahya's library is still open in the Great Mosque, the new *dar al-kutub* library is located in a separate new building outside the old city.

Modifications in the social organization of circulation also began in the imamic period. Although the intent of the old endowments was the beneficial use (*intifa'a*) of the books, there were frequently founder-stipulated restrictions regarding circulation. Two such types of stipulation are referred to in the 1925 decree. One is in the endowment of Muhammad bin al-Hasan, grandson of the famous Zaidi imam Qasim bin Muhammad (ruled 1598–1620), which is established not as a public endowment but rather as a private one for the benefit of his descendants. Because of the limited benefit that ensued, Imam Yahya ordered this collection joined to his new library. The descendants' endowment rights were upheld by the imam to the extent that they are permitted preferential, but no longer exclusive, borrowing privileges; and there is a further condition: they must give a security deposit, like every other borrower.[34] In the otherwise public endowment of al-Hajj Sa'd bin 'Ali al-Bawab al-Hashidi, there is a provision giving first borrowing rights to all sayyids. That provision is affirmed by the imam, again with the standardized obligation required of all borrowers of a security deposit.

Over the longer term, fundamental shifts in types of library book holdings and in related circulation patterns have mirrored the broader changes in the nature of knowledge and the social organization of its transmission. Simply stated, a genealogically modeled and status-sensitive circulation system has been largely replaced, especially in legislative theory, by a free-market type designed for a democratically conceived citizenry. The older "beneficial intent" rubric of the pious-book foundations has given way to nation-state language: the legislative mandate of the new administration is to open local libraries to help disseminate culture and knowledge to "all the people" (*li-kaffa afrad al-sha'b*).[35] Once mainstays of library collections, manuscripts have now been removed from circulation. Legislation envisions the encouraging of private individuals to "make gifts [of their manuscripts] to the Office, it being understood that their names will be associated with these gifts upon display in the museum."[36]

OFFICIAL HISTORY

I write what I have seen and heard.
AL-WASI'I (1928:278)

In the Author's Foreword to his *Selections*, a concise overview of
Yemeni history published in Cairo in 1951, 'Abd Allah al-Jirafi recalls
a former problem and its solution by Imam Yahya. The problem was
the perceived state of existing historical studies in Yemen. One aspect
of this concerned the fragmentation that had resulted from regional
accounts: "The historian of the (northern) mountains limited himself
to the history of the imams, and the historian of the Tihama and the
south of Yemen limited himself to others; no one managed to bring
together all the Yemeni historical sources and extract from them that
which would satisfy the spirit and give pleasure to the intellect." A very
different and also newly perceived part of the problem in the discipline
of history derived from the reliance upon "pens and inkwells." This
referred to the dangerous open interpretability of writing, the fact that
"the handwritten books[37] of Yemeni history were not secure against
misreadings and changed vowelings." As a consequence, according to
al-Jirafi, "the reader emerged from them with disordered views (*ara'
mudtariba*)." A still further dimension of the problem was the physical
frailty of writing and the extremely limited number of copies of manuscript works. Many histories had suffered the ravages of time (and
spiders), while in the case of others, "the hands of Europeans and other
visitors to Yemen of various eras had fallen upon them."

At the opening of his Foreword, before reviewing these detailed
aspects of the problematic scholarly situation that obtained in Yemen,
al-Jirafi offers a general testimony to the importance of the "art of
history" (*fann al-ta'rikh*):

> Noble in what is perpetuated of bygone days and related of peoples and
> races, employing to this end inkwells and pens, is the art of history, the
> link between the past and the present, the record of works small and
> great, the presenter of the monuments of societies in countrysides and
> towns, the expressive tongue for their sciences and their knowledges and
> their circumstances and their character and their culture and their
> beliefs, the truthful picture of their rise and their fall, and the oppression
> and justice and lowliness and honor involved.

He continues that it is, therefore,

> incumbent upon every society endeavoring to advance that it first turn
> attention to its past and the study of its history, learning what it has

consisted of in the way of events and catastrophes and what the causes
have been of rises and falls. This is because the life of societies is bound
up with their past, and their recent times are but the child of their distant
eras. For this reason it is said that a society that has neglected its past
and knows it not is like a man who has lost his memory.... The study of
history is a necessity of survival; knowledge of the society's history is itself
one of the greatest factors in progress, especially if in the society's history
there are excellent and glorious accomplishments.

According to al-Jirafi, Imam Yahya had "reflected on the problematic state of affairs" in Yemeni historiography and

he desired, following upon his [political] unification of Yemen al-Sa'ida,
to unify its history. To this end, he issued an official order to his son, his
Royal Highness Sayf al-Islam 'Abd Allah, the Minister of Ma'arif, to
establish a committee in the Ma'arif Ministry to study the history of
Yemen and publish a comprehensive book, containing a concise survey
together with political, literary, and social facts.

The history committee was appointed in A.H. 1356 [1937],[38] relatively late in comparison with the school, publishing, and library efforts
begun in the early or mid-twenties. The timing did coincide, however, with the beginnings of underground nationalist opposition. With
Sayyid Muhammad b. Muhammad Zabara as its head and Sayyid
Ahmad b. Ahmad al-Muta', Sayyid Ahmad b. 'Abd al-Wahhab al-
Warith, and Qadi 'Abd Allah b. 'Abd al-Karim al-Jirafi as members,[39]
the committee was composed of leading intellectual figures, all of
whom, except for al-Jirafi, are also commonly identified as important
early advocates of reform. Their mandated production of a "unified"
Yemeni history proceeded by first breaking the object of study down
analytically, by means of a classification into periods. In a parallel
division of scholarly labor, committee members undertook specialized
compilation and writing tasks in one of the four resulting great historical epochs: pre-Islamic history (pre-seventh century A.D.); from the
time of the Prophet to the beginning of the Banu Ziyad state in ninth-
century (A.D.) Yemen; from the Banu Ziyad to the end of the tenth
century A.H. [sixteenth A.D.]; and from the beginning of the tenth
century to the "present history" (*al-ta'rikh al-hadir*) of the fourteenth
[twentieth] century.[40]

Unlike several bracketed studies that stayed within the frames of this
new historical classification, al-Jirafi's own 1951 study is based on
materials that he "selected" from all four periods. He put the history of
Yemen back together again, reconstituting an unbroken chronology

that begins with sketches of the pre-Islamic Yemeni states of Himyar and Saba and concludes with details of the announcement of Imam Ahmad's cabinet in 1949. Unlike most contemporary Western historians, who by definition apply themselves to the study of other eras, Yemeni historians had always written most fully about the events of their own time. As with legal witnessing, the authoritative contributions of historical accounts centered on what the author had personally seen or had heard from reliable individuals. Historians used to open their accounts as if they were giving oral testimony: for example, "qala 'Ali b. al-Hasan al-Khazraji" (lit. "'Ali b. al-Hasan al-Khazraji said").[41] These were historians of the present, chroniclers, in the main, of their own times. Retaining something of this sort of authority, al-Jirafi is most expansive on the contemporary reigns of Imams Yahya and Ahmad.

At the same time, however, the rapid surveys of his earlier chapters establish a continuous identity for an entity called "Yemen," ruled by a long succession of states. Developments in history writing outside of Yemen were part of the backdrop for such new approaches taken by highland authors. A series of published universal[42] and national histories, from the Ottoman Sulayman Pasha (1876) to the Egyptian Jurgi Zaydan,[43] had been in vogue among Yemeni readers. Universal and Ottoman history had been taught in the Ottoman school curriculum in Yemen; a new "comprehensive history," developed by the imam's History Committee, was eventually introduced into that of the *madrasa 'ilmiyya* (al-Akwa' 1980:289).

Al-Jirafi's historical project is rounded out by introductory materials of an interdisciplinary nature: the first chapter includes, in his description, a "detailed account of the country of Yemen, including basic information about its land and its boundaries, its varied climates, its regions, its rivers and valley systems, its mountains, its most renowned towns and ports, its most important and ancient ruins, and something about its economy, its tribes, and its population." The inclusion of geographical, linguistic, genealogical, and folklore materials was, in part, a continuation of distinguished indigenous traditions of inquiry on these topics. The eclectic comprehensiveness of al-Jirafi's account would be reproduced—with a political adjustment from royalist to republican—in a series of works of similar scope—for example, al-Waysi (1962), Sharaf al-Din (1963), al-Thawr (1969), M. al-Akwa' (1971), al-Shamahi (1972), and al-Haddad (new ed. 1976; 1986), that began to appear about a decade later, in the early years of the Revolution. The original Yemeni study in this new genre was not by al-Jirafi, however, but by his distinguished predecessor as a quasi-official imamic historian, 'Abd al-Wasi' b. Yahya al-Wasi'i (d. A.H. 1379 [1959]).[44]

In his *History of Yemen*, published in A.H. 1346 [1928], al-Wasi'i deploys a two-part "organization" (*tartib*) described in his opening "discourse" (*al-khutba*): "The first part concerns the biography of the Prophet and [then] the imams of Yemen down to the time of the contemporary imam of this era"; the second is devoted to "the geography of Yemen and its politics." In a transitional fashion, the book combines, as in al-Jirafi, diachronic and synchronic classifications, an initially rapid chronology that later slows to give year-by-year detail together with a type of presentation, new to Yemeni letters, arranged in quasi-analytic categories. Subheads (in Part II, Section 1, for example: "Language," "Industry and Commerce," "Marriage Customs in Yemen," "The Color of Town Women," "San'a', Capital of Yemen") are of widely varying levels of abstraction and elaboration. A Yemeni reality is re-presented in an unfamiliarly objective manner: at the same time that the implicit is made explicit for Yemeni readers, communicable sense is made of Yemen for non-Yemenis. Subsections such as "Pastimes and Games [of women]," which explains that Yemeni women do not engage in "disgraceful" and "dishonorable" dancing but dance only among themselves, seem mainly to address the perspectives of a foreign, especially Egyptian or Levantine audience.

As print decisively altered the communicability of the new historians' writings, its fixity and reproducible qualities also stilled fears about the perilous alterability and perishability of longhand texts. While some external textual apparatuses, such as title pages, chapter headings, tables of contents, and indices, were not completely unknown in manuscripts, they became standard and much more elaborate in printed works. Other apparatuses were altogether new, either separated out from the main body of the text or positioned in a novel meta-relation to it. Al-Jirafi's history includes what may be the first bibliography (*maraji'*) of supporting references for a scholarly study,[45] and footnotes initially appeared in such works as al-Wasi'i's history and Zabara's edition of al-Shawkani's biographical dictionary. Very specific to printed books of the era are concluding lists of "mistakes and corrections." While revealing the fallibility of editing and the available typography, these errata lists (which later disappeared) also subtly pointed up the potential perfectibility, finality, and closure of the printed text. In comparison with the physical and conceptual openness of manuscripts, printed texts were to be related to in a new manner. Copying, of course, would be completely eliminated; reading would no longer be an open-ended process that required and invited corrective intervention and elucidating comment. While printed texts were more physically distanced from and conceptually independent of equally newly constituted readers, they also contained a new authority, a new truth value, enhanced by the definitiveness of the technology.

With al-Wasiʿi's book it is possible to speak of, and fairly precisely date, the birth of a new kind of Yemeni historiography. Not only were the previous generation of historians (e.g., al-Kibsi, al-Iryani, al-ʿArshi)[46] pre-political-unification writers, their works were manuscripts in both the physical and the discursive sense.[47] It was with al-Wasiʿi that a convergence occurred between an emergent nation-state awareness, new modes of constituting an account, and the availability of print technology. If al-Jirafi may be considered a second-generation representative of this new tradition, then the scholars of the first decade of the Revolution are a third and perhaps final one. With the 1970s and 1980s, Yemeni history writing began to merge with a new discursive era, that of the university-trained historian and of international standards of composition, citation, and publication.

Bounded by earlier, manuscript authors and the recent appearance of "trained" historians, this transitional Yemeni history writing is marked by still other distinctive features. These we know about largely because of the parallel continuation, in the twentieth-century period in question, of the great biographical-dictionary tradition. The principal reference here is to the astounding corpus of biographical compilation undertaken and published by al-Wasiʿi's contemporary, the other founding father of contemporary Yemeni history writing, Sayyid Muhammad b. Muhammad Zabara (d. A.H. 1380 [1961]),[48] who was mentioned earlier as the head of Imam Yahya's history commission. Almost simultaneously in the mid-1920s, the two men were the first Yemenis to publish their own historical writings.[49] The crucial source for understanding changes in scholarly activities over the past one hundred years (the fourteenth century A.H.) is the last of Zabara's biographical histories, "The Entertainment of the Gaze" (*Nuzhat al-nazar*), published posthumously in 1979.[50] It provides entries on all the key figures in the history writing of the period (including the last of the manuscript historians, such as al-Kibsi, and the men of the following print generations: al-Wasiʿi, Zabara, al-Jirafi, al-Warith, al-Mutaʿ, al-Waysi, al-Haddad, Sharaf al-Din, Muhammad and Ismaʿil al-Akwaʿ, etc.).

Chronicles and biographical dictionaries are the two main old genres of Muslim historical writing. In Yemen, the biographical works have taken various forms, including some imaginative reworkings by twentieth-century Yemeni authors. The initial impetus for such works was to "know the men," enabling the critical assessment of the passage of authoritative knowledge through time. Ibn Samura's early dictionary details the actual arrival in the highlands of key legal texts. A simple genealogical method specified the teacher-student transmission links between generations (*tabaqat*) of jurists and the texts they carried. In later centuries, as it became increasingly difficult to trace linkages, breaks in reported chains of transmission occurred. Despite the multiplication of human transmitters and the proliferation of texts, however, genealogical analysis, often much more limited in scope, persisted in historical accounts. Al-Shawkani's early-nineteenth-century specification of the transmission links for the entire corpus of his knowledge was exceptional.[51]

In Zabara's biographical collections, specific attention is given only to an individual's teachers and students, although it is possible, by means of cross-referencing, to follow intellectual links backwards and forwards through several generations. In addition, Zabara frequently quotes *ijaza*s in poetry, and these name in some detail the relevant backgrounds of men and texts.[52] More innovative than Zabara's dictionaries are books by al-Jirafi and Isma'il al-Akwa'. Al-Jirafi's *Tuhfat al-ikhwan* is an extended biography of the great Yemeni scholar and jurist, Husayn b. 'Ali al-Amri (d. A.H. 1361 [1942]), completed by biographies of his numerous students. Al-Akwa''s *Madaris al-islamiyya* shifts the conventions of foreground and background, organizing the presentation by particular institutions, giving biographical notices for the individuals who taught at each of these schools. The development of the specialized genre of autobiography is evidenced both in the personalized style of historical writing by al-Shamahi[53] and in *A Page From the Social History of Yemen and the Story of My Life* by Muhammad al-Akwa'. This last combines a literary account of growing up in Yemen (in some respects like Egyptian Taha Hussain's famous autobiography) with a folklorist's fascination for details of custom and colloquial expression.[54]

An item that first appears in Zabara's biographies beginning with the entry on al-Wasi'i is mention of activities connected with the official mission of "enlivening" the Yemeni textual intellectual legacy (*turath*) and introducing it to scholars elsewhere in the Middle East, mainly through publishing Yemeni works overseas. Trips were undertaken with an aim at once old and new: the "dissemination"/"publication" (*nashr*) of knowledge. "And he undertook to have printed," the biographical entries say, and lists follow of "his own writings" and titles of other Yemeni-authored works seen through presses in Mecca, Cairo, Beirut, Damascus, or Baghdad. Imams Yahya and Ahmad, al-Jirafi wrote, "ordered the publication of a number of Yemeni writings, which had a distinct impact throughout the Arab world and a beneficial influence."[55]

This official publication policy extended to more than Yemeni histories. Unlike the texts of the Shafi'i school, which were of far greater interregional and colonial significance and therefore found their way into print much earlier, most of the major works of Zaidi jurisprudence were published for the first time in the first half of the twentieth century. The men who handled these publication projects were the leading Yemeni historians of the day. Before he had printed any of his own works, al-Wasi'i was responsible for the 1921 publication of the text (*matn*) of *Al-Azhar*, the basic manual of the school; the key commentary work, *Sharh al-Azhar*, which appeared in four large volumes; and also *Majmu' Zaid bin 'Ali*, the early hadith-jurisprudence work by the school's eponym.[56] The *Azhar* text appeared in a collection of basic texts (*Kitab majmu' al-mutun*) that also included a brief inheritance treatise and a short *usul* jurisprudence manual (*Al-Ghaya*). The biographer writes that his subject "expended an enormous effort in seeing *Kitab al-majmu'* into print." Al-Wasi'i had also taken the Zaid bin 'Ali manuscript with him on his travels, "and undertook to present [it] to the scholars of Egypt and Syria, to obtain their poetic appreciations of it,[57] and to bring to their attention the Yemeni method in the religious sciences." In addition to efforts to get books by al-Shawkani and his own massive biographical studies published, Zabara was instrumental in having the important commentary on the Zaid bin 'Ali text, *Rawd al-nadir* by al-Sayaghi, published in four volumes in 1929.[58] For his part, and in addition to several other types of important texts he supervised at the presses, al-Jirafi was instrumental in the publication of *Bahr al-zakhkhar*, a five-volume comprehensive study of all the legal schools by Imam al-Murtada, author of *Al-Azhar*.[59]

This intensive publication activity represented an important new wrinkle in the centuries-old pattern of traveling for scholarly pursuits, although al-Wasi'i and Zabara,[60] at least, endeavored to study on their trips in something approaching the long-established manner. Inside

Yemen there was still some of the old circulation of scholars in search of particular teachers or local schools of note, although the newly centralized pull of the *madrasa 'ilmiyya* in the north and the *Ahmadiyya* in the south skimmed the cream of the advanced students. Another sort of *rihla* in evidence in the first part of the century was only a recent version of a venerable practice. This was the research trip. To the extent possible, historians endeavored to base their accounts on personal communications and eyewitness experiences. Thus al-Wasi'i reports in the first person on his findings among a tribe, significantly including the women and children, who spoke classical Arabic "instinctually."[61] On a trip to Ibb, Zabara interviewed Ahmad al-Basir about the family ancestor who originally came to Lower Yemen; and Abu Bakr al-Haddad was the source for the profile of his uncle 'Abd al-Rahman al-Haddad. Later, al-Waysi and Muhammad Yahya al-Haddad would travel extensively in the pursuit of geographical data and information about early Yemeni civilizations, while the Akwa' brothers "visited numerous locales in various regions of Yemen to inspect and study archaeological and historical sites."[62] Isma'il al-Akwa' has frequent footnotes identifying his eyewitnessed and personal communication material. In the early post-Revolutionary period, texts began to be supplemented by photographs, many of which provided further evidence of the author's presence on field trips.

On the title page of *Selections*, below al-Jirafi's modestly sized name and two smaller lines saying he held positions as an instructor at the *dar al-'ulum (madrasa 'ilmiyya)* in San'a' and as a representative of the Ministry of Ma'arif to Egypt, there appears, in large bold print: "ordered to be printed by His Royal Highness, King of the Mutawakkilite Kingdom of Yemen, Imam al-Nasr ... Ahmad bin Yahya Hamid al-Din." An association with power was nothing new for Yemeni historians, but some of these scholars of the first half of the twentieth century were "quasi-official," as Sayyid Mustafa Salim has put it,[63] in a period-specific sense. Salim singles out al-Wasi'i and al-Jirafi for their marked official backing and their privileging of the history of the Zaidi imams, but the phenomenon was general. Historical studies had become the subject of the organizational interest of an evolving nation-state, beginning with the Committee of 1937, continuing after the Revolution with a similar Committee for Yemeni History,[64] and following with the Center for Yemeni Studies founded in 1975–76.[65] While most Yemeni historians of this century have been closely tied to the state, as members of state history committees, as secretaries in the imamic diwan,[66] and as appointed officials, many were also active advocates of reform or political opponents of the regime.

For all the shifts of technological and political terrain, however, the scholars of the transitional generations remained generalists of the "old school." All were trained in a core of knowledge centering on shari'a jurisprudence, which provided the common intellectual foundation for historical as for other branches of scholarship. Thus it is recorded in biographies, that al-Wasi'i taught the *Sharh al-Azhar* to his son and authored a short treatise on *usul* jurisprudence; that Zabara studied jurisprudence with the leading jurists of his day and served as a judge for seven years early in his career; and that al-Jirafi studied the *Sharh al-Azhar* with two different teachers. The same sort of curricular and career profile was shared by the succeeding generation of early republican historians as well. Sharply distinct from the manuscript products of the preceding period, the scholarship of this transitional period in Yemeni historiography is also decidedly different from that of the emergent contemporary historical discipline. Jurisprudence and history have now begun to diverge, into unrelated, parallel fields of inquiry, separately housed in a law school and a department of history.

PART III

Interpretation

CHAPTER 7

Relations of Interpretation

Whoever hath absolute authority to interpret any written or spoken laws is he who is the lawgiver to all intents and purposes and not the person who first wrote or spoke them.

BISHOP HOADLEY[1]

THE MUFTI OF IBB

Men begin assembling in the semipublic upstairs sitting room in the Ibb mufti's house shortly after lunch. Some plan to settle in for an afternoon of qat chewing, others intend only to see the mufti briefly and then leave. They sit on mats or mattresses at floor level and lean on individual armrests with their backs supported by cushions lined up along the wall. Light enters the room through two large windows set low in one of the whitewashed walls. A simple wooden chest placed before sitting cushions marks the space to be occupied by the mufti.

Descending from private top-floor rooms, the mufti enters the sitting room, carrying his own bundle of qat and wearing indoor attire consisting of a white skullcap and herringbone vest over a long, pure-white gown buttoned up to his neck. His dagger, in its elaborate metal sheath and embroidered dagger belt, his scholar's turban, and his long outer coat and shawl are left hanging on a hook upstairs. He is a tall and physically strong man in his sixties, but both his sight and his hearing are weak, and he wears thick glasses and a hearing aid. Without ceremony he steps over the wooden chest on his way to his accustomed sitting place. Adjusting his spittoon and thermos of water, he begins to select leaves to chew; the shared hose of the water pipe is passed to him to smoke. The scene is much the same as in many other afternoon qat sessions in progress around the town, including those at judges' houses.

Aside from breaks associated with the two main ritual breaks of the lunar calendar and with the fasting month of Ramadan, the level of activity in the mufti's sitting room is geared to the annual agrarian cycle. As is true at the courts, harvesttime in late autumn is a slack period for the mufti. Many of the ten or so men who gather on a given afternoon are from rural districts, cultivators of the small curved terraces that rise in steps up the steep mountainsides of the southern highlands. This is indicated by their loosely wrapped cloth turbans, soiled and open shirts, rough cracked hands, and bare feet. When one of these "tribesmen" enters after the mufti has taken his place, he will utter an initial greeting at the door and then advance across the room to where the mufti is sitting. Unlike most townsmen, who are apt to shake hands, he stoops abruptly and endeavors to kiss the mufti's hand and knee.

Some men come to the mufti for his assistance in settling disputes out of court. In acting as an arbitrator the mufti steps out of his official role as mufti. "We are in your hands, decide between us," is the formula of this sort of request. Other uses of his legal expertise also are outside of his official work. For some he acts as a notary (*katib*) who prepares written legal instruments. Although he would never appear for a client in court as a legal representative (*wakil*), he does write claims, responses to claims, and appeals of decisions for his clients to present in court. In addition to his primary work of delivering opinions known as *fatwa*s, there are other categories of legal activity in which he engages in his capacity as mufti. Both rural and town people come to him for legal evaluations of physical injuries (*arsh*) (see fig. 8). Occasionally, he adds his signature to attestations of poverty or of incapacity presented by individuals seeking entry onto the public charity rolls, or he is asked to countersign a legal instrument.

But the main activity of the mufti is the writing of fatwas. A fatwa is the mufti's response to a question. Questions are posed in writing, by those who can write for those unable to, and usually by men for women, using such simple formulas as "what is your opinion about . . ." and the matter is stated, or in conclusion, simply, "give us a fatwa" concerning the matter. On the same piece of paper, usually in the space left above the question, the mufti writes his *jawab*, his answer, which is the fatwa, concluding with the formula "God knows best" and his signature.

For a mufti's questioner, obtaining a fatwa is an informational step, taken either to regulate the individual's personal affairs or with litigation or some other form of settlement in mind. Questioners appear as individuals, not in adversarial pairs; posing a question to a mufti and receiving his response is not a judicial procedure like that in a judge's

Figure 8. The Ibb mufti writes an evaluation of a cut on a young girl's face, 1976.

court. Also, in Yemen, fatwas are not presented in court cases.[2] Without being binding a fatwa authoritatively provides the fatwa seeker with a legal rule relevant to the matter in question. Fatwa in hand, the questioner is free to arrange his or her affairs accordingly or to seek redress if wronged.

While virtually all Yemenis these days use fountain or ballpoint pens, this mufti continues to use an old-fashioned carved reed pen (*shizza*), which he dips repeatedly in an inkwell. His fingers are long and smooth, accustomed to the discipline of this instrument. Papers are held not against a desk but between the base of his writing hand and that of his left hand; as he writes two fingers of his left hand glide along the back of the paper to meet the pressure of his pen. When he is finished writing, he gives the paper back to the questioner. No record is made, and the mufti has no secretary. While the mufti is paid as a matter of course for writing legal instruments and in dispute settlement, he does not always accept money for fatwas, or if he does, it is a very small sum, considered a gift rather than a fee. In his capacity as mufti of Ibb Province,[3] a title he has held since shortly after the Revolution of 1962, he receives a government salary through the local branch office of the Ministry of Justice.

When a question is posed, the mufti's response is always immediate. Far from pausing to refer to a legal manual or, seemingly, even to reflect, he answers all questions without hesitation. This is remarkable in view of the range and complexity of the questions he receives. In general terms, the fatwas he issues may be classified into marriage and divorce matters, inheritance and pious-endowment questions, other property issues, and miscellaneous. This last category includes the occasional fatwa sought about a ritual detail. The prayer leader from the mosque next door, for example, once came to the mufti's sitting while I was present to ask about the fine points of timing for the first call to prayer of the day. Fatwas concerned with support payments connected with divorce and estate divisions require calculation (as do wound evaluations). Part of this mufti's academic formation, however, is in the subjects of arithmetic (*hisab*) and the law of inheritance, both of which he taught at the Great Mosque in Ibb before the Revolution.

Questions connected with marriage conflicts are the most common type currently (1975–1980) asked. Aside from common questions about such matters as the validity of the threefold statement of divorce, the mufti received many questioners whose lives were influenced by the large-scale migration of Yemeni men to Saudi Arabia for work. Many marital legal problems are connected with the absence of husbands. In estate-related questions, many individuals want to know which relatives are heirs of a deceased person and what share each should receive. A significant subset of these fatwas deals with problems concerning endowments, especially of the type associated with descent groups. There are fatwas on such issues as the exclusion from endowment-revenue distributions of an out-marrying woman's descendants, in favor of descendants in the direct male line. Others deal with attempts to sell inalienable endowment property or problems with their supervision. There are also fatwas dealing with the invasion of property rights, or with whether an individual is allowed to retract a sale or exercise a right of preemption. For preemption matters this mufti now refers his questioners to a rule established by the Ministry of Justice.

Three queries and their associated fatwa-responses will serve to illustrate the Ibb genre. Concerned respectively with marriage, inheritance, and property rights, these texts appear concise and implicit in translation. Queries are often poorly phrased or confused, and fatwas often must be explained to their recipients. Sometimes the formulation of the question represents a simple description of circumstances as best they are understood; other times it embeds a stratagem the questioner wants to have evaluated. Further explication, which I do not attempt here, would require background on the particular conflicts and an excursus into such matters as doctrinal rules and customary practices concerning marriage, guardianship, and the structure of male-female relations; inheritance and patterns of kinship; and property relations connected with the contract of sale.

Question 1: What is your opinion (*qawl*), scholar of Islam, may God be pleased with you, about a woman who has a young virgin daughter and, following upon the absence of the full brother of this daughter, the mother undertakes to marry the girl without the consent of her brother, despite the fact that the brother wrote weekly? The contract was entered into under the auspices of the judge, and she had no guardian except him. He [the brother] was only in absence one month. Give us a fatwa.

Fatwa: The answer: the judge does not have the right to make a contract given the existence of her legal guardian, her brother, as long as he had not abstained from the contract. God knows best. Mufti of Ibb Province (signature).

Question 2: What is your opinion, scholar of Islam, about a woman who died leaving her daughter and her full sister. She also has a husband and a half-sister by her mother and a son of her father's brother. Give us a fatwa concerning the number of shares in this matter, and also who is legally entitled to inheritance and who is excluded, in detail. Prayers upon our master Muhammad and his people and his followers, and peace. February 4, 1976. Presented by (name and village).

Fatwa: The answer: to the husband a quarter, and to the daughter a half, and the remainder to the full sister, and nothing to the half sister by the mother, and nothing to the father's brother's son. God knows best. 4 Safar 1396 (1976). Mufti of Ibb Province (signature).

Question 3: What is your opinion, scholar of Islam, about a man who sold a piece of land, without knowing it and without knowing its value, to a buyer in whose possession the land was for cultivation, when it later became clear that the land was valuable and that he received less than half of its value. Does the seller have a right to reclaim his land? March 22, 1980.

Fatwa: The answer: there is no fraud when the seller is legally capable, except if a legal condition was placed upon the purchaser. God knows best. Mufti of Ibb Province (signature).

While most Ibb fatwas are brief and straightforward, lacking any explicit reasoning or citation of authorities, a few are more expansive and make reference to differences among the schools of law or among individual jurists. In one fatwa (concerning the triple-repudiation type of divorce) the mufti cites the uniform view of the four Sunni schools, notes that it is the same as the Hadawiyya (Zaidi) school with one condition, and then goes on to refer to a consensus of authoritative Yemeni jurists such as al-Shawkani and Muhammad Isma'il al-Amir, representing a different view.

His fatwas also make occasional reference to customary law (*'urf*). When he is specifying the level of support payments owed to divorced wives, for example, he details amounts of grain, money, rent per month, and clothes per annum "according to custom" (*bi-hasab al-ma'ruf*). Another type of question asks the mufti to evaluate a customary settlement from the perspective of the *shari'a*. In one such instance, a dispute arose over whether a woman was or was not a virgin at the time of marriage. The conflict was resolved by rural leaders in the form of a *sulh*, or customary compromise, rather than in court and according to the shari'a. In his fatwa, the mufti found several of the money payments included in the terms of the settlement to be without basis. This opinion was implicit, however, as he merely stated what the legal money payment should be.

THE MUFTISHIP

A mufti is a type of Muslim jurist who delivers a nonbinding legal opinion known as a fatwa, exercising in the process the form of legal interpretation called *ijtihad*. Across the Middle East and North Africa for many centuries, muftis great and small, official and unofficial have worked at the interface of shari'a text and practice. Analogues for the muftiship have been identified in both Roman and medieval Jewish legal institutions.[4] According to Weber (1978:798–99, 821) and Schacht (1964:74), the muftiship was originally a "private" institution that later became "public." Schacht correctly adds, however, that the later official muftis "had no monopoly of giving fatwas, and the practice of consulting private scholars of high reputation never ceased." As a consequence, a significant dimension of authoritative interpretation consistently eluded the purview of Muslim states.

Yemen had only indirect experiences of such early public institutional elaborations of the office as occurred in Mamluk Egypt (Tyan 1960:224) and in the central provinces of the old Ottoman Empire (Gibb and Bowen 1957:133–35; *EI* 2 art. "Fatwa"). An official muftiship was established in Ibb during the second Ottoman occupation, but its public quality was not pronounced. The three generations in the al-Haddad family (grandfather, two sons, and a grandson) held the town mufti post during the Ottoman period and into the following imamic period up to 1950.[5] Ahmad b. Muhammad b. ʿAli al-Haddad, the grandson, described his activities in the 1940s:

> The place of issuing fatwas was in the sitting room of my house, since there was no formal office place for any judicial or executive organ in the old days. Most of our time in those days was unoccupied and we spent it reading *Subul al-Salam* [by al-Amir (d. 1753) on Hadith] and other books during the afternoons. As for the mornings, we used to walk down into the valley, and if anyone came up to us with a matter, we used to answer him in any place he found us, in the street or in any other place. (Taped discussion, 1980)

Currently, there is a Mufti of the Republic in the capital city,[6] and questioners from around the country now also have media access to a "Fatwa Show" on the radio, and on Yemeni television bearded old scholars in robes and turbans answer viewers' questions in a similar format. But these new manifestations of the muftiship and the continuing efforts of old-style muftis in a few places such as Ibb exist in a changed interpretive environment.

Muftis served in Yemen both under the terms of official appointments and as private scholars, and they ranged in stature from the most noted jurists of an era, such as al-Shawkani in the early nineteenth century, to modest men practicing in the provinces.[7] Prior to the Ottoman occupation, the giving of fatwas was an informal activity of leading scholars. A scholar occupied himself in "studying, teaching, and giving fatwas" (al-Akwaʿ 1980:234). A common formula that identified a prominent scholar was *intahat ilayhi riyasat al-ʿilm*, with the sense being that the scholar in question was the final authority— literally, "the leadership of knowledge ended up with him." The separate strands of the composite identity of one local scholar are detailed in the same terms: he was the leading scholar in "legal knowledge, fatwa-giving and instruction" (*intahat ilayhi riyasat al-fiqh wa al-fatwa wa al-tadris* [al-Akwaʿ 1980:661]). This old idiom of scholarly preeminence (cf. Makdisi 1981:129–33) occurs in biographical history accounts mentioning local muftis going back to the twelfth century.[8] A scholar without peer in the locality was by definition, and simultaneously, the individual sought out for instruction and prevailed upon to issue fatwas.

Muftis are intermediate figures. In relation to the wider institutional scheme for the interpretive transmission of knowledge, muftis occupy a niche between the jurist as teacher and the jurist as judge, mediating in identity and function between the opposed spheres of the *madrasa* (school) and the *mahkama* (court)—between the cloistered, theoretical transmission of shari'a jurisprudence in lesson circles and the public, practical application of it in judicial proceedings. Many muftis were also teachers, but unlike the retiring purists among their professorial colleagues, muftis were jurists who projected their knowledge beyond the confines of the lesson circle to address the affairs of the community. A mufti's involvement with the mundane world was more restricted, however, than that of a judge. As jurists and as moral beings, muftis typically distanced themselves from the considerable ambivalence surrounding the judgeship itself, and the court, which many considered an arena of corruption, coercion, and error.

With regard to its institutional form, the muftiship has been the subject of systematic reflection by Muslim scholars. According to Ibn Khaldun (d. 1406), both the muftiship and the judgeship are classified among the "religious-legal" (*diniyya shar'iyya*) functions that fall under the authority of the (great) imam, the leader of the Muslim community (1958:448 sqq.). For al-Qarafi (d. 1301), "every (great) imam is [also] a judge and a mufti" (1967:32), while the reverse is not true. Although they were Shi'is (rather than the Sunni type specifically referred to by Ibn Khaldun and al-Qarafi), Zaidi imams fit this characterization. In addition to his responsibilites for the affairs of the "world," a Zaidi imam was both a mufti and a judge in identity and capacity, in addition to being in a position of authority over appointed muftis and judges. As muftis writ large, Zaidi imams issued their own fatwa-like interpretive opinions (*ijtihadat* or *ikhtiyarat*); as judges writ large, they represented the final source of appeal in shari'a procedure while occasionally engaging directly in formal judgment giving.

MUFTIS AND JUDGES

In the shari'a manuals, the muftiship (*al-ifta'*) and the judgeship (*al-qada'*) are distinguished. An initial contrast concerns the locus and extent of the coverage. In the methodological literature, the "roots" (*usul*) manuals (e.g., al-Juwayni), the muftiship alone is discussed, while in the applied "branches" (*furu'*) manuals (Abu Shuja' or al-Nawawi) a chapter on the judgeship is standard, but there is no equivalent chapter on the muftiship. This separate and unequal treatment of the two offices in the methodological and applied literatures is consonant with a divergence in the kind of interpretation engaged in by muftis as opposed to judges. Differences between the two offices are also expressed in the types of conditions set for candidates. In general, these are not so highly elaborated for potential muftis as for those who would become judges (Tyan 1960:223–28). Requirements that a judge be male, free instead of being a slave, and sound in sight and hearing, for example, are not explicit requirements for muftis. Moral uprightness and intellectual attainment alone are the determinants of suitability for the muftiship. But while these attributes of ʿadala (justness or probity) and advanced scholarly status enabling interpretation are absolute requirements for muftis, for the judgeship both admission to the office of an individual lacking in moral standards (a fasiq) and one relatively ignorant has been conceived of, if by no means desired.[9]

Further evidence of the conceptual contrast between the muftiship and the judgeship is found in an ambivalence that surrounded the judgeship from early times (Gottheil 1908; Amedroz 1910; Wensinck 1922; Coulson 1956). The honor conventionally attached to the post and its incumbents was disturbed by a number of "ominous" hadiths: for example, "Of three judges, two are in Hell" and "He who undertakes the judgeship slits his own throat without a knife."[10] These and other hadiths quoted to me in Ibb, colloquial proverbs ("If the disputants settle among themselves, the judge is angry")[11] and lines of poetry ("Half the people are enemies of the judge, and that is if he is just")[12] portray judges and their social reception unfavorably. In addition, biographical histories from across the Muslim world contain many examples either of reluctance to serve or of declined judicial appointments. These include such celebrated cases as that of Abu Hanifa (the eighth-century founding figure of the Hanafi school), who is reputed to have repeatedly refused offers and as a result was subjected to corporal punishment and imprisonment, leading to his death. Yemeni biographical histories also document the incidence of such refusals.[13] An Ibb judge of the thirteenth century left a legacy that his eldest son should not undertake the judgeship, and it is reported of a fifteenth-century jurist that "he was invested with the judgeship of the town of Ibb after vehement refusal."

The stigma attached to the judgeship even found expression in manual discussions. Opening his chapter on the office, al-Nawawi first notes that filling it is a duty incumbent on the community (fard kifaya). He then treats the sensitive issue of whether an individual should seek the position or accept it if offered. Al-Nawawi writes that uniquely qualified individuals alone must engage in active solicitation. There are opposed views, however, about whether an individual should accept appointment when a better candidate is known to exist. For ordinarily qualified individuals, al-Nawawi mentions opinions holding that "it is reprehensible (*makruh*) to seek it, or some say forbidden (*haram*)."[14] Accepting an appointment is permissible if one is as qualified as any other potential candidate, and it is positively recommended to accept if one is an "unknown" jurist whose appointment would serve to "disseminate knowledge" (*nashr al-'ilm*) or to provide a qualified man with a licit income. Al-Nawawi's own summary opinion is that active seeking of the office is *makruh*, reprehensible. Generations later, in what amounts to one of many small theoretical skirmishes in his larger effort to reinstate active interpretation, al-Shawkani argues against the received notion that the judgeship is in any way *makruh*.[15] In the numerous biographical entries on the men who served as judges, there are de rigueur formulaic expressions of social approval and integrity in office.

Judges have generally been held responsible for historical divergences of the ideal and the real, for the advent of procedures and rulings not solidly anchored in the shari'a. In contrast to the visions of Hell visited upon wayward judges, however, even the commission of error in the course of a mufti's interpretive work is positively rewarded. According to a well-known hadith from the Prophet, "If an interpreter is right he receives two rewards; if he is mistaken he receives one reward."[16] One trace of the sort of opprobrium heaped upon judges being extended to muftis is found in a hadith quoted by Ibn Khaldun, but not known in Ibb, concerning the active seeking of public office: "Those of you who most boldly approach the task of giving fatwas are most directly heading toward Hell."[17]

Muftis and judges also practice in differently constituted settings. While the mufti is sought out by single questioners for nonenforceable fatwas, a judge rules in contexts of two-party adversarial conflict, and his judgments are enforceable. Ibn Khaldun blends his discussion of the muftiship with the role of scholar-teacher, whose forum is the *madrasa*, the place of instruction. In Ibb this meant the main mosque. Muftis were associated with the world of teachers and with students, who led more or less sequestered lives. The judge's *mahkama*, or court, by contrast, is the quintessential public forum, a locus for the coercive exercise of state power. Judges were explicitly forbidden to hold court in mosques.[18] Differences in source of income reinforced the institutional separation. Like their earlier Ottoman colleagues,[19] Ibb muftis were supported by a specially earmarked pious endowment.[20] This form of support once again associated muftis with the madrasa and the mosque, which were exclusively funded by such endowments, and further distinguished them from judges and their profane income, whether derived licitly from state monies[21] or illicitly from corruption.[22]

If, in ideal terms, the mufti is an intermediate figure, retaining the purity of the madrasa while approaching the rough and tumble of the mahkama, actual muftis have varied in their approximation of the norm. The present mufti of Ibb retains an association with the madrasa (as a former teacher), and he has the retiring pious nature of a private scholar desiring to keep some distance from the boisterous arenas of public life. There are other exemplars of this posture. One was 'Ali Naji al-Haddad, the apical ancestor of the Ibb al-Haddads. In the late nineteenth century he was a teacher and a mufti, both activities based in the town madrasa, the Great Mosque. Another example is al-Shawkani. In his autobiography (A.H. 1348, 2:214–25), he describes his isolation from the world (*al-dunya*) during the time he was a mufti and prior to being, as he put it, "afflicted" with the judgeship. Speaking of himself in the third person, al-Shawkani says, "He did not stop at the door of a governor or judge, and he did not befriend any of the 'people of the world' (*ahl al-dunya*)."[23] Of his work as mufti he proudly states that he issued fatwas for free: "I acquired knowledge without a price and I wanted to give it thus."

Muftis who were so inclined, however, could be important actors in "the world." For the Middle East generally, there is in this century the notorious example of the mufti of Jerusalem, and there is evidence that at least some Ottoman muftis became wealthy in their posts (Gibb and Bowen 1957:137). Two Yemeni examples, again provincial and prominent, also demonstrate that the muftiship was no institutional straitjacket. As was mentioned earlier, 'Ali Naji al-Haddad's son 'Abd al-Rahman was a scholar-politician. While in the post of town mufti, he led the successful resistance to the 1904 siege by Imam Yahya's forces. In the capital, San'a', the official Mufti of the Ottoman Province of Yemen was a public official who sat on the High Administrative Council. Accounts of the political exploits of one of the holders of this office concern a man deeply involved in political intrigue, an individual who was anything but a retiring scholar.[24]

WORLDLY INTERPRETATION

The worldly activities of muftis and judges are distinct in subject matter and yet similar in structure to scriptural interpretation, the madrasa-based activity that includes Quranic exegesis and other forms of commentary upon texts. Before making connections to related madrasa techniques, the two genres of worldly interpretation, fatwas and judgments, must be distinguished.

Asked in writing to explain the difference between a fatwa and a judgment, the Ibb mufti responded, fatwa-style:

> The answer: the fatwa is a legal clarification (*bayan*) for the judgment, and the mufti is the ascertainer of the legal reference (*dalala*) and the clarifier in his response of (that which is) legal and illegal in the shari'a, but in it there is no enforcement. The judgment requires enforcement. God knows best.

In the same work in which he distinguishes the categories great imam, mufti, and judge, al-Qarafi (1967:30–31, 41) also offers a typology for the fatwa and the judgment. He contrasts the conceptual bases of fatwa-giving and judgment-giving in a manner similar to the mufti of Ibb. A mufti refers to *adilla* (from the same root as *dalala*, used by the mufti of Ibb), while judges refer to *hijāj*. *Adilla* are such sources of law as the Quran and the Sunna, while the *hijāj* include information about the world, such as evidence, testimony, a disputant's acknowledgment of an act, oaths, and refusals to swear an oath (cf. al-Qarafi A.H. 1344:129).

If both fatwa-giving and judgment-giving embody an interpretive bringing together of doctrine and practice—of jurisprudence and actual occurrences—they do so with different emphases. Their interpretive thrusts are diametrically opposed. What is "constructed" in a fatwa is an element of doctrine: a fatwa is concerned with and based upon doctrinal texts (*adilla*), although it requires the specifics of an actual case as a point of departure. What is "constructed" in a judgment is a segment of practice: a judgment is concerned with and based upon practical information (*hijāj*), although it requires a framework of doctrine as its point of reference. Fatwas use uncontested concrete descriptions as *given* instances necessitating interpretation in doctrine; judgments address the contested facts of cases as *problematic* instances that are themselves in need of interpretation. Fatwas and judgments are thus interpretive reciprocals: they come to rest at opposed points on the same hermeneutical circle.

While the construction of the practical world by means of judgments is a crucial activity in any society, equally fundamental is the interpretive augmentation of the basic corpus of legal rules. In the Anglo-American system, both are accomplished in judges' rulings. But in the absence of a formal precedent-recording system, Muslim judges' rulings were not built into a corpus of case law. The closest approximation in the shari'a to the weight of precedent cases in common law is to be found in the collections of nonbinding fatwa opinions rather than in court decisions. It has been argued that a "legislative" capacity is lacking in Islamic law and that this function has been filled by the institution of fatwa-giving (Tyan 1960:219; Schacht 1964:745). In the Muslim tradition, extending the body of the shari'a has been accomplished both through the activity of jurists, usually associated with madrasas, who engaged in the purely scholarly extension and elaboration of the "text" through original works or commentaries, and by some of the same jurists and others outside the academy, acting as muftis, who took as their ground of interpretive departure not earlier texts but the facts of the world.

The method of *ijtihad* that evolved is anchored in analogy. A Greek logical method (Peters 1968) was wedded to the methods and constraints of interpreting a body of sacredly constituted text (Quran and Sunna). As the basic tool, analogy (*qiyas*)[25] is used dialectically to interpret new facts with reference to existing text and, conversely, new text with reference to existing fact. In the "roots" manual of jurisprudential method studied in Ibb (al-Juwayni n.d.: 67–71), analogy is first defined in terms of relating "branch" to "root," that is, a question of positive law to a source of law (Quran or Sunna). Analogy is of three types: one that works through a "middle" term (*'illa*); one that operates through a direct "indication" (*dalala*—cf. usage by the Ibb mufti); and one involving a relation of "similarity" (*shabah*). In this form of interpretation the underlying analogy is of the *text* and the world, allowing the systematic handling of a double-edged problem—creating new text and regulating new cases.

Analogically based ijtihad emerged as the accepted interpretive method only against the staunch opposition of strict or literal interpretationists, who rejected it outright, comparing it in one instance to "carrion, to be eaten only when no other food is available."[26] Ijtihad was developed by jurists from a loose application of personal opinion to a comparatively strictly defined method based on several modes of reasoning. No matter how rigorously defined, however, ijtihad was still an exercise of a single individual's interpretive capacity, and therefore, by definition, as human, potentially flawed. Muhammad al-Shafi'i, the jurist credited with both the initial elaboration of the "roots" methodology and the grounding of ijtihad in strict analogy, recognized that divergent views were the necessary concomitant of the use of ijtihad (Schacht 1950:97, 128).

Interpretations individual in origin could be accepted as accretions to the corpus of the shari'a through a mechanism placed third among the fundamentals (*usul*) of jurisprudence (the first two being the Quran and Sunna as source texts, and the fourth being *qiyas*). This is the principle of "consensus" (*ijma'*),[27] which is exemplified and justified by a Prophetic hadith: "My community will never agree in error." Consensus, the means by which individual interpretations became integrated into the law, was also subject to a narrowing of definition until it became associated, not with the opinion of all members of the community, but rather with that of the scholars alone, those deemed capable of evaluating an interpretation, either rejecting it as wrong or accepting it as authoritative. Consensus has been characterized as "the foundation of the foundation of the law" (Hurgronje 1957:57; cf. Goldziher 1981:50f.). Seen in relation to interpretation, consensus is the mechanism through which the *parole* of the individual interpreter could become part of the collective, consensual *langue* of the shari'a.

According to the disputed view that the "gate of ijtihad" was closed, however, the successes of the advocates of active interpretation eventually came to naught. This supposed watershed (c. A.D. 900) in the development of the shari'a corpus is characterized by Weber as marking both a "crystallization" of the four great Sunni schools of law and, simultaneously, an end to further interpretive additions to the set corpus: "The crystallization was officially achieved through the belief that the charismatic, juridical prophetic power of legal interpretation (*ijtihad*) had been extinguished" (1978:819). To the extent that ijtihad was condoned at all, according to this doctrine, it could only address formulations set within the existing frameworks of the four schools, but could not directly address the Quran and Sunna. There were jurists in subsequent centuries, however, including such formidable legal minds as Ibn Taymiyya (d. 1328) and al-Shawkani in early-nineteenth-century Yemen, who rejected this doctrine and brushed aside the boundaries and ossified dogmas of the schools to advocate ijtihad and rethink their positions from first principles, that is, the Quran and Sunna. Aside from such prominent intellectual figures, however, it was the ordinary muftis of Islam, continuously and unobtrusively,

across region and time, who provided the shari'a with an interpretive
dynamism through the exercise of ijtihad in their fatwas.[28]

FATWAS GREAT AND SMALL

But how can the mundane content of the Ibb mufti's fatwas—"to the
husband a quarter ..."; "the judge does not have the right ..."; "there
is no fraud ..."; and so forth—be reconciled with the claim that ijtihad
entails the creation of new doctrine? Does the ordinary mufti merely
re-cite relevant text rather than interpret it? This question can be
approached with reference to a pair of madrasa-based interpretive
techniques, one recitational, one hermeneutical. The first involves a
comparatively simple one-to-one association of fact and principle; the
second a complex, systematic use of analogic reasoning. Despite the fact
that they are written, fatwas given by jurists such as the mufti of Ibb
have a pronounced recitational quality. Rather than engaging in a
reflective pause to "construct" (or consult references) that might mark
the novel interpretation of a *mujtahid*, the mufti responds immediately.
"Difficult matters were referred to him," the biographical historian
al-Burayhi (1983:100) writes of an Ibb mufti who died in 1430, "and
he would embark on answers to them without hesitation." Having
identified the issue (itself an interpretive act based, in turn, on an initial
construction on the part of the questioner), such a mufti essentially
recites relevant text. Although every recitation is an interpretation,
when neither fact nor rule is taken to be new, a simple or associative
type of reasoning is employed. Such worldly fatwa-giving is an activity
equivalent to *riwaya*, the oral transmission of a text by a scholar qualified to do so by virtue of his own prior oral acquisition of the text in
question. Involving the creative matching of comprehended practice
with an identified and then transmitted segment of existing text, such
fatwas are recitations.

A more complex hermeneutical technique, involving ijtihad proper,
is also related to an equivalent madrasa method. If the ordinary mufti
may be said to engage in an activity equivalent to madrasa recitation,
great muftis such as al-Shawkani interpret in a manner analogous to
the procedures of scriptural hermeneutics. Whereas the ordinary mufti
transmits text, one such as al-Shawkani creates it. The fatwas of qualified jurists were liable to be treated as authoritative because they
offered either an innovative formulation of the sense of a text or an
analogical extension—a "filling in of the gaps"—of the textual body.
More complicated than a simple association of known fact to known

text, the interpretive use of analogy spans a previously uncharted conceptual distance, from existing text to created text, departing from a new configuration on the level of fact.

Within the specialized sphere of the muftiship, where real-world questions are addressed, interpretation through fatwas is modeled on, or is a model for, madrasa-based hermeneutics. According to a now familiar hermeneutical model (Ricoeur 1971), it might be assumed that an analogic mode of interpretation originally applied to scripture was extended, in the hands of muftis, to the interpretation of the world. But the reverse—namely, that a style of interpretation applied to the world was adapted to address text—is not only equally plausible but is suggested, in part, by the oral-recitational qualities of the "text" in question.

Different categories of fatwas may be associated with this recitational versus hermeneutic dichotomy in interpretive method. While the doctrinal impact of fatwas delivered in Ibb has been negligible, that of those collected by al-Wansharisi for North Africa and issued by Muhammad ʿAbduh for Egypt, Ibn Hajar for Hadramawt,[29] and al-Shawkani for Yemen has been substantial. Ibb fatwas retain the genre's characteristic structural orientation toward *adilla*, but they are relatively unself-conscious about any import they might have regarding new doctrine. Despite their pedigree, these local fatwas have no greater ambition than to contribute to the regulation of the practical affairs of people in Ibb and its hinterland.[30] It was perhaps such muftis, their fatwas devoid of expressed reasoning, that Weber (1978:797) considered comparable to oracles.

The case of al-Shawkani is different. It should be noted, however, that he distinguished between his "shorter," presumably ordinary fatwas, which "could never be counted," and those he calls "epistles" and "investigations" (*rasaʾil* and *abhath*), which were collected as fatwas with the title *Al-fath al-rabbani fi fatawi al-Shawkani*.[31] He also tells us that requests for fatwas came to him from both the elite, presumably mainly scholars, and the common people. This breakdown according to source of query may parallel his distinction between his fatwa-treatises, preserved in book form, and the uncounted ordinary fatwas that were dispersed without leaving a documentary trace. The latter may resemble the fatwas delivered in Ibb, with the important caveat that al-Shawkani was not a scholar of modest standing, but an "absolute" interpreter, a *mujtahid mutlaq*, a jurist of interregional calibre exhibiting the highest realization of interpretive ability.

Al-Shawkani's fatwa-treatises retain the question-and-answer for-mat, but (as in al-Qarafi 1967) the questions tend to be, if not purely hypothetical, at least abstractions of practice rather than the rough-and-ready statements of circumstance found in the ordinary query. Formulated by other scholars, or adapted for didactic purposes, the questions address both important social problems of the era—such as tobacco usage, the status of saintly miracles, disregard for the shariʿa among country people—and theoretical problems in jurisprudence. Al-Shawkani acts as the scholar's scholar, the mufti's mufti. At this level of discourse, such jurists could provide both a decisive interpretation of the sources and, to the extent that such opinions had a bearing on practice, an impact as well upon the conduct of individuals.

For al-Shawkani (as for al-Juwayni, studied in Ibb) a mufti was by definition a qualified interpreter, a *mujtahid* (A.H. 1349:234; 1394:43–45). For this reason the muftiship is integral to the central thrust of al-Shawkani's work: the assertion of the obligation of *ijtihad* and the refutation of its opposite, the intellectual posture of unquestioning ac-ceptance (*taqlid*) of established doctrine—the posture associated with the assumption that the "gate of ijtihad" was "closed." Al-Shawkani brooks no exception to his argument that not only muftis but also judges must be mujtahids (1969:35). He musters theoretical-doctrinal justifications (the *adilla*) for his position; he provides biographical ex-amples of earlier Yemeni "absolute" mujtahids (A.H. 1348, 2:133; 1:360); and he presents a model program of essential study for a would-be interpreter (A.H. 1348, 2:81ff.). Articulated in highland Yemen, it was an advocacy of ijtihad that would be noted some decades later as Muslim reformers elsewhere began to revitalize the concept as a tool for reform.[32]

Schacht (1964:74) suggests that the continuing importance of muftis was linked to the essential character of the knowledge, resulting in a "constant need of specialist guidance." But the muftiship was not only an institution through which rarified scholarly disputes and the re-ceived wisdom of the jurists were brought down to earth in communica-ble form as "guidance" for the common people. It was also the channel through which mundane, earth-hugging realities, including new fac-tual developments, were formally noticed by and reflected upon by qualified scholarly minds, leading to analogical extensions of the body of legal knowledge. In a dialectical manner, locally generated questions were related to locally interpreted jurisprudence. Muftis were the cre-ative mediators of the ideal and the real of the shariʿa.

CHAPTER 8

Shari'a Society

The scholars are the heirs of the prophets.

HADITH

It is impossible for knowledge not to engender power.

M. FOUCAULT

Shari'a texts lived in social relations, in human embodiers and interpretive articulations. As a general requirement of their attainments, scholars were meant to give of acquired knowledge. A commonly cited hadith says, "He who learns knowledge and conceals it is bridled by God on Judgment Day with a bit of fire."[1] In Ibb, the specific justification for the muftiship was identified as the Quranic injunction (16:43) to ask the knowledgeable, literally to ask "those who remember" (*ahl al-dhikr*). The obligation to give of acquired knowledge, satisfied in teaching or when a man of learning acted as a mufti, was matched by its inverse, the requirement placed upon the uninformed to question the learned. According to the classic "roots" manual by al-Juwayni (d. 1086), the mufti and his questioner have opposed statuses in relation to interpretation: the mufti must be a qualified interpreter and cannot be an accepting follower of doctrine, while the questioner cannot be an interpreter (i.e., must not attempt to interpret) and must be among the "doctrinal followers" (*ahl al-taqlid*) who follow a mufti, through his fatwas (n.d.:38).

Some seven and a half centuries later, al-Shawkani wrote:

> He who is deficient in the requisite knowledges is required to ask an individual whom he trusts with respect to his religion and his knowledge about texts in the Book and the Sunna to ascertain what is required of him in ritual and transaction matters and in connection with all other things confronting him. He should say to the one he is asking, "Inform me on the best established indications (*adilla*)[2] so that I may act in accordance with them." (A.H. 1348, 2:89)

To combat a practice of *taqlid* that in his view had become degener-
ate, al-Shawkani advocates a revised version of the interpretive interchange. "This is not *taqlid* at all," al-Shawkani asserts of his revision,
"because he [the questioner] does not ask him [the scholar] about
his opinion but rather for his *riwaya*." As was noted in the preceding
chapter, *riwaya*, oral transmission, the simple form of reporting from
acquired authoritative knowledge, involves interpretation, but on a
level of matching rule to instance rather than full-blown *ijtihad*. "Inasmuch as, because of his ignorance, he [the questioner] does not com-
prehend the formulations of the Book and the Sunna, he must ask
one who comprehends them." The questioner is able to understand
and then go on to apply the requirements of the Quran and the Sunna
"by means of the intermediacy of (*bi-wasita*) the asked." Opposed in
status is the interpreter himself, who acts in applying his knowledge
"without intermediacy in understanding." In summary, according to
al-Shawkani, the ordinary individual who "relies upon questioning is
neither a *muqallid* [one who practices *taqlid*] nor a *mujtahid* [one who
practices *ijtihad*] but rather one who proceeds according to an authoritative indication (*dalil*) using the intermediacy of a *mujtahid*." Ideally,
al-Shawkani would have this practice of interpretive "intermediacy"
replace relations based on unquestioning *taqlid*, which entail "the
acceptance of an opinion of another without binding evidence."[3]
     An intractable social fact underpinned the interpretive relation.
From earliest times, as al-Shawkani observes, the number of scholars in
relation to nonscholars was always small. As an Ibb intellectual put it,
"scholars used to be as rare as shooting stars." From the scholarly
perspective society was divisible into two general categories of individuals, the *'alim* (pl. *'ulama'*), the scholar or individual who has knowledge
(*'ilm*), and the *jahil* (pl. *juhhal*), the individual without knowledge, an
"ignorant person." The opposed social categories of *'alim* and *jahil* and
their defining characteristics, knowledge and ignorance, are elaborated
in the "roots" literature (al-Juwayni n.d.). Related collective social
categories frequently used in scholarly discourse are "the special people" (*al-khawass*) versus "the ordinary people" (*al-'awamm*, sing. *'ammi*,
an "ordinary person"), or "the scholarly people" (*ahl al-'ilm*) versus
"the people of the mundane world" (*ahl al-dunya*).
     At the base of the wider shari'a image of the social world, however,
is a valued egalitarian ideal, contained in such frequently encountered
constructs as the notion of the *umma*, the community of Muslims; the

'ibad, the believers; and al-muslimin, the Muslims, as well as in the institution of the mosque, locus of collective gathering for prayers led by a
layperson (known as an imam). As its basic social feature, Islam launched
a form of egalitarian community of the faithful, which stood opposed to
the "tribal" and town-centered hierarchies of seventh-century Arabia.
This egalitarianism, an "insistence that all men [are] on the same level
before God,"[4] is a fundamental presupposition running through shari'a
discourse and is conventionally considered a hallmark of Islam itself.

Increasingly specialized and unequally distributed knowledge was
one of many problems posed for this egalitarian ethos. Specifically,
there was the potential conclusion that, as Rosenthal (1970:2) bluntly
put it, "'ilm [knowledge] is Islam." Rosenthal observes that scholars
"have been hesitant to accept the technical correctness of this equation." Their hesitancy is based on more than philosophical grounds,
however, for the equation of knowledge and Islam, and thus of 'alim
with Muslim, would entail exclusive and divisive hierarchical implications in a society where knowledge was neither universally accessible
nor evenly distributed.

The acquisition of knowledge, with jurisprudence as its centerpiece,
was an activity vested with honor. Committing the Minhaj of al-
Nawawi to memory, the Ibb student encountered the statement that
working to gain knowledge "is among the finest of pious deeds," while
the opening words of the text are that an individual who becomes
knowledgeable in shari'a jurisprudence is one whom God "has shown
favor to and chosen among the believers." Numerous hadiths, studi-
ously memorized and repeated by generations of jurists, articulate
related ideas: that seeking knowledge opens a road to Paradise; that
knowledge accrues to individuals as a sign of divine favor, and so forth.[5]
In the Quran there are related statements: "God raises up by degrees
(darajat) those among you who believe, and those who are given knowledge" (58:11; cf. 39:9, 20:114).

An important articulation of the scholar-commoner relationship is
contained in the principle of "collective duty" (fard kifaya) elaborated
by early jurists. According to this doctrine, the Muslim community as
a whole is kept on a legitimate and observing basis so long as a sufficient
number of individuals perform the necessary collective duties imposed
on the community by God. Some of these duties, including knowledge
of the law, are enumerated in a definition by al-Shafi'i:

> Only a few men must know the law, attend the funeral service, perform
> the Jihad, and respond to greeting, while the others are exempt. So those

who know the law, perform the Jihad, attend the funeral service, and respond to greeting will be rewarded, while the others do not fall into error, since a sufficient number fulfill the collective duty.[6]

While legitimizing a form of social difference in passing, al-Shafi'i nevertheless seeks to place a higher value in the foreground: the identity, responsibility, and cohesiveness of the collectivity. But the mechanism of unequally distributed ultimate reward entails the gain or anticipation of special status.

Al-Shawkani sought to refine the 'alim/jahil distinction itself. In his discussion of the "two statuses" (1969:2) he speaks of their respective "responsibilities." Despite the fact that the 'alim, because of knowledge acquired, carries additional societal burdens that set him apart from the jahil, al-Shawkani argues forcefully that in many important respects there are no differences between the two categories of individuals. "The 'alim," al-Shawkani writes, "is equivalent to the jahil as concerns legal and devotional responsibilities." In this manner, he endeavors to reassert fundamental equality, especially in regard to basic Muslim obligations, while at the same time recognizing and differentiating the "two statuses."

At the base of the scholarly treatment of the category of jahil and the condition of "ignorance" is an old understanding of human nature. "A human is an essentially ignorant being (jahil) who acquires knowledge," Ibn Khaldun (1958, 2:424) wrote in the fourteenth century, summarizing an earlier Muslim (and Greek) philosophical tradition. In Ibb, children before the age of maturity and discernment are known as juhhal (pl. of jahil), literally "ignorant ones."[7] For the scholarly, the achievement of maturity and discernment do not in and of themselves produce a change in jahil status. Rural people such as those who appear in the Ibb mufti's sitting room, townsmen of low status (the 'amma), and women,[8] all of whom did not usually receive instruction, therefore remained, in the technical view of scholars, in a quasi-childlike condition of ignorance. All were conceived of and are occasionally still referred to as juhhal by older-generation scholars.

Addressing the problem of rural people who, it was said, did not carry out such key ritual "pillars" of the faith as prayer and fasting, al-Shawkani (1969:39–40) states that they have the legal-moral status of people of the pre-Islamic age of ignorance, known as al-jahiliyya (from the same root as jahil). They were beyond the reach of both the state and the faith, and thus of the shari'a as well. Townspeople, residents of state-controlled centers, represented a more problematic category. While a negative conclusion concerning the imagined or actual conduct of populations entirely beyond the pale came easily to scholars, a more troubling assessment was required in connection with the intimately known, uneducated urban 'amma, the ordinary populace. In Yemeni historical writing, which is explicitly devoted to the lives of the "honorable ones," the 'amma figure only rarely as the faceless mob that rises up at junctures of political disarray.[9] According to al-Shawkani, urban people are mostly juhhal, and yet he notes that they are frequently observant and willing to receive instruction.

Conceptions about language further model the knowledge and power relationship of 'alim and jahil. Arabic is subdivided by scholars into a classical or literary language, called al-fusha, or simply "the language" (al-lugha), and a purely spoken language known variously as al-'ammiyya ("ordinary" language, i.e., pertaining to the 'ammi, the "ordinary person"), al-darija (a word related to the d–r–j root, which also gives the word for a "degree" of status difference), or lahaja (spoken dialect, a word carrying a literal association with the tongue). Scholars are associated with the classical written language; uneducated ordinary people, with spoken dialects (although, by definition, scholars know dialects as well). The most perfect example of "the language" is the Quran, "an Arabic Quran," as it describes itself. Grammar and the other language sciences pertain only to the written language. It is not that dialects have no grammar, of course, but that "grammar," the recognized formal discipline, is associated exclusively with what is defined as "the language." Beginning in Quranic school and continuing in the madrasa, the acquisition of adab entailed both a learning of appropriate behavior and an acquisition of the literate skills. Al-Akwa' (1980:11) remarks that the former Yemeni instructional method was beneficial for students in that it "helped them train their tongues with syntax so that they would not be ungrammatical in their speech." Although the prayer leader (imam) could be an ordinary member of the mosque congregation, developed language skills and textual knowledge were preferred. In the absence of anyone possessing recitational knowledge, it is legal for an illiterate individual to lead others in prayer.[10] But when an 'ammi prayer leader's incorrect knowledge of voweling patterns alters the meaning of the recitation, the prayer session can be invalid. Al-Nawawi cites al-Shafi'i's opinion to the effect that "it is not lawful for one who can recite to pray under the direction of an illiterate person."[11]

COMMON KNOWLEDGE

Although "simple" and "complex" forms were identified, ignorance was mainly defined with respect to two sorts of knowledge, the "necessary" and the "acquired." Acquired knowledge, the type marking the scholar, is based on the learned skill of rational deduction. Necessary knowledge, by contrast, characterized by the absence of any capacity for, or intervention of, deduction, is based on understanding derived from the five senses, supplemented by what is known as *tawatur*, the knowledge of received wisdom.[12]

Conveyed as "uninterrupted tradition," *tawatur* knowledge can be understood as an integral part of the commonsense level of culture (cf. Geertz 1983c). According to jurists, common wisdom is by no means always misguided, especially inasmuch as it contains an authoritative, if rudimentary, acknowledgment of a given world. Jurists give examples of the soundness of such wisdom: "the knowledge of the existence of Mecca," site of the Muslim pilgrimage and scene of the earliest historical events of the Islamic era, and also the recognition that there was a Prophet named Muhammad.[13] As a type of "necessary" knowledge, the received wisdom that is collectively held as *tawatur* is classified with the knowledge derived from sensory perceptions, which directly imposes itself on the intellect without having been arrived at through reflection or deduction. Like sensory perceptions in its immediacy, tawatur knowledge is not subject to doubt about its accuracy, but is simply taken as given in the order of things. Jurists were especially concerned with a narrow area of common sense that carried kernels of historically significant received wisdom or widely held ordinary knowledge of legitimizing relevance. Tawatur knowledge may be understood as a collective and popular version of transmitted knowledge, broadly communitarian rather than narrowly genealogical in character. It might also be related to an informal, commonsense form of consensus. Consensus, the decisive methodological tool, refers in al-Juwayni to the view of "the scholars of an era,"[14] but others considered it grounded in the collective understandings of the Muslim community as a whole.

Al-Shafiʿi distinguishes specialist knowledge and general knowledge (*ʿilm ʿamma*). The latter, a distinct dimension of authoritative legal knowledge, includes such things as awareness of the existence of the five daily prayers, the duty of fasting during the month of Ramadan, the obligation to give alms, and that adultery, murder, theft, and drinking wine are forbidden. "This kind of knowledge," al-Shafiʿi said, "may be found textually in the Book of God, and may be found generally among the people of Islam." As with tawatur knowledge, "the public relates it from the preceding public and ascribes it to the Prophet of God, nobody ever questioning its ascription or its binding force upon them. It is the kind of knowledge which admits of error neither in its narrative nor in its interpretation; it is not permissible to question it."[15]

Creativity is at issue in the differentiation of necessary and acquired types of knowledge: from the point of view of scholars, ordinary people are equipped, in a passive sense, for following or affirming known and established ways, but they are not properly prepared for actively ascertaining correct courses of action in novel circumstances. Such is the recitational or analogical reasoning-based interpretive task of the trained scholar. Al-Juwayni's definitions of knowledge and ignorance contrast disciplined thought and undisciplined "imagination": "Knowledge is the understanding of that which is known as it is in reality; ignorance is the imagining of a thing other than as it is in reality" (al-Juwayni, n.d.:28). At stake is an accurate and developed knowledge of "reality" (al-wāqi'). The link of this "reality" with Islam is indicated by the scholarly efforts to pin down its precise nature. As one commentator notes, "some say it [reality] is what God Almighty knows," while for others it is what is inscribed on the celestial "Hidden Tablets."[16] To acquire knowledge, then, is not only to realize human potential more completely but also to gain active access to an understanding of Creation.

Such authoritative social-classificatory thought had powerful consequences. The position of scholars vis-à-vis the uninformed was implicitly fused to the whole dialectic of the God to human relation, especially as this relation was replicated within the social order and through history. A necessarily passive commonsensical wisdom of the untutored is definitively represented by scholars as composing the characteristic mentality of ordinary people (although it must in some sense be shared by scholars as well). The condition of having this sort of simple wisdom alone is juxtaposed with a more complex, active, and analytic wisdom of the scholarly, which is portrayed as providing its practitioners with a more secure and far-reaching knowledge of "reality." Denigrated for its potential irrationality and vulgarity of expression, common knowledge is nevertheless constituted by jurists as a valued bedrock of legal authority. The combination exhibits a double-edged hegemonic efficacy: social difference is firmly constituted while subordinate knowledge is at the same time legitimated and appropriated. In his studies of hegemony, Gramsci was generally concerned with how an elite-developed "conception of the world" came to constitute the quietly constraining received wisdom of ordinary people. One facet of the complex workings of hegemony concerns scholarly efforts to anchor "ruling ideas" systematically in the thought of those who, as Marx put it, "lack the means of mental production."

HIERARCHY

A Quranic text (43:32) employs a general conception of *darajat*, or "degrees" of ranked difference (a notion also used with reference to differences in knowledge [58:11] and gender [2:228]): "We have apportioned among them their livelihood in the world, and we have raised some of them above others by degrees, so that they may take others in service." This recognition of the social fact of hierarchy based on worldly circumstances and of God as its author is immediately followed, however, by a powerful crosscutting qualification, which reaffirms a countervailing ultimate principle: "(But) the mercy of your Lord is better than that which they amass." Aside from the general, and constant, reiteration of such potent egalitarian categories as the "believers," "Muslims," and the "community," not only in the first sections of the manuals devoted to ritual but throughout the other chapters as well, there are particular doctrinal areas where egalitarian themes are further developed.

In the extensive chapters on "transactions" (*mu'amalat*), for example, the capacity to contract is a key issue. In this dimension of the jurisprudence there is a strong egalitarian emphasis based on the central but largely implicit construct of the individual. "Contractualism," according to Hodgson, through which "ascriptive status was minimized, at least in principle,"[17] is considered a characteristic thrust of the *shari'a*, and of Islamic society in general.[18] Being an adult and of sound mind are all that are required of an individual to enter into a binding shari'a contract. The "mind" that enabled the ordinary, sane adult, male or female, to contract may not be fully rational in the developed, reasoning sense defining the status of the educated, but it was taken to be rational enough for the routine conduct of affairs. As a form of "necessary" knowledge, common sense may be an imperfect rendering of "reality," but for purposes of legal undertakings it is considered sufficient. This may be understood in another way, of course, which is that far from serving to reduce or counteract hierarchical tendencies found elsewhere in the jurisprudence, the egalitarian-individualistic principles underpinning contractual capacity worked to mask, and indirectly support, actual inequalities between the parties engaging in the contract, in much the same manner, for example, as similar assumptions in the capitalist wage-labor contract (Engels 1972:136). The same sort of individualism is also behind unilateral dispositions in the shariʿa. Thus making a will is supposed to be an act radically open to all, including non-Muslims (but not slaves). It is a capacity, al-Nawawi states, "accorded by the shariʿa to everyone, whether Muslim or not, without distinction of sex, [inasmuch as the person is] adult, sane, free." Unstated here is the fact that making a testamentary disposition implies having an estate to dispose of: the circumstances that are assumed and addressed are those of the wealthy.

Knowledge and ignorance, and scholar and commoner distinctions were part of a wider social world of status ranking in the Muslim community according to honor, descent, occupation, and wealth. In addition to this legally imaged mainstream population, still wider social categorizations of "free" as opposed to "slave" and "Muslim" as opposed to "non-Muslim" entailed further hierarchical implications. As is characteristic of all status systems, a detailed consciousness existed of the interrelated hierarchical strands.[19] As some individuals were "raised up" by "degrees," a layered quality of social levels, known as *tabaqat* (e.g., in Ibn Khaldun, but also in Yemeni conceptions) was understood to be the social product. While recognizing the thoroughly Muslim, and at times and places egalitarian, character of Yemeni society, Western students of Yemeni social structure (e.g., Bujra 1971; Gerholm 1977; Stevenson 1985) have debated whether "caste" might be the appropriate designation for some of the sorts of hierarchical relations found in the highlands. Yemenis themselves have understood their own social order with communitarian, genealogical, and a diversity of "layer cake" type of conception, the last replete with elaborated social categories and associated strata terminology (Serjeant 1977; Dresch 1989:117–57). A modicum of social mobility was always part of the system, however. Status could be achieved through the acquisition of either knowledge or wealth. Limited possibilities of advancement along both avenues served, in practice, to defuse some of the outward rigidity of the social ranks. The social order was, in any case, far more flexible and complex than the indigenous layer-cake theory would have it. While descent groups of scholars, descendants of the Prophet, and tribal elites seemed uniform and enduring, there was always considerable variation among individuals, a sloughing off of unsuccessful segments, and long-term processes of rise and fall among leading families.

From the perspective of substantive doctrine, contractual orientations are frequently crosscut by the concerns of status. *Homo equalis* is confronted by *homo hierarchicus*. Witnessing is an example. In this doctrine, a predominant egalitarian formula, namely, that all Muslims are by definition persons whose legal testimony is admissible (*al-muslimun 'udul*), is subject to qualifications that open the door to the preoccupations of a hierarchical society. Al-Nawawi gives five general conditions for a witness: he (or she) must be a Muslim, free (not slave), discerning, of "irreproachable character" (*'adl*), and serious.[20] In the concision of Abu Shuja' these separate conditions become a single requirement of *'adala* (same root as *'adl*), that is, "justness" or "probity," based on irreproachable character.[21] The absence of any requirement bearing on knowledge or instruction is notable: the technically ignorant appear to be as good as any other witnesses. For a potential judge, to be sure, there are knowledge requirements, but in witnessing, the linchpin institution of legal processes, all (free, sane) Muslims, regardless of intellectual attainments, are equally eligible to give testimony. Even the normative concern for what is to constitute "irreproachable character" is tempered by a sensitivity to acceptable differences of person, time, and locale. Grave sins aside, respectable character is considered contextually relative, being exhibited in "one who models his conduct upon the respectable among his contemporaries and fellow countrymen."

In this Muslim version of the doctrine of the "credible witness," the concern is not so much with absolutes as with deviations from local societal or even personal norms, which are taken as indicative of an instability of character thought to bear on one's capacity as a truthful witness. Discussing concrete behaviors that can put a reputation in question, al-Nawawi gives a number of examples. While most of these pertain to the "common" people, in one instance there is a specific reference to jurists. This is the hypothetical case of a jurist (*faqih*) who wears a particular type of gown and raised turban, in a place where these are not customary for jurists. Al-Nawawi's other, equally culturally specific examples of an individual lacking in the requisite "seriousness" are one "who eats in public and walks there bare-headed"; "who embraces his wife or his slave in the presence of other persons"; "who is always telling funny stories"; or "who habitually plays chess or sings or listens to singing, or who dances for an excessively long time." These apparently puritanical examples are concluded, however, with the cautionary statement that "it is well to take into consideration that these matters differ according to individuals, circumstances, and places."

Following the relatively egalitarian orientation of this initial discussion of the qualifications of witnesses, al-Nawawi briefly raises a further issue and in doing so touches on concerns of a hierarchical nature.[22] The issue in question is the occupation of the potential witness. "Base occupations, such as blood-letting, sweeping, and tanning," al-Nawawi writes, "practiced by one of high social position for whom it is unseemly," disqualify the individual as a witness. Although social levels and conceptions of honor and dishonor are certainly involved here, there is no crude assertion that those involved in the "base" occupations are for that reason alone simply unqualified as witnesses. It is rather the *mismatch* of social position and occupation, the lack of conformity of background with work activity that cause a question to be posed about an individual's character. This is clear from al-Nawawi's next statement, which is that "if [such an occupation] is customary for the person, and it had been the craft of his father, then there is no disqualification." That truthfulness is thought to pertain to individuals of differing statuses, insofar as they are engaged in "suitable" activities and do not deviate from appropriate and established personal norms, is part of a larger, distinctive conception of justice as consisting of a balanced equilibrium of diversity. Injustice (*zulm*), Mottahedeh observes (1980:179), citing early Arabic dictionaries, is not so much oppression as "putting a thing in a place not its own" or "transgressing the proper limit."

Occupational difference also figures in textually established rules about suitable marriage partners. Within the extensive discussion of marriage rules, a subset is concerned with *kafa'a*, or "equivalence."[23] Rules about the status or honor equivalence of marriage partners can entail as their active consequence forms of stratum endogamy. Al-Nawawi's statement on marriage equivalence according to profession provides a concrete image of an entire stepped hierarchy structured in occupational terms alone:

> A man exercising a lowly profession is not a suitable match for the daughter of a man in a more distinguished profession. Thus a sweeper, a bloodletter, a watchman, a shepherd, or a bathhouse operator is not a suitable match for the daughter of a tailor; and the tailor is not suited for the daughter of a merchant or a cloth seller; nor they, likewise, for the daughter of a scholar or judge.[24]

Marriage mismatches here involve a man of lower rank seeking the hand of a woman whose father's occupation places her on a higher rung. The distinction between commoner and *'alim* is embedded in a series of fine-grained distinctions as the resultant social hierarchy runs from the lowest occupational level (sweeper, bloodletter, watchman, shepherd, bathhouse operator), through intermediate levels of tailors and merchants or cloth sellers, and finally to the highest level, that of scholars and judges. The concern with mismatches of status and occupation also figures in defining the "poor." "One may be legally called poor," al-Nawawi states, referring specially to scholarly endeavors, "even though [one is] able to gain a living by some work not suitable for one. Thus a learned man may be called poor though able, strictly speaking, to provide for his own needs by exercising some trade that would prevent him from continuing his studies."[25]

Hierarchical mismatches in court drew particular attention from the jurists. Manual sections on legal procedures before the shari'a court judge represent both an acknowledgment of the existence of social differences and a determined effort to reduce their impact, at least in this specific institutional setting.[26] The key principle articulated by both Shafi'i and Zaidi manuals is that in this forum the judge must treat pairs of disputants equally. Within the same phrase articulating the principle of "equality" (*taswiya*), however, a qualification is stated. Unequal, preferential treatment by the judge is appropriate if the two disputants are a Muslim and a *dhimmi*, a "protected" person of the Book, that is, a Jew or a Christian. The Muslim can be legitimately "raised" above the *dhimmi* in the attentions of the judge. Abu Shuja' says that the required egalitarian treatment of disputants is to be embodied in three things: space, word, and regard. The disputants should be seated together, in the same row before the judge; they should be addressed in an equivalent manner and be given the same opportunity to speak and be heard; and the judge should not look at one of the parties and not at the other. Al-Nawawi adds that the judge should treat the two parties equally in such detailed matters as standing up (or not) when one of them enters the court and in returning greetings. Judges are specifically forbidden to favor one side by suggesting how to make a claim or to word testimony, or to formally hear one party without the other's being present.

A further, recommended practice for the judge is couched in the language of "weak" (*da'if*) and "strong" (*qawi*), a social vocabulary used in Yemen and elsewhere to characterize, not physical, but rather status or honor differences between claimants. It is thus suggested in the Zaidi manual that the judge "advance" or give precedence to the claim of the "weaker" of two individuals each seeking to be the initiator of an adversarial proceeding. Directives sent to a judge in the early centuries of Islam advocate similar measures. Both equal treatment and advancing the cause of the weaker party are summarized in one version: "Act impartially between people in your audience-room and before you, so that the man of noble status (*sharif*) be not greedy for your partiality and the man of inferior status (*da'if* [lit. "weak"]) despair of justice from you" (Serjeant 1984:66). Another, probably earlier letter says, "Admit the man of inferior status (*da'if*) so that his tongue may be loosened and his heart emboldened" (Serjeant 1984:69).

This idiom of "weak" and "strong" also figures in al-Ghazzi's commentary on a discussion of the physical place where a judge ought to hold court. This place should be in the center of the town and well known, the jurist writes, so that both "the local person and the outsider, and the strong and the weak" will have access. To facilitate this open access, the judge should post no guards at the outside door to block or regulate entrance. To counterbalance the gender-specific inequalities that might constrain the behavior of women seeking access to the judge, special rules are established. Al-Nawawi says the judge should give priority to hearing women's cases, while the Zaidi *Azhar* manual recommends that the judge set aside a separate session for women's claims.

All such measures to reduce hierarchical influences focus on the relationship between the parties to a dispute. It is in this relation that a mismatch of status is considered especially problematic and where formal equality helps create the aura of judicial impartiality that legitimizes judgments. Some of the apparent clarity of the strategies to bring about the desired "equality" begins to dissolve, however, as one reads further in the more expansive commentary literature. Al-Ghazzi comments, "The judge should seat the two parties before him (lit. "in his hands"), if they are equivalent in honor (*sharaf*)." This ambiguous statement is only partially resolved as the commentator goes on to give as an important exception the case of a Muslim and a *dhimmi* (a Jew or Christian) appearing together as adversaries. A commentator on the *Azhar* follows the rule of "equivalence between the two parties," with this qualifying note:

> aside from the difference between the "high" (*rafi'*, lit. "raised up") and the "low" (*wadi'*), or between the believer and the sinner (*fasiq*), due to his [the judge's] respect for Islam. The privileging of the believer over

the [Muslim] sinner is not what is at issue in the principle of equivalence
in the judicial session.[27]

Issues of high and low status are reinserted in the discourse, while in
separating the righteous from the sinners, difficult problems, similar to
those previously discussed in connection with identifying "just" witnesses, are raised.

If hierarchy in the relationship between the claimants seems to slip
subtly back in despite the strong egalitarian principle advanced to
control it, another form of hierarchical relation in the courtroom remains unexamined, unquestioned. This is the relationship between the
judge and the claimant, which is likely to be one of *'alim* and *jahil*. The
Azhar recommends that the judge have other local scholars present at
his court, and al-Nawawi that he consult with them before arriving at
a decision. While the forum is to proceed on the basis of an egalitarian
attitude regarding the claimants, a necessary but understated form of
hierarchy based on knowledge is nevertheless essential to its overall
organization.

On the level of interpersonal relations in Yemen, status differences
are initially played out in greeting postures. In his private sitting room
an Ibb town judge receives a man who approaches him with *taqbil*,[28] a
kissing of hand and knee. In a nearly simultaneous gesture, the judge
brushes off the kisses and raises the man up to a seated position before
him. Sitting back on his haunches, the man says to the judge, "I am a
weak country person, I am in your hands." The term *haiba*, meaning
"awe," "fear," "respect," refers to the sensations aroused in one individual by another, and to the social atmosphere that obtains in interactions between superiors and inferiors (cf. Mottahedeh 1980:184f.).
Kissing the hand and knee is the correct gesture of status behavior when
a subordinate confronts the haiba not only of scholarly jurists, but also
the differently constituted haibas of teachers, imams, Sufi shaykhs,
descendants of the Prophet, tribal shaykhs, powerful landlords, and
fathers. There are structural analogies linking these several haibas, but
in another sense each represents a separate strand of hierarchical identity and a distinct type of encounter. A scholar's haiba is specific to his
knowledge: it is a haiba related to the text the scholar embodies and
interprets. Haibas are also contextually and historically specific, so that
a judge's haiba also depended on that of the state.

Scholars such as judges consciously strove to cultivate their haiba by
such means as their attire and demeanor, both of which receive comment in the legal literature. A proverb, "A tribesman's brain is in his

eyes," was cited to me by an Ibb judge to explain why he had to present himself in public as an imposingly attired figure.[29] Speaking critically of abuses in the early nineteenth century, al-Shawkani (1969:29) mentions the type of judge who wears a "turban like a tower." But he nevertheless refers in admiration to one of the noted judges of his era, saying, "His haiba was great in [people's] hearts" (A.H. 1348, 2:333).[30] Sternness in comportment, learned as part of a scholar's formative disciplining, was required, as the haiba of a judge served positively to create the properly serious atmosphere of the tribunal. But the haiba imbalances between opposing claimants had to be counteracted to ensure that the "truth" would emerge. The "equalizing" procedures functioned, in part, to reduce haiba effects. Thus the "weak" man's claim should be given preferential treatment so that "his tongue may be loosened and his heart emboldened."

A South Arabian proverb speaks, however, to the other side of the haiba behavior of respectful kissing: "A kiss on the hand means hatred of it."[31] The basic gesture of respect comprises a silent hostility. For those of subordinate status who live the ambiguity of inclusion and exclusion, of equality as members of the community of Muslims and inequality with respect to the relations of hierarchy among the same Muslims, an unvoiced resistance is embedded in the very recognition of stature. While haiba behaviors underline the conscious, calculated, and constructed quality of status interaction in the view of the elite, they also illustrate the ambivalent combination of rejection couched in acquiescence on the part of the subordinate.

The relations of power surrounding authoritative texts centered on the connection between interpretation and hierarchy. Shifting and ambiguous in the social image it conveys, and taking on the diversity of the individuals who embodied and transmitted it, shari'a discourse is characterized by a textual and lived heteroglossia (Bakhtin 1981). Despite strong egalitarian counter-currents, the shari'a understanding of the social order was anchored in the distinction between knowledge and ignorance, a distinction that concerned, not differences of intelligence, but rather control of the cultural capital acquired in advanced instruction. Associated with the relation of interpretation and hierarchy was a state and wider polity of the question and response, in which, like muftis, imams, governors, and judges made themselves available to answer petitions and claims.

CHAPTER 9

Judicial Presence

Islamic law still envisages the primordial method of starting an action, which consists of the plaintiff seizing the defendant and hauling him before the judge.
JOSEPH SCHACHT

MUWAJAHA

As his retainers leaned on their rifles and his secretary squatted nearby, men gathered around the judge in the open-air entranceway to his house. He sat on one of the little plaster benches built into the curved buttresses that direct rainwater away from the grain stores below Ibb houses. Framed by a grey stone facade, he was attired in a billowy white ankle-length gown, with his dagger in its inlaid silver sheath positioned at a distinctive slanted angle to one side of a wide belt decorated with brocade calligraphy. His scholar's *'imama*, a multicolored raised headpiece wound around with turns of sheer white cloth, rested on his head like a little crown. In coat and skullcap, the secretary was comparatively drab; the soldier-retainers wore knee-length men's skirts, crossed cartridge belts, heavy upright daggers sheathed in wood and leather, and wrapped dark turbans with a significant tail marking their profession left dangling down the back. The walled entranceway was open to the passing alley, and anyone could enter to join the semicircle that formed around the judge.

Such was the simple physical format of the *shari'a* court in session, held in the mornings and outdoors, in front of the judge's personal residence.[1] In some well-known disparaging comments Western jurists have made the Muslim judge, or *qadi*, sitting in this sort of court setting, stand for the absence of principled justice: for example, "The court ... is really put very much in the position of a Cadi under the palm tree" (Lord Justice Goddard), and "We do not sit like a kadi under a tree dispensing justice according to considerations of individual expedi-

Figure 9. A judge receiving men outside his residence in San'a', 1980.

ency" (Justice Felix Frankfurter).[2] For Schacht (1964: 197), a leading
student of Islamic law, the procedure involved is portrayed as something of an evolutionary survival: a "still" practiced "primordial"
method.

To Yemenis, judges in this type of open setting, accessible to the
public, appeared in a posture known as *muwajaha*, from *wajh* meaning
"face," the quintessential face-to-face encounter of official public life
(see fig. 9). Muwajaha was also the format in which the mufti received
afternoon *fatwa* seekers, and the same sort of generic activity was characteristic as well of both ruling imams and local governors. Direct
accessibility, based on a public presence that enabled personal encounters and personal solutions to problems, was a fundamental value of the
old administrative style.

Hakim, the standard term for "judge" (*qadi* was also used), as in
hakim shar'i or "shari'a judge," had another sense, which meant "ruler,"
as in the identification of Imam Yahya as *hakim al-yaman*, "ruler of
Yemen."[3] In this domain of overlapping terminology a verb from the
same h–k–m root, followed by *bainahum* (lit. "between them") can
mean "he governed" when used of an imam or, beyond the sphere of
the state, of an important rural shaykh, and "he adjudicated their case"

when used in reference to a judge. One is reminded of a similar double resonance of the English word "court," held by both kings and judges. While the categories judge and imam are not to be confused, it is also true that the activity of governing in Yemen was in general very much devoted to settling disputes, with only a specialized part of this activity being handled by the shari'a court variety of hakim.

Like Saint Louis under his oak at Vincennes, Imam Yahya was well known for his daily practice of making himself available to his subjects. The tradition went back more than a millennium to the conduct of the first Zaidi imam in Yemen, al-Hadi,[4] and the scene was nearly identical to that enacted on the local level by judges in twentieth-century Ibb. "Every morning," the historian al-Wasi'i (1928:295–96) writes, "the Imam himself sat in the courtyard of his palace, Dar al-Sa'ada, to hear for himself people's petitions." "Himself" is repeated to emphasize the physical presence of the imam. "The decrepit, the weak (*da'if*), women, children, the long-suffering came to him [and he met them with] a warm, sympathetic, solicitous and unpretentious countenance. This [activity] was the centerpiece of his desire to extend justice and equity."[5] Attentiveness to the needs and problems of the down-trodden and the people of lower status was a sign of just government in general[6] and a value in judicial procedure in particular, as expressed in the manual principle of giving precedence to the claim of the "weak."

Wajh, the "face," was also a man's "honor,"[7] however, and the face-to-face *muwajaha* was rarely an encounter of equivalent personas. The *haiba* behavior of kissing hands and knees that occurred as the "weak" related to the judge reached its zenith in relating to the apical figure of the imam, whose *haiba* was immense. The behavior of those received in public audience does not figure in the historian's account, however, which is only concerned with identifying the presence and generosity of the imam's countenance. Needless to say, it was easier for an imam or a judge to step down in demeanor and discourse than it was for an ordinary person to step up.

At noon, followed by a few soldier-retainers and a crowd of people, the imam would walk to the mosque, continuing to hear petitions even as he washed in preparation for prayer. After lunch, like the local mufti, judges, and governor in Ibb, the imam would appear in his *diwan*, the semipublic sitting room in his own palace-residence. There his secretaries would gather around him to engage in reading and responding to petitions that had arrived from around the country. Again, in a manner characterized by personal involvement with each and every case, he would "attend to the papers one by one, [including] the simple and the momentous."

In Ibb, the mufti of Imam Yahya's era was in the habit of taking long strolls in the morning, and he too would answer the people who came up to him. This casual availability in the morning complemented that of the more structured, principal time and place of giving fatwas, during afternoon qat-chewing sessions in his diwan. A daily morning walk around the town, during which he received requests and petitions, was also standard for Isma'il Basalama, the Ibb governor during the first part of Imam Yahya's reign, as was noted by the Syrian traveler al-'Azm (1937:291–92). The official routine of al-Qadi Ahmad al-Sayaghi, governor in the 1950s under Imam Ahmad, provides an example of some further modalities and also points in the direction of an eventual transformation of this administrative style.

Al-Sayaghi's daily schedule began indoors with a four-hour block of time devoted mainly to the general reception (*muwajaha 'amma*) of people who had come to see him, and also to replies to submitted petitions with the assistance of his secretaries. In his capital, Ta'izz, Imam Ahmad too had discontinued the regular morning open-air encounters of his father, taking this activity inside to a diwan.[8] Later in the morning, al-Sayaghi customarily went out to tour the town but mostly for the purpose of inspecting the work on the construction projects that were his real passion. During the afternoon qat session, he met with selected individuals (*muwajaha khassa*). On Friday afternoons, however, he conducted himself in the old manner. This one afternoon a week anyone could approach the Ibb governor, the deputy of the imam, who sat out under a tree next to the government offices for the reception (*muwajaha*) of those who otherwise might not have been able to reach him.

Central to the muwajaha format was the notion of responsiveness. An "official," *al-mas'ul*, was literally "the one asked." What was sought from an imam or a governor, a mufti or a judge, was an "answer" (a *jawab*). In the case of the mufti, a query was posed and the answer was the fatwa. For the other three dispute-handling public officials, the imam in the capital and the governor and the judge on the provincial level, the approach was made in the form of a complaint or petition, known as a *shakwa*. Historically, shakwas were the general means by which individuals initiated actions in which they wanted to involve the state.[9] Whether these were individual-state matters (employment, state credit, charity disbursement, tax matters) or individual-individual ones (disputes of all sorts) pursued through the state, the shakwa always represented the opening move.[10]

SHAKWA

It is absolutely necessary that on two days in the week the king should sit for the redress of wrongs, to exact recompense from the oppressor, to give justice and to listen to the words of his subjects with his own ears, without any intermediary. It is fitting that some written petitions should also be submitted if they are comparatively important, and he should give a ruling on each one.

NIZAM AL-MULK (11th century A.D.)[11]

The basic procedure for obtaining justice, for finding relief from injustice (*zulm*), through the state, was thus a direct appeal to an official, one of whom was the shari'a judge. In his well-known Hadith commentary al-Nawawi summarizes the pattern as follows: "The wronged person can seek relief from the sultan and the judge, and other appointed officials, asking for redress from the offending person, saying 'So and so has wronged me,' or 'So and so did this or that to me'" (quoted in al-Shawkani A.H. 1394:14). The vocabulary of *zulm*—the *mazlum* (wronged person), *zalim* (offending person), *zalama* (to wrong), *tazallum* (to complain or seek relief)—is precisely that utilized in shakwas.

In many Muslim states, from an early date, *mazalim* jurisdictions, as they became known (from the same z–l–m root), amounted to alternate or superior forums for handling disputes.[12] The existence of such competing forums partly contradicted the supposedly universal jurisdictional sweep of the shari'a court, especially if matters contained within the purview of the shari'a were as a consequence not dealt with by the shari'a judge. In imamic Yemen, this contradiction worked a bit differently than in the typical Sunni state, headed by a sultan or a king. Condensed in the identity of the imam were both a sultan's temporal capacity to handle grievances such as salary arrears, petitions for transfer of position, or complaints about an official's conduct, and the full shari'a capacity of the ultimate judge (and mufti) in the land. While there was for this reason no open contradiction or separation of powers at the apex of the imamic system of rule, at the local level of the governorates there opened up two distinct positions: the shari'a judge (*hakim*) and the governor (*na'ib*, *'amil*). These separate delegations (*wilaya*) of capacity, undivided in the identity of the imam, meant that dispute settlement on the level of the provincial town involved a division of labor between the hakim's capacity to handle shari'a matters and the governor's capacity to handle problems defined as being of another sort—roughly, the *mazalim* jurisidiction formula.

In ideal terms, as in the description of Imam Yahya by the quasi-official historian, the shakwa is oral, conveyed verbally by the petitioner and "heard" by the ruler—thus (al-Wasi'i): "to hear for himself people's petitions [shakwas]," "he walked and continued to hear shakwas," "and while washing and afterwards before the prayer he continued in this fashion hearing shakwas." An extreme and desperate version of the auditory connection was public shouting. It used to be possible to literally "gain the ear" of the Yemeni head of state by persistent shouting at his front door, and it is a strategy still occasionally employed from street level to get the attention of a local governor upstairs in the official residence. Interchange based on speaking (or shouting) and hearing might be initially understood as the only possible method for the presentation of the concerns of the illiterate downtrodden, and women and children. In another sense, however, the emphasis upon "hearing" is stylized and overstated. It is part of a system of representations centering on the value of "presence" situated at the heart of the face-to-face intimacy of the muwajaha formula. While a speaking-hearing mode for the communication of shakwas was valued as an ideal, a writing-reading mode was frequently the practical norm. The ideally oral quality of the shakwa fit the ideal character of the muwajaha, but underpinning such structures of apparent presence were practices of distancing and absence implemented through writing.

There was a further status twist to this. Petitions from the mass of lower-status individuals, which were supposedly "heard" in the public muwajaha, had in actuality to be transformed from their imprecise dialectial articulation into the discourse of the text in order to be dealt with. Elite petitions, those of the few, the individuals most accomplished in the literate skills, could be communicated in speech, but this occurred, not in the open public format, but rather in the relatively private afternoon diwan settings of the "special muwajaha" (*muwajaha khassa*).

Proper conduct of the muwajaha style of government depended on the elimination and avoidance of barriers between ruler and ruled. The barriers at issue were both physical—walls, closed doors, guards—and of the insubstantial, haiba sort, which caused ordinary petitioners to tremble and lose their words. To provide what he refers to in a section heading as a "Description of the Imams of Yemen," al-Wasi'i (1928:297) quotes an account that makes repeated use of verbs and nouns derived from the h–j–b root, which means to "hide," "conceal," "make a separation," and "to veil." In its various forms the h–j–b root expresses circumstances opposite to muwajaha, which depends on an unobstructed meeting of faces. According to the quoted text, the ideal imam is like one of his subjects in his simple style of life, and he "speaks to them and governs them, without regard to whether [the individual] before him is a noble or a commoner, strong or weak, without creating a barrier (*hijjab*). He does not delegate matters to ministers or chamberlains (*hujjab*). . . . [Such rulers] neither keep [others] out (*yahjibun*) nor seclude themselves (*yahtajibun*)."

An important connotation of the h–j–b root is feminine seclusion and veiling: in the public domain, proper and just "masculine" conduct is enacted through the regular presentation of one's face and through the secure medium of speech; improper and unjust ("feminine" for men) conduct, by contrast, relies on the concealment of the face and works through the dangerous medium of writing. An ordinary form of muwajaha wisdom similarly dictates that men come out of their houses every day, show their faces, and circulate in the town streets, or risk criticism and suspicion.

A negative assessment of a ruler, within the muwajaha idiom of statecraft, typically pointed to the practice of official distancing. Thus a republican historian criticizes the conduct of Imam Yahya's sons as provincial governors, including al-Hasan in Ibb, as follows: "They withdrew [a h–j–b verb] themselves from the people and distanced themselves from *hearing* their shakwas" (al-Akwa' 1980:295, emphasis added). By extension, Imam Yahya's general policy is critically characterized as one of "total isolation; he shut himself, and Yemen, off from contact with the outside world."

In practice, shakwas were virtually always written,[13] as were the responses, which were usually added in the form of a note atop the original piece of paper containing the shakwa (as is the case with the query and its fatwa-answer). To engage the official machinery even shouted claims had to be reduced to a concrete statement of the problem in the form of a written shakwa. To get around the soldiers who might block delivery, Governor al-Sayaghi placed a barrel with a slot in the top to collect hand-submitted shakwas at street level. The mail system, which functioned rather well in the post-Ottoman imamic period, served principally to carry shakwas, either to provincial governors or to the imam himself.[14] For those private individuals who could afford it, the telegraph system served the same end. Public writers, who continue to set up their boxtop offices outside the governorate offices in Ibb, specialize in writing shakwas for petitioners who cannot write for themselves.

On the receiving end, in the imam's diwan for example, shakwas were first screened and summarized by secretaries.[15] The secretary wrote a brief memo at the top indicating the subject matter and the action sought. The shakwa was then passed before the imam, who would add a quick note of refusal or permission, such as "nothing forbids this," or return the paper to the secretary to draft a brief order (*amr*) or a note of transfer to an appropriate official or other person. Transfers often carried a request for investigation or clarification of the complaint, and, if warranted, an order for implementation (*tanfidh*) or *dabt*, which entailed some form of arrest, seizure, enforcement, or restraint. One of the possible officials to whom a shakwa initially presented to an imam or a local governor might be transferred was the shari'a judge of the appropriate jurisdiction. The hakim too received shakwas directly, and also transferred them to others. The ideal administrator was one who not only was accessible, in the sense of receiving people's shakwas, but who responded to them quickly and decisively. For officials of all levels, reading and responding to the shakwa traffic was one of the principal tasks of day-to-day government.

Finally, the original shakwa document, now bearing a response, was returned to the petitioner. It was the petitioner who was responsible for effecting the physical transfer to another official or person if such was called for in the response. To have an order carried out, the petitioner had to take the shakwa with the order written on it to the official addressed in the response, such as, "to the governor of Ibb, for enforcement," or "to the shari'a judge, carry out the necessary shari'a procedures." The system depended on the initiative of petitioning individuals to keep their matters alive.

For the judge, the shari'a court itself, the *mahkama shari'a*, entailed a specialized form of muwajaha. The required openness of this event was defined in manual chapters on procedure. Court should be held in a well-known and central public place, while the rule against posting a doorman (*hajib*, from the h–j–b root) addressed a concern for unimpeded direct access. Reacting to the tumult of bodies crowding a contemporary (mid-1970s) Ibb courtroom and pressing forward to gain the attention of an old judge, his teenage son suggested that it would be desirable to create order by placing guards at the door to let disputants in one at a time, or in pairs. His father retorted sharply that a guard at the door led inexorably to people's being denied access and, as a consequence, being denied justice. Years after the opening of official courtrooms, older judges could still be encountered listening to disputants sitting outside at curbside or at the doorsteps of their residences before or after lunch. But the direction of new legislation concerned with judicial procedure is toward more "ordered" sessions, with access to the judge regulated by a doorman,[16] and also—diametrically opposite to the open-door format—private interviews, conducted under newly instituted prosecutorial auspices (Messick 1983b),[17] and closed sessions in certain circumstances. A final separation of house and court was mandated by the "Judicial Authority" legislation of 1979 (Art. 17): "Sessions are to be held in the court building, in specially designated rooms."

A shakwa presented to a judge, or transferred to him, is a way of bringing a matter to his attention for the first time. In giving attention to a shakwa, however, a judge is not engaging the process of adjudication. The shakwa represents only a petition by a single party, and this is different from a claim (*da'wa*) with which a formal proceeding opens. A da'wa involves two parties, one who makes the da'wa and a second who is also present and hears the da'wa and then responds to it, in an *ijaba*. The presentation of a shakwa is intended only to get the judge to issue a summons to the second party. If the shakwa is minimally plausible and the subject matter relevant to his jurisdiction, the judge will dispatch one of his soldier-retainers, a step known as *infadh*.[18] This occurs by means of a note written atop the shakwa by the judge, which says, "Bring so and so to give justice (*li-insaf*) to the petitioner." In addition to the task of maintaining order before the judge, the work of delivering summonses is the primary activity of the judge's soldier-retainers.

There were thus two distinct types of muwajaha that occurred as the judge sat before his house. The simple and far more numerous first type is the approach by the single party for the purpose of presenting a shakwa; it is the petitioner and the judge who come face-to-face in this instance. The second, more complex type, occurs "between" (*bain*) two parties and in the presence of the judge. It requires a claimant (*mudda'i*), who states the da'wa, and a defendant (*mudda' 'alih*), who first hears the da'wa and then makes an answer, an ijaba. In this instance the parties confront each other and together confront the judge. From the beginning, then, as a matter becomes a case and is adjudicated, a petition is answered by the judge, a claim is answered by the defendant, and a claim and a response (followed by evidence or oaths) are together answered by the judge in his ruling (*hukm*).

JUDICIAL KNOWLEDGE

A judge's personal knowledge of particular people and their affairs constituted an important and recognized basis for judicial action. Specifically, according to both Shafi'i and Zaidi manuals, except in *hudud* cases,[19] where evidence must be presented, a judge can give judgment based on his own knowledge (*'ilm*) of events; and, when the evidence of witnesses is presented, he can accept or reject it on the basis of his own knowledge (*'ilm*) of the justness or unjustness of the persons in question, without requiring further verification of their character.[20] Pragmatic and contextual, this circumstantial 'ilm was derived from worldly contact and experience rather than from teachers and set the practicing judge off from the more retiring among his fellow scholars. While 'ilm in the sense of knowledge acquired in the madrasa receives prominent mention among the fundamental conditions for assuming the judgeship—Abu Shuja', for example, enumerates six detailed subpoints —that of 'ilm in the informal, local sense is not developed. Without such contextual knowledge, however, that obtained in the madrasa could not be effectively implemented.[21]

Dealing as he does in worldly *hijāj*, that is, in evidence, testimony, acknowledgments, and oaths, the judge requires a down-to-earth understanding of people and their ways in his jurisdiction. And yet there was a constraint, at least in the perspective of the manuals, that restricted his purview to the surface of outward fact and verbalized intention, to the exclusion of deeper but unexpressed purpose or concealed motive. Shari'a court proceedings are meant to operate on the basis of *al-zahir*, a level of outward appearances and manifest meanings. Confronted, for example, by an oath confusing in its implications, a judge is instructed to follow the outward sense of the articulated statement.[22] Likewise, the import of an oath is never to be determined by the potential existence of a "mental reservation, or an interpretation contrary to the meaning of the words, nor a reservation made in an undertone which the judge cannot hear,"[23] any of which might be alleged subsequently by the oath-taker. In making the key initial decision about which of the two parties in a case is to be the plaintiff (and thereby assume the burden of proof), the judge is to apply the following rule of thumb: "The plaintiff is the individual whose claim conflicts with the appearance of things (*al-zahir*)."[24] Interpretation of a final ruling in a case is similarly restricted: the judge's decision is to be "implemented manifestly (*zahiran*) not implicitly (*batinan*)."[25] Fittingly for an encounter of "faces" (*muwajaha*), the proceedings are intended to function *zahiran*, or as we would say, "on the face of," issues, words, and rulings. Among the relevant specialists in appearances was the physiognomist, the student of faces and physical indications, who could be called upon by the judge to give evidence.[26]

Al-Nawawi offers some notes on how a judge should conduct himself in order to acquire information upon being appointed to a new and unknown jurisdiction. Before departure for the new post, he should make preliminary investigations "about the circumstances of scholars and persons of good repute in the district." He may expect to ask and receive advice from local scholars on matters of jurisprudence and also, from those with practical experience, information about locally accepted custom (*'urf*). Al-Nawawi recommends that the judge consult such local jurists before rendering his decisions. Persons of good repute could be relied upon to guide the new judge in discriminating the just and the unjust in the population and, together with the local scholars, provided prospects for staffing his court. The Zaidi manual likewise counsels the judge to have both scholars and other reputable people present at court sessions.

The new judge, al-Nawawi writes, should "enter on a Monday and proceed to the center of the town." He is then to carry out a series of initial inquiries to acquire necessary information concerning two main areas of judicial responsibility that extend beyond his duties as a trial judge. "First of all, he should look into the situation of individuals in jail. Those who say 'I was jailed justly' should remain so. If 'wrongly,' then his adversary must produce proof, and if the latter is absent he should be written to, to present himself." Then the judge should interview the local trustees of the several types: "He who claims a trusteeship should be questioned about it, and about himself and his administration. He who is found lacking in the requisite justness should have the funds taken away from him, and the less than fully competent should be supported with counsel."

Next the judge should see about appointing court functionaries to assist him, including both a secretary and an individual known as a *muzakki*, whose task it is to pronounce officially on the justness, or not, of individuals who appear before the court as witnesses. Known to both the Shafi'i and the Zaidi manual, the procedure of verification of witnesses, or *tazkiyya*, does not require the existence of a specific court official to be implemented. To the extent that court evidence is given as oral testimony by witnesses, however, a judge new to a place is largely dependent on trusted witness verifiers, official or not, to establish the necessary evidential basis for his rulings. As an institution, the muzakki represents a specialized form, and in the case of the existence of an actual court official, an important delegation, of one of the essential capacities pertaining to the judge himself. A judge who has come to know the local people, by contrast, is often able to engage this dimension of his official identity directly and verify the character of witnesses by means of his own information. A witness stands between the judge and unknown facts concerning persons and events, and a muzakki is a further intervening link in the human transmission of evidence, standing between the judge and an unknown witness. To eliminate the further mediation in the chain of evidence transmission, the judge may cultivate a personal knowledge of his constituents.

Intended for the circumstances of various times and places, including, for example, those that obtained in his native Syria, al-Nawawi's manual takes into consideration still another possible communicative intervention, a translator.[27] Judges in very large cities of the Middle East and elsewhere doubtless could never come to know the population of their jurisdictions well enough to forgo major reliance on the mediations of muzakkis, translators, neighborhood notaries, quarter heads, market and craft officials, experts of various types, sectarian representatives, and so forth. But in Ibb, and perhaps most if not all Yemeni towns, the population was, until recent years, small (e.g., for Ibb, ca. 5,000 in 1900), and the character of the interaction was "face-to-face"; people all "knew" one another in terms of names and social identity, if not on an intimate basis (i.e., *zahiran*, if not *batinan*). It was such knowledge, within the community and, potentially, between the judge and the community, that ideally structured a local muwajaha encounter. In recent decades, however, Ibb has expanded rapidly in surface area and population (ca. 17,000 in 1975), and town society is now marked by a rapidly declining degree of mutual "knowledge." Associated with the spatial and demographic changes, a shift is occurring to a pattern of interaction in which people interact for the first time in the presence of large numbers of townspeople they do not "know." Associated with this social change is a new state presence, represented by numerous new functionaries, including university graduate judges, who not only are different in formation and administrative style but who remain strangers to the town to the end of their often brief tenures in office.

Prior to the late 1950s, when the first expansion outside the old walls occurred, the "public" informational space had an immediacy indicated by such important auditory institutions as voiced calls to prayer (now loudspeaker assisted), public criers in the marketplace, and the sounding of horns by night guards on their rounds. The main alleys were informational channels, not only as the principal locale of everyday male interaction, but also for societal announcements: a convert to Islam was taken through the streets on muleback; wedding processions were accompanied by gunfire, fireworks, music, and ululation; a criminal act was publicized by drumming (or, in extreme cases, dragging) the culprit around the town. Town life was, in addition, a series of types of communication-rich assemblies of men. The paradigm of gathering was in the "place of gathering," the mosque (*jami*), both at the neighborhood level during the week and at the community-gathering level on Friday. The marketplace, especially the morning meat market and the afternoon qat market, was the main everyday public arena. By midafternoon, gatherings shifted indoors, for business in officials' sitting rooms and for pleasure or for special occasions in friends' reception rooms.

The circuitry of interpersonal knowledge in a small community such as Ibb carried information about reputation. Originally constituted "before the people" (*quddam al-nas*), reports concerning reputations circulated thereafter through dense word-of-mouth channels. A collectivity of informal (and potentially formal) witnesses for one another's conduct, the community was acutely sensitive to deviation from established personal norms. Conduct was evaluated with reference to a frame of known differences of social identity, occupation, personality, and so forth. As with the "mismatches" discussed earlier, it was mainly the nontypical for the type that was remarked upon. Feeding with special enthusiasm upon the novel, gossip nevertheless also confirmed in passing the already known.

That men's and women's networks intersect in the family and otherwise diverge is routinely recognized in Ibb. As part of a comprehensive separation of the sexes, women have their own neighborhood links, public bath days, visiting patterns, and an entire parallel world of afternoon qat-chewing sessions.[28] The existence of a social division of experience and related specialized knowledges that pertain especially to men or to women is acknowledged in the manual sections devoted to legal testimony.[29] There are, on the one hand, matters that "mainly males have to do with (lit. 'see')." These include legal undertakings from contracts to such public events as conversion, witness evaluation, and death. Al-Nawawi's sample list is "marriage, repudiation, remarriage with a repudiated wife, [conversion to] Islam, apostasy, challenging and certifying [witnesses], death, insolvency, agency, testaments, and secondary witnessing." In connection with such matters two men must give testimony, rather than the ordinary case possibility of one man and two women. "That which is restricted to the knowledge (*ma'arifa*) of women and which is not normally regarded by men," al-Nawawi writes, includes such matters as "female virginity, childbirth, menstruation, breast feeding, and [female] physical defects under clothes." Four female witnesses, without any males, can speak to such matters. From the position of (a male-constituted) jurisprudence, men ideally represent the *zahir* society of the streets, markets, and mosques; women represent that of the *batin*, ideally located in the house, concealed, and veiled.

Like "social honor" (*ihtiram, sharaf*) and "justness" (*'adala*), the inverse, established notoriety and, more technically, the status of "sinner"/ "unjust" (*fasiq*), are products of collective attribution and somewhat relative in content. While the first two guarantee that one's word as a witness will be relied upon, the latter have the opposite effect. According to al-Nawawi, when a *muzakki* is asked by the judge to report on a witness and the report is positive (i.e., the witness is just), the muzakki need not go into his reasons. But if he concludes that the witness is among the unjust and therefore challenges him or her, the grounds must be specified. These grounds can be either what the muzakki has personally observed or information gained through "*istifada*."

A word from the same root used in reference to water means to "overflow" and "flood"; the legal term means "spread widely" or "saturated" in reference to information. Another usage of the same term by al-Nawawi concerns how a local population comes to know of the appointment of a new judge. A written imamic order, accompanied by traveling witnesses, is one possibility, and *istifada*—whereby the appointment simply, but decisively, becomes widely known—is the other. Al-Ghazzi also uses the term in his summarizing comment on a list of the types of facts for which the testimony of a blind witness is acceptable.[30] The list includes knowledge of such things as deaths, kinship, and property rights, all of which al-Ghazzi says may be "established by *istifada*."[31] Al-Nawawi makes a similar argument in connection with testimony based on public repute (*tasamu'*). The term involved is derived from a root meaning "to hear," as is the general expression for "reputation," or "good reputation" (*sum'a*). In a non-direct manner, public-repute testimony can be used to establish descent (*nasab*), tribe (*qabila*) affiliation, or death, as well as such legal facts as marriage and the existence of an endowment or property rights.[32]

Al-Nawawi gives an instructive condition for the acceptance of this public-repute type of information: he says it must be "heard from a sufficient number of individuals to guarantee against collusion in a lie." Similar reasoning provides the foundation for another variety of information discussed earlier, the received wisdom known to jurists as *tawatur*.[33] What *tawatur* is to formal knowledge of important general historical matters (the existence of Mecca, etc.) and more technically to the science of hadith, *istifada* and *tasamu'* are to practical local knowledge about particular people and events.[34]

A microsocial and historical catalogue of particular actors and specific occurrences, the ever-shifting "known" of a place was tapped into by a judge in a special manner. In one respect his knowledge inevitably became deeper and wider than the ordinary person's as he became privy to otherwise guarded secrets exposed in situations of conflict. In another sense, however, he was barred by his position from some of the most routine but informative interactions of everyday life. Al-Nawawi says it is appropriate for the more narrowly specialized muzakki to evaluate justness based on personal knowledge derived from relations of friendship, neighborliness, or transactional dealings, but a judge is counseled not only to avoid buying and selling on his own behalf—interactions that would necessitate diverse ordinary contacts—but also to avoid doing so even through a known agent. For a judge friendship could also be problematic: he must be wary of gifts given him, and he is forbidden to give judgment in cases involving not only his own relatives but also individuals with whom he had any sort of formal association.[35] The stylized intimacy of the muwajaha encounter thus involved, on the part of the judge, a man at once unusually knowledgeable about the hidden aspects of people's affairs, yet also structurally distanced from many aspects of mundane social life. Although a judge could (and did) rely on the human resources of his household, including his wife, children, personal retainers, and secretaries for help in knowing about the community, he also had to exert himself to overcome the isolation of his position.

The Yemeni practice of not appointing judges to their home districts is not based on an explicit manual principle, but al-Nawawi's advice to a new appointee to make inquiries about scholars and reputable people implies a posting to an unknown place. The Yemeni appointment rule served the purpose of causing a new judge to start fresh, in a context free, at least initially, of both the demands of extensive family ties and the constraints of prior obligations and events. The paradox here is that while too much intimacy—such as would occur in a native district posting or if a judge attempted to conduct himself like an ordinary citizen—was to be avoided, a substantial degree of close contact was nonetheless essential for acquiring the local knowledge basic to judging.

CUSTOM

The requisite circumstantial knowledge of a judge was not just of persons and happenings, however, but also, in a more structural sense, of pattern and custom. The key summary term involved is *'urf*, which is often translated as "customary law." From the root '–r–f meaning "to know," *'urf* refers to known usage, both substantive and procedural.

In the most general sense, the 'urf of a place (*'urf al-balad*) refers to the established usages in all the domains of social life. An initial issue is the level of locale (*balad*) referred to. It might be possible to speak, for example, of the 'urf of Yemen, but what is usually highlighted by the term is regional difference, variation. The 'urf of a place could be said to be similar to (or even include) special linguistic usage, with 'urf differing from locale to locale in much the same way regional dialects shade one into the other. Measures are a good example: each highland region had its own terminology of particular linear and volume units. A judge posted to Ibb from somewhere in Upper Yemen had to learn the local terms and the measures indicated. It was not a difference of yards and meters, however; to the extent that the judge knew something of units of land and quantities of grain in his home district he would find similar types of measurement categories used in Ibb.

A judge had to concern himself mainly with 'urf that was relevant to the applied shari'a. Inasmuch as the shari'a is general or summary in its provisions, there are two basic ways it could be extended or given necessary detail. One is through the activities of interpretation, which "fill in gaps" in the shari'a's conceptual structure as needed. The other is by reliance on the existing detailed structures of local usage, or 'urf, a patchwork backdrop of practices that showed through the gaps in the shari'a fabric. Although "custom" as an integrated and elaborated

category of law was never elevated to a position of theoretical prominence by jurists, a widely accepted judicial attitude toward such usage
is summarized in a simple formula cited by Ibb judge al-Haddad:
"If no relevant [shari'a] text is found, then that which is known customarily is taken to be a binding condition" (*idh lam yujad nassan
fa-l-ma'ruf 'urfan ka-l-mashrut shartan*).[36] This view speaks not to situations of conflict between shari'a and 'urf, which are not tolerated by
jurists, but to areas of substantive concern about which the shari'a is
silent.

There are numerous substantive areas in the manuals where the
judge is specifically directed to supply necessary detail by reference to
prevailing custom.[37] Often this is by means of the expressions "'urf" or
"'urf al-balad," but the same sense obtains in a number of alternative
terms, used in the manuals and in Ibb practice, such as *al-ma'ruf* ("the
known"), *al-mashhur* ("the known"), *al-'ada* ("custom"—as in "Adat
Law" in Southeast Asia), *al-mu'tad* ("the customary"). Still other terms
reveal an openness to contextual grounding in the specifics of many
shari'a provisions. *Mithl*, meaning "like" or "similar," is often used to
this end. The amount of money that must be paid to the wife by the
husband as *mahr* is not set in the manuals; instead the amount is
characterized as *mahr al-mithl*, that is, a sum to be determined according
to what is locally appropriate for women of equivalent status. Another
example, mentioned earlier, concerns the "seriousness" (*muru'a*) of a
potential witness, which is to be evaluated relative to the standard of
seriousness current in the local community, that is, *muru'at al-mithl*.[38]
Many monetary and other questions are to be determined by reference
to similar local circumstances of "time and place," a frequently encountered manual formula that rhymes in Arabic (*zaman wa makan*).

Two specific and relatively bounded varieties of 'urf that an Ibb
judge usually knew something about and occasionally dealt with officially were the custom of the merchants (*'urf al-tujjar*) and "tribal"
custom (*'urf al-qabili*). The first is a body of detailed local practices
opened up around the core transactional forms of the applied jurisprudence (sale, lease, credit, partnership, agency, etc.). Ibb merchants
always tended to handle their disputes informally among themselves
rather than appearing in shari'a tribunals. With advancing commercialization in recent years, this separation was formalized with the
appearance of chambers of commerce (with arbitration functions) and,
a few years later, commercial courts (established in the three largest
towns).[39] The second type of custom concerns rules elaborated mostly

beyond the physical and conceptual bounds of the shari'a, although "tribal" practices such as the *hajar*, an animal sacrifice used to appease abused honor and preceded by a public procession, occurs fairly frequently in Ibb town.[40] In some regions, a judge was expected to be conversant with two discourses, to "provide shari'a rulings in shari'a matters and customary rulings for customary issues."[41]

'Urf is also procedural. Formal and official shari'a courts are paralleled in Ibb by an important alternative resolution format of an unofficial and customary nature. While shari'a court adjudication procedures result in winners and losers, the customary formula is compromise (*sulh*). Customary compromise represents a foil for the court in a sense that goes beyond the alternative that it represents to a state forum, substantive shari'a jurisprudence, and formal adjudication. Men gather in the sitting rooms of private houses for this compromise type of settling, and the meeting of faces involved is quite different from that in a public muwajaha. Whereas court procedure is based on extended and frequently damaging verbal confrontations between the adversaries, compromises work through separation and avoidance. Each of the parties is talked to alone; views are aired, and potential solutions are suggested. Mediators motivated by goodwill can cut through the posturing and lying that plague the tribunal. Unlike the cool and narrow effort to focus upon manifest facts (*al-zahir*) in the judge's court, mediators freely explore issues in breadth and in depth, "studying hearts," as one put it. It is only when a compromise has been reached that the parties are brought together to seal the agreement. At the session, usually over an afternoon of qat chewing, the matter at hand is not overtly mentioned. The final settlement is effected through writing. If there are last-minute hitches, mediators step out of the room briefly for further words. As the conversation in the room is steered in other directions, final documents are prepared and then unobtrusively passed along to the parties for their signatures. Others present—relatives, friends, and neighbors—add their names as witnesses. In this manner two "faces" meet each other in the presence of assembled men: the genius of sitting-room compromises is that they permit the intact honor of each man to confront the other, without either being put into question.

As venue types, courtroom adjudication and sitting-room compromise represent polar opposites: shari'a versus 'urf in substance, official and public versus unofficial and private in format. There are, in addition, intermediate types, the customary[42] but official dispute-handling activity of the governor (the *mazalim*, discussed earlier) and the shari'a-based but unofficial activities of consensual ruling and judicial arbitration (*hukm taradi* and *tahkim*).[43] Compromise itself is not an exclusive property of custom and the sitting room, however. The *Azhar* manual says a judge ought to "urge compromise (*sulh*)" upon the parties to a dispute.[44] A caveat is attached: the urging should occur especially when the correct solution is not apparent to the judge, whereas if the truth is clear, he should encourage a still simpler and, in Yemen, unlikely outcome, forgiveness.[45] In the perspective of jurists, compromise is generally permitted insofar as it does not, in the words of a famous hadith, render "legal the illegal, or illegal the legal."[46]

In a *hukm al-taradi*, the delegation of authority (*wilaya*) comes not from the state but from the parties themselves and depends on their prior agreement for enforcement. Al-Akwa' (1980:306) says of one twentieth-century jurist that "he undertook judging (*al-qada'*) by mutual consent (*taradi*) between disputing parties who came to him." In 1908, prior to the Treaty of Da''an and before Imam Yahya had won the right to appoint regular judges, he took advantage of a period of friendly relations with the Ottoman governor to dispatch a number of unofficial *taradi* judges to San'a'.[47]

In other than *hudud* and criminal cases, a judge who sees a possible solution can also ask the parties to empower[48] him to arbitrate (verb, *hakkama*; verbal noun, *tahkim*). Arbitration is recognized in the manuals, but al-Nawawi is anxious to give the procedure a formal shari'a footing by adding, "with the condition [that the arbitrator] has full judicial qualification."[49] Arbitration appears to have been very common in Ibb under the Ottomans, being both formally sanctioned and enforceable by the government,[50] and local examples also exist for the Zaidi imamic period.[51] An official shari'a court judge who also engages both in *taradi* judging (with individuals outside his regular jurisdiction) and in *tahkim* is specifically envisioned in an imamic appointment letter.[52] From the point of view of shari'a jurisprudence, however, all of these possibilities—compromise, consensual rulings, and arbitration—are delicate matters. All lead into the competing terrain of out-of-court settlement, which Muslim states, including the Y.A.R., sought to bring under the umbrella of official legitimacy and control.[53]

Finally, the formal court judgeship itself may be thought of as involving its own customary practices. Manual chapters on formal shari'a procedure list general procedural requirements, recommendations for judicial conduct (*adab al-qadi*), and actions that are forbidden. Although not mentioned in the manuals, experience (*mumarasa*) is understood to be vital. The transition from madrasa-trained scholar to trial judge was predicated on a learning of the professional ropes. Together with the varieties of local knowledge, including current 'urf, and the possibilities of extracourtroom procedure, experience was a further ingredient for successful in-court judging.

Many judges learned this aspect of their profession by beginning their careers as court secretaries, others by frequenting court sessions conducted by their fathers or relatives. Al-Shawkani had had neither sort of preliminary exposure when he was abruptly called and persuaded to take on the judgeship in early-nineteenth-century San'a'. He writes (A.H. 1348, 1:464) that he was immediately deluged by cases and that "the intellect worked hard, the mind troubled greatly." This was especially so, he says, because "I did not know the procedural usages (*umur al-istilahiyya*) in these matters. I had not ever been present with a judge in a lawsuit, and I had not even attended the litigation sessions of my father." The leading scholar of the era considered himself a novice when faced with the demands of the judgeship. His life of studying, teaching, and issuing fatwas, and his deliberate avoidance of public life, had left him uninformed about the world of the court. He felt a strong contrast between his predicament and the record of his predecessor in the post, the noted scholar and judge of the late eighteenth century, Yahya b. Salih al-Sahuli.[54] Al-Shawkani admires the exceptional precision of al-Sahuli's opinions, which he attributes not to his predecessor's excellent scholarly credentials but rather to his lengthy and comprehensive practical experience (*ikhtibar, mumarasa*).

For judges as for ruling imams, the basic public muwajaha, the open court encounter, implicitly required the acquisition of a spectrum of informal knowledges. As indicated in this chapter, there were both significant twentieth-century modifications of this system, from shifts in the administrative styles of imamic officials to the introduction of prosecution institutions and commercial courts under the republic, and important continuities, including some persistence of claimant receptions at private residences even after courtrooms were built and the guarantee of the right of complaint by shakwa in the republican constitution. A further assessment of changes and continuities in the shari'a courts, however, must take account of innovations introduced in the Ottoman period.

CHAPTER 10

Court Order

Head judge (*qadi*)	2,000
Head secretary	400
Second secretary	300
Third secretary	300
Secretary	300
Mufti	400
Judgment witness (*shahid al-hukm*)	150
Judgment witness	150
Religious studies instructor	200
Court usher (*mubashir*)	150
Court caretaker	60
Asst. Judge (*na'ib*), Jibla	300
Asst. Judge al-Makhadir	300
Deserving scholar	200

DISTRICT ACCOUNTS, IBB, 1916[1]

The twentieth century opened in Yemen with a judgeship recently modified in accord with Ottoman reforms. Behind the simple character of the 1916 Ottoman personnel list lies a template for a new way of thinking about the nature of the *shari'a* court. Although the more sweeping changes represented by the new Nizamiyya courts established in the central provinces of the empire were not instituted in the highlands, there were some significant innovations.[2] A modicum of "order" (*nizam*), on a scale reduced and adapted for the special circumstances of Ottoman rule in Yemen, was introduced into local judicial affairs, as it had been in the closely associated sphere of instruction. Like Ottoman schools, much of this new system would apparently be undone by Imam Yahya,[3] only to reappear in the institutional reforms of the republic.

Undramatic though they may now appear, the innovations signaled in the personnel list were elements of a comprehensive reformulation of the judicial process, and beyond, as in the case of instruction, of the state itself. The list embodies selected bits and pieces of a much larger Ottoman bureacratic scheme for a justice system, one roughly analogous in scope and detail to the legislation for judicial organization enacted in Yemen in 1979.[4] The 1916 Ibb court staff were implementing a style of bureaucratic behavior radically different from that of the patrimonial imamic state, one that would only begin to be fully elaborated conceptually and enacted in practice with the wave of legislation and accompanying generation of complex new state organs in the 1970s.

The most revolutionary qualities of the list are the routine elements and orderly features that make it, now for us, so mundanely cognizable as a segment of a typical bureaucracy. State employees are deployed in categories and grades of positions, each with specific duties and salaries. This last feature, fixed state salaries, had only been successfully instituted for the Ottoman judiciary in the latter half of the nineteenth century. Salaries replaced a much-abused practice of court fees, collected by judges directly from those who appeared before them.[5] The theoretical reorientation of the source of judicial income, away from individuals and to the state, is an important measure of an intended shift in the definition of state control and responsibility. In contrast to an old mode of income generation and expenditure entirely within the loop of particular organizational segments, through fees and other sorts of revenues collected and then disbursed internally, the state would come to mediate in these transactions. Under the Republic, this would occur by means of budgets, accounts, and salary disbursement managed by the Central Bank.[6]

Like Ottoman students separated into classes, and soldiers mobilized in their units,[7] local court functionaries were organized in ranked grades—head secretary, second, third, and so forth—in accord with a preexisting bureaucratic plan laid out in rationalized and abstract detail. Yemeni legislation would eventually conceive of bureaucratic employment in similar terms, according not only to set salary levels but also to requirements concerning age, educational attainment (with associated examinations and attestations), procedures for appointment, trial periods and inspections by superiors, rules about time in service and seniority, eligibility for promotion, transfer and retirement, and an array of position-specific duties. Bureaucratic work would become internally differentiated and specialized, increasingly organized and routinized.

With the transition, accelerated since the Revolution, from an agrarian to a commercially oriented state, the peak and slack annual work rhythms of the remaining old harvest-focused administrations (Endowments, Government Properties, and Tithe offices) now stand in sharp contrast to the regular, year-round activity pattern of the new offices such as the Central Bank and the Tax Office. Sons following fathers in their positions, and dense linkages of kinship and marriage characteristic of the old offices[8] are beginning to give way to a more achievement-oriented division of administrative labor. This, in turn, dovetails with the increasingly specialized advanced instruction of the contemporary educational system. Government of the household *diwan*, with men seated together on floor cushions before slant-topped writing desks, has been transformed into government of the public office building, with its separating walls, doors, and desks, and windows raised up to match the move from the floor to chairs. The all-purpose craftsman secretary (*katib*, lit. "writer") has given way to a panoply of titled functionaries with specific job descriptions. In the shift from a patrimonial to a bureaucratic state, initiated in Yemen by the Ottomans and then recommenced under the Republic, the old *haiba* of the person is dissolving into the alienated *haiba* of form.

The head judge for the district in 1916 was Muhammad Nuri, an Ottoman Syrian, while all the subordinate (and lesser paid) court positions were filled by men from the town and region.[9] At least two of the local men, one of the al-ʿAnsis and a man named Muhammad al-Yunis, received instruction in the Ottoman *Majalla*, the codified version of the official Hanafi school of jurisprudence discussed in chapter 3. It was the *Majalla*, its substantive provisions little different from the Shafiʿi school, that was applied in the Ibb court. As one product of the struggle between the Ottomans and Imam Yahya, the court configuration in Ibb was distinctly different from that which obtained in the Upper Yemen of the era. As Point Six of the Treaty of Daʿʿan, signed with the imam in 1911,[10] the "government," as it is referred to, had confirmed its right to "appoint non-Yemeni shariʿa judges in regions [such as Ibb] where the population follows the Shafiʿi or Hanafi school (*madhhab*)."

In his original negotiating position of 1906, however, the imam had not only demanded that "judgments be in conformity with the shariʿa," but also sought complete control of all judicial appointments.[11] At Daʿʿan, which was intended, as al-Wasiʿi says, to settle the affairs of those districts under the administration of the state (i.e., the Ottoman province of Yemen) but resided in by Zaidis, the first point agreed to is that "the imam will nominate judges of the Zaidi school, [then] inform the provincial administration, which will [in turn] inform Istanbul for the confirmation of this nomination by the Judicial Office."[12] In addition to dividing up the appointment of judges according to spheres of influence, the treaty provides (Point Seven) for the creation of "mixed courts" with "Shafi'i and Zaidi judges" to handle claims of "mixed schools."[13]

The 1916 court personnel list reveals a further distinguishing characteristic of Ottoman judicial organization: the position of the "judgment witness." According to the old shari'a manuals, both Shafi'i and Zaidi, the judgeship is conceived of as a single position,[14] while Ottoman courts in Yemen typically comprised a presiding judge and court "members" or "judgment witnesses."[15] This innovation was eliminated in Ibb with the return of Zaidi rule in 1919, but reappeared after 1962 under the Republic. In the judicial reorganization of 1972, judge Ahmad al-Haddad was moved from the Ibb district judgeship to become presiding judge of the new Second Court of Ibb Province, constituted in the Ottoman style with four court "members" and three secretaries.[16] When this sort of institution of a panel of judges "giving judgment by agreement or a majority view" was introduced in the nearby Sultanate of Lahj (by means of a 1949 Code adapted from the Egyptian Code of 1931), it proved very controversial.[17]

Within the Ibb district in the Ottoman period there was also a hierarchy of judges, represented by the two subordinate "deputy judges" (na'ibs) responsible for the subdistricts of Jibla and al-Makhadir. This judicial scheme was paralleled by that of the general Ottoman district administration, which was headed by a district officer (qa'immaqam) with subordinate subdistrict officers (mudirs) for Jibla and al-Makhadir. Earlier in the nineteenth century, al-Shawkani, like his late-eighteenth-century predecessor al-Sahuli, had been designated qadi al-qudat, literally "judge of the judges," but this was more an honorific than it was an expression of an elaborated judicial hierarchy. Noted scholars of the early twentieth century, such as 'Abd Allah al-Yamani (d. 1931) and Husayn al-'Amri (d. 1942), were referred to as Qadi al-Qudat and Shaykh al-Islam.[18]

The Ottomans also introduced the concept of appeal (ta'n), which is also unknown to the manuals.[19] Above the district level there was an Ottoman appeals court (known as majlis al-tadqiqat) located in the capital, San'a'. It originally had an Ottoman presiding judge and Yemeni associate judges, replicating the local pattern in Ibb. From San'a' appeals could be taken to the Sublime Porte in Istanbul. Appeal became deeply grafted onto Yemeni practice as a direct consequence of Points

Two and Three of the Treaty of Da'·'an. These provide for an appeals court (*mahkama istiʾnafiyya*), to be located in San'a' and staffed by a head judge and associate judges—all to be nominated by the imam and confirmed by the government.[20] The imamic appeals courts have a somewhat complicated subsequent history, involving a Ta'izz-based and sometimes more Shafi'i-oriented second branch. Soon after he took control of Lower Yemen from the Ottomans, Imam Yahya appointed 'Abd al-Rahman al-Haddad, the noted Shafi'i scholar from Ibb, to head the appeals court in Ta'izz.[21] Imam Yahya's son Ahmad, whose governorate seat and then capital as imam was in Ta'izz, operated with a branch (*shu'ba*) there and another in San'a'.[22]

Prior to the Ottoman period, however, there were neither multiple judges (in a single court) nor formal possibilities for appeal. The first of these innovations—like the Christian Trinity when viewed from the Muslim theological perspective—violated the essential oneness of the judicial presence, fracturing the unitary quality of the judge's face and voice in the *muwajaha* encounter. The second, the possibility of appeal, undercut the sanctity and finality of the judge's word, opening the door to continuing reinterpretation of decisions.

Problematic changes also occurred in the area of judicial writing. In Ottoman courts, judgment documents (*hukm*, pl. *ahkam*) were radically shortened.[23] The typical Yemeni style of judgment, spoken of as being "long and wide" (*tawil wa 'arid*), is apt to be a very lengthy (but quite narrow) rolled scroll made by joining together pieces of document paper. The separate parts in a judgment document are, from top to bottom, the claim and response (*da'wa wa ijaba*), the evidence section (*bayyinat*), the summary (*khulasa*), and the ruling (*jazm*). One feature of the preparation of such documents is distinctive: the first three sections usually were copied out by a court secretary, but the final ruling section, usually amounting to only a few lines, had to be in the handwriting of the judge himself, followed by his signature. Before copies of judgments are handed over to the two sides in a case, or before a judgment such as an execution is carried out, the text is "dictated" to the parties by the judge.

In such documents it was the evidence section that could balloon out of proportion in an effort to record all the verbatim testimony and quote from all the relevant documents. The Ottoman strategy was to shorten claims and counterclaims, often through rewording and condensing, and to record only a summary of the relevant evidence in the final document. It was a strategy, however, that violated the essential

purity of original words. The resistance to it might be understood as a
very minor version of the sort of outrage felt (in the 1940s) at the rumor
that adversaries had shortened the Quran (al-Maqbali 1986:67–68).
During my residence in Ibb in 1980, an Egyptian advisor attached to
the local courts was once again endeavoring to introduce a similar
reform: to reduce judgments "long and wide" to fit the single-page
format of new court registers.

IMAMIC JUDGES

According to the earliest Muslim sources, the Prophet's initial representatives to Yemen were sent as "judges." Thus ʿAli, later the fourth
caliph, is reported to have said, "The Prophet of God, May God's
Peace be upon Him, dispatched me to Yemen as a judge." At the
departure of Muʿadh bin Jabal, an exchange is supposed to have occurred in which the Prophet asked his emissary the famous question
"On what basis will you judge?"[24] Although the judgeship of the time
had yet to be differentiated and elaborated in the manner of the later
manuals of jurisprudence, the appointment of judges in the provinces
was a continuing theme in the exercise of authority.[25]

After the departure of the Ottomans, Ibb judges of the twentieth-
century imamate, appointed by Imams Yahya and Ahmad in the
period 1919 to 1962, were predominately Zaidis from Upper Yemen.
That this aspect of control of Lower Yemen was a political issue during
Zaidi rule is indicated by the line of questions posed to Ibb governor
Ismaʿil Basalama by the Syrian traveler al-ʿAzm.[26] Judges were appointed to district and subdistrict posts until 1946, when Ibb was made
a full province, formed from districts taken from the older provinces of
Taʿizz and Dhamar, at which time a judgeship of the province was
added. There was also a fourth local judgeship (known as *hakim al-
maqam*, lit. "judge of the seat") attached to the district officer and, later,
the governor.

The major exception to postings of northerners was a series of judges
appointed from the important al-Iryani "qadi" family, whose ancestral
home, Iryan, was located precisely at the meeting point of Shafiʿi and
Zaidi regions near the Sumara Pass. One contemporary member of the
family described the family's posture as a composite: Shafiʿi in ritual
matters and Zaidi in jurisprudence. Yahya b. Muhammad al-Iryani
was a distinguished scholar and Ibb district judge from 1919 [1337] to
1927 [1345].[27] To this extent Governor Basalama was accurate in his

response to his questioner that there were local men in the judgeships. After the Ibb post, Iryani retired briefly to his native Iryan to teach and give fatwas, but in 1930 he was appointed an associate judge of the appeal court in San'a', and later became the presiding judge of the first branch. He was a "second generation" student of al-Shawkani, since one of his teachers was the very distinguished al-'Amri, the first Yemeni presiding judge of the appeal court. Iryani was, in turn, the teacher of a number of men in Ibb during his tenure in the local judgeship, including the future mufti and Ibb judge Ahmad b. Muhammad al-Haddad. In addition to his accomplishments as a jurist, al-Iryani was a *hafiz*, one of those in his era who had memorized the entire Quran, and he is also noted for his poetry, some of which al-Akwa' (1980:300) characterizes as "nationalist." An independent and at times critical posture enabled the Iryanis to be among those intellectuals who were able to hold important positions under the imams and still make a smooth transition into leadership in the republican period. Two of Yahya b. Muhammad's sons, 'Abd al-Rahman b. Yahya[28] and Muhammad b. Yahya, both of whom had been judges in the greater Ibb region in the imamic period, were to become, respectively, president of the Republic (1967–1974) and presiding judge of the appeal court. Other Iryanis also served in Ibb both before and after 1962.[29]

According to the old administrative philosophy in Yemen, neither judges nor governors should be posted in their native districts. While it was normal for Zaidis to be sent anywhere in the imam's domain, Shafi'is under imamic rule could, at most, expect positions in Lower Yemen. Ahmad Muhammad al-Haddad's posting to the rural subdistrict of al-Mudhaykhira west of Ibb town fit this pattern. His post-Revolution appointment to the judgeship of the Ibb district, however, went directly against the old imamic practice. The only significant local exception to the rule during the imamic period involved the special case of the Ibb governor, Isma'il Basalama, who became district officer in the waning Ottoman years and retained the position under Imam Yahya.[30] Following this single exception, however, all subsequent Zaidi-period governors were northerners.

Lengthy postings could lead to permanent settling in the place of jurisdiction. Some judges, like others posted to Ibb during the earlier centuries of Zaidi rule, contracted local marriages for themselves and members of their family and acquired property, both of which entailed a continuing local rootedness. Others, however, remained somewhat aloof from Ibb society, living, for example, in rented houses for the duration of their tenures. Among the governors, al-ʿAbbas and Sayf al-Islam al-Hasan resided in the government seat, whereas al-Sayaghi married a number of local women and built a four-house compound as part of his wholesale transfer of residence to Ibb.

Despite some important exceptions in practice, there was in the imamic period a decided value placed upon the nonremoval of appointed officials who conducted themselves properly, which often led to lengthy tenures in the principal judicial posts. A number of Ibb judges actually died in office or shortly after retirement. According to the manuals, an imam's recognized capacity to remove or retire (ʿazl) judges is in fact meant to be limited. "The imam can remove a judge," al-Nawawi writes, "who has manifested a fault, or in the absence [of a fault], one who is better than he is, or is equivalent to him when his removal serves the general interest, such as in quieting sedition (fitna)."[31] After making this association between judges and fitna, al-Nawawi concludes with the sort of extremely concise, and weighty, turnaround phrases common in the manuals: wa-illa fa-la, literally "otherwise no." That is, the imam can remove a judge for the stated reasons, but otherwise must not. Proper or not, an order for removal should be implemented in any case, al-Nawawi continues. But a judge is not automatically retired or removed upon the death of the appointing imam.

In Yemen the preference for long postings is perhaps clearer with respect to Zaidi governors: the four who served in Ibb all remained in office about ten years.[32] The Zaidi ideal was in marked contrast to the rule under the Ottomans, who (prior to Ismaʿil Basalama in the final years) changed Ibb qaʾimmaqams every two years. Under the Republic, the turnover of local governors has been even more rapid than under the Ottomans. The (twentieth-century) Zaidi value placed on the nonremoval of officials as a hallmark of sound government is reflected in the treatment by the historian al-Wasiʿi of two contrasting imams of an earlier era, one considered exemplary, the other disastrous.[33] Thus Imam al-Mutawakkil Ahmad (d. 1815 [1231]) and "those before him" were noted for their practice of "appointing ministers of state (wazirs) and not retiring them until they were overtaken by death." As a result, "a minister attended to the affairs of state and the benefit of the people instead of looking to his own interests." The opposite was true of the succeeding imam, al-Mahdi ʿAbd Allah (d. 1850 [1267]), under whose chaotic rule (the "days of corruption" in Ibb) there were constant changes of officials. Each as a consequence "looked to his own interests rather than to those of the state" and "sought to amass wealth by any means possible." In the process, the state "got weaker every day." In the Ottoman Empire, the issue of the length of judicial tenure had once been viewed in a similar light. Originally held in perpetuity, judgeships in the empire were reduced to one-year tenures by the beginning of the eighteenth century. For Ottoman critics of that era such "frequent changings of office were seen to be the prime factor in the deterioration of the Ottoman judicial system and a cause of widespread corruption."[34] In Yemen, the long tenures valued by the imams would become, for the nationalist opposition, one of the policies indicative of corrupt rule. What had been appreciated as integral to a constancy and effectiveness of administration came to be seen as leading inevitably to the compromising of judges allowed to stay too long in one place.

It has been suggested that in contrast to an "impersonal" style of justice found in the West, Muslim justice was characterized by its "intimacy."[35] In patrimonially organized imamic Yemen, the local variety of judicial intimacy was just one expression of a highly personalized style of official life. The judiciary was not specialized: judges simply had more of the same training that governors and other educated individuals had received. Under the imams, the courts showed only the earliest signs of a specialization that would lead to such jurisdictions as a traffic court under the Republic. Intimacy was augmented by lengthy tenures: substantial time in a locale made it possible to acquire the sort of detailed background and awareness for knowing interchanges.

This sort of judicial identity was based on other related features: the unitary quality of the judicial presence, the open accessibility of the muwajaha encounter, the personal-residence setting for court, and the immediacy and (ideal) responsiveness of the process. By contrast, the sorts of changes introduced, first under the Ottomans and later under the Republic, all pointed in an "impersonal" direction: short tenures in office, limited dependence on local knowledge, plural judgeships and multivoiced majority rulings, a physical shift from open-air entranceways and residence sitting rooms to specialized public courtroom spaces, strict controls on access to the judge, and the elaboration of time-consuming procedural steps. More narrowly specialized in their training, competencies, and assigned jurisdictions, judicial personnel also became more interchangeable. In an emergent new perspective, the goal of impartiality was associated with impersonality, which was based on the primacy of the role rather than on the old primacy of the person.

CRITICAL TEXTS

Despite several administrative reshufflings, court reform did not get firmly under way in the Republic until the important legislation of 1979 (see chapter 3). In the 1960s, while the civil war raged in the northern highlands, unresolved legal disputes were piling up in Ibb. The response, as the appointment letter translated below demonstrates, was both old and new: the appointment of highly respected, shari'a-educated men to constitute a special "committee," or joint court, to handle difficult cases. In the absence of the requisite legislation, which was more than a decade away, the substance and tone of the letter are distinctly reminiscent of appointment letters for judges in the imamic era.[36] Mentions of ministry authority, legislated (*qanun*) law, and the republican government intertwine with a litany of older concerns about abuse and injustice.

> Yemen Arab Republic
> Ministry of Justice
> Office of Judicial Inspection

Date: 16-6-[19]67 A.D.
Equiv.: 7-3-[13]87 A.H.

In the Name of God, Merciful and Compassionate

In view of the heavy work load of the Court of Ibb Province, and the stalling of cases in it, and the numerous complaints (*shakwas*) received from the citizens at the Ministry of Justice, it has been decided to appoint the learned qadis 'Abd al-Hafiz al-Ghazzali, Muhammad bin Yahya al-Haddad and Muhammad Naji al-Wahhabi [to establish themselves in the provincial governorate] with their joint task being to settle cases concerning property, homicide, honor, and the "rights of God," and to protect ordinary people from losses and tyranny, and to treat disputants equally, and relieve the oppressed from his oppressor by means of the truth, and give succor to the troubled, and protect the lofty position occupied by adjudication, with consciousness of the great responsibility pertaining to it. And to avoid corruption, and apply that which is set down in the Book of God Almighty, and that which is found in the correct and clear Sunna—and that which has been decided by the Ministry of Justice as rulings of legislated shari'a and qanun law based on the Book of God and on the Sunna of the Prophet of God. And to order that which is right and to prohibit dangerous wrongs. And strengthen the community, and guide the ordinary people, and instruct all the people in their responsibilities to God and to the government of the Yemen Arab Republic, as concerns obedience and compliance. And

promote relations of goodwill and brotherliness and concord among the
citizenry, and generalize justice and ease for the population. And provide for the Shari'a of Muhammad its rightful place, as established by
God Almighty (may the Prophet be blessed). And avoid any obstruction
of access for the weak and the oppressed and the troubled, and forbid
those who would profit, and unscrupulous legal representatives, and
those of corrupt motives from gathering at the court to prey upon people.

The ministry has confidence that the aforementioned men will carry
out their responsibilities with fidelity and good faith as is in accord with
their characters.

It is understood that the provincial government has its own administrative responsibilities. The appointees are required to observe these and
work within them. As it sees fit, the Ministry will transfer cases that have
proved difficult to settle for the judges of the subdistricts and districts.
The hope is that the court will undertake its duties in the most resolute
way, and God is responsible for causing all to undertake what is required
toward the shari'a of God and toward the community. Please accept our
wishes for good luck and success.

'Ali Nu'man
[signature and seal]
Deputy Minister, Ministry of Justice

An entirely different register of critique is represented by publicly
performed skits, such as "Education in the Old Days," which opens
chapter 5. The following translation is of a skit written by the local
master of the art, a primary-school principal named Muhammad Zain
al-'Awdi, who was mentioned earlier as the Ibb orphan who studied
Zaidi jurisprudence on an imamic government stipend. An active and
imaginative man, al-'Awdi has written numerous skits that go back to
the early days of the Revolution. As a teacher he was instrumental in
introducing curriculum reforms into new post-Revolution Ibb schools.

Skits are always newly created for particular events, which become
the occasions for their only performance. The event for this skit was
the first anniversary of the 1974 Correction Movement initiated by
Ibrahim al-Hamdi, then the Yemeni head of state. Just as the skit
presented earlier is reminiscent of the famous account of the Quranic
schoolmaster in the memoirs of Egyptian writer Taha Hussein (1981),
so this skit recalls Tawfiq al-Hakim's novel *The Maze of Justice* (1989),
which concerns a prosecutor in a rural district. As in the novel, the skit's
critique is biting but humorous, referring to specific and well-known
corrupt practices in Yemeni shari'a courts. Although the title refers to

pre-1974 circumstances, the Jewish characters of Scene Two place the objectionable behaviors (by Muslims) farther back in time. A blunt concluding narration, however, assures that the contemporary relevance of the message is not lost.

"The Courts Before the Correction Movement"

Scene One: The judge seated on floor cushions with qat before him and his mouth full. The water pipe mouthpiece is in his left hand as he smokes; his right hand rests on his upright knee. Soldiers are to his right and left.
[Two men enter.]

—[one of them]: Greetings sir, my brother here and I each have half of a piece of land and between us there is a boundary marker. Yesterday my brother here displaced the boundary marker from its rightful position and moved it a foot into my property.

—[the other]: Don't believe him, sir, the only one who moved anything was him, he took a foot of my property.

—We can pledge, me and you, fifty-fifty, to have the Judge come out to measure what's mine and what's yours and find the extra foot.

—Perfect, that's it, the Judge will come out and God's will be done. When will you come, sir?

—[Judge]: Tomorrow, God willing.

—God willing. [They leave, and soon they encounter a mutual friend from the village.]

—Hey, what have you two been doing?

—[one of them]: We have asked the Judge to come between us and measure and give a judgment, with his expenses divided equally between us.

—Get hold of yourselves, the way (to your place) is by the foot, and each foot is two riyals. You're going to waste two thousand. You're crazy and that's all.

—It doesn't matter if we waste money. Better than being wronged.

—Hey, listen, you would be much happier if you agreed to settle between yourselves for nothing and avoid the expenses.

—How's that?

—I'll go out and take a look at the original place of the boundary marker and its place now, and we'll divide the foot in half. You should act as brothers, whereas shari'a [proceedings] only create among you enemies and killing.

—That's good advice, and God is our advisor.

—So, okay, go back to the Judge and tell him, "We have settled, so there is no reason any more for your coming."

—Let's go, brother!

[Before the Judge]

—[one of them]: Sir, we have agreed and settled, so you don't have to come out.

—Who settled the matter for you?

—Someone from our village.

—Who is this evil one, son of an evil one, who would involve himself in the Shari'a of God?!

—Ah . . . , ah . . . , we settled for ourselves, sir. So you won't have to come.

—It's not so easy. They say don't come—but the heart has already traveled. Muhammad, saddle the mule!

—There is no power and no strength save in God! [They leave, forlorn.]

—[Their friend]: So what happened, did you convince the Judge or not?

—No.

—Why not?

—Because he said "the heart" had already traveled.

—Go back to him and give him fifty riyals, and tell him this is the fee for the heart.

—[returning to the Judge] Sir, here's fifty riyals fee for the heart, so you won't come.

—[Judge]: And fifty riyals fee of the soldiers.

—Here's fifty riyals for the soldiers.

—And fifty riyals for the fee of the mule.

—What, even the mule's heart traveled?

—Yes, and fifty riyals fee for the assistants.

—Why, this is too much, how do the functionaries get dragged in? Only cursed ones would have to pay into government hands just for the adjusting of turban coils.

—Pay, and I don't ever want to see you again.

Scene Two

—[Advocate]: Sir, yesterday Salim Hayyim died.

—[Judge]: Who's that, the one who works in silver?

—Yes.

—Hmm... wealthy by God. Hey, get up, you and the soldier go and bring his two sons in and I'll divide his estate.

—They've already divided it, sir.

—Impossible, according to what religion did they do the division. Come on, get up, bring them in now.

[A short time later]

—[Sons of the Jew]: Yes sir, what can we do for you?

—Nothing, except that we asked you to come so we can divide for you the estate of your father.

—We have divided it, sir, may God protect you.

—How's that? According to what community and what religion. Don't you know that the government that governs you is an Islamic government?

—Yes, sir, we divided according to the Islamic shari'a, riyal by riyal, rug by rug, water pipe by water pipe, and acre by acre.

—That's not the way it is. The shari'a of Muhammad requires appearance, and that appearance is before the courts where I will divide for you justly.

—You are welcome to do so, sir.

[The second day they appear in court and with them they brought their money.]

—Divide the money into three parts.

—But we are only two, sir, why should it be divided into three?

—The third is the fee of the Judge, Jew, understand or not?

—That's not permitted to you by God, sir.

—It's required according to an imamic order.

—Have fear of God, sir, that's oppressive.

—[the second son]: Shut up my brother, we should consider that the deceased left three.

[narrator]: This is how the shari'a was in former times, but up to the present we don't see a great difference, except for some of the judges. As for the others, they disgrace the reputation of the Republic, but the People are watching them.

PART IV

Inscription

CHAPTER 11

Evidence of the Word

O believers, when you contract a debt
one upon another for a stated term,
write it down, and let a writer
write it down between you justly,
and let not any writer refuse
to write it down, as God taught him;
so let him write, and let the debtor
dictate, and let him fear God his Lord
and not diminish aught of it. And if
the debtor be a fool, or weak, or unable
to dictate himself, then let his guardian
dictate justly. And call in to witness
two witnesses, men; or if the two
be not men, then one man and two women,
such witnesses as you approve of,
that if one of the two women errs
the other will remind her; and let the witnesses
not refuse, whenever they are summoned.
And be not loth to write it down,
whether it be small or great, with its term;
that is more equitable in God's sight,
more upright for testimony, and likelier
that you will not be in doubt. Unless it be
merchandise present that you give and take
between you; then it shall be no fault in you
if you do not write it down. And take witnesses
when you are trafficking one with another.
And let not either writer or witness be
pressed; or if you do, that is ungodliness in you.
And fear God; God teaches you, and God has
    knowledge of everything.
And if you are upon a journey, and
you do not find a writer, then a pledge
in hand. But if one of you trusts another,
let him who is trusted deliver his trust,
and let him fear God his Lord. And do not
conceal the testimony; whoso conceals it,

> *his heart is sinful; and God has knowledge of*
>   *the things you do.*
> *To God belongs all that is in the heavens and*
> *earth. Whether you publish what is in your hearts*
> *or hide it, God shall make reckoning with you*
> *for it. He will forgive whom He will,*
> *and chastise whom He will; God is powerful*
>   *over everything.*
> QURAN (2:282–84, TRANS. ARBERRY 1955:70–71)

One of the most revealing expressions of the relationship between the spoken and the written word concerns the use of documents and the rules of evidence. Supplemented by other, less pointed passages, the Quranic text quoted above is the principal source for approved usage of documents. There are also hadiths indicating that the Prophet himself used written legal texts. Among them is one in which the Prophet is reported to have used a document in connection with a sale in which he was the buyer. The gist of the hadith is that a Companion of the Prophet shows a document (*kitab*) that the Prophet either wrote himself or had written to embody his purchase of a slave from the Companion. Together with the Quranic verses, this hadith is among those cited by al-Tahawi (Wakin 1972:5 [Arabic text]), a jurist of the ninth and tenth centuries who was deeply concerned with the status of written legal instruments.

The concern of such scholars as al-Tahawi stemmed from an interesting contradiction. Legal documents had been integral to the conduct of affairs prior to the rise of Islam, but although they continued to be widely and routinely used in the Muslim era, their evidential value was not established in doctrine. The manuals do envision witnessing acts associated with the preparation of written instruments, as in the quoted Quranic text, but they do not take such further steps as requiring documentation for specific types of undertakings[1] or recognizing the value of witnessed documents as evidence in court proceedings. "Bearing witness (*tahammul al-shahada*) is a collective responsibility (*fard kifaya*)," al-Nawawi states, "in marriage, and also in acknowledgments, financial transactions and the writing of documents."[2] While witnessing in general is identified as a key social duty, documents so witnessed were not constitutive: "Legal obligations exist whether or not they are spelled out in the documents" (Wakin 1972:30).[3] In al-Nawawi's sections on evidence and court procedure, the ruling assumption is that evidence is oral, mainly taking the form of spoken testimony (plus confession and oath). Deprived of the doctrinal legitimation that would render them admissible in court actions, yet considered crucial to the everyday conduct of affairs, legal documents remained "ambiguous" (Wakin 1972:4).

Ordinary contracts of sale, lease, debt, credit, loan, and so forth, the most mundane of all legal writings, raise issues, by now familiar, surrounding the relationship of the spoken and the written. A structural tension in the sphere of evidence between testimony and text, resulting in a decisive but unstable privileging of the former, is a further very specific instance of the wider valuation of the unique authority of the spoken word. Within the specialized domain of evidence, the unity and certainty, Derrida would say the embodiment of "presence," of the testifying human witness, stood opposed to the dangerously open interpretability, and the human absence and alienation of the written text. The particular transition from speech to writing that occurred in the creation of legal documents carried a trace of the debilitating general stigma associated with the move from the divine to the human.

Al-Tahawi, a Hanafi by school, was one of a number of distinguished jurists who authored works in what became known as the *shurut* (lit. "stipulations") literature. Cognizant of the gap that existed between the thrust of the formal-evidence doctrine and the ongoing, widespread use of legal documents in practice, scholars such as al-Tahawi developed formularies, or practical guides for notaries. An even earlier guide is attributed to al-Shafi'i, although the later jurists of his school would be the most reluctant of the four in giving any sort of formal recognition to documents.[4] Containing model document texts for the various types of contracts (cf. Wakin 1972), the *shurut* works might be seen as direct subversions of the formal rules of evidence, although the works and their authors were esteemed rather than condemned. Many jurists managed to make contributions on both sides of the issue, writing at times within the constraints of *shari'a* doctrine, at other times addressing the diametrically opposed requirements of necessity.

This dual approach to the question of legal instruments persisted down to the period of modernist legislation in all of the schools of Islamic law except one, the Maliki school of North Africa. There the institution of the precertified, "reliable witness" was successfully grafted by jurists onto that of the notarial profession, making possible what

Tyan (1959:84) has characterized as the "triumph" of the legal document as formally admitted evidence. Elsewhere, it was not until the late-nineteenth-century promulgation of the Ottoman *Majalla* (Art. 1736) that legal documents were given cautious recognition.

Under Ottoman rule in Yemen, court registration of legal documents was introduced in the main towns. New to the highlands, it was a practice consonant with the changed attitude of the *Majalla*. In addition to formally legitimizing the use of documentation, court registration also involved the key innovation of providing state backing for private acts. With imamic rule in 1918, however, there was a return to older documentary practices, but a similar type of registration was reintroduced following the Revolution of 1962.

THE PRESENT WITNESS

In the commentary by al-Ghazzi, the section on evidence rules opens with a brief discussion of words derived from the sh–h–d root, used in connection with the activity of witnessing. "Witnesses" (*shuhud*, sing. *shahid*) are initially defined as "those present" (*al-hudur*).[5] This fundamental quality of presence actually has two aspects: witnessing involves both presence at the word or deed borne witness to and presence at the moment of the process between the adversaries before the judge. In line with the ideal structure of all such *muwajaha* encounters, the witness must have physically seen or heard, according to the nature of the thing witnessed. Witnessing is an activity grounded in the immediacy and authenticity of the senses. Following this logic, the deaf can testify to seen acts, and the blind to heard ones. A blind person's testimony is accepted provided an individual "makes a statement acknowledging something into his ear and then accompanies him until he gives it as testimony before the judge."[6] On the judge's side, evidence is commonly characterized (as in Western systems) as "heard."[7]

Witnesses "carry" testimony, ideally embodying (memorizing) the evidence involved securely within themselves from the moment of its original apprehension to the moment of its communication to the court. The same terminology (from the root h–m–l) is applied to bearing testimony, the Quran, and academic knowledge, including hadiths. Bearing witness, as was noted earlier, is one of the formal collective obligations of social life. This obligation is also expressed in the quoted verses from the Quran (2:282): "and let the witnesses not refuse, whenever they are summoned." As with learning in the academic context, however, there are two sides to witnessing, the original receipt of information and its later transmission to others. This last, the obligation to give evidence, is analogous to the obligation to give of knowledge acquired; the same verb (k–t–m: to conceal, hide, keep silent, hold one's tongue) is used to refer to the equivalent faults of withholding testimony and not passing on knowledge.[8] "And do not conceal the testimony; who so conceals it, his heart is sinful" (2:283).

Witnessing is implicitly construed on a recitational model related to the acquisition/transmission format of formal learning. It represents a (usually) short-term, horizontal, and single-node version of the long-term, vertical, and multiple-node transmission of academic knowledge or hadiths. Witnessing pertains to the contemporary bonds of a social community; knowledge and hadiths to the historical links of genealogy. The theory of witnessing also contains an analytic concern for the qualities of the human conveyers that directly parallels the "science of men" on which the theory of hadith evaluation is based.[9] The same specific critical method of *jarh wa ta'dil* ("disparaging and declaring trustworthy")[10] is applied to both witnesses and relayers of hadiths. The accuracy of reports about words or deeds, whether of the Prophet or of an ordinary contemporary individual, depends on ascertaining the appropriately trustworthy and upright character (the *'adala*) of the human medium. The characteristic problems—fabrications of hadiths and false testimony—represent equivalent adulterations in the transmission of authoritative truth.

The manual treatment of the special case of "testimony on/about testimony" (*al-shahada 'ala al-shahada*) is instructive. Unlike Anglo-American "hearsay" evidence (French, "oui-dire"), which is generally deemed untrustworthy and lacking in evidential value, certain types of carefully defined instances of valid evidence transmission between trustworthy primary and secondary witnesses are permitted. One example al-Nawawi gives is when a witness says to another, "I am a witness concerning such and such and I make you a witness (*ushhiduka*, lit. 'I en-witness you')."[11] The mechanism involved here is based on a refined and ideal form of direct, human-to-human verbal transmission. Predicated on the justness of the two individuals, and on the face-to-face quality of their encounter, this is an evidential version of the crucial linkage of *isnad*, the essential uninterrupted "chain" joining and guaranteeing the accuracy of the human transmission of hadiths. A second example of such testimony about another's testimony having validity concerns evidence heard as it was given under oath before a judge.

Validity in this instance is anchored in the privileged circumstances of the muwajaha encounter itself. Beyond such pure instances, the evidence of secondary witnesses becomes suspect and inadmissible. The vocabulary of "original" and "secondary" (*asl* and *far'*), used for these two categories of witnesses, echoes the textual relation of original (Quran, Sunna) versus supplement (*fiqh* jurisprudence).

Aside from the general requirement of witness probity, rules against testifying by interested parties (enemies, relatives) and warnings to watch out for individuals who seem either gullible or overly anxious to testify, a number of precautions are meant to further guarantee the purity of words spoken in the judicial session.[12] For example, a judge is forbidden to suborn, harass, or confuse an individual making statements. Likewise, the judge should refrain from verbal assistance, such as providing appropriate wording or suggesting a type of plea. To assure the integrity and fullness of an individual's words, questioning by the judge should occur only after a statement is complete. Once uttered, a claim or testimony can be retracted only under strict conditions. The legal-ritual purity of evidence transmission is couched in a sworn (*shahada*) formula, "I bear witness to God" (*ashhadu lillah*), which is also the opening of the fundamental "testimony of the faith" (also *shahada*) by which Muslims bear witness to the uniqueness of God and the status of Muhammad as His Prophet. On the receiving end, and with regard to his active part in the judicial encounter, it is understood that the complete and attentive presence of the judge may be impaired by disruptive physical states (extremes of anger, hunger, satiety, thirst, sexual desire, illness, need to urinate or defecate, sleepiness, and being hot or cold).[13]

Ideally, the tribunal is seen as a meeting of a judge and opponents who are ordinary individuals; no specialized speakers, such as the articulate and court-wise "shari'a representatives" who frequently appear in Ibb,[14] are envisioned. The Shafi'i evidence doctrine operates according to a marketplace theory of free circulation of witnesses, and thus of words.[15] Just as restraints on trade—monopolies, hoarding, unfair advantage, illegal weights, and so forth—are combatted in economic provisions of the jurisprudence, so the proper functioning of the market for truth depends on eliminating barriers to the free flow of testimony. In contrast to the institution of the prerecognized "reliable witness," which came to dominate proceedings in many large Middle Eastern towns,[16] and which evolved into the certified notary of the Malikis, is al-Nawawi's dictum "It is forbidden to rely only on designated witnesses to the exclusion of others."[17]

THE CHASTITY OF DOCUMENTS

Replicating in court a pattern found in the sphere of instruction and elsewhere, an oral core is complemented by a written surround. As in instruction, where the recitational forms of *darasa* were supplemented by reading and writing, an ideal, oral-testimony form of evidence is situated at the center of court processes, which in actuality relied heavily on the services of the written word. Together with orally expressed claims and responses, the recitational *shahada* (testimony) represented the key theoretical source text of formal judicial procedure, the basic *matn* subjected to the *sharh* of judicial interpretation. Given this theoretical emphasis, one that was reinforced by the weight of an entire system of such emphases, it becomes clear why legal documents had to be written out of the evidence doctrine. As was noted earlier, the manuals discuss witnessing support for documents, but they do not consider documents to be potential evidence. Various other court-related writings are mentioned in the manuals, however, and these provide an instructive entrée into the distinctive written environment of the court.

It is perhaps appropriately enigmatic to cite here Abu Shuja''s fourteenth requirement for the post of judge, namely, that the candidate must be able to write (*an yakun katiban*), together with the reverse view, inserted immediately thereafter by his commentator. Al-Ghazzi recognizes that the opinion that a judge should be able to write is "sound," but then goes on to say that the "more correct [doctrine] is the opposite." Al-Nawawi is silent on this detail, except for what might be implied in his requirement of "the Arab tongue, [both] in formal language and grammar."[18] That a judge should be assumed to have the capacity to write would seem to fit both the practical circumstances of his academic training and the requirements of his post, unless a truly oral transmission of knowledge and conduct of court were possible.

Court is otherwise portrayed in the manuals as a place of paperwork: transcripts and records are made of proceedings, and judicial memoranda, correspondence, summonses with seals and judgment documentation are produced, copied, and archived.[19] As part of his court staff, a judge should have a secretary, a *katib* (a "writer"). In contrast to the judge himself, this functionary's job description involves an unambiguous capacity to write: "It is required that he be a Muslim, just, and knowledgeable in the writing of transcripts and records; desirable also are [knowledge of] jurisprudence, abundant intelligence, and excellent script (*khatt*)."[20]

If, in many routine respects, the shari'a court of the manuals seems the familiar, document-handling institution one might expect, in turning to some further details of its documentary practice one reencounters the characteristic precautions associated with writing. An example is judge-to-judge correspondence. Abu Shuja' says, "A writing (*kitab*) from a judge to another judge concerning rulings is not accepted [is not to be relied upon] except after the testimony of two witnesses [who] bear witness concerning what is in it."[21] The two individuals, the commentator adds, must bear witness to the document's contents both at the creation of the document by the writing judge and then again before the judge written to. Al-Ghazzi takes the opportunity here to provide an example of what such a document might look like, making a digression in the mode of the *shurut* authors. His model document text inserted at this point in the commentary concerns a claim and a resultant judgment in the first judge's jurisdiction against an absent party (*gha'ib*),[22] resident in the second judge's jurisdiction. Two pairs of witnesses are involved.

> In the Name of God, the Merciful and Compassionate. Present before us, may God forgive us and you, is so-and-so. He made a claim against so-and-so, [who is] absent [and] resident in your district, concerning such and such a thing. He brought forward two witnesses, they are so-and-so and so-and-so; their probity was established before me. I had the claimant swear an oath and [then] I ruled in his favor for the amount. I had so-and-so and so-and-so witness the document.[23]

An essential stipulation is connected with these last-mentioned individuals, the "document witnesses." Al-Ghazzi writes that "their justness must become apparent before the judge written to"; an original acceptance by the writing judge does not suffice. Mobile witnesses, who travel with the text (and whose probity must be so manifest, so little context-dependent, as to be apparent even in districts where they are not known), are the ultimate conveyers of truth. Such traveling witnesses also figure in another type of writing, a judge's appointment letter from the imam.[24] When the imam writes to the appointee, two witnesses must witness the letter (*kitab*) and then "go out with him to the district." An ordinary, unaccompanied letter is specifically ruled out.

Remembering, the presence of the memory to itself, is the greatest authority. Al-Nawawi writes concerning the judge that "if he sees a document (*waraqa*) containing his judgment or his certificate . . . he should not implement it . . . until he remembers." Neither should witnesses ordinarily depend on the prompting of a document. There are contested opinions, however, that maintain that certain types of documents can be given limited weight as reminders. These include a "protected document" (*waraqa masuna*), one "well guarded," "chaste," one with virtue intact because it has been kept in an archive and not allowed to circulate. Certain types of oaths can be made, based on one's personal writing or that of one's father; others concerning inheritance rights may be made by an heir on the basis of a writing of the legator, "if one is confident of his script and of his sincerity." Al-Nawawi concludes this section by holding for the "permissibility of the relating of speech (*riwayat al-hadith*) on the basis of a writing securely kept (*mahfuz*) in one's possession."[25] A text can support *riwaya*, oral transmission, if one can relate to it as one's own proper writing or through the bonds of written kinship, and if it is kept well guarded at home and not permitted to be loose in the world.

Texts "loose" in the world are, like *jahil* individuals, in trouble and troublesome. Socrates observed (in *Phaedrus*) that unlike its "parent," which is "living speech,"

> once a thing is put in writing, the composition, whatever it may be, drifts all over the place, getting into the hands not only of those who understand it, but equally those who have no business with it; it doesn't know how to address the right people, and not address the wrong. And when it is ill-treated and unfairly abused it always needs its parent to come to its help, being unable to defend or help itself. (Plato 1952:158)

TEMPTATION OF THE PEN

Under Zaidi imams, guidance on certain selected points of law was exercised through personal but authoritative interpretive opinions (*ikhtiyarat, ijtihadat*). Among the twenty-two opinions published in this century by Imam Yahya Hamid al-Din, one concerns the old problem of legal documents. Originally articulated by the imam as concrete rules, and kept as a reference list at the Appeal Court,[26] the collection of imamic opinions was also rendered (by another scholar or scholars) into the form of a poem, which had to be accepted by the imam as an accurate rendering of his views. When the imam accepted the formulation of the poem he also authorized the preparation of a more extensive prose commentary based on it. The relevant section of this multi-authored text (published as al-Shamahi A.H. 1356 [1937]:31–33) begins with two lines of poetry in which the principle of the imamic position concerning the status of documents is stated. It is this condensed poetic statement that is elaborated upon in the commentary: "The evidence of just writing, we know, is accepted; / It is humanly transmitted, in an unbroken chain." This acceptance of legal documents as evidence hinges on the key term "just" (*'adl*), which directly echoes the wording of the Quranic passages "and let a writer write it down between you justly" and "let his guardian dictate justly." *'Adl* also refers to a just person, and in the formulation *shahid al-'adl* means a "just witness," one whose testimony is accepted as evidence. By extension, especially in Maliki North Africa but elsewhere as well, an *'adil* was a notary. The second line of the poem employs words (*mu'an'an*, "orally transmitted," and *musalsal*, "linked in a chain") that directly invoke the science of hadith. Through this use of hadith terminology, the evidence contained in written form is characterized as "handed down" or transmitted via a continuous human "chain" in a manner that is asserted to be analogous to an authentic and, therefore, legally binding hadith. There is an attempt to overcome the alienation of writing, the break it causes in the human transmission of truth, by grafting onto it the established theory of the chain of just transmitters.

The commentary itself begins with a historical eulogy of *khatt* ("script" or "writing"):

> Writing is one of the pillars of human undertakings (*mu'amalat*), one of the ways of human communication. It is one of the two tongues; in fact, it is the more sublime. With it traditions are conserved; with it the circumstances, customs and history of earlier generations are known; with it laws and jurists are learned about. It is the most important medium, the greatest mediator between those who are living and those who have passed away. Prophets utilized it in the dissemination of their messages to the blacks and the whites, to those near and far. With it they raised their protests against the kings, including caesars and khosraus; with its proclamations they called the nations, Arab and foreign, until the Truth became clear and God's order appeared.

Characterized as "one of the two tongues,"[27] writing is assimilated to speech and yet differentiated from it. Writing stands "between"; it is a "medium" and a "mediator" linking, as in an unbroken chain, the past and the present, the dead and the living. The commentator goes on to describe the Muslim appropriation of writing, moving from the pre-Islamic period (*al-jahiliyya*) to the Islamic era:

> As they embraced the religion, the pious generation of Companions and Followers took it on, rendering it a Muslim practice. Using it they

delivered their *fatwas*; into its texts [*mutun*, pl. of *matn*] went their intellectual disciplines; on its wings their arguments took flight; on its evidential
meanings were built their legal principles, while at the same time they
used it to settle their cases. They regarded writing as their safeguard for
what is uttered by the lips, enunciated in the eloquent sessions of legal
interpretation, and articulated as assembly addresses on traditions and
proofs.

Writing is a "safeguard," it permits the preservation of life, memory,
speech, event; and yet, as becomes apparent later, it harbors within a
separation and a threat of falsehood. There was a recognized fear of
"loss" without writing.[28] As a protection against death, however, writing was itself predicated upon a kind of death. It is both a remedy and
a poison. The evidence for the role and general importance of writing,
according to the commentator, is strong:

> The Sunna on this is abundant, and the hadiths agree and are numerous;
> they are without condition limiting the breadth of support for it, without
> restriction regarding the influence of its evidence.

The writer (*katib*) and his writing (*khatt*, *kitaba*, *rasm*) then are associated and equated with the witness and the oral activities of giving
dictation and testimony:

> As for the science of the writer and his character, he is among those of
> cautious procedure and justness. If we know his writing with certainty,
> then it is just as we take his dictation or as we value his testimony that
> we take and value what comes to us as his document and his writing.
> There is no difference between them.

This formulation of an identity between writer and the dictating
teacher or testifying witness is ideal and yet duplicitous, especially in
view of what the commentator is about to say. The text begins here
to deconstruct itself as the commentator presents opposing positions
which, together, serve to define the problematic of legal writings.

> The views of scholars are divergent concerning the reliance upon the
> judgment and contract documents [lit. "sale documents" (*basa'ir*, sing.
> *basira*)] of judges and notaries. One group holds that they are absolutely
> unreliable, for the reason that writing leads to the potentiality of play,
> and the temptation of pens and geniuses, in the domain of composition
> and practice. It [writing] is therefore weak with respect to its value, aside
> from its positive qualities, in establishing legal possession and other
> matters. Another group holds for the necessity of valuing it [writing],
> and for the reliance upon it without restriction.

An opposition is now fully opened: writing that earlier served as a vital "safeguard" here also becomes something dangerously open to "play" and "temptation." The two contrary positions constituted for the sake of the argument are now subjected to criticism.

> In both of these two points of view there is immoderation and negligence. And the deleterious effect in the realm of justice is great, resulting in the spoilation and squandering of wealth. The two positions may be refuted. As for him who has said it is absolutely wrong to accept documents, the manifest position of the Sunna, and its clarity and concreteness, already mentioned, refute him and defeat him. As for his mentioned reasoning that assumes the potentiality in writing of play and temptation, etc., the reason is ailing, and the potential is distant. It is nothing but the creating of doubt, since a potentiality does not dislodge the manifest and its meaning. As for the falseness of the position of him who holds for the valuation of documents without restraint, this is obvious. Because if the door of unlimited acceptance of them were opened, the wealth of the community would be lost and people's possessions would be removed from the permanence and security of their hands. In this position there is immoderation and a disdain for principles, because any claimant can make for himself what he wants in the way of documents, proceeding with craft and skill in reproducing the papers he thinks will advance his circumstances.

In good dialectical fashion, the constitution, and then refutation, of opposed positions opens the argument space for a resolution through the synthesis of the imam's interpretive opinion.

> Therefore the Commander of the Faithful, may God protect him, has taken a position more just than the two positions. It amounts to a middle position, as was indicated in the lines of poetry, and that is that it is absolutely necessary in the reliance upon writing to have knowledge of its writer and his character and his justness, and of the fact that the writing to be relied upon is his writing; or to have knowledge that the writing in question is well known among the old writings for which there is no suspicion of falsehood or forgery. If we were to give up the utilization of such documents it would entail the loss of rights and properties whose (sole) records these old documents are, their writers unknown and unknowable. This ascertainment is entrusted to the jurisdiction of the judge. He is required to undertake a thorough examination to gain knowledge of the locally prominent writings and documents. With detailed inspection and enlightened thought he must distinguish among the writings, and know the valid ones from the false ones. For the practitioners of forgery are skilled in imitation and cleverness in ren-

dering documents for presentation and copying them in the guise of scripts of individuals who can be trusted. What is required is the examination of the script and (the finding) that it pertains to one of those individuals who can be relied on and trusted. This is what accords with the spirit of the shari'a, and what is called for to maintain order and protect civilization. This opinion finds its greatest legal support in the thrust of the Sunna of Muhammad.

The threat of misrepresentation through documents can hardly be considered alleviated by the formulation of this imamic opinion. Writing is addressed with a mix of respect and mistrust; writings remain both indispensable and dangerous. There is just writing and there is false writing, but it is the latter that has prompted this discourse. False writing redoubles the already problematic status of writing: false writing is to just writing as writing in general is to speech. Forgery wears a guise of truth.

The solution proposed for the use of documents rests heavily on knowing—of men by men. The two mandated forms of guarantee are, first, that found in the science of hadith where "accepting the hadith means knowing the men," and second, the critical capacity of the judge to assess the triple link between writing, writer, and legitimate intent. Such guarantees imply the long-term judicial tenures common under the imams.

As articulated in this commentary, the problematic of legal documents has a feature that distinguishes it from the situation of writing in most other domains and genres. The documentary transition from speech to writing is twofold: it involves both the representation of a verbally constituted human contractual undertaking in the form of the document text, and the representation of the legitimizing act of the human notary-witness in the form of his handwriting. There is a double process of representation, in both "his document and his writing," with the worth of the former subordinate to that of the latter. Script, it is assumed, conveys (as precisely as a fingerprint) the person, whether just or forger; the mark of the pen transmits the qualities of the human witness. While it may be difficult, it is not impossible to distinguish the mark of the just writer from the mark of the forger. This sort of double connection between calligraphy and character is not at issue, for example, in the more anonymous identity of the manuscript copyist. The power and mystery of the legal document resides in the nature of writing as human signature.

In the recent legislation of the Yemen Arab Republic,[29] however, a template is provided for a new world of document writing, one in which the weight of authority is shifted from the notary to the state. The legislation embodies a local version of the "triumph" of the legal document as acceptable evidence. Accordingly, "writing" (*al-kitaba*) takes its place (after testimony and oral acknowledgment) as the third of eight modes of "shari'a proof" (Art. 33). This resolution, in legislative theory at least, of the old problem of legal documents is part of the thoroughgoing reconceptualization of the shari'a itself. Two categories of documentary form are identified (Arts. 118–43): "official writings" (*muharrarat rasmiyya*) and "customary writings" (*muharrarat 'urfiyya*).

Both are new conceptions. The first represents the design of a type of secure instrument required by a contemporary capitalist society, in which the state, through the authorizing signature of an official (such as a court functionary), backs a standardized text. Under the direct colonial influence of the British, this transformation occurred years earlier in nearby Lahj.[30] According to the new legislation, documentary evidence really refers to this type of "official" document. In the case of sale documents, the result is an instrument approximating a Western deed. The second, the "customary" document, is a new incarnation of the old legal document. It issues from "ordinary people" (Art. 120) and can be treated as "official" once the judge has satisfied himself (along the lines suggested earlier by Imam Yahya) as to its authenticity. The "customary" document is actually broken down into three separate subtypes (Art. 124), only the third of which represents the centuries-old standard. Unlike the first two subtypes, which envision parties to the agreement preparing and signing, or at least signing, their own documents, the third subtype alone is the classic form: a document prepared privately by a notary and signed by him (and sometimes other witnesses), but not signed by the parties. In the legislative text (Art. 127) concerned with this venerable old genre of document, there is a clear echo of a former problem and a former solution:

> If the customary document is written in the handwriting of an "other" (*al-ghayr*), and is unsigned by the party, it requires witnesses for its contents to be accepted, except if the writer of the document has a reputation for justness and reliability and good conduct, and if his handwriting is known to the judge because of its [local] renown, or if he acknowledges before the judge that he is the writer of the document and bears witness to the accuracy of its contents, then it is permissible to accept the document's contents.

THE CONSUMPTION OF TEXTS

It would be difficult to overstate the high regard ordinary Yemenis have for legal documents.[31] People care for and protect their own papers as the most vital of personal effects. Held in private hands, documents are folded or rolled into narrow scrolls, placed in individual protective tubes or tied together in bunches, and then stored in cloth bundles or in wooden chests. In this originally agrarian society, the basic property documents pertain to land and buildings. These include the two main types of instruments of private ownership, namely, sale/ purchase contracts and inheritance documents; separate testaments for property held as endowments; leases, which are the basic instruments associated with the exploitation of both private and endowment prop- erties; and related fatwas, judgments, or settlements. Associated with every one of the thousands of individually named terraces that climb the mountainsides and fan out across valley bottoms in the Ibb hinter- land are one or more such legal texts.

In times of turmoil in the town, people sent their documents out to secure locations in the countryside for safekeeping. In its long history Ibb has been plundered many times, and personal documents were often either lost or destroyed. In an account of a raid that occurred in 1708, for example, the destruction of property documents is specifically mentioned.[32] When such disasters befell the town, members of the community gathered afterward at the judge's house to remake their documents. Because of their value, documents are also stolen.[33] In contrast to the equivocal treatment of such writings in the manuals and the imamic opinion, a more straightforward attitude prevailed in everyday contexts. Sound documents are known to have considerable legal weight: they decisively demonstrate ownership rights and are brought forward to that end in transactions and in disputes or court cases.[34]

Some people fear having personal documents taken away from them when they must be examined in a dispute. An extreme example of this fear's being realized concerns a modest cultivator who endeavored to assert an ownership right to a piece of property in conflict with a powerful local shaykh. In a meeting between the two, the cultivator brought out the document in question as proof of his ownership. The shaykh proceeded to extinguish the man's right in an unusual manner: he ate the document. As a precaution, intermediaries are used. These are people to whom documents may be revealed in security or who can carry copies of documents to show to an official or adversary. One of the most common disputing ploys is to say that someone "has documents" supporting his contentions. It is understood that if such documents do in fact exist, they may not be brought into play until the last moment. The possibilities for bluffing are similar to those in a card game. Withholding documents is a frequently used and effective disputing stratagem. In court, a claimant will either present documents he holds or bring witnesses to the effect that the defendant has the relevant documents.

If an individual's personal documents are not in his or her possession, other people may be holding them. Marriage gives rise to crisscrossing inheritance and endowment-share claims that are frequently the subject of dispute. An expression of this on the documentary level is a precautionary practice whereby husbands and wives keep their personal documents separate. In theory, there is no mingling of assets between a husband and wife, although if the relationship is strong, and especially if there are children, household finances are usually handled jointly. Since women are sometimes in danger of losing control of their personal documents—and thereby the property in question—to their husbands, many keep their documents at their father's house. If a wife's documents are kept at her husband's house, they are often stored in her own locked trunk.

Another standard source of disputes in Ibb pits an oldest brother against his siblings. Younger brothers and sisters are supposed to act respectfully toward their oldest brother; when the father dies, it is said that the oldest son takes his place. Fathers often tried to favor this first son with special benefits from their estate. Documents typically figure in the oldest brother's exercise of family power. At the death of the father, it is the oldest brother who takes control of the estate documentation. At best, he oversees the estate properties and allows the other heirs revenue from their rightful shares. But he will frequently keep his siblings' inheritance documentation in his own hands. This might not be so serious except for the fact that disputes among siblings over inheritance matters are among the most common sources of conflict in Ibb. In this and other types of cases it is essential to have access to the relevant documentation.

Some of these issues of document control are illustrated as an Ibb man discusses a dispute over a town lot that the local governor had been told was unowned.

At the time I didn't have the ownership documents for the property, since they were in the hands of my older brother, who had died. I went to his house and asked his wife if I could look through some papers to find the documents. She gave me a few papers and I found the documents for the lot. I went to the mufti's [al-Haddad's] house to present the documents to him. I asked him to go up to see the governor, which he agreed to do. He went but the governor was preoccupied and he was unable to to bring the matter up. In the meantime, friends of mine made a bond (*kafala*) to be offered the governor whereby I would be asked to show what papers I had in my hand. I took my documents to Qasim al-'Ansi [a friend who was also one of the governor's secretaries]. I told him the governor wanted to see them, but that I was afraid he would take them from me. I wanted al-'Ansi to take copies up to the governor's office, and he said he would. He told the governor, "This man is correct in his ownership claim, he and his grandfather and the generations before." (Taped discussion, 1975)

If personal documents are not in an individual's possession and are not with a father or an older brother, one other person may be expected to have them: the local judge. If a judge holds an instrument for very long, it may never be returned. A number of people told me they had lost the documentation for one property or another when an old judge died. In an active dispute, individuals who have initiated court proceedings frequently must bring their documents to the judge for examination. When asked to return such documents after the settlement, the judge will be expected to require the payment of a small fee. Once considered an unsolicited "gift," this fee is now viewed as an abuse. To protect originals and to avoid this payment, many people take advantage of technology that has been available in Ibb since the early 1970s and make photocopies to leave with the judge.[35]

Documents change hands at transaction times. In a land transfer, a sale document (*basira*) is prepared to spell out the terms of the contract. When the parcel has been the subject of previous sales there will be at least one old document extant. This ought to be given to the new owner at the time of the sale.[36] In one instance, I was shown a series of such documents, relating to a string of sales of the same plot going back nearly three hundred years, all in the hands of the current owner. When a sale involves inherited property, however, the relevant existing document is the person's inheritance instrument (*farz*). In such cases a sale contract is written for the current sale and kept by the buyer, and a notation is written adjacent to the entry for that property on the seller's inheritance document: "The contents of this document (section) are transferred to the buyer X according to the sale document (*basira*) in his hand. Written by Y (date)." The inheritance document, listing properties still owned, stays with the seller. Other documents that ought to change hands at transactions are those resulting from disputes. A man who had purchased both halves of a plot divided as a result of a dispute had two related judgments, copies of the same court decision held by each party to the old conflict. Old settlement documents are often viewed as positively dangerous. One particularly ferocious family conflict over inheritance terminated with the intervention of Imam Ahmad. He saw to it that the final terms were set down in a series of formal documents bearing his authentification and seal and, significantly, that all the previous documentation generated in failed resolution efforts was burned.

In complex undertakings, each of the component transactions can become the subject of a separate document (cf. Wakin 1972:11). In a land sale I observed, the preparation of the final sale instrument was preceded by that of two earlier instruments. Since the buyer did not have the full purchase price on hand, the first of the two prior documents was a fictitious receipt of the full amount of the sale, while the second embodied a loan equivalent to the sum that actually remained to be paid. This maneuver on paper was necessitated by a desire to keep the final sale contract document "clean," that is, unencumbered.[37] It is not always the case, however, that the full transaction terms are recorded in the document. An example is the *tanazul*, in which an individual "steps down" as supervisor of an endowment. The associated document makes no mention of the money paid to the retiring individual by the new supervisor. Likewise, marriage documentation only mentions the sum known as *mahr*, which is not actually paid until divorce or at the time of the husband's death. Two other immediate payments to the bride's family are far larger but are not noted in the documents. Dispute settlements usually take the form of transaction documents. In such situations documents can also serve initially as settlement tools: as opponents are brought together, a document writer, acting also as a mediator, will prepare a succession of documents, ever more closely approximating the finally agreeable terms.

There are instances of transactions without documents. While land sales are virtually always placed in writing, in the case of an "oral sale" (*bay' lisanan*) no document is prepared and the entire burden of support for the undertaking rests upon witnesses. Their witnessing act is not reinforced by mention in an instrument or by signatures. Such documentless land transfers are rare, occurring, if at all, among the co-residents of small rural villages. One important sector of legal-economic activity in Ibb is regularly undocumented: commerce. Petty retail sales occur, of course, without any documents (except receipts in recent decades), but the same has also been true of wholesale transactions between the members of Ibb's tightly knit commercial community. Trust alone underpinned even high-value deals between established trading partners. Undertakings such as land sales or estate divisions lack the repetitive character, not to mention the trust, that makes documents dispensable among local merchants. One is reminded here of the exception mentioned in the above-cited Quranic text requiring written documentation: "unless it be merchandise present (*tijara hadira*) that you give and take between you." Documentation is on the rise among merchants, however, especially for use in their increasing dealings at a distance with agents and firms representing international business interests.

In their constitution, documents can range the legal gamut from unassailable to weak. The difference often depends on the nature of the social relationship between the contracting parties. A man who had recently moved to Ibb from a village might lend considerable sums to someone from that village with no document or, at most, an extremely simple IOU. But in loaning even a small amount to a townsman he would need a full-fledged written instrument. In general, the soundest documents prepared by the leading document specialists in town tend to be associated with undertakings where the relationship is relatively insecure. Poorly written documents, often authored by nonspecialists, are sometimes found in dealings between friends or close associates. In transactions between some categories of relatives, the documentation may also be less than complete. Full and strict documentation is more likely within a nuclear family than between distant cousins. Relatives are not apt to be casual about their documentation if they are joint heirs to an estate or common beneficiaries to endowment revenue. Trusting behavior between brothers, for instance, is as highly valued as it is rare; in their legal affairs brothers relate to one another with the formalities and legal trappings of total strangers. In undertakings with actual strangers or local individuals with bad reputations, the soundest documents are sought.

Documents can win legal contests, and disputants in Ibb frequently build their strategies around written evidence. In one lengthy, extended-family dispute over an endowment, a man was able to fend off repeated legal attacks by the rest of the family because of his possession of a single clear-cut text that supported his cause. Through fifteen years of litigation, judgments repeatedly returned to this original document as the basis for findings. But outcomes are not always sure. In one case I followed, secure documentation did not carry the day. Despite his presentation of extensive and sound supporting documents, a man widely perceived as a scoundrel was unable to get a firm ruling in his favor.

Beyond the internal legal construction of the text, a document can be strengthened in external ways. More witnesses than the two normally required for a contract may be used. The bottoms of some very important older Ibb documents are filled with the names of numerous socially prominent witnesses, reading like a local who's who of the era. It is also possible to seek a countersignature from a legal official, the governor, or sometimes even the head of state. Such an authentification (known as a *tasdiq* or *i'timad*) is always located in the large space left at the top of the document. A consequential signature and the date are typically preceded by a simple, one-line affirmation of "what is written below." When such documents are examined, a reader's attention gravitates to the significant space above the text. (It is also in this space that transfers are noted, giving information about the intervening history of the document.) Until about thirty years ago, personal seals, containing the document writer's name and the date of the seal, were also de rigueur. Official seals remain extremely important. In court, a document with an official seal—Ottoman, imamic, or republican—represents an exceptionally strong piece of evidence.

To *qayyad* a document means to have a copy of it entered into a court register, either between records of judicial decisions or in a separate register. This can be done to increase the security of the instrument. An entry number (giving page number and volume) is placed in one corner of the original. In the Ottoman period, registration was required, and inheritance and land sale documents from that period (1872–1918) bear Ottoman revenue stamps as evidence of the collection of a recording fee (*rasmiyya*). Registration, in the form of the authoritative "official writings" legislation referred to earlier, has been reinstituted under the Republic, but it is a phenomenon far removed from the world of the manuals. As Emile Tyan observed, "an essential characteristic of the Muslim notarial system is that it involves neither an authentification furnished by the intervention of public authority, nor the publication of juridic acts."[38] An Ibb scholar concurred: "Why should we register

documents? We have a system based on custom and knowledge that has
lasted for one thousand four hundred years." In his view, nothing of a
legal nature was added to a document by registration, and, he maintained, no one would ever require that a document be registered to
accept it as valid. Goody (1986:154–59) has discussed the advent of
registration of title comparatively, especially in connection with the
spread of writing and with such associated developments as new patterns of land alienation. In Yemen, where writing itself is not new,
document registration is one aspect of a comprehensive extension of
state authority into formerly private domains.

Prior to the advent of state intervention in documentary practices, a
writer was the first line of defense for the documentation. When documents figure in legal proceedings, it is the writer's identity that must
hold up in court. Documents seem to stand alone as pieces of evidence,
but this is only due to a judge's intimate acquaintance with the local
men who have produced them. In many cases handwriting alone is
sufficient for an Ibb judge to know who wrote an instrument; a new
judge, however, will rely on his secretaries, who are local men, and in
some cases writers are summoned. Old attestations added to documents
typically said that the writer is "known to me in person, script (*khatt*),
and signature/seal ('*alama*)."

Among men who handle documents frequently, whether they are
members of the judiciary, bureaucrats, document writers, or wealthy
private individuals, there is an extremely acute sensitivity to imperfec-
tions, internal or external, in a text. It is impossible to say how much
documentary forgery occurs in Ibb, but it is certainly well known. Once
I was given what was described to me as a three-hundred-year-old
document. Reading it with me later, a scholarly friend suddenly held
it up to the light. This revealed two things to him. First, the paper was
yellowed on one side only, suggesting that it may have been aged in a
smoker. More significant, however, was the watermark, indicating a
brand of heavy document paper (*bayyad*) that had not come to Yemen
from Istanbul until the early 1920s. Other features of what turned out
to be an incompetent forgery were adduced: there was no government
seal (not strictly required), there was no writer's signature, the ink
was "new" on the paper, and the script style was relatively modern.
Another mode of falsification is the reuse of seals: in an especially
crude example I saw, an old seal had been cut out and pasted on a fake
old document. Antedating and postdating are more subtle and widespread abuses. In general, if a judge finds a document to be blotted

(*matmus*) or altered (*mughayyar*), or otherwise determines that it is forged (*muzawwar*),[39] then he will not rely on it.

Katib, meaning writer, refers to several categories of professionals in Ibb, one being the legal-document specialists.[40] Document writers might be confused with the petition (*shakwa*) or letter writers, also known as *katib*s. As in many countries of the Middle East, these men set up their boxtop desks outside government buildings. They are not qualified, nor would anyone approach them, to write or interpret a formal legal instrument. In their work, these boxtop writers are highly visible, while legal-document writers tend to work in private sitting rooms out of the public eye. Maktari (1971:96) states that in the former Sultanate of Lahj, with the British in nearby Aden, document writing was performed by *wakil*s, legal representatives. In Ibb there are two distinct occupational identities. Since they assess supporting documentation, formulate court claims, and study opposing evidence and claims, wakils should ideally be as well educated as the document specialists. But Ibb wakils tend to be better known as specialists in the public spoken word; they know how to "weigh their words." Until the recent legislation establishing the new profession,[41] the skills associated with a lawyer in the West were subdivided into spoken and written specializations. In Ibb, wakils have ranked distinctly lower in public esteem. They are thought to prey on naive disputants, seeking them out in helpless moments before entering court. The Prophet's dictum "The representatives [are] in Hell" (*al-wukala' fi al-nar*) is cited in Ibb, and in the early postrevolutionary years they were specifically condemned and banned from the courts.[42]

Document specialists, by contrast, are considered scholars (*'ulama'*) who are sought out by their clients rather than the other way around. As was true in the Middle East generally, document writing in Yemen has been considered a high-status, honorable profession.[43] The reputation of such men had to be solid, that is, the community had to produce men of unquestioned stature, for the authority of the crucial documents they wrote depended squarely on their knowledge, honor, and personal probity. Honor was established and maintained before the community (*quddam al-nas*), in the course of everyday interaction. As is true for members of the judiciary, appropriate decorum was essential. Notaries cannot engage in frivolity, must be of stern comportment, and ought to wear appropriate attire. Unlike the judiciary, but like wakils (until the new legislation establishing the profession of lawyer), document specialists were not appointed or regulated by the state. Their performance of document-writing services depended exclusively on their public acceptance. Public opinion was sensitive in these matters: if any doubt arose concerning a writer's integrity, his writing activity fell off abruptly.

Ahmad al-Basir,[44] a scholar in the classic mold, from his *'imama* turban and hennaed beard to his knowledge of jurisprudence and his love of poetry, was the last of the older generation of Ibb document writers. At the height of his career as a writer, the sitting room of his house was filled every day with people seeking his professional assistance. Unlike all the contemporary document specialists, this was for many years his exclusive occupation. His importance as a writer is attested to by the frequency with which his handwriting and signature are encountered on Ibb documents of the last forty years.

There are numerous occasional writers of documents in contemporary (1980) Ibb, but ten men are identified as professionals. In this group are two *faqihs*, two part-time merchants, and a court scribe—all of whom handle a small volume of documents. Four other men account for the weightiest and the majority of documents produced in town. One is the mufti, for whom private-document writing is one of his unofficial activities. Two hold positions under the full-judge level in the local judiciary. Neither spends more than an hour or two per day in his official capacity. Like many men in the town today, they retain a government position basically for the sake of the monthly salary. They are primarily document specialists, and it is this work that occupies most of their time and provides the bulk of their income. The last of the four principal writers, however, seems to indicate a new direction for the profession. He lacks the scholarly depth of the others, yet he is technically proficient. Out of a shop in the marketplace he operates what is virtually a real estate business, dealing with all manner of transactions and disputes relating to land. With the advance of commercialization in Ibb, the volume and value of land sales have increased dramatically, and this specialist has been in the midst of the action. Another new direction, suggested in the legislation, is that literate private individuals may increasingly prepare their own documents and then have them registered at court. This is attractive because document specialists become privy to their client's legal acts. That such information is sensitive is illustrated by the appeal of a poster boosting education: "Become educated and protect your secrets."

Transactions, especially those involving real estate, generate income for witnesses, intermediaries, and document writers. The writers receive a fee (*ujarat al-tahrir*) paid by the buyer in the case of a sale contract.[45] The fee is nominal for instruments such as marriage contracts or leases, some of which are written for free by nonprofessionals, but land sales, inheritance matters (the province of the judge or his delegate), and dispute settlements may bring the writer, for no more than an hour's work, more than a government functionary earns in a month. A writer's status underlies the pattern of payment. Tyan's discussion of payments to historical Middle Eastern notaries applies to the Ibb case as well. It was customary not to stipulate the fee in advance, but rather to allow the responsible party to set the level of the payment. "Because of the dignity of the profession, notaries avoid, 'out of modesty,' speaking of money at the time of the performance of one of their official acts, which could give rise to bargaining of the sort that occurs in low-status professions and crafts."[46] A reluctance to appear motivated by a base concern for money fits with the aura of noble bearing actively projected by the old educated elite. While such a sentiment may be quite genuine among some document specialists (and others), the younger generation now ridicules what they perceive as the greed of most such men, whose covetousness the young see as only barely veiled by a dignified manner. A writer will accept whatever a client pays and would seek more, if necessary, only after the fact and through an intermediary. Fees are generally customary, varying with the overall value of the transaction and according to whether the writer performed any services beyond the preparation of the document.

THE ABSENT WRITER

The meaning process of writing and creating texts such as legal documents rests on parallel movements. The first is from the shari'a to text, from the manual to the document; the second is from the world (as event) to text, from a specific human undertaking, such as a sale, to the document. The first progression, from the shari'a as divinely constituted, to the shari'a as humanly interpreted in the jurisprudence, and then to the shari'a as implemented by notaries in their documents, is a divine-to-human trajectory, the progress of a scriptural word into a fallible human world. The second progression is a parallel, world-to-text movement, which may be similarly broken down into one that proceeds from the "intention" (*niyya*)[47] of the parties, through their spoken agreement, to the document in which the agreement is embodied. This trajectory is from a pure idea in the mind, to speech as the sign of the mental idea, and then to writing as the "sign of a sign" (Derrida 1974:29). Although the two movements appear distinguished by their separate starting points in the shari'a and the world, their trajectories from divine to human and from intention to textual representation are analogous. The perfection of the divine and the clarity of the idea together come to rest in the imperfect form of the document.

Behind a given document text is the law, in front of it is the world: a document represents a bringing together of socially constituted and enduring legal principles with individually constituted and ad hoc negotiated terms (respectively, Durkheim's "contract-law" and his "contract" [1933:211–25]). Through his document text, the writer mediates both the reproduction of the law and the incorporation of the world. The document emerges as he considers both the dictates of the law and the facts of an undertaking; he must be both a specialist in this area of shari'a drafting and intimately conversant with the affairs of his society. The notary is a figure in between, and each contract is an interpretation.

In Ibb there were no models for notaries to follow, except for other documents of the same genre. No formularies were in circulation, either of the old *shurut* type or of the more contemporary practical guides (the *tawthiq* or *watha'iq* literature) used in North Africa. The chapters on sale in the manuals contain no example documents and there was no formal instruction in the preparation of written instruments. The reproduction of the local version of the documented contract of sale is thus based on knowledge gained through practical experience in handling local transactions. It is a text model that exists only in its human transmitters, the notaries, and in the concrete examples of their writing—that is, particular, historically contingent documents.

Take as an illustration the sale/purchase instrument, the *basira*, the basic ownership document for the fundamental type of privately held (*milk*) property predominant in Ibb.[48] It was specifically these documents that the imam's commentator had in mind as the troublesome records of Yemeni "rights and properties," the documents essential to "maintain order and protect civilization."

These documents all begin with the phrase "In the Name of God, the Merciful and the Compassionate," written above the body of the text. In this opening of the sale document there is an invocation of God and, at the same time, an invocation of the whole of the Muslim textual tradition. This same phrase initiates the paradigmatic Muslim text, the Quran, as the first words at the beginning of the first *sura*, itself known as "the opening." The genealogical connection to the authoritative original text is explicit. The *basmala*, as the phrase is known, opens up a textual space for "writing" in the broader Derridian sense, in which literal writing is only one specialized form. It is employed not only to commence Muslim writings as diverse as books, personal letters, and amulets, but also for lintel inscriptions at building entrances and to orally bless and begin actions, such as crossing the threshold upon entering a house, taking the first bite of food at a meal, putting the plow into the earth, or engaging in sexual intercourse.

After this invocation, the text proper begins with a verb, following the standard word order in Arabic sentences. This first word, "bought," one of the distinctive lexemes of alienation, immediately makes apparent the identity of the document as a contract of sale (*bay*').[49] As a third-person, past-tense verb, "bought" also embodies the transformative textual mediation of the notary. Having heard the uttering of the binding contractual statements, made in the first person by the seller and the buyer, he then records the already existing undertaking in the form of the document text, using the third-person voice of a third-party observer. The documentation of the contract thus involves a complex shift of person and medium: from first-person-oral to third-person-written.

Like Geertz's "ethnographer," the notary "'inscribes' social discourse; he writes it down. In so doing, he turns it from a passing event, which exists only in its own moment of occurrence, into an account, which exists in its inscriptions and can be reconsulted" (1973:19). However different ethnographic and notarial writing may be as practices of writing, they share a transformative, and problematic, relationship to the "said" of the world. In his act of inscription of a contract between two parties, the notary acts as an outsider, a nondirectly participant "other"—the "*al-ghayr*" of the customary document in Yemeni legislation. His voice, which is not that of a person in direct address, takes instead the third-person pronominal form known in Arabic as "the absent" (*al-gha'ib*).[50] The writing intervention of an "other" thus results in a text characterized by an "absence." The only shifts within the document text to the first person occur if the notary refers parenthetically to his relationship to another text, an inheritance document, for example, which might be examined to ascertain property boundaries. While the notary is an outsider with respect to the private transaction, he is an insider with respect to the law and its texts.

The manuals envision the two parties actually meeting each other (a *muwajaha*) and uttering reciprocally binding statements, and this conforms with Yemeni practice. Examples are provided by al-Nawawi of appropriate first-person, past-tense utterances, such as "I sold to you" and "I bought." *Basira* documents are records of what occurred at an encounter; specifically, they embody undertakings that were constituted as past-oriented, executed contracts (as opposed to future-oriented, executory contracts) from the moment of the binding statements. A verbal agreement alone, employing such statements and made before the required two witnesses, constitutes a sale contract. As is assumed by the statement examples, no writing is foreseen in the perspective of the manuals. In a notary's text, the fact that the necessary binding statements were made is signaled by the formula that the sale was concluded "with the offer and acceptance."

The moment of the sale transfer is reenacted in document texts. A parcel of land, originally the *milk* property of the seller, figures in the text as the "sale object." A series of formal steps, including the requisite words of offer and acceptance, an affirmation of the completeness of the sale, and then the physical receipt of the price money by the seller from the buyer, lead up to the moment of transfer. First the seller is said to let go, he "surrenders" his property, "guaranteeing" (consecrating) it as it leaves his possession. Then, conveyed in textual representation by the pivotal, third-person past-tense verb *sar* ("became"), the property, once again, this time in the absent form of the document, is alienated: it becomes the *milk* property of another individual, the buyer. The relevant section of an Ibb *basira* reads:

> The seller received the entire purchase price from the hand of the buyer at the session, completely and perfectly. The seller surrendered his sale object, vacating legally and guaranteeing any legal fault concerning all the rights of the sale object, and its trees and stones. And at that moment the aforementioned sale object became the individual property of and right of the aforementioned buyer, among the group of his properties to be disposed of as he desires.[51]

Unaltered in actuality by these solemn proceedings, the land in question is "transferred"—through semiotic maneuvers that embody an exchange relationship between humans.

A final section of the document begins with the words "This was written with the witnessing of." There are actually three levels of witnessing that occur in the "witnessing clauses." The names of the standard two witnesses required in the shariʿa for a valid contract are stated. These are the eye and ear witnesses to the oral contract, individuals who could ideally come forward to testify in the event of a contested outcome. God is mentioned as "sufficient witness," suffusing the human undertaking with ultimate authority. And, finally, there is the notary himself. Although not explicitly referred to as a witness, the notary is the witnessing linchpin of the textual representation of the contract.

The chain of witnesses, as the imam and his commentator asserted, constitutes the legitimizing support for the written document. Witnessing supplements writing by situating it in an ideal chain of spoken utterances, in a fictional genealogy of human witnessing links. But as the imam knew, witnesses could both lie and die. The buttressing of writing through the supposedly sound institution of witnessing actually served to cover up the fact that the burden of potential falsification associated with writing attached to speech as well. *Lapsus calami* conceals *lapsus linguae*.

A textual change is in progress, however, as this old style of document is being transformed into something we would recognize as a title deed.[52] Associated with the birth of a new notion of the state, this transformation has involved public regulation of the formerly private activities of notaries[53] and the advent in Yemen of lawyers and legal drafting of the Western type. All this involves the displacement of the notary from a central role in constituting the authority of a document. Notaries will still write, but it will increasingly be the state that legitimates. In older sale documents, the names of the parties to the contract and the two witnesses were essential to record, but their signatures never appeared, simply because these were considered to have no legal effect (cf. Wakin 1972:51n, 68n). The buyer and the seller did not sign, because it was the notary who translated the undertaking into a permanent text—a text that was his product. The signature of the notary established the link in the chain of truth. Recently, however, sale documents have appeared bearing, in addition to the signature of the notary, those of not only the witnesses but also buyers and sellers. Together with the requirement of official registration, these newly appearing signatures confirm the onset of a decisive epistemological transformation in the nature of the documentary text.

CHAPTER 12

Spiral Texts

The handwriting of the Arabians in the common business of life is not legible.
CARSTEN NIEBUHR, *TRAVELS* (1778)

"It is worthy of mention," a Syrian Arab traveler of the late 1920s observed, "that the method of writing in Yemen differs from the method of writing among us." "I saw some documents," he explains, "and they begin the writing on all of them with: 'In the Name of God the Merciful and Compassionate,' then they write a few lines beneath the *basmala*." Compared with "traditional" Arabic writing practices elsewhere in the Middle East, the description was thus far unremarkable. But the conclusion to the sentence brought his readers a genuine surprise: "then they rotate the writing around these lines in the shape of a spiral."[1]

A visual image, a spatial metaphor. The physical features of such "spiral texts" provide insights into the general nature of calligraphic practices and the course of discursive changes. Structures and developments similar to those exemplified by spiral texts are identifiable in related domains of textual practice, including two further examples to be discussed, administrative bookkeeping and the use of official seals. This poetics of written space then can be extended to general domains of spatial organization: towns, architecture, and the space of the state. Finally, earlier observations about changes in the *shari'a* and in instruction are recalled as a bridge is constructed between alterations in physical space and discontinuities in what Foucault (1970) has called the "space of knowledge."

While the Syrian traveler (an exemplar of the print world, a graduate, with a literature major, from the American University in Beirut, and a writer of newspaper travel pieces on Yemen) did not report what sort of documents he had come in contact with, these could have been

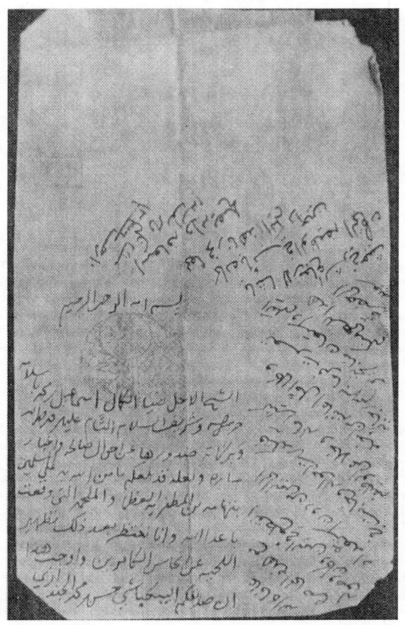

Figure 10. A spiral letter from Imam Yahya to Ibb governor Isma'il Basalama, 1917 [A.H. 1336].

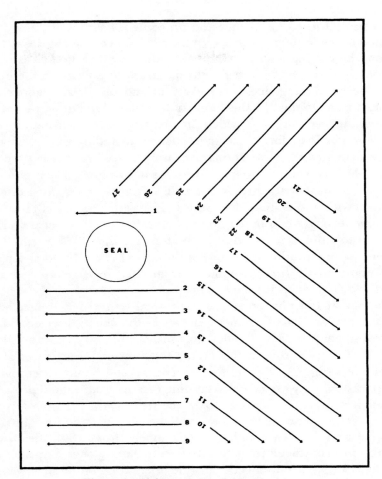

Figure 11. Movements of the spiral text.

as diverse as memoranda, official correspondence, legal opinions, testaments, or sale instruments. All such handwritten texts were apt to exhibit the characteristic spiral form he describes. Given a blank page, a Yemeni writer of the period commenced far down on the page and indented radically toward the center. Since Arabic is written right to left, this meant roughly within the lower left quadrant. When the bottom was reached before the writing was finished, the spiral effect came into play. In short texts, completed at or before the bottom edge, there was no spiral, but a very wide margin remained to the right and across the top of the page. When the text continued, however, writer and writing turned the corner and proceeded, nearly upside-down in relation to the initial lines, back up the right side of the page. Continuing on, the writing might pivot again, adjusting direction so as to arc diagonally through the upper right quadrant to a finish in the upper left. The concluding lines were likely to end up directly above and perpendicular to the "In the Name of God the Merciful and Compassionate," the *basmala*, with which the text began. In their nautilus-like spiral proportions, formal correspondence, including official imamic letters, provided the most dramatic examples (see fig. 10, diagrammed in fig. 11),[2] but there were many versions of this type of spatial movement in Yemeni writing. A local mufti's *fatwa*-answers, for example, spiraled within the space left above the written query. Staid legal instruments might end in long tails of text that ran in reverse up right margins to culminate in twists at the top (see fig. 12). Lengthy legal judgments ran continuously on long scrolls of carefully joined paper and might finally turn over the bottom edge to conclude in a few upside-down lines on the back.

To look at this phenomenon in historical terms,[3] recall once again the humble land-sale document known as the *basira*, discussed in the preceding chapter. Many older documents of this type, dating from periods of imamic rule in this or the last century, bear traces of the spiral effect (fig. 12). By contrast, recent but still handwritten basiras are quite obviously organized according to a different spatial principle. In sale instruments from the 1970s, the text begins near the top and appears centered on the page, located between equal and straight-ruled margins drawn in by hand. In a document from 1991, the text is entered on a contract form, which has printed margins and lines for text (see fig. 13). No rotation occurs in the orientation of the new writing; the text proceeds downward in regular horizontal lines, moving margin to margin until completion. In these contemporary documents the writing is constrained in a manner familiar to Western legal instruments; the spiral is harnessed and the lines are straightened and centered. These sorts of changes are also evident with typing, as in the shift from spiraling imamic letters to the standard margin and paragraph form of republican correspondence.

The physical alteration from spiral to straight-ruled text is clear enough at a glance, but what is its significance? In the case of the basira it has to do with changes in the basic epistemological structure of the document, with the principles underpinning the document's construction and its authority. These have to do, in turn, with a backdrop of

Figure 12. Upper portion of an old sale contract, dated 1856. Writing in right margin is upside down.

changing relations of production and advancing commercialization.[4] Spatial shifts in such documents are closely linked to the evidence cited in the preceding chapter concerning such interrelated changes in documents as the advent of official court registration, the appearance of

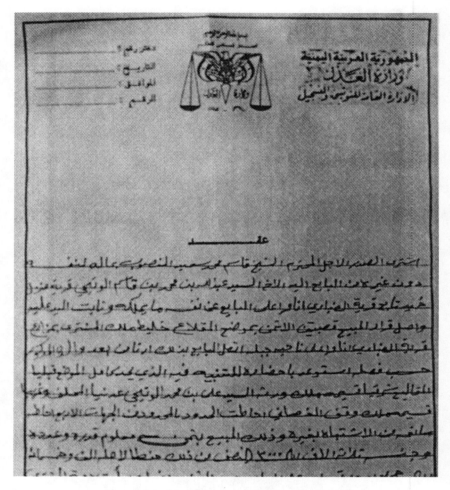

Figure 13. New sale document, dated 1991.

signatures by the parties to the contract, new evidence rules, and most recently, the licensing of writers, all of which have brought an extension of state control and a displacement of the private notary from his once central role as the legitimizing author-witness. With this displacement it has for the first time become conceivable for a basira to be entered on a printed contract form or even typed; handwriting, formerly the crucial mark of the notary's identity and his authoritative presence in the text, was becoming less relevant.

Physical differences between spiral and straight texts involve more than a simple matter of design, of curved versus not curved. Ruled or printed margins on the new documents, which are prepared or exist in advance of the actual writing, are an important clue to differences in textual construction. In contemporary documents, writing fills a pre-defined space between parallel lines, while in spiral texts there is no such prior demarcation of the textual space (beyond page-size constraints). The physical space occupied by the text in such older, spiraling documents is instead produced in the course of the writing itself. Another way of putting it is that behind straight and spiral shapes, and filled versus produced space, lie quite different relations of form and content. In the new, straight documents, form is separate from, prior to, and more determinate of the shape of the textual contents. In the old spiral texts, by contrast, form and content are not clearly separable, and it appears that, if anything, it is textual contents that determine form. That is, in spiral texts, the ultimate shape depends on the physical extent of what has to be said.

Cassirer (1955, 2:84) contrasts two modes of spatial organization along similar lines. In differentiating "geometric space" from "mythical space," he points to differing form and content relationships. While the construction of geometric space is predicated upon the separation of form and content, the opposite is the case with mythical space, in which form "is not something that can be detached from content or contrasted with it as an element of independent significance; it 'is' only insofar as it is filled with a definite, individual sensuous or intuitive content." Cassirer's opposed epistemologies may be related to the contrasting methods of the "scientist" and "bricoleur" in the work of Lévi-Strauss (1966:22). These differ according to the "inverse functions they assign to events and structures as ends and means, the scientist creating events... by means of structures and the bricoleur creating structures by means of events."

SCRIBAL REGISTERS

These small techniques of notation, of registration, of constituting files, of arranging facts in columns and tables that are so familiar to us now, were of decisive importance in the epistemological "thaw" of the sciences of the individual.
M. FOUCAULT, *DISCIPLINE AND PUNISH*

Consider now the example of the property and accounting registers kept by the old agrarian state bureaucracies. This apparently dry material—the "ignoble archives" of bookkeeping, files, lists—is given

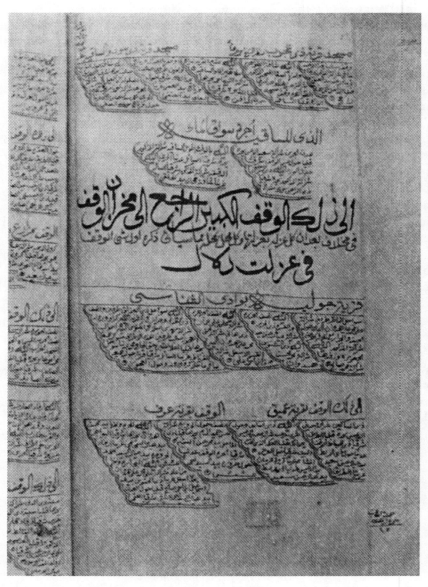

Figure 14. Register (*musawwadat al-'abbasiyya*) of endowment land pertaining to the Great Mosque of Ibb.

pride of analytic place in the work of Weber,[5] Goody,[6] and Foucault. In some details of textual procedures, the local record-keeping tradition[7] exhibits a history of recent transition parallel to the shift from spiral to straight texts. By the turn of the century the Ottomans had introduced new "international" (*duwali*) bookkeeping methods in all the Ibb offices except the endowments (*awqaf*) administration.[8] There an older format continued until reorganization efforts of the late 1940s and 1950s.

A typical page in an old-style endowments register, made (as a copy) in 1928 (see fig. 14),[9] reveals a form determined by content relation similar to that found in spiral texts. Although the pages as a whole are ruled, individual entry texts are hemmed in, after the fact, by curved and scalloped lines. Instead of the physical regularity that results from filling in the standardized, printed entry forms currently in use, here each page, even each entry is particular in appearance. Scalloped form follows content: it is the physical extent of the writing, generated by the substantive detail on tenants and tenancy, area measurements, property names and boundaries, that determines the final shape of entries and, cumulatively, the overall appearance of register pages. In their layered arrangement, the property entries in such registers resemble nothing so much as the physical appearance of the curved and stepped terraces they refer to.

Subdivisions in the body of the register are marked by headings done in large decorative script in red and black ink. Together with literary embellishments such as the rhymed prose (*saj'*) found in introductory sections, this sort of calligraphy is absent in the more austere and "business-like" contemporary land registers. Similarly, the rounder hand of the old *katib* contrasts with the sparse, specialized, and more standardized administrative (*diwani*) script introduced by the Ottomans and the angular Egyptian-influenced hand that has now become the norm. Although individual items in the old foundation register are separated by scalloping, they are linked grammatically. The register reads continuously, using conjunctions and connecting phrases, from the fancy headings, into and through a series of entries to the next heading, and so on, from the opening *basmala* to the last word. In addition to the scalloping, a register's integrity was physically ensured by such protective marking devices as small nucleated circles or pairs of dashes, inserted to plug gaps. In the bottom corner the total number of entries on the page is stated in script and in numerals, and the first word of the next page is given.

The writer certified that upon completion the register was free of smudges or other signs of alteration and that his copy was an exact, word-for-word replica of the original. Attestations are included in the original register text, and others are added to the copy. These also bear witness to an exact agreement of copy and original (mentioning the *muqabala* comparison procedure),[10] specify the total number of entries, and quote the first and last entries. An important attestation of this volume is by Imam Yahya and includes his seal over a brief, physically slanted statement written by a secretary. It reads (referring initially to the previous attestation):

> In the Name of God, the Merciful and Compassionate. What the Judge of the Endowments, the distinguished scholar Qasim bin Ibrahim bin Ahmad bin al-Imam may God protect him, has stated is attested to. The copy has taken on the authority of the original and is to be used accordingly. This register is to be kept free of alteration and erasure as it is on this date, the 19th of the month of Ramadan the honored, the year thirteen hundred and forty-six Hegira [1928].

The phrase "has taken on" is my rendering of the pivotal verb *sar*, encountered in connection with the sale instrument of the preceding chapter. Translated there as "became," it was central to the discursive enactment of a transfer of property. Here the register copy becomes equivalent to the thing itself, a fragile and authoritative original in its own right. Aside from the necessary avoidance of alteration, the register's integrity hinged on the physical and hermetic contiguity of its text and on the indication of a scribal presence, conveyed by a distinctive script. As a "copy" it is virtually the same thing as the original, not because it "looks like" the original in the photo-identity sense accomplished by mechanical reproduction (cf. Benjamin 1968), but because it has passed through an authoritative process of human reproduction and collation. Although they apparently accomplish the same task, manuscript copies and print copies work with differing technologies and epistemologies.

Like the sale instruments of the period, old registers bore the personal mark of a particular *katib* and displayed the artistry of his scribal craft. The text was suffused with the human presence, the *haiba*, the prestige, dignity, and awe-inspiring quality of specific men who concretely embodied the state. This was reinforced and perpetuated by kinship relations of descent and marriage among functionaries and officials (see Messick 1978). While the *haiba* of such a register was highly personalized, the authority of new bureaucratic texts is relatively depersonalized. Like that of the nation-state to which it pertains, a new register's authority rests on its diffused formal abstractness, implemented through the standardized printed forms now available for all official acts. Like the displaced notary in relation to the new registered documents, the contemporary functionary lends little of his person to the forms he fills.

Forms, that is, documentary blanks to be filled in, appeared in Ibb with the Ottomans. At the local telegraph office, for example, one of the earliest of these forms had a crescent seal at the top, headings in Ottoman Turkish and French, boxes for office use, and lines to contain the message.[11] Such blank forms proliferated in the Ottoman bureaucracies as they would later under the republicans. The commercial receipt, another type of printed form to be filled in, was introduced via Aden. Prior to the "order form" itself, the written purchase-requests Ibb merchants sent to Aden were connected narrations by a scribe (concluding with *qala*, "said," and then the writer's name).[12] Their internal arrangements were similar to the scalloped entries of the old foundation register. Existing apart from and prior to any particular written content, forms are the mechanical templates of the new age of writing.

As with the Ottomans earlier in the century, the principal goal of the Egyptian advisors attached to Ibb offices in the late 1970s was to facilitate a bureacratic movement in a new direction, to assist functionaries in separating what had formerly been lumped together, to itemize what had been recorded whole. While old accounting registers were predominantly horizontal (written) in orientation, the new exhibited a more vertical (numerical) alignment. Thus while the pages of a tax collector's manual from early in the century contained entries strung across the page like laundry on a line, a comparable manual from circa 1955 had two prominent axes, one of grain types, the other of terrace names, creating a grid for entering the relevant figures. Vertical orientations facilitate whole-page summations and are associated with a new emphasis on the efficient extraction and display of numerical data, which used to be embedded in written text.

SEALS OF STATE

As a second example of a related phenomenon also recently transformed consider contrasts in official seals. A consistent presence on this century's texts of state, Ottoman, imamic, and republican, state seals have differed markedly in their significative technologies. Imams of the early nineteenth century did not use seals and simply signed their correspondence;[13] the later use of seals by the Hamid al-Din imams coincided with the Ottoman presence. As an element of "tradition," this seal usage was not inherited from time immemorial but was of relatively recent adoption.[14] Imams Yahya and Ahmad utilized round seals about the size of a silver dollar, applied in red ink in the space at the beginning of official texts.[15] In a letter, the *khatm al-sharif*, the royal seal, was placed just under the *basmala*, and above the beginning of the text proper, like the eye of the spiral (see fig. 10). When used elsewhere, such as on judgments and attestations, a seal was typically accompanied by a few words of affirmation, written at a slant and sometimes in the imam's own hand.[16] Following the completion of the writing and the fixing of the seal, a red powder (called *hamura*) was applied by the imam himself. This red dusting left a long-lasting trace indicating the document's lofty source. Anthropologist Carleton Coon, on a visit to Yemen in 1933, witnessed the process one afternoon in Imam Yahya's sitting room. The imam was working with al-Qadi 'Abd Allah al-'Amri.

> He and the Imam had little heaps of papers in front of and between them, and after we were seated went back for a while to their discussion of these documents. Some of them the Imam signed, and dipped his fingers in a pot of red pigment to smear diagonally across them. This is the Imam's official sign, and is as important as his seal or his signature. Every document we received from him was crossed by four of these rosaceous smirches.[17]

It is of relevance for what follows regarding detailed changes in seal usage that, contrary to what Coon reports, there were in fact no signatures by the imam.[18]

Twentieth-century imamic seals are composed internally of off-center circles or ovals, with the largest of the crescent-shaped spaces thus created bearing the title "Commander of the Faithful" together with the imam's personal title, chosen and assumed upon accession. The next crescent within contained the imam's name and family name (e.g., Yahya Hamid al-Din); in Ahmad's seal this is preceded by "the Imam" and followed by "God make him victorious" (see fig. 15). This last phrase appears in the smallest circle in Imam Yahya's seal, whereas in that of Imam Ahmad there is the *basmala*. Like the silver currency minted in San'a' after 1926,[19] which they closely resemble in design, imamic seals were composed entirely of writing. As with the flourishes of the old registers, this was calli-graphy, beautiful writing, elegantly interwoven and sensuously curved to fit the crescent spaces. It also carried authority as the mark of the ruling imam.

Figure 15. Seal of Imam Ahmad on Appeal Court ruling, 1958 [A.H. 1378].

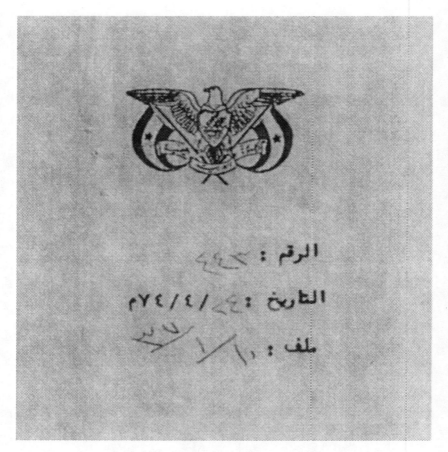

Figure 16. Republican seal printed on official stationery, 1974.

Official seals continued in use after the Revolution of 1962, but both
the seals themselves and their methods of employment were different.
Aside from the shift from imamic red to republican blue, the most
apparent of the semiotic changes is from script to emblem. The new seal
of state bears the image of an eagle (*nasr*), head in profile and wings
spread, together with the national flag and the legend "Yemen Arab
Republic." According to one republican writer, this emblem "represents the power of the people."[20] While the imamic seal bore the personal name of the imam, the living embodiment of the patrimonial
state, the republican seal bears a symbol and the name of the nation-

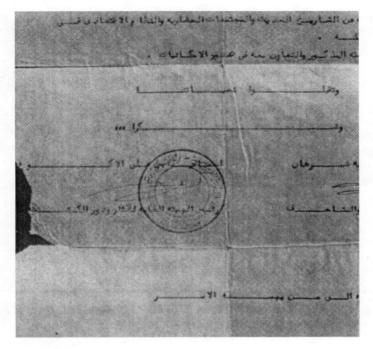

Figure 17. Signature and seal of republican official.

state. In use on official texts, the imamic seal, as was noted, was applied without a signature, or rather, it was itself the mark of the patrimonial imamic ruler. Aside from their appearance at the top of official stationery (see fig. 16), republican seals implement a separation of office and officeholder (and an interchangeability of incumbents) and are always accompanied by signatures: the official signs first, then the seal is placed over the signature (see fig. 17). In imamic states, the name of the state and, potentially, even the location of its capital, the imamic "seat," could change with each new ruler (e.g., the move from San'a' to Ta'izz in this century). In the nation-state conception, by contrast, the name of the state and the location of its capital are not normally subject to such alteration.

The recent appearance in the highlands of the notion of an emblem that is meant to "stand for" the state is traceable to the Ottoman period. In the year 1901, for example, according to the historian al-Wasi'i (1928:180), the Ottoman governor of Yemen had a tall column

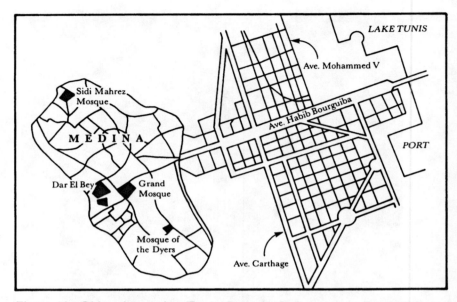

Figure 18. Old and new city, Tunis. From L. C. Brown, ed., *From Madina to Metropolis* (Princeton: Darwin Press, 1973), p. 29.

erected outside the main gate of San'a'. "At its top he had placed the image of a crescent moon, like those put atop minarets, made of copper plated with gold." It was the same symbol that appeared on the printed forms used at telegraph offices. The historian goes on to say that it was the governor's intention that the column with the crescent should serve as "a memorial for the government" (*tadhkaran lil-hukuma*).

THE CALLIGRAPHIC WORLD

Speculatively extending this "spiral" analysis to the articulation of space in a wider sense, an excellent example is found in a comparison of the physical layouts of towns, old and new. As was true of *madinas* from North Africa to central Asia, the old walled town of Ibb was a labyrinth of closely packed multistoried houses on narrow and winding alleys and culs-de-sac. The new quarters, by contrast, are characterized by relatively straight-line, wide thoroughfares with some space left between the buildings. The growth of these newer parts of Ibb is governed, in theory, by a municipal zoning and building "code," which involves plans for the expansion of the town and endeavors to regulate standards of construction. There was no colonial period "ville nouvelle" or European section here,[21] but the form taken by Ibb's more modest new growth has followed a related pattern. Visually, the curvilinear urban script of walled Ibb contrasts sharply with the roughly rectilinear format of the new quarters. While passageways in the old town were mostly the residual, irregular spaces left and defined by the construction and expansion of buildings, streets in the new have been drawn in first on planning maps and then residential and commercial construction has followed. Although more dramatic in the monumental, whole-city plans set forth for a colonial Rabat,[22] Tunis (see fig. 18), or Cairo,[23] an equivalent separate specification of a projected urban layout and its determination of the possible subsequent locations of houses and shops has occurred in Ibb. Reversing the relation that obtained in the walled town, this new separation and precedence of urban form over urban content is analogous to the changeover from spiral texts to their straightened successors.

On a smaller scale, within the urban setting, architectural innovations carried out related alterations. Ottoman military buildings were among the first representatives in the highlands of a new type of public construction. An impressive barracks complex, housing infantry, cavalry, and artillery units was constructed outside the main gate of San'a', and a large military hospital and a well-run pharmacy inside, while in Ibb a small complex that also included a military bakery and a dispensary were constructed on a hill facing the walled town. These buildings were "new" in that they were physically separated from the old urban contiguities and highly specialized in function.

As a concomitant to the rise of a civil service in Yemen, there occurred a local version of the classic separation of "the bureau from the private domicile of the official."[24] Just as the imam's government operated from the courtyard and the upstairs *diwan* of his residence, so the local governor's house in Ibb was also the governorate office, with functionaries upstairs and the jail downstairs. Shari'a court was held in front of the judge's home, and, as at the mufti's, petitioners were received in the afternoon sitting room. Although there were some important earlier examples (the Treasury Office, built in the 1940s, and, among residences, Governor Sayaghi's innovative four-house modular complex of the 1950s), specially designed offices became the norm only after the Revolution. The handling of administrative registers, which were always retained at home as the personal effects of officials or secretaries, also changed. As was true of many of the details of the former system, this individual control of registers came to be viewed as an abuse: old registers were called in for deposit in new office file

cabinets, and their removal from the office was forbidden. The transition to work in offices was not abrupt, however: older judges were
inclined to receive claimants outside the court building, and many
functionaries continued to save exacting bookkeeping tasks for afternoon qat chewing in their own sitting rooms.

Just as the house became more specialized as a home, so the mosque
became more specialized as a place for "religion." Instead of being
located around pillars in the prayer room of the Great Mosque, schools
moved out to separate places for the specialized activity of instruction.
A variation on the progression from spiral to straight was again involved: the shift was from class space as the lesson circle, its size and
shape produced by the particular daily gatherings of students, to the
classroom, a permanent rectilinear space, with rows of desks, positioned
like the lines on a form, to be filled with different student content. In
the case of military barracks a related separation took place: learning
from the Ottoman example, Yemenis eventually made the changeover
from a reliance on occasional armed forces, quartered as they moved or
living in their own residences, to a standing professional army, uni-
formed, constantly under a disciplinary regime, and housed in specially
demarcated facilities (Foucault 1977; Mitchell 1988).

On a larger scale, a version of the shift from spiral to straight fits
the changing physical-conceptual reality of the state. As with the *harka*s
of sultans in Morocco (Geertz 1983; El Moudden 1983), the space of
an old imamic state was, in part, created through the movements
of the imam and his armies through the countryside.[25] Contrasting
with this, in a relation, again, of produced versus filled space, are
the fixed or claimed frontiers of the nation-state. Some maps were
narratives that consisted of a listing of contiguous places rather than
a grid filled in with reference to the four cardinal points. Asked for
a sketch map of Ibb town, an old scholar replied by dictating a string
of markets and mosques that one would encounter in a walking tour.
Without stopping, this "map" continued to one of the town gates
and then on out into the countryside and a long series of similarly
connected places. Within government "seats" such as Ibb, the local
presence of the state was constituted as officials made daily rounds
of the markets and streets. Supplementing the physical movements of
the patrimonial imam were such extensions of his person as his sons
holding provincial posts and (prior to telephone and television) the
circulation of texts bearing his seal and the red *hamura* applied by his
fingers.

THE "SPACE OF KNOWLEDGE"

To conclude this excursus on "spiral texts" I want to sketch some further connections between physical and conceptual space, specifically, between the sorts of detailed changes identified in the space of writing and general changes that have occurred in the "space of knowledge." This last is characterized by Foucault as "an epistemological space specific to a particular period" (1970:xi).

Spiral texts were elements of a reasoned, ordered, and internally consistent intellectual world that was neither convoluted nor unevolved. The basic knowledges involved were bodily ones, and the basic transitions that have occurred involved disciplinary routines normalized at the level of the body. As the fundamental mediating site for the articulation of the physical-conceptual, the body was fully engaged as spiral texts were produced and used. Pivoting bodily movements and a rhythm of page rotation were required either to write or to read such a text. As a group, these and many related bodily techniques for reproducing space were distinct from the types of physical disciplines involved in filling in forms, typing, or working at a computer screen. Opposed to the emphasis on the physical contiguities of produced space (both between writer and text and within the text) are the expected separations that attend the world of filled spaces. The strong indexicality of the old texts, in which writing was a nonarbitrary mark of the person, is distinct from the character of texts, printed and not, in which writing itself ceased to be the mediating bearer of authority. "The relation of the sign to the signified now resides in a space in which there is no longer any intermediary figure to connect them: what connects them is a bond established, inside knowledge, between the idea of one thing and the idea of another" (Foucault 1970:63).

Academic knowledges such as shari'a jurisprudence were understood to be embodied. Both the internal inscription of memorization ("on the surface of the heart") and the human presences and linkages in authoritative knowledge transmission ("between me and the author are two men") were physically conceived. The authoritative knowledge of recited texts lived more in its human interpreters, al-Shawkani maintained, than "in the bodies of pages." In terms of a simple dichotomy between literacy and nonliteracy, it is possible to state that literacy "enables a society to accumulate culture hitherto preserved in embodied form" (Bourdieu 1977:187). But a literate tradition in which knowledges were contained both in human "carriers" and in books represents an alternative situation to either exclusively "embodied" or strictly "decontextualized" (Goody 1977) forms of knowledge.

Within the sphere of formal knowledge, specifically within the discourse of the shariʿa, the codification shift discussed earlier had a structure parallel to that occurring between spiral and straight texts. In a manner analogous to the change in the form/content relation of spatial ordering in writing, the (casuistical) old discourse differs from the (abstractly rational) new. Whereas the former developed principles within cases (form following content), the latter elaborates principles independently of and prior to the cases to which they are subsequently applied (content following form). In the disenchanted thought of shariʿa legislation, the old primacy of the concrete instance has given way to a new primacy of the rule. Having cut its ties to the older forms of human embodiment, the shariʿa of the legislated code relies instead on an authority internal to the new discourse itself. The "straightened" (Bourdieu 1977:169) thought that has appeared entails a changed character of knowledge, a new locus for truth, and a different relation to and among humans.

Conclusion

Identified at the outset as both a polity and a discursive condition, the calligraphic state was a phenomenon anchored in the complex authority relations of a spectrum of writings and associated institutions. Varying in their stylistic constraints and applications, genres ranging from shari'a treatises and scholarly histories to judicial opinions, court rulings, scribal records, official correspondence, and ordinary contracts shed light on different dimensions of the polity while also revealing regularities and diversity in the discursive formation.

Where the sword served to threaten or coerce, the authority of the pen concerned the conveyance of "ruling ideas." The hegemony of these ideas was initiated in childhood as an integral part of the inculcation of a particular world. From birth rituals to Quranic school formation, textual embodiment was a process intended to install the general templates of shari'a society. Relations of interpretation were predicated on hierarchies of the learned and the ignorant, although there was a complex understanding of the intricacies and legitimizing significance of ordinary common sense. Associated with these hierarchical relations of interpretation was a state and wider polity of query and response, in which imams, governors, muftis, judges, and respected scholars acted as the providers of answers for a populace that appeared before them as individual petitioners.

But textual domination was more than a matter of the message. An additional strength concerned the structuring of the medium. A textual habitus, a set of acquired dispositions concerning writing and the spoken word, and the authoritative conveyance of meaning in texts, was reproduced in homologous structures and practices across the different genres and institutions. It was the resulting, partly implicit, experience of coherence amid diversity, the reaffirming of basic orientations through multiple forms and sites of expression, that enhanced the natural qualities of the dispositions themselves. From domain to domain, the quiet redundancies of discursive routines were mutually confirming.

A culturally specific paradox informed the grounding of spoken words in written texts. From the recording of Revelation to the documentation of property rights, attempts to inscribe original speech, considered authentic and true, resulted in textual versions of diminished authority. The other side of the paradox was that speech events were fleeting and evanescent. Despite the staggering retentional capacities of human memories, the spoken word needed the services of writing to endure. Writing rescued words from perishing, but only at the cost of another death, that of the original meaning conveyed by speech. In its written form speech was absent, altered, and open to a potentially infinite number of interpretive readings. Although the lack of transparent meaning in written texts was acknowledged, links of authoritative communication, similar to those that underpinned instruction and witnessing, enabled some writings to claim to be true representations of original words.

Associations of the spoken word with presence, truth, and justice, and of the written word with absence, falsehood, and injustice, held mainly in connection with the various authoritative texts of the discursive core. By contrast, such associations figured little, if at all, in the large textual surround of the more peripheral intellectual disciplines and in ordinary written usage, where the more familiar (to Western practice) activities of reading and writing prevailed. At the heart of this "written tradition" stood a corpus of texts construed as recitations. Despite the fact that its principal attributions of textual authority depended on privilegings of spoken communication and requirements of human presence, the discursive formation as a whole was thoroughly literate. Since logocentric conceptions in instruction and other institutions quietly presupposed a reliance on reading and writing techniques, the theory of recitational practice did not always coincide with the facts of that practice. But, to invoke Maine once more, this was the sort of theory that "produced consequences of the utmost importance."

My structural approach to this discursive formation was complemented by diachronic concerns, representing a move toward what Todorov (1981) has termed a "historical poetics." The discursive shifts examined within this complex textual tradition occurred in the course of a move from a particular local manuscript culture to a world of print technology. The new writing that has emerged is more separately assured, more authoritative in and of itself. No longer must writing so regularly call upon speech, its "parent," as Socrates called it, for support. The new authority of writing has to do with the appearance of independent forms and frames (Mitchell 1988) and with the spread of a host of other separations that developed across the polity and within the discursive formation. While many of the distinctive images linger, the old ideals of voiced presences are being replaced by the multiple alienations of a newly shaped and differentiated society.

In scope, the polity described by authoritative texts was considerably broader than the old state. In addition to their vital contributions to the regional and local dynamism of the shari'a, private scholars acting as interpreting muftis represented an important range of textual authority outside of state control. The drafting activity of notaries also functioned without state supervision until the recent advent of document registration. Alternative dispute-resolution procedures likewise flourished beyond the bounds of state jurisdictions, and although this troubled jurists of earlier eras, it was the nation-state that took steps to bring such arbitration and mediation mechanisms under official aegis. Although shari'a instruction frequently had an intimate relation to state power, legal education at the university today is under far more complete state control.

Once the central discourse of the Muslim polity, the shari'a was decisively repositioned within nation-state frameworks. My characterization of the shari'a as a general societal discourse rather than as "Islamic law" placed emphasis on a historical transition to the codified and legislated form of law. The decisive move from the old manuals to legislation, from open to closed shari'a texts, represents both the key instance of discursive transformation and an important backdrop for changes that have occurred in other institutions. Alteration in the form of the shari'a has changed the nature not only of interpretation, but also of government.

As the simply organized patrimonial imamate gave way to proliferating bureaucratic segments and to the beginnings of representational government, and as a face-to-face society of witnesses and known reputations yielded to a citizenry of equivalent strangers, so individualized licenses for the transmission of specific texts were replaced by standardized state diplomas, the unitary opinion of the judge by the collective voice of members of a bench, and the stand-alone authority of the notary's hand by official registration. In the process, the social basis of the polity is shifting from reckonings by status and kinship (including such manifestations of the latter as tribes, intellectual genealogies of shari'a scholars, and the descent lines of the imams) to the imagined simultaneity and homogeneity of a national citizenry. Whereas distinguished lives once became text in a manner that recalls Emerson's dictum that "properly there is no history, only biography," recent histories of the "people" mark the birth of a new "descending" individualism.

The account presented here has emphasized the advent of novel forms of order. Shari'a codification, new methods of instruction, changes in court procedures, and legal-document registration are among the diverse expressions of a fundamental reordering of Yemeni society. Many significant new institutions, some of Western origin, were introduced in mediated form by the Ottomans; others were based on examples from British-controlled Aden. Taken over by Yemenis, these new forms and techniques were rephrased, first as the hybrid institutions of twentieth-century imamic rule and then, on a far more comprehensive scale, as the postrevolutionary innovations of the republic. The appearance of stand-alone "forms" and a new relation of form and content were integral to the technologies of signification at the heart of the reorderings. This transformation was not an evolutionary event but a historical one, part of the gradual incorporation of Yemen into the structures of the world system. In a world influenced in different ways by the imperial and colonial West, highland Yemen represents a situation at one extreme of the continuum of possibilities, in which change occurred at a pace marked by an unusual absence of outside intervention.

While necessarily concerned to invoke and address family resemblances found in other places and times, a discursive history of the type attempted here must also be resolutely specific. Ultimately, these spiral texts pertained to Yemen alone—even the Arab traveler found them exotic. While it is possible to speak generally of the Islamic "discursive tradition," looked at in local-level detail even regional versions fragment into multiple histories. While they exhibit important shared structural regularities, the phenomena that compose a tradition also put its cohesiveness in question. For diverse structural and political reasons, the constituent genres and institutional domains changed in different ways and at different rates. Also, as the spiraling correspondence of the imams and the concurrent straight texts of the Ottomans illustrate, practitioners of old and new coexisted. Dichotomies such as opposed epistemes have the heuristic importance of succinctly summarizing the scope of change. But there are neither clear epistemological poles nor all-inclusive watershed points in specific discursive histories. Just as there was no original society of stationary traditional institutions, there is no terminus reached, no modern society completely achieved. There are only intervals of multiple transits, each composed of continuities, discontinuities, and ambiguities. In this regard, the "calligraphic state" is itself a construct, referring neither to a specific polity and its dissolution nor to a particular discursive moment and its transformation. It is instead a composite of historical materials and must finally give way to the phenomena out of which it was built.

BIOGRAPHICAL GUIDE

Abu Shuja', Ahmad. Author of shari'a jurisprudence manual, Shafi'i school; died after 1107; lived in Basra

Ahmad b. Yahya Hamid al-Din. Imam of Yemen 1948–1962

al-Akwa', 'Ali b. Husayn. Zaidi scholar; father of Muhammad and Isma'il; posted to Ibb as a teacher in early 1920s

al-Akwa', Isma'il b. 'Ali. Published scholar; Director of Antiquities; Ibb resident in the 1930s and 1940s

al-Akwa', Muhammad b. 'Ali. Born 1903. Published historian; former cabinet minister, judge, and teacher in Ibb; leader in 1940s of early opposition movement in Ibb

al-'Ansi, Salih. Ibb judge; student of al-Shawkani; died 1875

al-'Awdi, Muhammad Zain. Ibb school principal and adib

Basalama, Isma'il. Governor of Ibb (under Ottomans and Imam Yahya); shaykh; leading merchant; died 1934

al-Basir, Ahmad. Ibb teacher and notary; died late 1970s

Faqih al-Nahi. Ibb scholar; died 1171

Faqih Sa'id. Saintly figure; executed in Ibb in 1841

al-Ghazzali, Abu Hamid Muhammad b. Muhammad. A leading Muslim intellectual figure; died 1111

al-Ghazzi, Ibn al-Qasim. Commentator on the text by Abu Shuja'; died 1512

al-Haddad, 'Abd al-Rahman b. 'Ali Naji. Shafi'i scholar and public official in the Ottoman period; born in Ibb 1876; died 1922

al-Haddad, Ahmad b. Muhammad b. 'Ali Naji. Ibb mufti and judge; died 1981

al-Haddad, 'Ali Naji. Ibb scholar and mufti; died 1893

al-Haddad, Muhammad b. Yahya b. 'Ali Naji. Published historian; Ibb resident

Hamid al-Din. The line of Zaidi imams that included twentieth-century imams Yahya, Ahmad, and al-Badr

Ibn Khaldun. North African scholar and jurist; author of *Al-Muqaddima*; died 1406

Ibn Samura al-Ja'adi, 'Umar. Yemeni historian; died 1190

al-Iryani, 'Abd al-Rahman b. Yahya b. Muhammad. Ibb judge, local coup leader in 1948; president of the Republic, 1967–1974

al-Iryani, Yahya b. Muhammad. Scholar, Ibb judge, presiding judge of the Appeal Court; died 1943

al-Juwayni, "Imam al-Haramayn." Shafi'i scholar; teacher of al-Ghazzali; author of an usul manual studied in Ibb; died 1086

al-Murtada, Imam Ahmad b. Yahya. Author of *Kitab al-Azhar*; died 1432

al-Nawawi, Muhyi al-Din. Shafi'i jurist; author of *Al-Minhaj*; native of Syria; died 1277

al-Shafi'i, Muhammad b. Idris. Jurist; founder of the Shafi'i school; died 820

al-Shawkani, Muhammad b. 'Ali. Yemeni scholar; died 1834

al-Wasi'i, 'Abd al-Wasi' b. Yahya. Yemeni historian; died 1959

Yahya Hamid al-Din. Imam of Yemen (declared 1904–, ruled 1918–1948)

Zabara, Muhammad b. Muhammad. Yemeni historian; died 1961

Zaid b. 'Ali. Fourth-generation descendant of the Prophet; founder of the Zaidi school; died 740

GLOSSARY

adab	intellectual culture, correct comportment
'adala	justness, probity
Aden	port city on Indian Ocean; former British colony and former capital of South Yemen
adib	man of letters
'alama	signature/seal
'alim, pl. 'ulama'	scholar
'ammi, pl. 'awamm	common person, uneducated person
arsh	wound evaluation
asl	original, source
al-Azhar	mosque university in Cairo
(*Kitab*) *al-Azhar*	basic fiqh text of the Zaidi school
basira	sale document
basmala	term for the phrase "In the Name of God the Merciful and Compassionate"
batin	internal; implicit meaning
bulugh	physical maturity
da'if	weak, in social identity; its opposite is qawi
dalil, pl. adilla	indication; legal reference, in a source text
daraja, pl. darajat	degree, step; used in the Quran in connection with social difference
darasa (noun)	advanced instruction
Dhamar	town on highland plateau; provincial capital; old Zaidi scholarly center
diwan	semipublic sitting room in a residence; work place of official and secretaries
dustur	constitution
faqih	scholar, one knowledgeable in fiqh; Quranic school teacher

far', pl. furu'	derived rule (*see* asl); pl. the "branches" literature, the works of applied jurisprudence
Fatiha	opening sura of the Quran
fatwa	nonbinding opinion of a mufti
fiqh	jurisprudence
furu'	*see* far'
gha'ib	absent party; term for the third person pronominal form in Arabic
hadd, pl. hudud	Quranic punishment
hadith	an oral report, especially concerning the Prophet's words or deeds; also the name of the science of such reports
hafaza (verb)	memorize
haiba	awe, fear, respect
hajaba (verb)	hide, conceal, veil
hakim	judge
Hanafi	school of (Sunni) shari'a jurisprudence; official school of the Ottoman Empire; named after Abu Hanifa, died A.D. 767
Hazr	residence of advanced students in Ibb
hijāj, sing. hujja	evidences from the world, bases for judgment
hudud	*see* hadd
hukm	binding ruling of a judge, a hakim
'ibadat	ritual rules; opening section of the fiqh works
Ibb	town in Lower Yemen; provincial capital
ijaza	license received in advanced instruction
ijma'	consensus
ijtihad	interpretation
ijtihadat	interpretive opinions; another term for imamic ikhtiyarat
ikhtiyarat	lit. "choices"; personal opinions of Zaidi imams, applied in their courts
'ilm	knowledge
imam	spiritual-temporal ruler of the Muslim community; also a prayer leader in a mosque
'imama	turban of a scholar
isnad	"chain" of human transmitters in oral transmission
jahil, pl. juhhal	ignorant person; a child
jawab	answer; a mufti's fatwa is one specialized type
katama (verb)	to conceal, hide; used in connection with knowledge and evidence
katib	writer
kitab	text, scripture, book, document

khatam	ceremony at the leaving of Quranic school
khatm	seal
khatt	handwriting, script, calligraphy
luha	writing board used in instruction
ma'arif	public instruction
madhhab	doctrinal school of shari'a jurisprudence
madrasa	school
mahfuzat	memorized texts
mahkama	court
Majalla	the Ottoman civil code promulgated in 1876
malaka	term used by Ibn Khaldun meaning "habitus"
Maliki	(Sunni) school of shari'a jurisprudence named after Malik b. Anas, died A.D. 795
maqru'at	recited texts; *see* qara'a
masmu'at	heard texts
matn, pl. mutun	text, basic text; a manual of fiqh jurisprudence
mi'lama	Quranic school
milk	private ownership
al-Minhaj	shari'a jurisprudence (fiqh) manual, Shafi'i school, by al-Nawawi
mu'amalat	transactions; a section of the fiqh works
mufti	deliverer of nonbinding legal opinions known as fatwas
muhājirin	advanced students
mujtahid	interpreter, one capable of ijtihad
al-Mukhtasar	"The abridgement"; title of many works, including the Shafi'i fiqh manual by Abu Shuja'
muqabala	meeting; muqabala bil-asl: collation of copy and · original
mutala'a	reading; *see* tala'a
muwajaha	encounter, face-to-face meeting, audience
muwatin	citizen
nass	text, source text
nizam	order; used in connection with nineteenth-century reform movements
nuskha	copy
qadi	judge; also, in Yemen, a scholarly individual or member of a scholarly family of other than sayyid descent
qanun	Ottoman administrative law, legislated law; as "Qanun San'a'," town market regulations
qara'a (verb)	recite (also "read" in contemporary usage)
qat	plant, *Catha edulis*, chewed in afternoon qat sessions
qawi	strong, in social identity; its opposite is da'if

qawl	spoken word, opinion
qira'a	recitation
qiyas	analogy
riwaya	oral transmission
rushd	intellectual maturity, adolescence
Rushdiyya	Ottoman advanced primary school; *see* rushd
Sa'da	town in the far northern highlands
San'a'	capital of Yemen
sar (verb)	became
sayyid, pl. sada	descendant of the Prophet Muhammad
Shafi'i	school of (Sunni) shari'a jurisprudence, named after Muhammad b. Idris al-Shafi'i, died A.D. 820; also used in reference to a follower of this school and to an inhabitant of Lower Yemen
shahada	testimony of the faith; testimony; diploma
shahid, pl. shuhud	witness
shakwa	complaint or petition presented to an official
sharh	commentary
Sharh al-Azhar	commentary on the Azhar fiqh manual
shari'a	God's plan for the Muslim community; the central societal discourse; Islamic law
Shi'i	lit. "faction"; those holding that leadership of the Muslim community should pertain to the direct descendants of the Prophet
shura	consultation
Sinna	title for Quranic school teacher
siyasa	statecraft
sulh	compromise
sunna	authoritative practice of the Prophet Muhammad
Sunni	those holding that leadership of the Muslim community need not be restricted to the direct descendants of the Prophet; an adherent of one of four standard schools of shari'a interpretation
tabaqat	social levels; intellectual generations
tabib	doctor
Ta'izz	city in Lower Yemen; capital in the 1950s
tala'a	to read; *see* mutali'a
taqlid	acceptance of established doctrine
tawatur	knowledge that has the status of received wisdom
Tihama	coastal plain along the Red Sea
'ulama', sing. 'alim	scholars
umma	the community of Muslims
'urf	custom

usul, sing. asl	sources; *see* far'
usul al-fiqh	the methodological ("roots") branch of the jurisprudence literature; *see* furu'
wakil	legal representative
waqf, pl. awqaf	endowment
yad	hand; handwriting
Zabid	town on Tihama coastal plain; old scholarly center
zahir	outward appearance, manifest meaning
Zaidi	(Shi'i) school of shari'a jurisprudence; named after Zaid b. 'Ali, died 740; an adherent to this school or, generally, an inhabitant of Upper Yemen
zulm	injustice

NOTES

CHAPTER 1

1. Ibn Samura 1957:213. Faqih al-Nahi was reckoned in the seventh generation of Yemeni jurists. On the town, see art. "Ibb," *Encyclopedia of Islam* (hereafter the first and second editions will be cited as *EI* 1 and *EI* 2; the *Shorter Encyclopedia of Islam* will be cited as *SEI*).

2. Al-Shirazi, died 1083 (all dates are A.D. unless A.H. is indicated). See *EI* 1, art. "Al-Shirazi." The text was *Al-muhadhdhab*; cf., for Yemen, Ibn Samura 1957:126f., 171, 217; al-Khazraji 1911:368, 1914:343–44; al-Burayhi 1983:86. For Yemeni historical materials, see al-Hibshi 1972, 1983; Sayyid 1974:33–34. On the intellectual culture of eleventh-century Baghdad, and *shari'a* jurisprudence as the "queen" of the scholarly disciplines, see the important study by Makdisi (1981).

3. For the usage of '–m–d root terms to characterize authoritative texts, Ibn Samura 1957:126, al-Nawawi 1882:2, 6, 7; al-Shawkani A.H. 1348, 2:394; I. al-Akwa' 1980:9–10. Some texts had *Al-mu'tamad*, "the relied upon," as a title; in al-Nawawi's work, the subtitle was *Wa 'umdat al-muftiin*.

4. The writing of Bakhtin (1981:342f.) on "authoritative discourse" is relevant here: "The authoritative word demands that we acknowledge it, that we make it our own; it binds us, quite independent of any power it might have to persuade us internally; we encounter it with its authority already fused to it. The authoritative word is located in a distanced zone, organically connected with a past that is felt to be hierarchically higher. It is, so to speak, the word of the fathers."

5. There are early exceptions—e.g., for the Shafi'i school, *Al-Mukhtasar* of al-Muzani (d. 877).

6. Ibn Khaldun 1958, 3:290–91.

7. The Arabic term *malaka* (pl. *malakat*) is a borrowing via translation of the Greek *exis*, which was also translated into Latin as *habitus* (Rosenthal

1958:lxxxiv). For Pierre Bourdieu (1977; 1984), a comparable notion of "habitus" is the central concept in his poststructuralist sociology of practice. Similarities between the two analytic usages include an emphasis on the bodily basis and implicit qualities of the dispositions involved, reference to language models, and emphasis on the importance of repetition/practice for inculcation and reproduction. For Ibn Khaldun a distinct habitus pertains to each art or "craft," a concept that includes scholarship as one of many varieties. As a person is decisively "colored" by a habitus, the acquisition of one makes that of another difficult or impossible. For Bourdieu (1984:170–75) there is a separate habitus associated with each of the class-based "conditions of existence" of modern societies. Drawing on the cultural specificity of Ibn Khaldun and the poststructuralism of Bourdieu, I examine the internal differentiation and cross-genre and cross-institution homologies of a textual habitus, a set of generative dispositions structuring (and structured by) discursive practices.

8. *SEI*, art. "Al-Shafi'i"; for a biography by a Yemeni, see Ibn Samura 1957:134–42.

9. Zabara 1979:347–48.

10. All citations are from the three-volume Arabic text of Van Den Berg (al-Nawawi 1882–83–84); cf. art. "Al-Nawawi" in *SEI*.

11. Keyzer (Keijzer) trans. (Abu Shuja' 1859). I have used the Arabic text of the Van Den Berg translation of the commentary by al-Ghazzi (1894) with the *Mukhtasar* of Abu Shuja' embedded. For the biography of Abu Shuja', see the article in *EI* 2.

12. Burton 1893, 1:103n.

13. Al-Nawawi 1914.

14. See Calder 1990, for references and for discussion of how the Prophet's illiteracy became a figure in discursive theory.

15. Hurgronje 1931:168n.

16. See Graham 1985, 1987; Fischer and Abedi 1990a, 1990b.

17. *EI* 2, art. "Kira'a."

18. Cited in Juynboll 1969 and 1983 in his discussions of *tadwin*, the recording of hadith. See also Powers 1986.

19. Goldziher, quoted in *SEI*, art. "Hadith," p. 120.

20. See *EI* 1 and 2, arts. "Kur'an"; as-Said 1975.

21. Ibn Samura 1957:190–91. Sayf al-Sunna's tomb and an associated, within-the-walls cemetery are well-known landmarks in Ibb town. Many later scholarly biographies refer to burials near Sayf al-Sunna.

22. See the article "Muslim b. al-Hadjdjadj" in *SEI*. The author of *Al-Minhaj* was a principal commentator on the *Sahih* (al-Nawawi 1929).

23. Al-Shafi'i's *Risala*, trans. Khadduri (al-Shafi'i 1961:239), translation modified; cf. *Risala*, ed. Shakir (al-Shafi'i 1940:370–71).

24. While it is generally recognized that early Semites invented the pho-

netic alphabet, it has been argued that the Greeks significantly "perfected" it by developing vowel letters (Ong 1982:89, 91; for a review of recent literature, see Goody 1987:40ff). Alphabet issues have figured centrally in a much larger claim, however—namely, that "writing has transformed human consciousness" (Ong 1982:78). How writing has done so, it has been argued, has depended, in part, on the alphabetic technology available. The work of Eric Havelock (1963), comparing the oral versus literate intellectual styles of Homer and Plato, has constituted a crucial point of departure both for Ong and for Goody, the leading anthropological student of literacy and writing. Within literate civilizations, it is maintained, different alphabets have differing capacities to promote such things as "analytic thought." "It does appear," Ong (1982:90) writes, "that the Greeks did something of major psychological importance when they developed the first alphabet complete with vowels." He follows Havelock in the view that "this crucial, more nearly total transformation of the word from sound to sight gave ancient Greek culture its intellectual ascendancy over other ancient cultures." Goody, however, has reconsidered his earlier use of the Greek case as a model for cross-cultural comparison. He now finds it "necessary to challenge certain notions about the uniqueness of the West as far as the explanation for the emergence of the 'modern' world is concerned" (1986:xi). In particular, "the 'alphabetic' writing of the Greeks is no longer seen as so unique an achievement" (1987:xvii–xviii). The whole constructed legacy of Greek originality, including the alphabet thesis, has been critiqued by M. Bernal in his *Black Athena* (1987). For a view of Arabic writing that considers vowels "a peculiar European invention" rather than as "something 'missing' from Arabic," see the discussion of grammatical "movement" in Mitchell 1988:148–49.

25. The history of the Arabic alphabet is relevant here. The Quran was placed in definitive written form "before the development of an Arabic orthography that could indicate with some precision how a text actually reads"; as a consequence, this early manuscript's "defective consonantal form allows for variant readings not only of internal vowels and inflectional endings, but even of many of the wholly unpointed consonants themselves" (Graham 1985:34; cf. Ibn Khaldun 1958, 2:382). For an example of the ensuing interpretive complexities, see Powers 1986.

26. Both are mentioned in the biography of 'Abd al-Rahman al-Haddad (Zabara 1979:347–48). Among the Malikis of North Africa the text by Ibn Malik was one of several "memorized by all educated men" (Eickelman 1978:497n).

27. See al-Burayhi (1983:85, 87, 98, 102) for use in Ibb. Ibn al-Wardi's text was a versification of the manual by al-Qazwini (d. 1266); cf. *SEI*, art. "Al-Shafiʿi," p. 514; and I. al-Akwaʿ 1980:9.

28. According to al-ʿAmri (1985:191), these categories are eulogy, censure, self-glorification, criticism, and politics.

29. Aside from major manuals, a variety of brief compositions were versified. Two examples are a twentieth-century collection of imamic opinions (al-Shamahi 1937 [A.H. 1356]) and an official schedule of damage awards for physical injuries (Zabara 1956:66–67). The opening of the former declares that "among the most important of obligations/[is] Memorization of the opinions of the Imam of the Arabs"; the latter begins, "Memorization of knowledge is a facilitation/For its student, so memorize the verse-text/Of injury penalties." Commentaries could also be versified: al-Suyuti's thousand verses are a commentary on an embedded verse text, while the legal manual by Ibn al-Wardi is a verse-commentary on a prose *matn* he "decided to versify." On the margins of the Ibn al-Wardi text, an author of other verses explains his treatment of still another text, saying he "versified it, summarizing its expression, rendering simpler its comprehension and its memorization."

Verse both serious and light and on a wide spectrum of subjects has been a constant of highland scholarly activity. A few artful lines by a man of repute could release a torrent of rhymed replies, offerings of augmenting verses, and interstitial flourishes. For a number of years, Ibb literati engaged in a protracted poetry duel with their counterparts from the neighboring town Jibla. When Muhammad al-Shawkani (see chap. 2) passed the night in al-Makhadir just north of Ibb, he composed two verses in praise of the evening scene. In them he introduced a legal metaphor that played on the name of a nearby qat-producing area called al-Bukhari, which is also the name of a famous compiler of hadith. The poem caught the attention of other poets, including two *adibs* from the al-Basir family of Ibb. One of these set about adding both further verses and interstitial rhymes in a different meter, all based on the original metaphor (see Zabara 1931:391). Excerpts from the Ibb-Jibla poetic duel are in Zabara (1941:206ff.). In 1922 Imam Yahya took time from a busy schedule during the fasting month of Ramadan to compose a long poem on the virtues of qat (Rihani 1930:210–11). Gatherings to chew qat and to hear the lines of old poets sung by musicians have always been a frequent pastime in Ibb. In Arabian society generally, poetry is "a major art, perhaps the supreme art" (Serjeant 1951:1), and its "tribal" practitioners have begun to receive the attention they deserve (Caton 1990; Dresch 1989; Meeker 1979).

30. Khadduri, trans., in al-Shafi'i 1961:15. On the similar composition of al-Shafi'i's longer work, *Al-Umm*, see al-Mahmassani 1961:28. For a general discussion of this phenomenon, see Pederson 1984, chap. 3. In a very different intellectual environment, Saussure's *Cour de Linguistique Generale* was also created from student notes.

31. Imam al-Mahdi Ahmad bin Yahya al-Murtada composed his *Kitab al-Azhar* during the years 1392–1399 while in jail (al-Shawkani A.H. 1348, 1:126).

32. Rosenthal (1947:7) notes that "the historian and theologian entirely relies upon written material. Memorized knowledge has no longer any place in his work." The conventional classifications of the Muslim intellectual disci-

plines are also relevant to the boundaries of the recitational complex. See *EI* 2, art. "*'Ilm*"; al-Azmeh 1986:146–97. On medicine in Ibb, see chap. 4, n. 16.

33. In his ground-breaking work on Muslim education in Morocco, Eickelman characterized the pedagogical style as "intermediate between oral and written systems of transmission of knowledge. Its key texts existed in written form but were conveyed orally, to be written down and memorized by students" (1978:487; 1985). Al-Azmeh (1986:155) terms such systems "composite."

34. Al-Shafi'i 1961:265. I have modified the translation; cf. al-Shafi'i 1940:431.

35. Al-Shafi'i 1961:239–40. Translation slightly modified; cf. al-Shafi'i 1940:371.

36. Ibn Samura (1957:157) mentions a man who had five hundred volumes, and al-Akwa' (1980:194) one with two thousand. As al-Akwa' (1980:7) notes, it was common for rulers and powerful individuals to establish libraries in connection with the schools they founded. (On library reform, see chap. 6.) Small personal libraries were common in Ibb, although many were lost when the town was plundered in 1948. For a survey of all aspects of the Muslim culture of the book, see Pederson 1984. On calligraphy in particular, see *EI* 2, art. "Khatt," and Schimmel (1970; 1984), which include extensive bibliographies.

37. Al-Khazraji 1911:56.

38. Cf. Ibn Khaldun 1981:755, where the collation process is described as *al-riwaya wa al-dabt*, i.e., "oral recitation and checking."

39. Cf. Beeston 1983:24. Bakhtin (1981) discusses the protective framing of authoritative discourse.

40. In the case of *Al-Minhaj*, two important commentaries studied in Yemen are by Ibn Hajar 1897 and al-Ramli 1967; in that of *Al-Mukhtasar*, the main commentary is by al-Ghazzi 1894, and an important gloss is by al-Bajuri 1974.

41. For details, see *SEI*, art. "Al-Shafi'i."

42. Two well-known Prophetic hadiths elaborate this assumption: "Difference of opinion in my community is a [manifestation of Divine] mercy," and "My community will become divided into seventy-three sects."

43. Al-Nawawi 1883:4. Here and in other citations of al-Nawawi and of Abu Shuja' /al-Ghazzi (1894), I have consulted the French and (in the case of *Al-Minhaj*) the English renderings but have generally made my own more literal translations.

44. According to the doctrine of abrogating and abrogated sections, there are some contradictory positions in the Quran. In the exegesis (*tafsir*) literature, the sacred text is opened up to the interpretive efforts of human commentators. The definitive written text of the Quran was established, and enforced by 'Uthman (cf. *EI* 2, art. "Kur'an"; as-Said 1975), and seven standard recitations were later authorized (ibid.; *EI* 1, art. "Tadjwid").

CHAPTER 2

1. There are Shafi'is in some of the western mountain districts in the north; see Gerholm 1977:33–35. There are also important Isma'ili groups, and formerly there was a large Jewish population.

2. *EI*, art. "Al-Zaidiya," and Serjeant (1969:285); cf. al-'Amri (1985:6 and refs. cited).

3. Al-'Amri 1985:127. To these may be added the nonrecognition of both the practice of *taqiyya*, dissimulation of religious identity, and the existence of the "*nass*," a written bequest from the Prophet identifying 'Ali as his successor (*EI* 1, art. "Al-Zaidiya"; Serjeant 1969; Stookey 1978:83–85).

4. *Al-Azhar*, "Kitab al-siyar" (al-Murtada 1973:313–28). Cf. renderings of the list of attributes in Strothman 1912:80; Rihani 1930:108; Stookey 1978:83–85; Serjeant, in Serjeant and Lewcock 1983:77.

5. Quoted in Stookey 1978:84. An imam should be courageous (*miqdam*) but not foolhardy (al-Murtada 1973:314).

6. Rihani 1930. In Arabic al-Rihani (1951) wrote *rabb al-sayf wa al-ijtihad*.

7. See al-Hibshi 1979. In the Preface to this work, Serjeant writes, "There can indeed be few countries of the world where so many rulers have not only written, but made a significant contribution to learning" (ibid., p. vii). Cf. al-'Amri 1985:6 and refs. In the absence of an individual with the appropriate scholarly credentials, a caretaker figure, known as a *muhtasib*, was envisioned (al-Murtada 1973:313–28).

8. E.g., "Whatever our master the Imam al-Mahdi...and the scholars pronounce is to be acted upon for it is shar'." Cited Serjeant and Lewcock 1983:430.

9. See *EI* 2, arts. "Imam," "Khalifa"; Emile Tyan 1954, 1956; Arnold 1924; al-Mawardi 1915; and cf., the "Mirrors for Princes" literature, e.g., al-Ghazzali 1964. With reference to the Ottoman Empire, see Gibb and Bowen (1950:27–38). On early-twentieth-century reformist thinking about the imamate/caliphate, see Kerr 1966.

10. The Prophet's specific descent line was part of the larger Hashimite clan, which was one of ten such clans that composed Quraysh.

11. Al-Nawawi 1884:202–3. Al-Nawawi makes occasional use of the terms *sultan* and *imam*. There are no requirements listed for a sultan, a position mentioned in passing in connection with public Friday prayer, alms (*zakat*), the enlivening of land, marriage responsibilities (as ultimate guardian), and responsibility for miscarriages in one type of circumstance. Aside from the list of requirements, an imam figures in matters connected with warfare (permission for raids, distribution of booty, dealing with rebels, jihad, prisoners, financing the military), distribution of charity (*sadaqa*), criminal punishments (crimes against persons, capital punishment, and the *hadd* crime of adultery), and responsibility for a well.

12. Ibn Khaldun 1958, 3:314 on "hukm al-sultani."

13. On women scholars, al-Shawkani A.H. 1348, 2:24, 25, Appendix 104; cf. *shaykhat* mentioned in intellectual genealogy of Ibn al-Jawzi, cited al-'Amri 1985:107.

14. "The commentary which students have relied upon until the present" (al-Shawkani A.H. 1348, 1:394).

15. Van Arendonk 1960; Stookey 1978; Gochenour 1984.

16. Dresch 1984:154, cf. 1989; Caton 1990; Stookey 1978.

17. In a circular dated 1774 [A.H. 1188], Imam al-Mahdi al-'Abbas (born in Ibb in 1719 [A.H. 1131]) requires all judges of his realm to apply Zaidi school principles (reproduced in al-'Alimi 1989:256–57; cf. p. 128).

18. Ibn Samura 1957:79–80, cited in Maktari 1972:4.

19. Sometimes referred to as *'asabiyya*. Northerners use the disparaging term *lughlughi* to refer to the speech of Lower Yemen, while in Ibb there is sensitivity to "San'ani dialect." One distinguishing feature is that the letter *qaf* is pronounced with a *q* in Lower Yemen and *g* in Upper Yemen.

20. For movements during the Qasimi period, see Messick 1978:48–50, 268–69. The phenomenon began centuries earlier; see Dresch 1989 and Stookey 1978:153.

Two families provide examples of contemporary town descent groups which began in Ibb with eighteenth-century judicial postings. Muhammad al-Shuwaytr (d. 1758) was from Dhamar, the northern plateau town about the size of Ibb, located on the route to San'a' and famous as a center of Zaidi scholarship. He is credited with a commentary on the text of the *Azhar*, and he also served three different imams in five judicial appointments in Lower Yemen, to the time of his death in Ibb. His son followed him as judge of Ibb, and his grandson, in a branch of the al-Shuwaytr family by then well rooted in Ibb, was born, lived, and died (1796) in the town. But during his student days this grandson was sent north to the family's ancestral Dhamar to study Zaidi jurisprudence. Back in Ibb as a teacher, it is noted in his biography that he taught inheritance law and gave instruction in the key Zaidi text-and-commentary, the *Sharh al-Azhar*. The same fundamental work figured as well in the formation of scholars of the al-Mujahid family. The elder al-Mujahid (d. 1763) grew up in in the far northern town of Sa'da, the original Zaidi toehold in Yemen, where he was exposed to a wide number of subjects before concentrating on rhetoric and the *Sharh al-Azhar*. He later managed to get appointments, first to the ruling imam's elite circle of secretaries, and then to a judgeship in Lower Yemen. The last sixteen of a total of thirty years of judicial service were spent as the judge of Ibb. Although raised in Ibb, his son was also sent to Dhamar to finish his instruction with a prominent jurist (another al-Shuwaytr) with whom he studied *Sharh al-Azhar*. Sources: al-Shuwaytr (Zabara 1958:716, 727; 1931:314), al-Mujahid (Zabara 1958:171; 1931:394; al-Shawkani A.H. 1348, suppl.:153).

21. For a discussion of the man and his work, see al-'Amri 1985.

22. Al-Shawkani A.H. 1348:2–3; cf. al-'Amri's (1985:146) translation of

the first part of this text and his comments on al-Shawkani as a historian (pp. 188–91). As al-'Amri notes, al-Shawkani (A.H. 1348, 1:3–4) also offers a critique of historiography, specifically the biographical history form.

23. See al-'Amri 1985:106–10, for a discussion of this work and a useful genealogical table.

24. Stookey 1978:83.

25. On al-Juwayni, known as Imam al-Haramayn, see *EI* 2, art. "Djuwaini." His *Kitab al-Waraqat* (al-Juwayni n.d.) is also included in a commentary by al-Mahalli (n.d.) and is translated by L. Bercher (al-Juwayni 1930).

26. Al-'Amri, p. 129, based on al-Shijni.

27. Zabara 1958:14; al-Shawkani A.H. 1348, 1:287, with note 1 by Zabara; cf. al-'Amri 1985:128. According to al-'Ansi family sources in Ibb, he was al-Shawkani's son-in-law. Al-'Ansi's poetry is found in the biography of 'Ali Naji al-Haddad, in Zabara 1956:149.

28. Biography in Zabara 1979:347–48. Zabara based his account on local family sources, especially 'Abd al-Rahman's noted brother Abu Bakr. The biographical sketch that follows is derived from Zabara and from oral sources in the contemporary al-Haddad family.

29. He is credited with treatises on such diverse subjects as *jihad* (in connection with the dual threats of the Idrisi ruler of the 'Asir and the Christian powers); on miracles attributed to saints, and a biographical work on the "kings" of the 'Uthman line (Zabara 1979:348). None of these works were available to me.

30. Al-Jirafi 1951:258n; al-Akwa' 1980:295. Issued sometime before the death of al-Haddad in 1922, Imam Yahya's *ikhtiyarat* were initially a simple prose list kept at the courts (al-'Alimi 1989:258–59). They were later reversified, commented upon, and published in al-Shamahi 1937 (see chap. 11 below). An example of such opinions from previous Zaidi imams is the *ikhtiyarat* of al-Mu'ayyad billah Muhammad b. al-Qasim, 1602–1644 (Serjeant and Lewcock 1983:79). In about 1950, Imam Ahmad invited scholarly comment on the poetry version (*manzum*) of his own *ikhtiyarat*. One who replied was Ahmad b. Muhammad al-Haddad, mufti of Ibb. The imam subsequently wrote to al-Haddad, "Your letter of commentary on our honored *ikhtiyarat* arrived clothed in eloquence and originality as it derived the Quranic *adilla* [see chap. 7 below] and the Prophetic hadiths, and we thank you for that" (photo in my files).

31. A short list of such works would include, in the field of hadith, the two early *Sahih*s of Muslim and Bukhari, commentaries by the Shafi'i al-Nawawi and the Zaidi Ibn al-Amir (*Subul al-Salam*); al-Zamakhshari and al-Baydawi in *tafsir*; and Ibn Hisham and Ibn Malik in grammar.

32. According to al-Jirafi (1951:96) there was "chaos" after the fall of the Qasimi state. Al-'Amri (1985:3) is of the opinion that al-Mahdi al-'Abbas (d. 1775) "was the last important imam in the whole history of the imamate."

33. Shaykh Ahmad 'Ali Sa'd and son Sa'id were of northern tribal ancestry

(oral sources: their descendants, Shaykh ʿAli Muhsin Pasha of al-Mudhaykhira and son Shaykh Sadiq; cf. Zabara 1929:159; Playfair 1970 [1859]:126).

Faqih Saʿid claimed to be the imam and the awaited mahdi and took the important state-formation step of coining money in his own name. A full spectrum of labels have been applied to this figure, viz.: *faqih* (jurist), *sufi*, *wali* (saint), *imam*, *mahdi*, and, in the view from British Aden, "fanatic" (Zabara 1931:226–27; al-Jirafi 1951:197; al-Shamahi 1972:157–59; Playfair 1970 [1859]:147). In oral history, Faqih Saʿid is attributed with control over the jinn, and he is said to have assured his forces that no harm could come to them when fighting for his cause. After treachery and defeats, his demise came in Ibb where he was beheaded by order of the imam.

This last of the great saintly figures of Lower Yemen (see notes 36, 37, and 39 below) appeared in the unlikely environment of Wahhabi influence combined with existing Zaidi opposition to such "idolatry." A nineteenth-century Yemeni historian saw Faqih Saʿid as an originally benign and ascetic "sufi" who, had he been offered the world, would not have taken it. "For forty years he remained in studious retirement, isolated from the people of wealth and power" (al-Hibshi 1980:92). For a contemporary Yemeni historian, the rise of Faqih Saʿid is closely connected to the chaotic situation of the region, which included foreign occupation of the Yemeni coast. Faqih Saʿid is seen as having overcome the quietistic bent of the sufi (asserted to be a typical Shafiʿi reaction to trying times) to lead a popularly rooted rebellion seeking social reform (al-ʿAmri 1984:291–99).

34. On the period, see al-Sayaghi 1978. Cf. Stookey 1978:159; Serjeant and Lewcock 1983:89, 90, 191n; Playfair 1970 [1859]:4, 29; Gavin 1975:132.

35. A full assessment of the Ottoman period in Yemen must await a study of Ottoman sources. These include archives in Istanbul and such records as the Ottoman court registers available in Yemen. In 1980, Jon Mandaville and Muhammad al-Shuʿaybi collected registers from al-Hudayda, Bajil, al-Zaydiyya, Kamaran Island, and Turbah and deposited them in the Central Library of the Ministry of Justice in Sanʿaʾ. Studies of turn-of-the-century census data note, however, that the census was not "extended to the Yemen, the Hecaz, Tripoli of Libya, and Bengazi, where regular Tanzimat provincial administration was not yet established" (Shaw 1978:332).

Also remaining to be investigated are the early-twentieth-century Arab world interconnections. James Gelvin, who is working on Salafiyya connections, kindly provided me a copy of an account by Muhibb al-Din al-Khatib of a trip to Yemen (al-Khatib 1972).

36. A *qada* administration, headed by a *qaʾimmaqam* was established in Ibb, replicating a structure found throughout the empire. This district officer, with his secretary and an assistant, oversaw the directors of the subdistricts of Jibla and al-Makhadir and Ibb town offices that included treasury, education, a district court staff, a company of gendarmes, and a section concerned with "orphans and military and civilian pensioners." (Source: Ibb *qadaʾ* financial

summary for 1916, original in my files; I thank Jon Mandaville for help with
the Ottoman Turkish of this document.) Also functioning at the time, but
not mentioned in the summary, were the Municipality Office and the Pious
Endowments Office. Until the last years, the staffing was Turks and Ottoman Arabs at the top and town men occupying the middle and lower rungs.
A small indicator of the special circumstances of Ottoman Yemen is the
effort to institute standardized official attire. In the mid-1890s, Yemeni functionaries were required to wear Turkish attire, replacing the 'imama turban
with the tarbush, but the requirement was soon dropped (al-Wasi'i 1928:161,
176).

37. Many tombs of awliyya (sing. wali) still stand in Lower Yemen, including twelve in Ibb town. These include al-Kazami, Shaykh Musa, Sayf al-
Sunna, Shams al-Din (Fairuz), al-Nasr (formerly at the main gate and now
gone), al-Muqri, al-Khatib, Sadat al-Barashi, Beni Mufaddal (in a house), 'Ali
b. 'Umar al-Azhar, al-Daghdagh b. Ayyub (in Mansub house), al-Shammal
(in al-Mahatta); al-Bayhani and al-Humazi are founders' names only (source:
Ahmad al-Basir, 1975). Saint tombs were visited, mainly by women, on Thursday night (Friday eve) until such practices were banned by twentieth-century
Zaidi governors.

Yemeni saints from Lower Yemen are the subject of a fifteenth-century
biographical history by al-Sharji (n.d.). Where other works, such as that by
Ibn Samura, specialized in shari'a jurists, al-Sharji's intent was "to gather
together a book in which I single out for mention the awliyya among the people
of Yemen." He writes that he had looked through the available sources, "but
I did not see in any of them a presentation of a biography of a single individual
among the veritable sufis and ascetic scholars of Yemen. They mention only
the people of Syria and Iraq and North Africa, and such places, and this could
lead someone who did not know about the circumstances of this blessed clime
to suppose that there was no one worthy of mention, nobody who could be
described as a wali." In his entries on particular men al-Sharji undertakes to
cover "their characteristics, their sayings, their virtues, and their miracles."
The status of saintly miracles (karamat) is a central issue, one that men such as
al-Shawkani and 'Abd al-Rahman al-Haddad addressed in their writings.
After his opening remarks, al-Sharji's first section is devoted to the "miracles
of awliyya and their verification in the Quran and Sunna." He concludes the
section by saying that an accepting consensus on the status of miracles exists
among the four Sunni schools and that only the Mu'tazilites "and others like
them among the heretics" deny the existence of miracles. This last point is
especially significant, for the Zaidis are Mu'tazili in theology.

Among the Ibb men mentioned by al-Sharji (n.d.:60–61, 76) are two
fourteenth-century descendants of Sayf al-Sunna, the early hadith scholar.
They are described as jurists and awliyya. The first is a mujtahid to whom a
posthumous miracle is attributed: "Every night a light was seen to rise up from

his grave into the sky, causing the ignorant (*jahil*) to think there was a fire." The second, a teacher noted for his unusual patience with students, is referred to as a jurist and a sufi, a man who "joined two paths, who received the honor of both houses." The most famous *wali* in Ibb is al-Qudsi (d. 1289), whose white-domed tomb-and-mosque complex is located on the mountainside just north of town. A descent group still in possession of his giant-sized, crooked walking staff is one of the town's leading families (cf. al-Sharji n.d.: 107; al-Khazraji 1911:251; al-Burayhi 1983:82).

38. The Rifaʿiyya Order, brought to the town by al-Qudsi (cf. n. 37), was defunct. Al-Qudsi (from al-Quds, Jerusalem) began receiving instruction in the order at age twelve. After his studies and initiation, he was directed to make the pilgrimage to Mecca and then continue southward to Yemen, where he was to spread the order and set up lodges. According to Shuman (1960:55, n. 35), sufi activity began to decline by the Tahirid period. On sufi activity in the Hadramawt, see Serjeant (1957:20).

Berkes (*EI* 2, art. "Islah," p. 168; cf. 1964:259) states that there was a general revival of Sufi orders in the Ottoman Empire in the period 1876–1909. The Shadhiliyya Order, well known in Egypt and North and West Africa, was active in Ibb. The local shaykh came from Upper Egypt. The brothers had as their distinctive attire a white gown, white ankle-length pantaloons, special slippers, prayer beads, and a piece of wood used to clean the teeth before prayer, which at other times stuck out of the turban. They gathered in their lodge near the Great Mosque during the first morning hour after the sunrise prayer and again in the first hour of the evening after the sunset prayer. They recited two set texts of supplication (*al-mashishiyya* and *al-yaqutiyya*), then they began the *dhikr* (lit. repetition) of the name of God. This they commenced slowly and clearly, in seated positions, but then they rose in a circle to repeat rapidly the letters "alif" and "haʾ," the first and last letters of the word "Allah." In 1975 Ahmad al-Basir explained this repetition by reference to some lines of poetry: "Alif is the beginning of the name, Haʾ is the end, the two Lams are without body / All the letters come out and with them the heart rises and soars." There is now an important work by ʿAbd Allah al-Hibshi, *Al-Sufiyya wa al-fuqahaʾ fi al-yaman*, 1976, which I have not been able to consult.

39. Zabara 1956:149–57. One poem says, the Prophet "did not order us / To play the drum, the pipe, the flute." One senses a revulsion in these Shafiʿi jurists closely approximating sentiment among Zaidi scholars. Firmer still are lines that say, "To the call of Satan, you are responsive" and "Your religion is a wicked religion." These jurists rejected what they saw as claims of superiority ("They are beautiful and the rest are flawed") and of special insight ("They are the knowers of the shariʿa in truth"). Instead, the sufis are portrayed as sinners and liars, who in fact know nothing of the rules of ritual obligations, the hadiths, or the shariʿa. Especially galling for the proper jurist was the presence of the sufi music and, worse, dance in "our mosques," which

are appropriately "the places of manuscripts and books." More practically ominous, since these jurists manned the judicial posts, is the line "He who dances is not to be considered just in his testimony" (cf. al-Nawawi 1884:401–2). In Zaidi Ibb, most music would again be banned. The spiritual exercises of the sufis did not rule out participation in the conventional ritual of daily prayer. Also, men like Ahmad al-Basir, *fiqh* teacher and notary, could join a brotherhood without a conflict of identity. Except for the testimony of al-Basir, we know little of the local sufis in this period from their own perspective. It is significant that al-Haddad's and his teacher's verses are quoted in a Zaidi-authored biographical work, which describes the poetry as "written on the subject of the sufi heretics."

40. Serjeant 1969:297; cf. al-'Amri 1985:69 on an earlier instance of tomb destruction. The large surrounding mosque complex was not destroyed. In 1937, Ibn 'Alwan's views had been cited in the official newspaper *al-Iman* to counter "pantheistic" (*hululiyya*) doctrines said to be propagated by Aden-based propagandists (Rossi 1938:572–73).

Ahmad Ibn 'Alwan (d. 1266) was a contemporary of al-Qudsi, but his background was quite different. Al-Sharji (n.d.:19–21) explains that he had intended to follow in his father's footsteps as a royal scribe and to that end studied grammar, language, and related subjects in the field of letters. On the very day he was to assume his father's post, as he was en route to the palace, the course of his life was abruptly changed: "A green bird landed on his shoulder and extended its beak up to his mouth. He opened his lips and the bird put something inside. He swallowed it. At that instant, he turned around in his path and went immediately into seclusion, staying in retreat for forty days." His spiritual genealogy went back to Abu Bakr, the first caliph, whom he spoke of as his shaykh. Ibn 'Alwan was known for his preaching, in the manner of Ibn al-Jawzi (cf. Giffen 1971, esp. 27–29), for his discourses and poetry on sufi themes and for speaking in tongues. In one cited discourse he makes a classic sufi distinction regarding the shari'a, stating that there is a conventional "outward" (*zahir*) meaning and a "truth" (*haqiqa*), or inner meaning. Hodgson (1974:403) has written generally that "as the several forms of Islamic piety became more clearly articulated, the more shari'a-minded came actively to distrust the Sufis and were inclined to persecute the less cautious of them for heresy; and the Sufis, though respectful of the shari'a and of the hadith-minded circles from which their movement had arisen, often privately looked down on the more shari'a-minded 'ulama' scholars as concerned more with the husks than with the kernel of truth."

In 1821, the Zaidi imam of the day was apparently about to visit Ibn 'Alwan's famous tomb, but was counseled not to do so, perhaps by al-Shawkani who was with him at the time (cf. al-'Amri 1984:231–32; al-Hibshi 1980:32–33). Hunter (1968 [1877]:175) says that one of fourteen annual saint's visitation festivals in Aden was that of Ibn 'Alwan. According to Ahmad al-Basir (Ibb, 1975), there used to be a *zawiya* for Ibn 'Alwan in Ibb, located in the present al-Mukhalata Mosque. There were also practices such as dedicating the firstborn animal, visitation of his tomb for cures, and pious beggars who circulated in his name.

41. See Messick 1978:62–65 for detail.

42. Al-Wasiʻi 1928:140. These same "people of Yemen" are characterized by their "affection" for the imam (1928:202). Due, in part, to the uniqueness of al-Wasiʻi as a published source, this Zaidi-imamic historical view has been widely reproduced in Western scholarship. The different reception of Ottoman rule in Shafiʻi as opposed to Zaidi areas of the highlands has been obscured. Stookey (1978:164, 283), for example, says that "resistance to Ottoman rule had been a salient aspiration of the Hamid al-Din imams, shared by much of the population irrespective of sect," and he refers to "a struggle by the Yemeni people under Imam Yahya's leadership against the Ottoman occupation." Serjeant (1969:295) identifies the source when he writes, "Both Zaidis and Shafiʻis considered the Turks as foreigners, oppressors, and bad Muslims —so the Yemenite historian al-Wasiʻi sums up the Yemeni view." Elsewhere in his text al-Wasiʻi is quite laudatory of specific Turkish governors, praising them in terms that approach those of ideal imamic rule. Serjeant (Serjeant and Lewcock 1983:97) also notes that, among Zaidis, "old men not infrequently speak well" of the Turks, and Gerholm (1977:35) mentions intermarriage in Manakha.

43. Al-Wasiʻi 1928:141.

44. Schacht 1964:89–90. It was Schacht's view that in the Ottoman Empire, the shariʻa received "the highest degree of actual efficiency which it had ever possessed in a society of high material civilization since early ʻAbbasid times."

45. Al-Wasiʻi 1928:233–34. Al-Wasiʻi himself was the speaker at the Great Mosque of Sanʻaʼ in 1910 [A.H. 1328] in an assembly ordered by the Ottoman governor following receipt of a telegram from Istanbul that said the Italians had declared war on the empire and were attacking Tripoli. Al-Wasiʻi urged the assembled people to "act in accord with the responsibilities of unity and agreement and leave behind differences and divisions."

46. These are unlawful intercourse, false accusation of unlawful intercourse, drinking wine, theft, and highway robbery.

47. This "Ottoman law" was known as *qanun*. The existence of this corpus of promulgations by the Ottoman sultans was based on the theory that *qanun* rules were elaborated only beyond the bounds of what the shariʻa set forth (Berkes 1964:14; Schacht 1964:91; Gibb and Bowen 1950:23). Schacht writes that the first *qanun*, dating from the fifteenth century, "presupposes that the *hadd* punishments are obsolete and replaces them by *taʻzir*." *Taʻzir* is a form of discretionary punishment meted out by the judge. According to the nineteenth-century Ottoman Criminal Code, based on the French and modified by the Italian code, the *hadd* penalty of cutting off the hand of the thief was not recognized (al-Mahmassani 1961:42).

48. Al-Wasi'i 1928 :197. The phrase on *fasad* is a quotation of Quran 5:33.

49. In the Treaty of Da''an, signed in 1911 (text in al-Wasi'i 1928:236–39; cf. Stookey 1978:163–64).

50. In al-Wasi'i 1928:207–10.

51. Others, aside from jihad, included the collection of the tithe (*'ushur*, zakat) and, negatively, the collection of an illegal "market tax" (*maks*).

52. Al-Murtada 1973:315; cf. al-Nawawi 1884:215, 217. The *hudud* are treated in a separate *Azhar* chapter (1973:286–93), which covers the *hadd*s of unlawful intercourse and, in special sections, false accusation of unlawful intercourse (*qadhf*), wine-drinking, and theft, including highway robbery. They are distinct from the *jinayat*, the punishments associated with wounds and including legal retaliation (*qisas*) for murder, which are the subject of the following chapter in *Al-Azhar*.

53. In San'a' in 1913, with the imam exercising greater control, and with a *firman* issued from the sultan confirming a return to pure shari'a rule (Bury 1915:16), "a thief who had broken into a house was taken into custody. He acknowledged what he had stolen and his hand was cut off as a *hadd* after judgment against him. And a man who had drunk wine was brought before the judge and he legally acknowledged what he had drunk and after this was established the *hadd* was administered. And the shari'a *hadd* was applied to an adulterer after this was established by acknowledgment and fulfilling the conditions. And a murderer was brought for execution (lit. 'retaliation') and a great crowd gathered outside San'a' at the Yemen Gate" (al-Wasi'i 1928: 256–57).

54. Rossi 1938:568; Obermeyer 1981:181–82, where the following quotation is cited.

55. Al-Jirafi 1951:258n.

56. For an entire index of such categories, see M. al-Akwa' 1971:539.

57. Al-Wasi'i (1928:243–44) was aware of the rise of nationalist movements among Arab populations in Syria and Iraq.

58. "It is the Christians who say there is a difference between Zaidis and Shafi'is. But they are ignorant in these matters because they even say that the Shafi'is do not want to be ruled by the Zaidis. Now, who could believe this?" Quoted in Obermeyer (1981:186; cf. Rossi 1938:569).

59. In al-Rahumi et al. 1978:225.

60. I. al-Akwa' 1980:294.

61. Sharaf al-Din 1968:37.

CHAPTER 3

1. Quoted in Berkes 1964:167.

2. *Al-Majalla*. Arabic translation. Third printing. Matba'at al-Jawa'ib: Istanbul, A.H. 1305 [1888], p. 4. Most of the introductory report of 1869 is translated in Liebesny (1975:66–69).

3. Liebesny 1975:65.
4. *Majalla*, p. 3.
5. *Majalla*, p. 6.
6. Onar 1955:294.
7. *Majalla*, p. 4; Liebesny 1975:67.
8. *Majalla*, p. 5. Quoted in Liebesny 1975:68.
9. *Majalla*, Art. 14. Cf. Liebesny 1975:100 (referring to Iraqi Civil Code, Art. 2, the same as Art. 14 of the *Majalla*): "Where there is a text (*nass*), independent interpretation cannot be applied."
10. Kerr 1966; *EI* 2, art. "Islah."
11. Schacht 1964:73; Coulson 1964:234.
12. Cevdet Pasha, quoted in Berkes 1964:167.
13. Al-Mahmassani 1961:45; Chehata quoted in Liebesny 1975:99; Udovitch 1970:86; Wakin 1972:38n.
14. Quoted in Liebesny 1975:68–69.
15. Liebesny 1975:93.
16. Onar 1955:296. Outside of Turkey, the *Majalla* served for many years as the basic civil law of a number of successor Arab states (Liebesny 1975:89–93; al-Mahmassani 1961:46–48, where several commentaries on the *Majalla* are mentioned).
17. *Majalla* report, pp. 3, 9.
18. Al-Mahmassani (1961:45) notes that limitations on the freedom of contract were eliminated by Art. 64 of the Ottoman Code of Civil Procedure, as amended in 1914.
19. Anderson 1959:81. Cf. Gibb (1947:108), quoted in Said (1978:281), "petrified." Other examples of "immutability": Liebesny 1975:4; Crone 1987:18. Turner (1974:105) refers to the shari'a as a "fixed code." Gellner's reference to the shari'a as a "blue print" is appropriately criticized by Asad (1986:3, 14).
20. See Eickelman (1978) for citations; Goody (1968:14) writes that "under these conditions book-learning takes on an inflexibility that is the antithesis of the spirit of enquiry which literacy has elsewhere fostered."
21. Maine 1861:10–11, emphasis in original.
22. Compare Weber 1978:821, "The sacred law could not be disregarded; nor could it, despite many adaptations, be really carried out in practice."
23. E.g., Weber 1978:815–22; Schacht 1964:1, Anderson 1959:2.
24. Quoted in Liebesny 1975:94.
25. Vesey-Fitzgerald 1955:85; Schacht 1964:1; cf. Hodgson 1974:74.
26. Anderson 1959:4.
27. Schacht 1964:112–14.
28. E.g., "heart" (Anderson 1959:15, 82); "core" (Berkes 1964:169, 467).
29. Schacht 1964:76; Udovitch 1970:7; Liebesny's concentric circles (1975:56).
30. On this complex theme, see Goitein 1968; Rosenthal 1947:5; Peters

1972:13–19; and, with specific reference to the shari'a, the debate about possible Roman law origins, Weber 1978:818–19; Vesey-Fitzgerald 1951; Schacht 1959; Liebesny 1975:33–36; Crone 1987.

31. Quoted in Bennoune 1976:205.

32. Hamilton 1870 [1791]:xxxi. Cf. Said 1978:75, 77–78; al-Mahmassani 1961:49.

33. Anderson 1959.

34. See Johsen 1987:112–14. One late manifestation was seventeenth-century Roman Catholic confessional works. From the time of Pascal's devastating attack in 1663 on Jesuit casuists, the method has "carried the opprobrious sense of moral sophistry" (1987:113), and dictionaries now define casuistic thought as "intellectually dishonest" and "disingenuous." Maine recounts the fall of casuistry in the West in the following terms: "Casuistry went on with its dexterous refinements till it ended in so attenuating the moral features of actions, and so belying the moral instincts of our being, that at length the conscience of mankind rose suddenly in revolt against it, and consigned to one common ruin the system and its doctors" (1972 [1861]:207). The specific critique of casuistry was integral to the wider rejection of earlier discursive modes associated with a fundamental shift in the episteme of Western culture (Foucault 1970:51–52).

35. Schacht 1964:121. Examples of casuistic approaches in Islamic law are given in Schacht 1964:205–6; cf. Weber 1978:821, and Liebesny 1975:31–33, where Roman and Muslim texts are compared. There is, however, a concept-oriented *alfaz* literature, concerned with definitions and linguistic usages—e.g., al-Nawawi n.d.

36. Mitchell 1988; Ziadeh 1968:19; Abu-Lughod 1963; Said 1978.

37. Quoted in Liebesny 1975:79–80.

38. For a view of the subsequent history of the new codes in Turkey, see Starr 1978, 1989; Starr and Poole 1974.

39. Schacht 1964:87. A similar attitude was behind the abolition of the legal authority of custom for the Muslim population of British India by means of the Shariat Act of 1937 (1964:96).

40. Van Den Berg 1894:viii. Hurgronje (1957 [1898]:267) maintained that the study of Islamic law was important for "practical purposes." "The more intimate the relations of Europe with the Muslim East become, the more Muslim countries fall under European suzerainty, the more important it is for us Europeans to become acquainted with the intellectual life, the religious law, and the conceptual background of Islam."

41. Compare the attitude of commentator al-Ghazzi to the existence of versions of the Abu Shuja' *matn*. As Keyzer (Keijzer) notes (1859:xxx), al-Ghazzi incorporates frequent references to alternative wording found in different manuscripts. This inclusive method contrasts with the exclusive approach of the Western translators, who were concerned to create a monovocal definitive "text."

42. Bousquet 1935:193. Keyzer was also an early translator (in 1853) of al-Shirazi's *Kitab al-tanbih*, later translated by Bousquet (1949). In his "Introduction," Keyzer (1859) provides a history of Dutch scholarship on such legal texts. While the French specialized in Maliki law, and the British in Hanafi, Dutch colonial interests dictated that they would be the main early translators of the key Shafi'i works. Like those after him, Keyzer looked back critically upon the work of earlier translators, including a translator into Latin who was "not up to his task" (xxvi). In his own work he says he follows the approach of Perron, the French translator of Khalil.

43. Van Den Berg 1894:xi.

44. Bousquet 1936. Van Den Berg was also harshly attacked by Hurgronje for his work on al-Nawawi's *Minhaj*. See Schacht and Bousquet 1957:xii–xiii.

45. *Al-hai'a al-'ilmiyya li-taqnin ahkam al-shari'a al-islamiyya*. Created by Laws number 4 and 7 of 1975; an Ibb judge was among those appointed. A new panel was appointed by Decree 59 of 1988. Cf. Hubaishi (1988:30, 55).

46. *Al-Thawra* newspaper (San'a'), Sept. 26, 1974.

47. Compare the Egyptian Constitution of 1971 and the United Arab Emirates Provisional Constitution of 1971, in which shari'a principles are a "major source" for legislation, *Middle East Journal* 26 (1972).

48. *Al-Tashri'at*. Throughout the period of important legislative efforts in the Y.A.R., Husain 'Ali al-Hubaishi served as the influential Legal Advisor and Director of the Legal Office (see al-Hubaishi 1988:143–45).

49. Laws number 24, 42, 77, 78, and 127 of 1976, all published in *al-Tashri'at*, vol. 4.

50. Procedure: number 121 of 1976. Civil Code: numbers 10 and 11 of 1979 (*al-Jarida al-Rasmiyya* 14, no. 4 [1979], Appendix). Al-Hubaishi (1988:99) includes 27 of 1979 and 17 of 1983 as included in the four-part Civil Code. Two other laws drafted by the commission were on Shari'a Evidence and the Conduct of the Judge (number 90 of 1976) and on Building Rents (number 27 of 1976).

51. Al-Hubaishi (1988:45–46). He also refers (1988:99) to the Civil Code as "mixed," combining "shari'a rules and secondarily Euro-Arab Civil Codes." French law, mediated through Egypt, was the source for the new Public Prosecution legislation (Messick 1983b). Article 1 of the Y.A.R. Civil Code may be compared (in Liebesny 1975:95) with articles 1 and 2 of the Syrian (1949) and Libyan (1953) codes, which it resembles, and the Egyptian (1949) and Iraqi (1951) codes, from which it differs in that the latter place custom ahead of the shari'a. Unlike the Syrian and Libyan codes, however, in the Y.A.R. code there is no reference to natural law, and both custom and equity are conceived in fiqh categories and as shari'a constituted (*al-'urf al-ja'iz shar'an* and *al-'adala al-muwafiq li-usul al-shari'a*).

52. Hubaishi 1988:119, in reference to Family law. Speaking of the Civil Code, he says (1988:99n), "The legislator did not try to be strictly obligated

to either school [the Zaidi or Shafi'i] and resorted to other schools when necessary."

53. Civil Code, Book 2, chap. 1, Title. Cf. note 59 below.

54. Civil Code, Arts. 36, 87.

55. Law 39 of 1976, *al-Tashri'at* 4:319–458. Although they do not figure in the new Commercial Code, Yemen has a lengthy tradition of market regulations, including both *hisba* works and the *Qanun San'a'* (al-Sayaghi 1964; trans. Serjeant, in Serjeant and Lewcock 1983:179–240).

56. Law 45 of 1976, *al-Tashri'at* 4:459–75.

57. Law 40 of 1976, *al-Tashri'at* 4:772–76.

58. Yemen Arab Republic (1971). See also, al-Abdin 1976:115–25. Cf. *EI* 2, art. "Dustur."

59. Yemen Arab Republic (1971); al-Abdin 1976:119.

60. I prefer Pickthall (1976) to the translations in the *Middle East Journal* document, in which there are two errors in the verse numbers. It is 159, not 15, of Sura 3, and 38, not 78, of Sura 27.

61. Kerr 1966:134; cf. Berkes 1964:232–33; Tyan 1960:230–36.

62. Yemen Arab Republic (1971), chap. 4, part I, arts. 44–71.

CHAPTER 4

1. In addition to his autobiography (n.d., ca. 1979), which covers his early years, there is a brief biographical sketch of al-Qadi Muhammad on the back cover of his general history (1971). He taught at the al-Ma'ain madrasa in the village of the same name near Ibb, and he served as judge in Dhi Sufal and as a member of the *hai'at al-shari'a* in Ta'izz.

2. Al-Nawawi 1884:248. The verb used is from the same root that gives *ta'zir*, the discretionary punishment capacity of the judge, although the judge has a different sort of responsibility for these acts. Cf. Eickelman (1978:494) on the positive understandings of such punishments.

3. On "*adab al-mi'lama*," specifically Quranic school comportment rules, see M. al-Akwa' n.d.:46ff. Yemeni works on *adab* include al-Husayn b. al-Qasim, *Adab al-'alim wa al-muta'allim*, San'a', 1926, and M. al-Shawkani, *Adab al-talab*, 1979. See also Metcalf 1984.

4. On the rights and duties of child care (*hadana*) and custody, see al-Nawawi 1884:97–103; 1883:158–59; and Abu Shuja'/al-Ghazzi 1894:536–41; on guardianship, al-Nawawi 1883:22–23; on legal incapacity (*hajr*) and minority and majority, al-Nawawi 1883:16–18; Abu Shuja'/al-Ghazzi 1894:98–99, 112–13; on rites for the newborn, including the first cutting of hair and an associated sacrifice (*'aqiqa*), al-Nawawi 1884:310–11, Abu Shuja'/al-Ghazzi 1894:648–53; on circumcision for females and males, al-Nawawi 1884:251; on the commencement of praying, al-Nawawi 1882:63–64, Abu Shuja'/al-Ghazzi 1894:112–13.

5. There are seven conditions for a woman to have this right of *hadana*: she must be discerning or rational, free (not slave), of the appropriate religion, chaste, just or trustworthy, have a fixed residence, and be separate (from her husband and not remarried).

6. The important structural parallel of Quranic school with craft apprenticeship is noted in Eickelman (1978:491, 494). Ibn Khaldun considers the study of *'ilm* as "one of the crafts" (*min jumlat al-sana'i'*).

7. Al-Nawawi 1883:18. The examination should be repeated two or more times, before *bulugh* according to some jurists and after it according to others.

8. "Les êtres vivants sont 'mis en texte,' mues en signifiants des regles (c'est une intextuation), et, d'autre part, la raison ou le Logos d'une société 'se fait chair' (c'est une incarnation)" (De Certeau 1979:3).

9. The term *'aqiqa*, according to al-Ghazzi and Abu Shuja' (1894:648–50) refers in the language to the hair on the head of the newborn, and in the shari'a to the sacrifice. A child's first haircutting is another important ritual mode of physically marking a social being. The general rules of sacrifice are elaborated in another manual section.

10. These are known as the *humada*, *shikma*, and *kiswat al-wafa'*, respectively. For a twentieth-century Yemeni "folklore" account of childbirth customs, see al-Wasi'i (1928:308).

11. M. al-Akwa' (n.d.:78–88) discusses children's games; cf. Serjeant (Serjeant and Lewcock 1983:525–28).

12. Cf. Fayein 1955.

13. On the *khatam* generally, see the article in *EI* 2; in Morocco, the ceremony often marked the complete memorization of the Quran; cf. Eickelman 1985. The *khatma* was a handwritten or printed (in Hyderabad) copy of the Quran bought for school memorization purposes (M. al-Akwa' n.d.:40).

14. *Qadi* means "judge" in Arabic, but in Yemen the word also refers generally to educated individuals of other than *sayyid* (descendant of the Prophet) background.

15. On this usage specific to instruction, see Serjeant and Lewcock 1983: 316; for another meaning, *SEI*, art. "al-Muhadjirun." On the related concept of *hijra*, concerning the separation and protection of people (*muhajjarin*) and places, see Serjeant and Lewcock 1983:40–43; Dresch 1989. Travel for knowledge was an old practice; cf. chapter 1 and, generally, Eickelman and Piscatori 1990. For al-Juwayni, *ghurba*, foreignness, or absence from one's native place, was considered one of the "requisites of knowledge" (Makdisi 1981, frontispiece).

16. *Tibb*, medicine, is an example of a branch of learning acquired outside the *madrasa*, generally without teachers, directly from books and personal experience. In an imamic order of 1719 (original in the possession of Ahmad al-Basir), an Ibb man named Ibrahim al-Basir is described as a *tabib*, a doctor, a "curer (*mudawi*) of the inside and the outside." Although nothing further is

known about this man's training or skills, his medical tradition was an old and distinguished scholarly specialization.

Qasim Shuja' al-Din was one of the *tabib*s of twentieth-century Ibb. Born in a rural village, he had come to enroll as a poor student in the Ibb mosque school in 1917, the last year of Ottoman rule. Although he attained full competence and esteem in the core fields—jurisprudence, hadith studies, and the language sciences—and was locally recognized as an *'alim* and teacher, Qasim's particular intellectual inclination was toward medicine and the curing arts. This combination of a jurist's training with medical interests is not unusual (e.g., al-Khazraji 1914:93); even Imam Yahya wrote cures (Rihani 1930:133). Shared assumptions, terminologies, techniques, and the analogical method connect the two fields.

Qasim's principal textual sources were the well-known authoritative compilations of simples by Ibn al-Baytar (d. 1248), a botanist and pharmacologist from Malaga, and Da'ud al-Antaki (d. 1599), a doctor born in Antioch. A third major source was the compilation by the Yemeni Rasulid Sultan al-Muzaffar (1975). Through Ibn al-Baytar, Qasim was familiar with al-Razi and Ibn Sina, among the Muslim doctors, and Discorides and Galen among the Greeks. When I knew him, Qasim was also an avid collector who climbed the mountainside or wandered along the margins of terraces, head down in search of plants. His interests were the prescription of simples, dream interpretation, dietary regulation, and both recitational and written cures, for possession, impotence, and other problems. He had no expertise in such licit techniques as bloodletting and cauterization, the second formerly practiced in Ibb by Jewish moris; practices he considered illicit, such as some forms of magic; and still others he did not credit, such as hypnotism, occasionally attempted by one of the town judges. He dated his interests in curing to an event that occurred before he began to study medicine. One of his students fell into a seizure, with hands flailing and head bobbing. Qasim recited to him the "Chair" verse (2:255) and then the Cave and Hatab chapters (18, 111) from the Quran, both of which mention "fire." A jinn cried out "You've burned me" and was expelled to end the seizure. Up to that point Qasim only knew what everybody knew about the jinn, that they existed (cf. Quran 55:15). As a student of the shari'a, he was also conversant with the legal incapacity implications of being possessed (*majnun*). Qasim was not among those, including a *nazila* from Ibb, who tranced or otherwise summoned the jinn (e.g., al-Shawkani A.H. 1348, 2, appendix, p. 208). His standard curative technique involved a specialized type of recitation, mobilizing potent words. Qasim's written cures included amulets and writing on plates, using either Quranic text or formulae composed of the names of God, or combinations of words, letters, and numbers. He mastered the subsciences connected with the names of God, the letters of the alphabet, and numerical squares. Amulets are worn directly on the patient's body or written on objects that come into direct contact with the body, such as a woman's comb. The writing placed on plates is dissolved by a liquid, and the word is incorporated.

17. Rosenthal 1970:82.

18. For comparative examinations of the *madrasa*, see Fischer 1980, on the "scriptural school," and Makdisi 1981. The use of *darasa* as a noun with this voweling occurs early in Yemen (Ibn Samara 1957:227). Cf. also *darsa*, meaning "student" (M. al-Akwaʿ n.d.:44, 46); *al-darsiyya*, "the lesson," ibid., p. 53.

19. Ibn Khaldun's view of the Quran as the "basis of instruction, the foundation for all the habits (*malakat*) acquired later on" (1958, 3:300–301), quoted at the beginning of this chapter, is complicated by a second passage, which states, "no [scholarly] habitus can originate from the [study of the] Quran, because no human being can produce anything like it" (ibid., p. 303). These two views are consistent with my argument in chapter 1. The Quran is, paradoxically, both the end and the beginning of the *kitab*. The general scholarly problematic is one of crafting texts in the world of the Text.

20. Eickelman 1985:63; cf. 56, 62.

21. Such an individual could become a specialist in Quranic recitation or seek employment as an imam of a mosque (cf. I. al-Akwaʿ 1980:187, quoting a document stipulating that an imam must be a *hafiz*).

22. Because of the presence of blind students, the Hazr in Ibb is sometimes called *dar al-makfufin*. Biographical histories contain many entries on blind scholars, who are usually identified as "al-darir."

23. Disputation was taught in Yemen (Zabara 1956:45; al-Shawkani A.H. 1348, 2:219).

24. He used the word *ijtihad* here. For such usage (i.e., *mujtahidan fi talab al-ʿilm*) in the context of studying efforts, al-Burayhi 1983:87, 102.

25. Al-Shawkani A.H. 1348, 2:215.

26. See chapter 6 herein, on libraries.

27. Zabara 1956:114; al-Akwaʿ 1980:11. In the town of Zabid, al-Akwaʿ notes, this practice continues. In the northern highlands in the same month it was customary to recite works on inheritance.

28. Al-ʿAmri (1985:132, n. 11) where further references are provided.

29. Al-Shawkani A.H. 1348, 2:218.

30. Al-Shawkani, biography in A.H. 1348, 1:360f.

31. Al-ʿAmri 1985:107: "The idea of the *ijazah* was at first purely concerned with the Hadith and its science."

32. Al-Burayhi 1983:99.

33. On *waqf*, see article in *SEI*; and in connection with instruction, Makdisi 1981. For further details on *waqf* in Ibb and Yemen, see Messick 1978, chaps. 7, 8; Serjeant and Lewcock 1983:151–54, 315–16, 427–31. There were also less permanent forms of support. A common formula of support was *itʿam al-taʿam*, to provide board, literally "food," but also sometimes clothing, supplies, and expenses (see I. al-Akwaʿ 1980:188, 194, 202). In about A.D. 1300, according

to al-Khazraji (1911:265), a noted teacher from nearby Ta'izz moved with his students to Ibb. His lesson circle had expanded to over a hundred students, and the mosque where he had been teaching was too small. The people of Ibb (*ahl ibb*) undertook to provide for the expenses (*kifaya*) of the teacher and his large following.

34. In 1975, according to Ibb Endowments Office records, there were twenty-two active, endowment-supported mosques and nineteen that were former or inactive mosques (including those in ruins, displaced by construction, or used only as Quranic schools). Three were women's mosques, with women imams and caretakers; two other mosques originally had separate men's and women's sections. Three were recent, located in new quarters. At least seven contain tombs of "saints" or founders, the most famous being that of Sayf al-Sunna in the Sunni Mosque. There were also several privately administered mosques.

35. *Musawwadat al-darasa*, Maktab al-Awqaf, Ibb. I wish to thank al-Qadi Muhammad al-Ghurbani, al-Qadi Yahya al-'Ansi, and al-Qadi 'Abd al-Karim al-Akwa' for assistance.

36. The *'aqil* for a somewhat later period said there were as many as two hundred muhajirin during his tenure. Eligibility for endowment support and for residence in the Hazr was obtained through a document of attestation, signed by the mufti and other notables.

37. Compare a text quoted in al-Akwa' (1980:187–88) on instruction in Shafi'i jurisprudence in a mosque-school in Rasulid Ta'izz.

38. Compare al-Akwa' (1980:281) on reading to a founder's soul as part of an Ottoman (founder d. A.H. 967) period endowment in Zabid for the study of both Shafi'i and Hanafi jurisprudence.

39. That of Isma'il Basalama, written in a plague year; he actually lived another thirty years, so these particular endowments were not enacted. The charitable acts of his father Muhammad b. 'Abd Allah Basalama (d. 1889) included repairing waterworks and minarets in Ibb, Jibla, and surrounding villages; providing daily allotments of bread to the poor at his house; providing clothing for widows and orphans; creating cemeteries; and establishing endowments for the Great Mosque and for darasa in Ibb (Basalama family sources; al-Akwa' 1987; cf. I. al-Akwa' 1980: 255). His brother Ahmad 'Abd Allah also founded a darasa waqf for Ibb (*musawwadat al-darasa*, Maktab al-Awqaf, Ibb).

40. Also on the "private" side of the waqf institution is another very important category, the "descendant's endowment" (*waqf 'ala al-dhurriyya*).

41. This type of document is known as a *tanazul*, a "stepping down" from the position of *nazir*, administrator. In an Ibb document dated A.H. 1363, the position is transferred to a man, "and his descendants (*awladihi*) after him." The recitational duty, which is always detailed, here includes reciting one-half of a section (*juz'*) of the Quran every day, to the soul of a woman and her brother.

42. I have the documentation for recitational waqfs that were the subject of extended legal battles in several Ibb families.

43. In local instruments, the following lines are found: "As for him who transfers or alters [the waqf], I am his adversary, in the hands of God"; or, "As for him who transfers or alters [the waqf], upon him is ... the curse of God and the curse of all the people"; or, "As for him who transfers or alters or corrupts it [the waqf], ... he is exposed to the wrath of God and has become like those afflicted with helplessness by the spirits (*shayatin*) of the earth."

Al-Akwa' (1980:256–60) quotes the text of a Tahirid prince, who also undertook charitable works in Ibb. The following litany of rhymed prose threats is aimed at those who would subvert his endowment: "He who desires to alter this, or some of it, or corrupt it, or invalidate it, whether guardian or peasant, or interpreting scholar, or judge or heir, whether by open expression, or concealed sign, or violent seizure, or out of greed or fear—he will .bring ruin upon himself, and invalidate his integrity. Agonizing will his boldness be for him: he will deviate from his religion, scorn that which is sacred to him, and distain his pledges. He will justify the curse upon him, the curse of the prophets, the curse of the cursers among his good fellow men, ... and he will draw near to Satan, the evil one, with the lowest of the lowly. God will not accept from him either transactions, legal acts, religious duties, or supererogatory works."

Once created, endowments often suffered from the depredations of administrators, officials, and rulers. Al-Akwa' (1980:12) summarizes the fate of many early schools and their associated endowments as follows: "Most [of the schools] fell into ruin through neglect by the endowment administrators and officials; some rulers took over the endowments, appropriating them for their own use. Also, the majority of the pious endowments created by the kings and princes for their schools were illegal [in the first place]."

CHAPTER 5

1. Author unknown, Arabic script in my files. I want to thank Ahmad b. 'Abd al-Karim al-Akwa', an Ibb teacher and a frequent actor, for his assistance with this and other skits.

2. Al-Wasi'i 1928:118, 175. After A.H. 1295 [1878], the Ottoman governor of Yemen, Isma'il Haqqi Pasha, established both schools and new military units; after A.H. 1315 [1897], Governor Husayn Hilmi Pasha founded the Office of Ma'arif and Schools (*makatib*), a teachers school (*dar al-mu'allimin*), a vocational school, and a secondary school. An Ottoman Annual for the Province of Yemen for A.H. 1304 [1886] mentions the existence of *rushdiyya* and secondary schools (Salname, p. 201 [SOAS Library call no. E. Per 280670]).

3. Young 1905, 2:352–88; cf. Lewis (1968:83–89, 113–14, 181–83), Berkes (1964:99–121, 173–92), Shaw and Shaw (1977:106–15, 249–51). The

Memduh Commission of 1904 found that by 1900 the Ottoman Public Education Law was in application in Yemen and that the system worked well (Mandaville 1984:24–25).

4. *EI* 2, art. "Ma'arif"; Berkes 1964:99–110.

5. According to the famous Educational Dispatch of 1854, British colonial officials considered it "a sacred duty to confer upon the natives of India those vast moral and material blessings which flow from the general diffusion of useful knowledge." Quoted in Furnivall 1948:375; cf. 371–407.

6. Al-Wasi'i 1928:118; cf. Bury 1915:171, 180—Ottoman military education was German influenced. The first new units of Yemeni troops (known as the Hamidiyya) were almost immediately disbanded. According to al-Wasi'i (1928:119), "there was no benefit to their having existed." While the Ottomans instituted military colleges in the three largest towns, the training of Yemeni troops remained limited. Imam Yahya later endeavored to build upon the important idea of a standing professional army. Among the publications of the imam's press were two military instruction manuals (Rossi 1938:574–77). Cf. Mitchell (1988:36–39) for a discussion of an early-nineteenth-century Ottoman military pamphlet.

On official occasions, the local Ottoman detachment in Ibb, totaling (according to the district accounting summary of 1916) sixty-seven men in ten ranks and composed of Turks, Arabs, Circassians, Kurds, Albanians, and Laz, paraded with flags and sang martial songs to the accompaniment of a military band. The two most important military events of the period for the town were the 1904 Zaidi siege and World War I. The first was lifted with the arrival of a strong Albanian force, which impressed townspeople both with armaments (new Mausers, machine guns, and a six-inch German field gun) and techniques (signal corps, encampment in tents, and the carrying of dried field rations). When Sa'id Pasha (see fig. 4) attacked the British in Lahj, his force included both regular companies and irregular levies recruited in the Ibb-Ta'izz districts.

7. Based on a new education tax adopted in 1884 (Lewis 1968:182). Art. 195 of the Public Instruction budget legislation provided for the use of *awqaf* funds, however, but these were newly managed (Young 1905, 2:364). On the school taxes levied in Yemen, see Mandaville (1984:24).

8. The document, for *qada' ibb*, has a section for *da'irat al-ma'arif*, listing monthly salaries of 800 *ghurush* for a first-grade *mu'allim rushdiyya*, 400 for a second-grade teacher, and 100 for the caretaker.

9. Cf. Heidborn 1912, 1:252.

10. Rihani 1930:88, 121, 131, 152; al-'Azm 1937, 1:37; Bury 1915:73, 205; Scott 1942:166; Fayein 1955:48; Stookey 1978:187–88; Serjeant and Lewcock 1983:112–14.

11. Mitchell 1988:63–94.

12. Berkes (1964:102–8; 173–76). Although not instituted throughout the

empire until later, the *maktab rushdiyya* schools were contemplated as early as 1838 (Lewis 1968:84, 182).

13. Young 1905:369.

14. Telegrams of the era were received on forms printed in Ottoman Turkish and French. I have photographed examples that were sent from Lahj to Ibb in 1915 (for published examples, see Salim 1982). Bury (1915:164–65) says French was used on the San'a'-Hudayda line, but only Arabic characters (i.e., Ottoman Turkish) on the internal, San'a'-Ta'izz (via Ibb) line.

15. Young 1905:369, Art. 20.

16. Compare Meccan circles of Shafi'i students in the latter part of the nineteenth century: "We are first of all struck by the great difference of ages: in the same circles sit greybeards and beardless boys, striplings and grown men" (Hurgronje 1931 [1888–89]:186).

17. Published in al-Rahumi 1978:228–35. Cf. Article 20 of *Al-mithaq al-watani*, published by the opposition in 1956: "Yemenis enjoy the right of education" (al-Muwafiq 1970:74).

18. Young 1905:367, Art. 9.

19. Young 1905:367, Arts. 11, 12.

20. Young 1905:370–71.

21. R. R. Tronchot, "L'enseignement mutuel en France," cited in M. Foucault (1977:315, n. 5), and Mitchell (1988:70).

22. Class work represents 25 percent and written exams 75 percent of the final grade in each subject. The subjects and their relative weights for a fourth-grade elementary school student in 1975 were *al-tarbiyya al-islamiyya* (150), *al-lugha al-'arabiyya* (100), *al-riyadiyat* (100), *al-mawadd al-ijtima'iyya* (60), *al-'ulum wa al-sihha* (40), *al-tarbiyya al-fanniyya* (20) (*al-tarbiyya al-riyadiyya*, *al-suluk*, and *al-muwazaba* are categories left blank). The report card also has sections for class rank and for attendance.

23. Rihani 1930:131–32.

24. Al-Rihani, cited in Stookey 1978:188 .

25. Al-Wasi'i 1928:293. I follow Salim (1971:590), in his characterization of al-Wasi'i as "quasi-official."

26. Wenner (1967:58, 94), Stookey (1978:210–11), Peterson (1982:86–87).

27. The Ottomans also had a normal-school for teacher training that operated in Istanbul; for his part, the imam opened a *dar al-'ulama' wa al-mut'allimin*. Al-Wasi'i (1928:293) says that "an individual who obtained a degree was sent to one of the villages as a teacher."

28. Al-Wasi'i 1928:207.

29. I. al-Akwa' 1980:284–310; al-Maqbali 1986:44–47. The school was later known as *dar al-'ulum*. I follow the description of al-Akwa' in the following paragraphs. On the house used, cf. Zabara 1956:13.

30. These numbers are from al-Akwaʿ; al-Wasiʿi (1928:293) gives a figure of three hundred students for the early years.

31. Al-Wasiʿi 1928:293.

32. The school's endowment, including properties that produced an annual yield of about a half million old riyals, was constituted out of the redirected revenues of endowments pertaining to (1) saints' tombs (*waqf al-turab*), which were located mainly in Lower Yemen; (2) endowments for mosques that were either deserted or ruined; (3) other endowments of uncertain designation; and (4) properties confiscated from the Ismaʿili community. A new Endowments Office was opened the same year as the school (I. al-Akwaʿ 1980:300–301; cf. Messick 1978).

33. Al-Akwaʿ (1980:291–92) provides a list of these employees and their salaries. For details on students, 1980:290–91.

34. Al-Wasiʿi 1928:293. In reference to the orphans' school, he comments that the program for their instruction exhibits the "utmost order (*ghayat al-nizam*)." On his travels, al-Wasiʿi (1928:5n) studied in Mecca and traveled often to Egypt and Syria; Rossi (1938:580n) says al-Wasiʿi went subsequently to India, Dutch India, and Ethiopia, and was at the time of Rossi's visit about to go to Italy to visit a son who was a student there.

35. A listing of the "most important" books is given in I. al-Akwaʿ 1980: 288–89. The subjects of study, given as the categories of the book listing and in a sample class report card (p. 290), include tawhid, fiqh, usul al-fiqh, faraʾid, balagha, tafsir and ahkam, mustalah al-athar, falak, nahw, sarf, mantiq, hadith, sira, adab ʿilm al-qiraʾat, taʾrikh (one book), and maʿani and bayan.

36. I. al-Akwaʿ (1980:287n) gives an example text. This is virtually identical in structure to military *kafala*s I have for a company (*buluk*, a Turkish term) raised in Ibb in the 1950s.

37. In addition to al-Akwaʿ, see al-Wasiʿi 1928:293–94.

38. Scott (1942:166–67) on a march-past on the ʿid, the Great Feast; Fayein 1955:48.

39. Al-Shawkani 1969; cf. al-ʿAmri 1985:122; Dresch 1984:161,163;1989; Obermeyer 1981; Serjeant 1969:291.

40. Al-Wasiʿi 1928:261. Serjeant (Serjeant and Lewcock 1983:99) quotes this verbatim and without citation. This practice is frequent in the excellent historical summaries in *Sanʿaʾ* and is justified for the sake of brevity and to avoid further burdening an already heavily referenced text. But with a writer such as al-Wasiʿi, this can entail the uncritical reproduction of an imamic line.

41. Cf. the biography on the back cover of Qadi Muhammad's *Al-yaman al-khadraʾ* (al-Akwaʿ 1971). According to Qadi Ismaʿil al-Akwaʿ (taped interview, Feb. 27, 1976), their father was appointed to the Maʿain post in A.H. 1341 [1923]. Among the former Ibb students I knew were ʿAbd al-Karim al-Akwaʿ and Muhammad Yahya al-Haddad, who said he studied at Maʿain with Muhammad al-Akwaʿ in the years A.H. 1351–1364 [1932–1944].

42. Another small Ibb-area madrasa active in this period was at Jarafa, located in what is now one of the town's new northwest quarters. Qasim Shuja' al-Din, the former Great Mosque scholar and Hazr resident and *tabib*, was posted, somewhat against his desires, as the resident instructor. A later instructor was Muhammad al-Wahhabi. While al-Akwa''s school offered advanced instruction similar to that in the Great Mosque, at Jarafa the program was more elementary. The waqf for Ma'ain is known as al-Ghaythi, and represents one of the largest single endowments in the Ibb region at approximately 6,000 *qadah* of annual revenue. The special waqf for Jarafa is Hushaybri.

43. *Jami'at al-islah.* Cf. M. al-Akwa' 1971, back cover; al-Shamahi 1972: 192–96; al-Abdin 1979:36–48; Wenner 1967:91–93; Stookey 1978:216; Peterson 1982:77–80; Douglas 1987. Its members included 'Abd al-Rahman al-Iryani, later to become president of the Republic; 'Abd al-Karim al-'Ansi, a third-generation descendant of al-Shawkani's student Salih and later a republican cabinet minister; and 'Abd al-Rahman b. Muhammad Basalama of the powerful merchant family that had risen to political prominence under the Ottomans.

44. Taped interview Feb. 27, 1976; cf. al-Shamahi 1972:194–95.

45. Jailing attached no permanent stigma to those detained. Upon release, for example, Muhammad al-Akwa' was appointed to a judgeship in Ibb province, and then served briefly on the Ta'izz appeal court.

46. Al-Shami 1975:43–60.

47. Hunter (1968 [1877]:148–51) and Gavin (1975:192–93) for early educational efforts in Aden. For a summary, Luqman 1972:255–68. For details on the later period, see issues of the Colonial Office, *Annual Report on Aden.*

48. Hunter 1968 [1877]:149.

49. The school was located in a converted mill in al-Mashanna, the quarter outside the town walls to the east. There were some sixty students and one teacher, with two classes per day. When the student body increased, assistant instructors were added. The school continued until six months after the 1962 Revolution, at which time it was transferred to the confiscated house of Muhammad Ghalib (a *sayyid*) which became known as *qasr al-jumhuri* (republican palace). At Mashanna, according to former students, the program included religion (*din, tawhid*), history, language sciences, poetry, arithmetic, calligraphy, morals, and Quran recitation (*tajwid*).

50. Gavin 1975:290, 316.

51. E.g., Cahen and Serjeant (1957:25–26); al-Khazraji 1914:381. In the list cited earlier, al-Wasi'i (1928:261–62) includes mention of hostages taken by Imam Yahya.

52. In an autobiographical sketch, the historian Sharaf al-Din (1968, end page) says he studied in the *dar al-'ulum* in Sa'da, circa 1945–50. Ahmad al-Wasi'i, the historian's son, was the director (al-Jirafi A.H. 1365:51).

53. Al-Waysi states (1962:44) that in Ibb and Jibla "there were madrasa

'ilmiyyas on the model of the dar al-'ulum school in San'a'." Cf. on al-Waysi, Serjeant (Serjeant and Lewcock 1983:101).

54. See Messick 1978.

CHAPTER 6

1. Berkes 1964:500f.; Shaw and Shaw 1977:376; Lewis 1968:359.

2. Sabat (1966:327), cited in Obermeyer (1981:180); cf. Serjeant and Lewcock (1983:98, n. 284). Ottoman Annuals (e.g., *Salname* A.H. 1304 [A.D. 1886]) were printed at the press in San'a'.

3. Niebuhr 1792, 2:261. He comments, "The Arabians value chiefly a species of elegance, which consists in their manner of joining the letters, the want of which makes themselves dislike the style in which Arabic books are printed in Europe" (1792, 2:261).

4. Lewis 1968:50–51; Berkes 1964:36ff.; there was also a ban on the importation of printed books (Gibb and Bowen 1957, 2:151).

5. Cited in Lewis (1968:41). In a 1925 speech at the opening of the law school in Ankara, Mustafa Kemal (Ataturk) reflected on the old resistance to printing: "That same might and power, which in defiance of a whole world made Istanbul [from 1453] for ever the property of the Turkish community, was too weak to overcome the ill-omened resistance of the men of law and to receive in Turkey the printing press, which had been invented at about the same time. Three centuries of observation and hesitation were needed... before the old laws and their exponents would permit the entry of printing into our country" (Lewis 1968, 274).

6. Berkes 1964:195.

7. Harris 1893:197; M. al-Akwa' n.d.:40.

8. Mitchell 1988.

9. Mitchell 1988:92, 133–34.

10. Stookey 1978:188.

11. Rossi continues, "Also the children of the elementary school have few printed books available to them; they mostly learn on [wooden] boards which they use like slates or they take notes in notebooks under dictation from the instructor."

12. Among those interviewed were an al-Musannif from Jibla and Muhammad Yahya al-Haddad, from Ibb; al-Haddad was a former diwan secretary for Imam Ahmad and later a republican cabinet minister and published historian (al-Haddad 1976; 1986). He is a third-generation descendant of 'Ali Naji al-Haddad. Muhammad was always very generous in responding to my questions during my years in Ibb.

13. There were a few commentaries on advanced works published in Yemen. On the curriculum list given by I. al-Akwa' (1980:288–89) for the

madrasa 'ilmiyya, four works were available in editions printed by the government press in San'a': two were commentaries on a Zaidi *usul al-fiqh* treatise known as *Al-kafil*, by M. b. Yahya Bahran; one was a commentary on the *usul* work *Al-ghaya*; and one was a work on tafsir by M. b. al-Husayn b. al-Qasim; cf. Rossi (1938:571–72, 578); Renaud (1980–82:317). Two other books published outside of Yemen at early dates are also on the list: *Subul al-salam* by al-Amir on hadith (also studied in Ibb), published in Delhi in 1884, and al-Shawkani's *Nayl al-awtar*, published in Cairo in 1928.

14. Ong (1982) gives a concise analysis of the shift from manuscript to print culture in the West.

15. Al-Haddad went to Dhamar after an initial meeting with al-Wazir in Ibb. In a biographical entry on al-Wazir (Zabara 1979:368–69) it is reported that this imam of the abortive 1948 coup was appointed judge in Dhamar in 1915, later given further responsibilities, and finally transferred elsewhere in 1920. In 1920–21, he took charge of the annual *zakat* collection in Ibb. Al-Haddad left al-Wazir's service after the death of his uncle 'Abd al-Rahman al-Haddad in A.H. 1340 [1922]. Al-Wazir's desire to have the history text in question copied had to do with its prominent treatment of an imam in the al-Wazir line.

16. Rossi 1938:579 . The rate of pay was a thaler (a riyal) per sixteen-page unit (*kurrasah*, pl. *kararis*).

17. The old jurisprudence manuals (e.g., al-Nawawi 1883:159) mention copyists (*warraq*) in sections on the hire (*ijara*) contract. Just as the tailor and the kohl specialist are not responsible for providing thread and kohl when their services are hired, so the copyist is not responsible for providing ink.

18. Examples in al-Shawkani A.H. 1348, 2:219–20; Shuman 1961:43–44. Cf. Makdisi (1986:185) on Islamic "autograph diaries," which consisted of "notes kept by the author for use in writing other historical compositions."

19. Rossi 1938; Obermeyer 1981.

20. Al-Wasi'i 1928:348, 350.

21. Serjeant and Lewcock 1983:101; Serjeant 1979:90. In the Ottoman period, according to Bury (1915:166), Egyptian newspapers were available.

22. Al-Wasi'i 1928:295.

23. On the press in Aden, see Luqman (1972:264–68); some fourteen papers had fleeting existences from 1940 to 1952. In 1877 (Hunter 1968 [1877]:85), there were two printing machines in Aden, one of which was run by the prisoners in the jail, but there were no newspapers.

24. *Sawt al-Yaman* and a newspaper published in Cairo are mentioned by al-Jirafi (1951:257). Cf. Wenner (1967:92–93, esp. n. 17) on this press and its output.

25. Salim and Abu al-Rijal 1976.

26. Rossi (1938:574–77) gives background detail on the Yemeni military of the period.

27. Rossi (1938:580) continues, "The first reading book in use in schools in San'a' in 1937 was the syllabary called *Qa'ida baghdadiyya* (printed in Cairo by 'Isa al-Babi al-Halabi) with annexed brief sections of the Quran."

28. Text of A.H. 1343 [1925] reproduced in *Fihrist kutub al-khizana al-mutawakkiliyya* n.d. [circa mid-1940s]:327.

29. Husayn b. Yahya al-Wasi'i is named in the imamic decree of 1925. There is a brief biographical notice in I. al-Akwa' (1980:300–301); he is also mentioned in the biography of his brother in al-Jirafi A.H. 1365:94. According to al-Akwa', he also taught at the *madrasa al-'ilmiyya*.

30. This appointee is not named in the decree of 1925, but according to al-Akwa' (1980:301) this was al-Qadi Muhammad b. Ahmad al-Hajari, author of *Masajid san'a'* (A.H. 1361 [1942]) and a short tract on Yemeni history (al-Jirafi 1951, "kaf").

31. Zabara 1979:126.

32. A centimeter is defined on p. 342 of the *Fihrist* as "a tenth of a tenth of a meter, which is equivalent to a *dhira'* and a half of the known *dhira'*."

33. Al-hai'at al-'amma lil-athar wa dur al-kutub, founded in 1977 by Command Council Law No. 51 (*al-Tashri'at*, vol. 4, pp. 91–97).

34. The imam refers in this context to an early ruling by Imam al-Mutawakkil 'ala Allah Isma'il (ruled 1644–1676), which also holds for no lending to the descendants in question without a security deposit.

35. Law 51 of 1977 (*al-Tashri'at*, vol. 4), Art. 1, p. 91.

36. Law 51 of 1977 (*al-Tashri'at*, vol. 4), Art. 2:6, p. 92.

37. *Al-kutub al-khattiyya* rather than *al-makhtutat*.

38. Notices section in *Oriente Moderno* signed V.V. (1938:91), citing the official newspaper *al-Iman* of Shawwal, A.H. 1356 [1938]. Al-Jirafi later wrote that the committee was formed in A.H. 1361 [1942] (introduction to Zabara 1979:18), and an editor's footnote corrects this to A.H. 1356.

39. List given in al-Jirafi 1951, "ba'," and notes 1–4 same page. Al-Muta' is called "Father of the Revolution" and credited, in the same years as his official work, with the founding of the first organized opposition group (al-Shamahi 1972:176–84; cf. Stookey 1978:214–16; Douglas 1987:33). In addition to a book written as part of his History Committee activity, he wrote for the newspaper *al-Iman*. He was executed in Hajja for his role in the unsuccessful 1948 coup (Zabara 1979:55–57). Al-Warith edited and wrote for the journal *al-Hikma al-yamaniyya*, which was suppressed by the imam (Zabara 1979:108–10; al-Jirafi A.H. 1365:95). I. al-Akwa' (1980:278–79) writes that "his discussions in his house and his regular articles in *al-Hikma al-yamaniyya* annoyed Imam Yahya Hamid al-Din," and, insulted and depressed by the resulting restrictions imposed upon him, he fell ill and died in 1940 at age twenty-seven. His book on Imam Yahya was "lost" after his death. For his part, the committee head Zabara was "perhaps the first to raise his voice" (Peterson 1982:77) in demands for reform.

40. Breakdown given in al-Jirafi 1951, "b," with footnotes on how this worked out in terms of committee members' writings.

41. Al-Khazraji 1911:1. Cf. al-Jirafi in his opening remarks in Zabara 1979.

42. "Universal" refers to a new, nationalist-era cast to comprehensive histories. On earlier universal histories, cf. Gibb (1962:126).

43. On Sulayman Pasha, see Lewis (1968:347); cf. S. Hurgronje (1931: 165n) on the book "History of the Moslim Conquests," a new "universal history from the Moslim point of view from the time of Muhammad til the year 1885," written by the Shafi'i mufti of Mecca and published there by the government press during Hurgronje's stay.

44. Biographies: al-Jirafi A.H. 1356:94, where al-Jirafi says al-Wasi'i wrote him an *ijaza*; Zabara 1979:410–11; I. al-Akwa' 1980:298; by his son Ahmad in the 4th ed. of *K. al-Azhar* (al-Murtada 1973), before his *Tahdhib al-'uqul*, appendix pp. 39–43; and cf. his own *Al-durr al-farid li-mutafarriqat al-asanid*, with details on his teachers and with an introduction by his son.

45. The bibliography appears at the beginning, before the title page, while later bibliographies are placed at the end. There is an embedded listing of references at the beginnings of Zabara (1929 and 1931:note).

46. Cf. Introduction to Zabara 1979:6–7.

47. In some cases this included being in colloquial. Al-Jirafi's bibliography on page "waw" mentions a history by al-Harazi, and he says that "most of it is in colloquial expression."

48. Biography in Zabara 1979:7–15; cf. also an autobiography referred to.

49. In A.H. 1343 [1924] in San'a', Zabara published *Ithaf al-mustarshidin bi-dhikr al-a'immat al-mujaddidin* (title in text of Zabara 1979:21 differs from bibliography title given p. 13). In A.H. 1345 [1927], al-Wasi'i published in Cairo a work *Al-Badr al-muzil li huzn fadl al-yaman wa mahasin San'a' dhat al-minan*. Al-Wasi'i's *Ta'rikh al-yaman*, which I have repeatedly referred to, followed the next year, and two years later Zabara published both al-Shawkani's famous biographical history *Al-Badr al-tali'* and his own *Nayl al-watar* in Cairo. Several important early Yemeni histories had already appeared in European editions or translations (al-Hamdani 1884–91; al-Janadi 1892; al-Sharji 1903; al-Khazraji 1906–8).

50. The book was completed with the assistance of Zabara's son Ahmad, mufti of the Y.A.R., and was edited by the Center for Yemeni Studies and Research, with the participation of al-Jirafi.

51. *Ithaf al-kabir bi-isnad al-dafatir*. Hyderabad, A.H. 1328 [1910]. Cf. al-'Amri 1985:106–10.

52. Two examples: Zabara 1979:380–81 (an *ijaza* for al-Jirafi, through Muhammad b. Yahya al-Iryani, going back to al-Shawkani); p. 609 (an *ijaza* for one of the Haddads of Ibb, by Sayf al-Islam Ahmad b. Qasim Hamid al-Din).

53. *Al-Yaman: al-insan wa al-hadara*, 1976. Al-Shamahi has been criticized by Western writers for putting himself too much in the forefront of events.

54. In his *Al-madaris* Isma'il al-Akwa' (1980) refers often in footnotes to his own unpublished memoirs.

55. Al-Jirafi 1951, "jim."

56. All published at al-Manar Press in A.H. 1340 [1920–21] with financing provided by Shaykh 'Ali bin Yahya al-Hamdani. Sources: al-Murtada 1973, biography before *Tahdhib al-'uqal* in appendix; al-Jirafi A.H. 1365:94; Zabara 1979:411. Serjeant 1979:124, n. 84, says *Al-Azhar* was printed in Cairo in 1910.

On Zaid bin 'Ali and his *Majmu'*, see references provided in Renaud (1980–82:310–12), and comments and further references in Kazi 1962: 36–40. Zaid's authorship is disputed: Schacht (1950:337), for example, refers to the book as "wrongly ascribed." The publication by Eugenio Griffini in 1919 of a critical edition of the *Majmu'* (*Corpus Juris di Zaid Ibn 'Ali*. Milan: H. Hoepli) was connected with Italian colonial interests of the era in the Red Sea region.

57. *Taqrid* (poetry) or *taqriz* (eulogy), could accompany the text in publication much like excerpts from favorable reviews. The five scholars approached, whose names are listed in the biography, are said to have praised and lauded the work, to have verified the soundness of the method, and to have given Imam Zaid the recognition he deserved. Source: biography in *K. al-Azhar* (al-Murtada 1973, appendix).

58. Al-Jirafi, "Foreword" to Zabara 1979:17, and n. 3.

59. I. al-Akwa' (1980:305); in Zabara 1979:399, it is indicated that the minister of Ma'arif, Sayf al-Islam 'Abd Allah, was involved as well. The date of publication, according to the bibliography in Serjeant and Lewcock (1983) was A.H. 1366–68 [1946–48].

60. On Zabara's many trips, see a section on "rihlatihi," pp. 11–12 in introduction to Zabara 1979, and also details in the biography on p. 585.

61. Al-Wasi'i 1928:318. Al-Wasi'i, who was wearing glasses on his visit, was amazed by the fact that children he encountered cried out in unison, "He has two jewels in his eyes," using the classically correct dual form "naturally."

62. Zabara 1979:564–65 on Muhammad; Isma'il, p. 196. Zabara says Isma'il attended his lessons given in the al-Filayhi Mosque in San'a', "and he asked from me an *ijaza* and I gave him one." See Douglas (1987) on the scholarly-political circles at the al-Filayhi Mosque.

Muhammad al-Akwa' (1971:190–202) discusses earlier generations of scholarly travelers to Yemen. He also describes several trips in search of early inscriptions. In one case he was after one which "the hand of research had not reached" (1971:252, 367n).

The pre-Islamic history of the highlands involves a series of complex "inscription states," polities based on trade, agriculture, and hydraulic expertise.

These early states are known for, in addition to standing architecture, their epigraphic remains, written in an angular, upright South Arabian script that later Arab scholarship would refer to as *musnad* (Ibn Khaldun 1958, 2:381; cf. Pederson 1984:3–5).

63. Salim 1971:590–96, "observations on the sources."

64. Called *lajnat al-ta'lif wa nashr* or *lajnat al-ta'rikh al-yaman*, it was constituted in 1962 with M. al-Akwa' and Ahmad Sharaf al-Din among its members.

65. Established by Command Council Order No. 7 of 1975 and by Order No. 7 of 1976, revised by Order No. 23 of 1977 (these last two published in *al-Tashri'at*, vol. 4, pp. 928–29 and 82). A list of fourteen organizational members (including the Egyptian historian of Yemen, Dr. Sayyid Mustafa Salim) is given, p. 928. An original tie to the Ministry of Education was changed in 1977 to the *ri'asat al-dawla*, the head of state's office. The description of the CYS is as follows: (Art. 1) "The Center for Yemeni Studies is concerned with human and natural studies in the country in the past and the present and the future, and with everything connected with the Yemeni intellectual legacy *(turath)*."

66. Among the future historians who worked as secretaries *(kuttab)* in Imam Ahmad's diwan were al-Shamahi, al-Haddad, Sharaf al-Din, and al-Waysi.

CHAPTER 7

1. Cited negatively by H. L. A. Hart (1961:137) and positively by Stanley Fish (1990:9–10).

2. Cf. for the districts around Aden, Maktari (1971:32) and Anderson (1970:33).

3. I am indebted to Muhammad al-Wahhabi, the mufti of Ibb, for allowing me to spend many afternoons in his diwan. In 1980 he responded to my written request for information about his life with a virtual biographical-history entry: "My life—my birth was in the town of Ibb in the month of Safar in the year 1331 [1912]. When I reached seven years of age I entered the Quranic school and learned the Quran and recitation *(tajwid)* with teachers, among them al-Faqih Muhammad 'Abd Allah al-'Amr and al-Faqih Muhammad bin Muhammad al-Shuwab. After the completion of [these] studies I transferred to the madrasa of the Great Mosque of Ibb and learned the basic principles of jurisprudence, grammar, inheritance, and calculation. Then I transferred to the second class and studied jurisprudence, grammar, rhetoric *(al-ma'ani* and *al-bayan)*, hadith, and usul al-hadith with shaykhs at the Great Mosque school, such as al-Shaykh al-'Allama Qasim bin Naji al-Darasi, al-Faqih al-'Allama Ghalib bin 'Abbas al-Musannif, al-Qadi al-'Allama Ahmad bin 'Ali bin Salih al-'Ansi, his brother al-Qadi al-'Allama 'Abd Allah bin 'Ali bin Salih al-'Ansi, al-Qadi al-'Allama Ahmad bin 'Ali al-Basir, al-Qadi al-'Allama Yahya bin 'Ali bin Naji al-Haddad, al-Qadi al-'Allama, the current Head of the Second

Court of Ibb Province, Ahmad bin Muhammad bin 'Ali al-Haddad, and others. Then I was appointed repetitor (*mu'id*) in the madrasa of the mosque of Ibb, then teacher (*ustadh*) in the madrasa of the mosque of Ibb, then teacher of the madrasa of al-Jarafa outside the town, and I remained a teacher there until my return to the madrasa of the mosque of Ibb as a teacher replacing its greatest teacher al-Faqih Qasim bin Naji al-Darasi [d. 1943]. I stayed in instruction until I was appointed official mufti of Ibb Province; then I was appointed a member of the First Court of Ibb Province, then came my return to the fatwa function for the province. And I have continued to be mufti until this hour." For further detail on twentieth-century Ibb scholars, see al-Akwa' 1987:154–55.

4. As a public institution, the muftiship resembles the Roman *jus publice respondendi* (Weber 1978:797–99; Tyan 1960:221), while in its unofficial aspect, the muftiship is similar to the responsa-delivering Jewish *rav*, a function distinguished from the position of judge and held by such men as Maimonides (Goitein 1971:212, 325).

5. 'Ali Naji al-Haddad (d. A.H. 1311 [1893]), biography in Zabara (1956:148–57); 'Abd al-Rahman b. 'Ali al-Haddad (A.H. 1293 [1876]–1340 [1922]), biography in Zabara (1979:347–48), mufti from the death of his father in 1893 for about eighteen years; Abu Bakr b. 'Ali al-Haddad (A.H. 1307 [1889]–1351 [1932]), biography in Zabara (1979:39–40), was mufti in Ibb until the death of his brother 'Abd al-Rahman in A.H. 1340 [1922]. Ahmad b. Muhammad b. 'Ali al-Haddad (d. 1981) was mufti from 1922, replacing his uncle Abu Bakr, until about 1950.

6. Sayyid Ahmad b. Muhammad Zabara (b. A.H. 1325), son of the famous historian, was appointed to the muftiship in San'a' by 'Abd al-Rahman al-Iryani during his tenure in the late 1960s as president (biographies in al-Jirafi A.H. 1365:53; Zabara 1979 [written by al-Jirafi]:148–51). He married a daughter of Imam Ahmad's and taught the imam's son Muhammad, the future Imam al-Badr. The mufti of the Province of Yemen under the Ottomans was Muhammad Jughman, and before him, Hasan b. Hasan al-Akwa' (biography in Zabara 1979:214–16).

7. See numerous references to early fatwa-giving in I. al-Akwa' 1980; for more recent times, see Zabara 1956, 1:61, on a Hanafi mufti of Zabid; 1956:113–15, mufti of Bayt al-Faqih; 1956, 2:264, mufti of San'a' (d. A.H. 1316 [1898]); 1956:378, mufti of Hadramawt; and 1979:122, Shafi'i mufti of al-Hudayda.

8. Two famous lines of local muftis are from the al-Burayhi and the al-Mufti (al-Hubayshi) families (Ibn Samura 1957:190; al-Khazraji 1914:82; al-Burayhi 1983:100, 112, 117; Zabara 1941:772; 1929:95, 385; 1956:148; cf. al-Akwa' 1980:66). The fatwas of both Muhammad 'Abd al-Rahman al-Burayhi (d. 1459) and 'Abd al-Rahman 'Umar al-Hubayshi (d. 1388) were collected (cf. Brockelman 1943, 2:442; al-Akwa' 1980:156–57; al-'Amri 1985:108–9; Zabara 1958:58).

9. On *fasiq*, al-Nawawi (1884:365, 368). On relative ignorance (*jahl*): "Abu Hanifa expressly permitted the investiture of a Cadi, even if he were not deeply versed in the subtleties of the law" (Gottheil 1908:393; cf. Tyan 1960: 227). But *'adala* and *ijtihad* are both ideally required of a judge by al-Nawawi (1884:364) and al-Ghazzi (1894:672), with some explicit limitations.

10. Cited in the commentary on the *Minhaj* of al-Nawawi by al-Ramli (1967, 8:236-37); cf. Wensinck (1971:118-19). Another hadith, described by an Ibb judge as even more severe, is that "the judge is taken to the edge of Hell, there to either perish for his wickedness or be saved due to his justness." For an evaluation of such hadiths, see Juynboll (1983:77-95).

11. Cf. I. al-Akwa' 1968:89.

12. A longer poem critical of judging during the era of Imam Yahya is reproduced as Appendix D in al-Abdin (1975:291). See also the skit from Ibb translated at the end of chapter 10 herein.

13. Ibn Samura 1957:94, 219, 247; al-Khazraji 1911:58; al-Burayhi 1983: 98; al-Akwa' 1980:272.

14. Cf. a hadith to the same effect in Wensinck 1971:118.

15. Cf. al-'Amri 1985:161.

16. Schacht 1950:96; for Ibb, al-Juwayni n.d.:39.

17. Ibn Khaldun 1958:452. Compare the institution of the imam, or prayer leader (*EI* 1, art. "Salat").

18. Abu Shuja'/al-Ghazzi 1894:676; al-Nawawi 1884:374. Cf. *Al-Azhar* (al-Murtada 1973:283).

19. Gibb and Bowen 1957:137.

20. An agricultural plot with the name al-Jadil was a *waqf* providing annual income for the holder of the Ibb muftiship.

21. According to *Al-Azhar* (al-Murtada 1973:285), the *ujra* of the judge comes from the *mal al-masalih*.

22. In ibid., this is one of the grounds for dismissal.

23. Compare the description of an Ibb judge of the ninth century A.H. (fifteenth A.D.): "He did not pay attention to the leaders (*ahl al-ri'asa*)," al-Burayhi 1983:99.

24. This was Muhammad al-Jughman. See al-Wasi'i 1928:173-74, 201-4; Zabara 1979: 577.

25. See Schacht 1950:98-132; *EI* 2, art. "Kiyas." Hallaq (1989, 1990) argues that *qiyas* comprises more than analogical arguments.

26. Quoted in *EI* 2, art. "Kiyas," p. 239.

27. See art. "Idjma'" in *EI* 2; Hallaq 1986.

28. Through the "nonmotivated" responses of muftis the evolution of the theoretically immutable law occurred "silently" (Tyan 1960:219; cf. Schacht 1964:73; Coulson 1964:142-43).

29. Maktari 1971:33.

30. Twentieth-century muftis surveyed in the former Aden Protectorate reported that when acting unofficially, and when asked for a general opinion

(i.e., not simply for the opinion of their school), they exercised a type of ijtihad they called *bil-fatwa*, which was the lowest of four types (Anderson 1970:38, 370).

31. Al-Shawkani A.H. 1348, 2:223; Brockelmann 1943:819. For other remarks on his mufti activity, see A.H. 1348:219.

32. See *EI* 2, art. "Islah."

CHAPTER 8

1. Wensinck 1971, s.v. "knowledge"; cf. Quranic verses 2:159; 2:174, which use the same k–t–m verb (hide, secrete, conceal).

2. Cf. the usage of the terms *dalala* and *adilla* by the Ibb mufti and al-Qarafi, cited in the previous chapter.

3. This notion of "intermediacy" is also defended by reference to the relations that obtained among individuals of the early generations, who were neither "followers nor interpreters."

4. Hodgson 1974, 1:281; cf. Rahman 1968:3, 19.

5. See Wensinck (1971), s.v. "knowledge"; Rosenthal (1970:78ff.).

6. Al-Shafi'i 1961:87.

7. Cf. M. al-Akwa', "*juhhal al-atfal*," used twice (n.d.:41).

8. The term *daraja*, already mentioned as meaning a "degree" of status difference based on knowledge, refers elsewhere in the Quran (2:228) to a "degree" of difference based on being male instead of female.

9. Examples: al-Hibshi 1980:95; al-'Amri 1985:115f.

10. Beyond the language issues, a long list of social-category and hierarchy-sensitive preferences guide the determination of who should lead the collective prayer. Among these, al-Nawawi (1882:134–37) states, negatively, that "neither a man nor a hermaphrodite may lawfully pray under the direction of a woman or a hermaphrodite"; otherwise preference exists for such things as irreproachable character, scholarly attainment, age, and nobility of descent. "Where two persons are equal in all these respects preference will depend on cleanliness of clothing or body, sonority of voice, nobility of profession, etc." Al-Nawawi goes on to mention preference for the owner of land over an imam who owns nothing, the master over the slave, the lender over the borrower, and the legitimate governor over either the scholar or the landowner.

11. Al-Nawawi 1882:133. Van Den Berg and Howard translate *qari'* as "lettre" and as "one who can read and write"; I have rendered it as "one who can recite." According to al-Nawawi, the untrained are apt to violate recitational purity by omitting a consonant, by not properly pronouncing the doubling of a letter, by pronouncing two distinct letters as one in stammering, or by substituting another letter for the appropriate one.

12. *Sharh al-waraqat* (al-Mahalli n.d.:24, gloss). Jurists differed on the matter of classifying *tawatur*, some identifying it as a type of "acquired" knowledge.

See Zysow (1984) for a discussion of these different points of view. See also the important discussion in Weiss 1985.

13. Al-Mahalli n.d.:24, in gloss.

14. Al-Juwayni n.d.:34.

15. Al-Shafi'i 1961:81–82; al-Shafi'i 1940:357–59.

16. Al-Mahalli n.d.:22, gloss.

17. Hodgson 1974, 2:352. Hodgson says elsewhere (1974:348) that "there were *traces* of inequality both in shari'a and in custom" (emphasis added).

18. Contractual and related idioms (exchange, bargaining, negotiation) have figured prominently in anthropological accounts of North Africa (e.g., Geertz 1979; Rosen 1979, 1984).

19. For an insightful discussion of this "transparency" in a Yemeni context where inequalities were "on display," see Gerholm 1977:188.

20. Al-Nawawi 1884:400f. "Serious" is a rough translation of *muru'a*, which refers to the ideal manly qualities.

21. In al-Ghazzi 1894:700. See the discussions of witnessing in Geertz 1983 and Rosen 1987.

22. Al-Nawawi 1884:402–3.

23. Al-Nawawi 1883:332; cf. Ziadeh 1957. Occupation is one of five criteria to be taken into consideration to determine if a suitor is an appropriate match. The other four are physical defects, free status (instead of being a slave), character, and status according to descent (*nasab*). This last criterion, descent, is dealt with in numerous places in the shari'a manuals. It is one of many elements of the hierarchical context in which Islam emerged not fully revised by communitarian principles. While jurists tended to view the "tribal" as a purely opposite foil for Muslim civilization, many "tribal" structures are integrated into shari'a discourse.

In the marriage-rule context, at the highest level of generality, descent difference means that "a non-Arab is not the equivalent of an Arab woman," but it can also mean that an individual not of Quraysh, the Prophet Muhammad's tribe, is not appropriate for a woman of that group, or, more narrowly still, that one not of the Prophet's immediate descent lines is not suited for a woman of those lines. A variety of status honor is derived from descent, and this is an issue in determining appropriate marriages, both in general and with respect to the exemplary, and specific case of individuals known as "descendants of the Prophet" (*sada*, sing. *sayyid*). In Yemen and elsewhere in the Muslim world blood descendants of the Prophet have often occupied the highest rung of society, exhibiting the purest realization of honor through lineage. In practice, in places such as Ibb, strict endogamy was frequently violated among the *sada* themselves, while endogamy has generally obtained on the level of the elite as a whole considered in relation to the lower social ranks (cf. Bujra 1971).

24. Al-Nawawi 1883:332–33.

25. Al-Nawawi 1883:302.

26. Al-Nawawi 1884:377f.; Abu Shuja'/al-Ghazzi 1894:678; al-Murtada 1973:282.

27. Al-Murtada 1973:282n.

28. For the use of this term in the Hadramawt, cf. Serjeant 1957:14.

29. For an important study of the relation of attire to social hierarchy, see Mundy 1983. See also M. al-Akwa' (n.d.:159–60) for a discussion of the attire of the "three classes" (*tabaqat*).

30. Cf. al-Burayhi 1983:98: "There was love for him in people's hearts, and fear (al-haiba)."

31. Cited in Serjeant 1977:238. In some circles, scholars were objects of disparagement. Amin Rihani's soldier escorts filled his ears with negative comments about jurists.

CHAPTER 9

1. On holding court in houses, cf. Mandaville 1969:72; and *EI* 2, art. "Masdjid"; Tyan 1960:277; al-Murtada 1973:283 n. 2.

2. These perspectives and Weber's "kadijustiz" are criticized in the light of Moroccan shari'a court ethnography in Rosen 1980–81; 1989:58–59.

3. E.g., al-Wasi'i 1928:295, but also in colloquial usage.

4. Serjeant and Lewcock 1983:145, citing *Sirat al-Hadi ila al-Haqq*.

5. Observed by Rihani (1930:89; cf. 90, 104, 129), who is quoted by al-Wasi'i, same page. Also observed by Salvador Aponte, quoted in Salim (1971:478); and by al-'Azm 1937:180–81. Reported also in the official newspaper (Obermeyer 1981).

6. Cf. al-Wasi'i 1928:126–27, on a Turkish wali who is described in the same formulas.

7. On *wajh* as shaykhly honor, see Dresch 1989; 1990.

8. Imam Yahya stopped making himself available in his later years (Obermeyer 1981:189).

9. Starr 1978:115, 122, 189–91, 208, 231, 261, 269; Liebesny 1975:108; Berkes 1964:165. Ottomans in Yemen: al-Wasi'i 1928:175, 211; in earlier periods, al-Khazraji 1911:231; in the nineteenth century in the era of Faqih Sa'id (al-Hibshi 1980:95).

10. Normally, shakwas concern individual–individual matters, although they can represent claims against officials (e.g., al-Wasi'i 1928:178, 211). A right of complaint against judges and other officials had long been fundamental in the Ottoman Empire (cf. *EI* 2, art. "Mahkama: 2. The Ottoman Empire, i. The earlier centuries," pp. 3–5). In Ottoman Ibb, the *shakwa* was known as an *'ard hal*; in Egypt, there were *ardhaljis*, writers of complaints (Ziadeh 1968:22). The Constitution of the Yemen Arab Republic affirms this right (Art. 44): "Yemenis shall have the right to complain to any state organization concerning violations of the laws by public officials or their negligence of the duties of their office."

11. Nizam al-Mulk 1960:14.

12. *EI* 2, art. "Mazalim." Cf. Schacht (1964:51, 54, 189) for *mazalim* jurisdictions as courts of complaints, on *siyasa* as a synonym, and as appellate courts. In the Ottoman Empire the *mazalim* jurisdiction was for more serious criminal and civil cases (Gibb and Bowen 1950:116). A court of complaints was estabished in Saudi Arabia in 1954 (Schacht 1964:88). In preprotectorate Morocco, pashas acted as judges in criminal and civil matters (Rosen 1979:76). Maktari (1971:94) mentions "ruler's tribunals" in the nearby Lahj sultanate. Cf. *EI* 2, art. "Mahkama: ii. The Reform Era (ca. 1789–1922)," pp. 5–9.

13. In 1980 I collected shakwas and inventoried their volume, origin, and type at the two main shakwa-receiving offices in Ibb, those of the governor and of the subdistrict officer.

14. I have a collection of about 100 shakwas delivered to Ibb by mail from outlying districts in about 1950. (Cf. Ibn Khaldun 1958, 1:389f. on mails and the political danger of obstructing them.) One shakwa, dated 1950, is of relevance. It concerns the desired return of five familiar books (identified simply as Diwan Hafiz, Kitab al-Insha', Muluk al-Muslimin, Rihla Nazih Bek, and Kitab al-Shifa') which the petitioner originally gave as a deposit for a now repaid loan of six riyals.

15. A former secretary to Imam Ahmad was my principal source, although this activity has also been described by travelers.

16. *Hajib*—Law 121 of 1976: Art. 104 (*al-Tashri'at*).

17. My study of cases from the Ibb *niyaba* office concerned the first months of its operation in 1980. National *niyaba* case volume from 1981 to 1986 is given in al-'Alimi 1989:218, table 9.

18. Cf. Gerholm 1977:74, 195, n. 7.

19. Unlawful intercourse, false accusation of unlawful intercourse, drinking wine, theft, and highway robbery.

20. Al-Nawawi 1884:376, 379; cf. 418 (accepting secondary testimony), 430 (on a minor a judge might know to have been found); al-Ghazzi 1894:684; al-Murtada 1973:284.

21. See the important comparative discussion of "local knowledge" in Geertz 1983. For Morocco, Rosen has examined the general and specifically judicial patterns of "acquisition of knowledge about other people" (1984:18; 1989).

22. Al-Nawawi 1884:4 (but see p. 329).

23. Al-Nawawi 1884:436. Here I follow Van Den Berg as translated by Howard (Al-Nawawi 1914).

24. Al-Nawawi 1884:427.

25. Al-Nawawi 1884:376.

26. Al-Nawawi 1884:450–51. This specialization was also required to determine the identity of a foundling's father. On the science of *firasa*, see Mourad 1939; Fahd 1966, chap. 3.

27. Also envisioned in the new legislation—*al-sulta al-qada'iyya*, Art. 21.

28. Dorsky 1986; Makhlouf 1979; Myntti 1979.

29. Al-Nawawi 1884:408.

30. Al-Ghazzi 1894:708, 710.

31. Al-Ghazzi 1894:710.

32. Al-Nawawi 1884:446 gives an example concerning establishing the religion of one's parents, which may well be "known."

33. A "standard definition" from al-Qarafi (1967:349) is "the report of something sensible by a group of people whom experience precludes from acting in concert" (quoted in Zysow 1984:14).

34. In the *Majalla* (Arts. 1732–35, p. 250) *tawatur* is used to refer to evidence.

35. A *sharik* could be a partner in commerce, or a tenant farmer, or a co-resident, etc.

36. Cf. *Majalla*, Art. 43: "*al-ma'ruf 'urfan ka-l-mashrut shartan*," perhaps being quoted by the judge.

37. See the cautions in Schacht 1964:62; and counter views in Udovitch 1970.

38. Abu Shuja' 1894:702; al-Nawawi 1884:402. Cf. chap. 8, 20.

39. See Udovitch 1970, 1985. Ibb Chamber of Commerce founded 1974; commercial courts enacted by Law 40 of 1976 (*al-Jarida al-Rasmiyya* 11, no. 3 (1976):4–5. This material will be presented in detail in a later work.

40. See Dresh 1989. The Ibb material will be covered in a later work.

41. Wa yajibu 'ala al-hakim an yahkamu bil-shar' fi mudu' al-shar' wa al-man' fi hukm al-man' (Rossi 1948:33, cited Adra 1982:166).

42. See the discussion on state *qanun* or law as a type of custom, in *EI* 2, art. "Mahkama."

43. These types may be diagrammed as follows:

	official	unofficial
shari'a	court	judicial arbitration
custom	governor	compromise

44. Al-Murtada 1973:283 in Bab al-qada'; cf. Bab al-sulh, pp. 279–80.

45. In *Sharh al-Azhar*, Ibn Miftah A.H. 1357:317, *adab al-qadi* section. The "so long as judgment is not clear" formula occurs as well in the early letters, which also advocate compromise (Serjeant 1984).

46. Quoted, al-Murtada 1973:279n, and in the early letters (Serjeant 1984).

47. Al-Wasi'i 1928:219.

48. *Tafwid* entails various possible categories of powers.

49. Al-Nawawi 1884:366. Al-Nawawi cites both a position that holds it

totally impermissible and a wider view that allows it only when there is no state judge in the district.

50. In an Ibb *tahkim* judgment dated A.H. 1332 [1913], for example, the resolution occurred under shari'a court auspices and included a formal presentation of evidence by witnesses. The mutual agreement of the two parties with the finding is noted at the end of the document. Cf. *Majalla*, pp. 266–67 on *tahkim* rules.

51. Case document dated A.H. 1379 [1959], using the related formula of *ikhtiyar* ("choice")—of the shari'a judge of nearby Dhi Sufal in this instance—as the arbitrator.

52. Published in 'Afif 1982:261 (*wa min warada ilayhi bil-taradi min ghayrihim*); p. 265 (*tahkim shari'at allah*).

53. In 1980, legislation was pending on *tahkim*. Cf. "Mashru' qanun al-tahkim," Lajna Taqnin Ahkam al-Shari'a al-Islamiyya, Majlis al-Sha'b al-Ta'sisi, n.d. (mimeo, 4 pp.), and "Al-Mudhakkira al-tafsiriyya li-mashru' qanun al-tahkim," Ministry of Justice n.d. (mimeo, 11 pp. with an attached 4-page ministry version of the "mashru' "). Copies in my files.

54. Cf. biography in al-Shawkani A.H. 1348, 2:333.

CHAPTER 10

1. Personnel referred to as *ma'murin al-'ilmiyya*, lit. "'ilm officials." Salaries are monthly (in *ghurush*).

2. See *Majalla*, Book xiv, on "actions"; xv on "evidence and decisive oaths"; and xvi on "court organization, judgments, and arbitration" (cf. Liebesny 1975:69; Onar 1955:306–7). These sections were replaced in 1880 by the Code of Civil Procedure, based on French law. Nizamiyya courts were not instituted in Yemen or the Hijaz (*EI* 2, art. "Mahkama").

3. A document dated 1936 [A.H. 1355] summarizes the procedural and organizational rules to be followed in Imam Yahya's court system. This handwritten copy of the original text is reproduced in al-'Alimi (1989:265–71), who remarks that it blends rules derived from abolished Ottoman law with others from *adab al-qadi* in the shari'a.

4. For the Ottoman background, see *EI* 2, "Mahkama: 2. The Ottoman Empire, i. The earlier centuries"; *EI* 2, "Mahkama: 2. The Ottoman Empire, ii. The reform era (ca. 1789–1922)." The Y.A.R. legislation (discussed in chap. 3): republican decree Law No. 5 of 1979, *al-sulta al-qada'iyya* (judicial authority), in *al-Jarida al-Rasmiyya*, vol. 14, no. 2, Feb. 1979, pp. 15–31.

5. Source: *EI* 2, "Mahkama," pp. 3, 6.

6. This began in 1975. For background on the shift from zakat taxes and grain accounting in the old Treasury Office to commercial taxes and cash accounting under the Central Bank, and details on such old offices as the Awqaf, Baladiyya, Amlak, Sadaqa, Anbar, and Wajibat, see Messick 1978.

7. The 1916 Ibb district accounting document also has a section for the Ottoman gendarmes stationed in Ibb, with sixty-seven men in ten ranks.

8. Detailed examples given in Messick 1978.

9. Local men mentioned on the personnel list are from the al-Haddad, al-'Ansi, al-Mufti, and al-Akwa' families—all leading non-sayyid (or "qadi") descent groups in the town. There are two members of local sayyid families. Another important "qadi" family, al-Mujahid, and sayyids from two local descent groups are represented on the district list of "political stipends" (cf. al-Wasi'i 1928:112).

10. Al-Wasi'i 1928:236–39.

11. Al-Wasi'i 1928:207–9, Points One and Two.

12. While Point Six clearly covers the Ibb case, there is some ambiguity in the treaty about whether Lower Yemen might be considered among the regions where the imam could make his Zaidi appointments. In connection with negotiating Point Thirteen, al-Wasi'i (1928:209) mentions "Ta'izz," which at the time included Ibb, and Point Ten of the treaty says that "the government will appoint judges for the Shafi'is and Hanafis except in the mountains (*al-jibbal*)," which could mean only in the coastal plain, the Tihama. That "Ibb town" and Ta'izz were actually considered part of the purely Ottoman sphere is indicated by the biographer of al-'Amri, who was one of the mediators (see al-Jirafi A.H. 1365:139).

13. I have no information about whether these were ever implemented.

14. The dictum of al-Shafi'i (1940:419) is "Muslims have agreed that the Khalifa is unitary, the judge is unitary, the amir is unitary, and the imam." Multiple judges, with separate jurisdictions defined by place, time, or type, are known. Even judges with the same jurisdiction are possible, so long as they do not judge a single case together (al-Nawawi 1884:367). A deputy judge (*mustakhalif*) is also envisioned, with conditions (al-Nawawi 1884:365–66). A judge is advised to consult jurists (al-Nawawi 1884:374). Cf. *EI* 2, art. "Mahkama."

I have translated *mubashir* on the Ibb personnel list as "usher," but there is also a position envisioned in the Da''an Treaty (Point Eight) for *mubashirin* of the "circuit courts," which are supposed to circulate in the rural villages to settle shari'a claims. I have no information concerning the implementation of this treaty provision.

15. Cf. al-Wasi'i 1928:159, where the court personnel in San'a' prior to the Treaty of Da''an were a head judge, who was a Turk, members (*a'da'*), and judgment witnesses.

16. According to an autobiography he wrote for me, al-Haddad's first judicial position was as Ibb mufti. After more than twenty-five years in this post he was appointed (not on his request, he added) to a posting appropriate for the few Shafi'is of "qadi" families fortunate enough to have judgeships: he was sent west of Ibb to the subdistrict of al-Mudhaykhira, where he remained

a judge for eleven years. With the Revolution, he returned to Ibb and turned down the first offer made to him, which would have sent him away from town again. Not long afterward, he was appointed to the judgeship of the Ibb district, a position he held for about ten years, until the judicial reorganization of 1972. At that time he became presiding judge of the new Second Court of Ibb Province. At the same time he was also made head of the Judicial Council of Ibb Province. After the abolition of the district level of administration in 1976, and the consequent reduction of the court structure to two levels, the provincial court (as of 1979, Appeal Court) and subdistrict court (as of 1979, court of first instance), al-Haddad headed the second, until he was retired in 1980.

17. Anderson 1970:32.

18. Al-Yamani's title Shaykh al-Islam was a *laqab* (al-Akwaʿ 1980:297; cf. Zabara 1979:438); al-ʿAmri is referred to as both Shaykh al-Islam and Qadi al-Qudat by his biographer (al-Jirafi A.H. 1365:6).

19. A judgment may be reversed (*naqd*) only if it contains important mistakes: "If he judges by ijtihad and it then becomes clear [that this is] significantly, not subtly, contrary to a text of the Quran or the Sunna or Consensus or Analogy, [then] he or another [judge] should reverse it" (al-Nawawi 1884:376; cf. Schacht 1964:196). Cf. al-Nawawi 1884:406, concerning *naqd* when testimony turns out to have been given by infidels, slaves, or minors (or if both are *fasiqs*, in one opinion).

20. Al-Wasiʿi 1928:237–38. Point Two says, somewhat ambiguously, that the court will handle "shakwas" directed to it by the imam. As al-Jirafi says (A.H. 1365:142), however, the work of this court was to "reconsider rulings of judges, and [either] confirm (*ibram*) or reverse (*naqd*) them." Both terms later became part of the official name of the court, which was initially known simply as *diwan al-istiʾnaf*. Point Four of Daʿan states that judgments requiring the death penalty must be sent to Istanbul for confirmation.

The last Ottoman presiding judge was Khalil Asad, and the first man appointed by Imam Yahya was Husayn al-ʿAmri, who had served as a mediator for the Treaty (al-Wasiʿi 1928:231; cf. p. 219 where al-Wasiʿi refers to al-ʿAmri as his teacher; full biography of al-ʿAmri in al-Jirafi A.H. 1365, with a reference to the appointment on pp. 142–43). Al-Jirafi (biographical notes in al-Akwaʿ 1980:305–6) was one of al-ʿAmri's secretaries at the court. Succeeding presiding judges under Imam Yahya were Sayyid Muhammad Zaid al-Huthi, Sayyid Zaid b. ʿAli al-Daylami (bio. notes in al-Akwaʿ 1980:297–98), al-Qadi Yahya Muhammad al-Iryani (formerly judge in Ibb), and Sayyid Qasim Ibrahim (bio. notes in al-Akwaʿ 1980:302–3). Additional sources: interview with Sayyid ʿAbd al-Qadir ʿAbd Allah, presiding judge of Y.A.R. appeal court, June 22, 1980 (cf. bio. notes, al-Akwaʿ 1980:308), and sources in Ibb.

21. Zabara 1979:348.

22. Among the presiding judges, in San'a', were Sayyid Muhammad Hasan al-Wada'i, Sayyid Yahya Muhammad al-'Abbas, and Qadi 'Ali al-Anisi; and in Ta'izz, Sayyid Ahmad Zabara and Qadi 'Abd al-Rahman al-Iryani. The court in Ta'izz was known for a period as *al-hai'at al-'ilmiyya*, and is said to have ranked higher than the Appeal Court in San'a'. (Sources: same as preceding note.)

After the Revolution, the Appeal Court was consolidated in San'a', until 1979, when additional, province-level appeal courts were instituted as part of the general policy of decentralization. Procedures for appeal were legislated in 1976 in *Qanun al-murafa'at* (Law of Procedure), No. 121 of 1976, published in *Al-Jarida al-Rasmiyya*, vol. 11, no. 8 (Aug. 31, 1976), arts. 188–225, pp. 32–34.

23. This from old men in Ibb and from a limited number of judgments from the period held in private hands. The Ottoman court records themselves have yet to be examined.

24. Both discussed in Sharaf al-Din 1968:13–14.

25. Premodern histories from Lower Yemen abound with mentions of men holding Ibb judgeships (e.g., Ibn Samura 1957:235f., including a list; al-Khazraji 1911 and 1914; al-Burayhi 1983:83–116). Upper Yemen sources for the later Zaidi period down through the nineteenth century provide more scattered notices about individuals posted to southern highland towns and districts. European travelers, who began to arrive in Ibb by the early seventeenth century, were often received by the town judge. In 1609, John Jourdain was so hosted, as was Niebuhr in the 1760s. Niebuhr remarked of judges that "in Turkey, they are reputed very corrupt and selfish: but in Yemen, we found them persons of great worth and integrity, earnest to do prompt and candid justice."

26. Cf. chapter 2.

27. Born 1882 [A.H. 1299], died 1943 [1362]. Biographies in al-Akwa' 1980: 299–300; al-Jirafi A.H. 1365:132; Zabara 1941:203; 1931:391. Al-'Amri (1985:176) refers to al-Iryani as a second-generation disciple of al-Shawkani and mentions that he is author of a work edited by his son 'Abd al-Rahman.

28. He was Hakim in al-Nadira and, later, Hakim al-Maqam in Ibb. He was also married to a woman from an Ibb family and was one of the local leaders of the *jami'at al-islah* and during the Dusturiyya coup of 1948.

29. Both 'Abd Allah b. Muhammad and Hasan b. Ahmad served as Hakim al-Maqam in Ibb in the decade before the Revolution, and the latter made the transition to become hakim of the province after it, while his son and other Iryanis continued to hold local judicial positions in the 1980s. According to his son, Hasan al-Iryani was born ca. 1906 [A.H. 1324] and died ca. 1968 [A.H. 1388]. He worked initially as a court secretary, then his first judgeship was in Ma'bar in ca. 1931 [A.H. 1350], for five years; this was followed by Milhan (Mahwit), eight years; Khaban (Sadda), two years; Sha'ir (Ba'dan), two years; Yarim, five years; then Ibb pre-Revolution, eight years, and post-Revolution, five years. I have a short *hukm* of his from Yarim dated 1949 [A.H. 1369].

Other judges appointed to Ibb in the imamic period were virtually all Zaidis from the northern highlands, including both sayyids and qadis. Under Imam Yahya, al-Iryani was followed as Ibb district judge by Sayyid Hasan al-Warith, from the plateau town of Dhamar. Al-Warith had been among the judges of the diwan of Imam Yahya and was in the Ibb post when he died in 1934 [A.H. 1353], after having previously served in several other towns. He was followed by Sayyid Isma'il al-Marwani, said to be related by marriage to Imam Ahmad. Judges of the Ibb maqam in this period were al-Qadi Muhammad al-Hamdi (father of another national leader), al-Qadi Muhammad al-Ghashim, and al-Qadi Salih al-Fadali. Sayyid Isma'il b. 'Abd al-Rahman al-Mansur, from al-Ahnum, was initially judge of the district and then, under Imam Ahmad, of the province; Sayyid 'Abd Allah b. Ishaq, from San'a' and Hamdan, was judge of the district; and al-Qadi 'Abd Allah b. Salih al-Fadali, from 'Anis, was judge of the subdistrict. In addition to the two Iryanis, al-Qadi Ahmad b. Muhammad al-Wada'i also held the judgeship of the maqam. Both al-Ghashim and 'Abd Allah b. Ishaq were graduates of and former teachers at Imam Yahya's madrasa al-'ilmiyya in San'a'.

An outside judge who figured in a few of the most intransigent local legal battles of these years, involving several powerful town families, was al-Qadi 'Abd Allah b. 'Ali al-Yamani, the son of the former "Shaykh al-Islam" (Zabara 1979:438). Described by Zabara (1979:378) as "one of the greatest scholars of the era," the younger al-Yamani intervened in Ibb cases in the 1940s and 1950s, from his post of "judge of the seat" in Ta'izz, first with Ahmad as governor, then as imam.

30. See Amin Rihani 1930:49 (photo facing p. 52); al-'Azm 1937:289–92. In a document from the early years of Zaidi rule Basalama signs himself, transitionally, as Ibb "district officer"—in both Ottoman and Zaidi idioms—*qa'immaqam 'amil Ibb*. Of Hadrami merchant background, Basalama was a state official (formerly head of the municipality), an active merchant, and a powerful landholding, but town-based, shaykh.

In rural areas under at least nominal state control there tended to be both state officials (district officer and judge) and shaykhly authority. In the immediate Ibb area, Isma'il Basalama managed to combine both types of authority; and in the Shafi'i districts newly acquired by the imam this was sufficient to guarantee his continuance in office.

Although they often accepted appointments as state officers in other districts, shaykhs from Lower Yemen did not relinquish authority over their home districts.

31. Al-Nawawi 1884:368–69. A Sunni imam is intended by al-Nawawi.

32. Isma'il Basalama, Sayyid al-'Abbas ibn al-Imam, Sayf al-Islam al-Hasan, al-Qadi Ahmad al-Sayaghi.

33. Al-Wasi'i 1928:61–62.

34. *EI* 2, "Makhama: 2. The Ottoman Empire, i. The Earlier Centuries," p. 3; cf. further references in Gibb and Bowen 1957:122.

35. Gibb and Bowen 1950:121.

36. E.g., in 'Afif 1982.

CHAPTER 11

1. Cf. Schacht 1964:193, "There are no legal acts which must be embodied in a document."

2. Al-Nawawi 1884:414–15.

3. Compare the perspective in which a document "gives formal expression to a legal act or agreement, for the purpose of creating, securing, modifying, or terminating a right" (*Black's Law Dictionary*, 4th ed., p. 941).

4. Schacht 1964:82–83.

5. Al-Ghazzi 1894:670.

6. Al-Nawawi 1884:411.

7. Al-Nawawi 1884:366; al-Ghazzi 1894:696.

8. Cf. hadith cited in chapter 7.

9. See Shafi'i 1940:240–50; on the formula *al-riwaya shahada*, see Brunschvig 1976:205.

10. Juynboll 1983:264.

11. Al-Nawawi 1884:417f.

12. See al-Ghazzi 1894:680–82.

13. Abu Shuja' (al-Ghazzi 1894:678–80). A judge should specifically avoid giving a judgment in such circumstances. Anger (*ghadab*) is equally dangerous in distorting the words of a witness, p. 702. Cf. the principle of *al-tanassum* in the Zaidi manual (al-Murtada 1973:283).

14. *Wakil*, pl. *wukala'*. An important manual chapter is devoted to "agency" (*wakala*).

15. See Geertz 1979.

16. Ibn Khaldun, cited in Wakin 1972:8; Tyan 1959:12.

17. Al-Nawawi 1884:379.

18. Al-Nawawi 1884:365; cf. Abu Shuja' (al-Ghazzi 1894:674–75).

19. Al-Nawawi 1884:372–77, 379, 384, 391.

20. Al-Nawawi 1884:373.

21. Abu Shuja' (al-Ghazzi 1894:686).

22. Al-Nawawi (1884:382–92) devotes an entire chapter to this important and problematic category of ruling.

23. Al-Ghazzi 1894:686.

24. Al-Nawawi 1884:371–72. See chapter 9 above, on the other possibility, common knowledge.

25. Al-Nawawi 1884:376–77, 436. Cf., for Lahj, Anderson 1970:32.

26. The original list was dated 1934 [1353]. The rule in question, number fourteen, stated, "Reliance upon handwriting is accepted, if the handwriting is known and its writer known for probity" (al-'Alimi 1989:258). See chapter 2, n. 30.

27. A common expression. See, for example, the section "Writing" in M. al-Akwa' 1971:251. Compare also the section in Ibn Khaldun (1958, 2:356), which is cited and discussed in Mitchell 1988:150ff.

28. On this "fear" and on the notion of "loss," see Ibn Khaldun 1958, 3:312, and al-Ramli 1967, 8:321.

29. Command Council Ruling, Law 90, of 1976 (*al-Tashri'at*, 4:805–30).

30. Anderson 1970:32. An office for deed registration was established in Aden in 1871 (Hunter 1968 [1877]:131, 134).

31. The generic word for all types of legal instruments is *mu'amala*, pl. *mu'amalāt*. A notary is a *katib al-mu'amalat*. Other frequently used general terms for documents are *wathiqa* (pl. *watha'iq*); *hujja* (pl. *hujaj*); *waraqa*, (pl. *awraq*). Some types have specific names, and some of these are peculiar to Yemen, or Ibb: for example, a sale contract document is known as a *basira* (pl. *basa'ir*); an individual's inheritance document in Ibb is called a *farz* or *fasl*. Records and some types of receipts are referred to as *sanad* (pl. *sanadat*); or as registers (*daftar*, pl. *dafatir*).

Mu'amala refers colloquially both to the undertaking itself and to the written document in which this is set down. The word has a range similar to the English "transaction," including both "behavior" and, in a technical sense, "pecuniary transaction" (Schacht 1964:145). In the manuals of jurisprudence, the subject matter is broken down into two major sections, the opening *'ibadat* (ritual obilgations) section followed by the longer *mu'amalat* (transactions) section. In the *Sharh al-Azhar*, for example, the first volume contains the *'ibadat* and volumes 2 through 4 the *mu'amalat*.

32. Zabara 1956:875–77, "They burned books and *basa'ir al-amwal*."

33. One instance of theft of *basa'ir* occurred in a case (no. 26 of 1980) heard in Ibb by the new office of the *niyaba* (cf. Messick 1983b).

34. See Frantz-Murphy (1985) for a summary of the state of research on early document use in the Middle East.

35. Local photocopy studios are expert at reproducing documents. Lengthy scrolls are copied by skillfully joining copy sheets together and placing studio seals on the back for security.

36. Serjeant (Serjeant and Lewcock 1983:487b) refers to a practice of *ta'til al-basira*, cancellation of an old sale document by the judge.

37. For a discussion of the legal stratagem, the *hila* (pl. *hiyal*), see Schacht 1964:index, s.v. Al-Nawawi uses the term, e.g., 1884:432.

38. Tyan 1959:13, my translation.

39. Cf. recent legislation touching on documents and forgery: *Qanun al-ithbat al-shar'i wa wajibat al-qadi wa al-tahkim*, Command Council no. 90 of 1976 (*al-Tashri'at* 4:805–30, esp. pp. 819–23).

40. Known more specifically as *katib al-mu'amalat*, or in some contexts, such as marriage, as the *faqih*. Another type of *katib* mentioned earlier is the government administrative assistant or functionary.

41. *Tanzim mihnat al-muhamah.* Command Council Law 81 of 1977 (*al-Tashri'at* 4, Appendix, 57–61). Point 48 concerns the former *wakils.*

42. Ministry of Justice judicial appointment letter of June 16, 1967, translated in Chapter 10 (photocopy in my files): "and forbid those who would profit and unscrupulous legal representatives (*wukala'*) and those of corrupt motives from gathering at the court." Cf. Ziadeh 1968:21; Tyan 1960:262–75.

43. Ibn Khaldun, cited in Tyan 1959:41.

44. See elements of his biography discussed above.

45. Cf. Wakin 1972:41, n. 2. Writers may also be entrusted with a client's documents and keep money on deposit until a transaction is consummated (cf. Schacht 1948:521).

46. Tyan 1959:29, my translation.

47. For *niyya,* cf. Schacht 1964:116; Rosen 1985, 1989.

48. *Milk,* the shari'a category of individually held and alienable land figures in manual sections on the sale contract. Yemen is distinctive (Lebanon being a comparable Middle Eastern case) in the overwhelming historical predominance of the *milk* property form, estimated at between 70 and 80 percent of all cultivated highland land (Dequin 1976, cited in Gerholm 1977:59). The two other significant categories of land rights, endowments (*waqf*) and state lands (*miri*), also have, in Yemen, a close relation to *milk.* Endowment land legally presupposes the prior existence of *milk* rights, out of which an endowment is constituted. While *miri* refers to a type of usufruct holding with ultimate title vested in the state (as in the central Ottoman Empire), in Yemen the small amount of such land is mostly the confiscated former *milk* holdings of the ruling Zaidi imams of this century.

49. Manuals contain chapters on sale, the most important of the "transactions" (*mu'amalat*). The sale contract has been described as a model for the other types of bilateral contracts (Schacht 1964:151–52).

50. Cf. Benveniste 1968:199–200; applied to anthropological discourse in Fabian 1983:82–85 and Fernandez 1985.

51. For the full text, see Messick 1989:36–37.

52. From a comparative perspective, Goody (1986) states that "when writing appears, the concern with truth in time becomes closely linked to the use of written evidence" (p. 154) and, specifically, that "written evidence in court is characteristically given greater truth value than oral testimony" (p. 152). This view is accurate here only to the extent that (1) documentary evidence was always very important in practice, and (2) that it has very recently become important in theory. In this instance the stronger association of writing and truth that has emerged is connected, not with the advent of literacy, but with integration in the Western-framed discursive culture of the world system.

53. Law 72 of 1983 on the regulation of notaries (*umana'*). Qualifications for

the position include being able to read and write; a general understanding of the shariʿa; "being proposed by the citizens of his jurisdiction"; and an examination for those without a degree in shariʿa law. The profession is to be supervised by the judiciary (Hubaishi 1988:174).

CHAPTER 12

1. Al-ʿAzm 1937:164. Salim (1982:25) writes that "the lines of a document turn around themselves such that the last appear inverted in relation to the initial ones." See also the discussion in Khatibi 1974.

2. For other examples of such spiraling correspondence, see Salim 1982.

3. In contrast, Ong (1982:100) gives a quasi-evolutionary theory of changes in the movement of writing. Semitic right-to-left writing is the most "primitive," followed by the back and forth of boustrophedon, then the vertical mode of stoichedon, and "finally" the "definitive left-to-right movement on a horizontal line."

4. In Ibb sale instruments over the last two hundred years, the manual-derived legal terms for the alienation of land and the clause organization of the text are largely invariant. There seems to be no representation in the legal formulas of changing relations of production. For a preliminary discussion of this problem, see Messick 1989.

5. Weber's interests in double-entry bookkeeping and the bureaucratic file are famous (see Weber 1978). Wittfogel (1957:50) writes, "The masters of hydraulic society were great builders because they were great organizers; and they were great organizers because they were great record keepers."

6. In earlier work Goody (1977) developed the comparative significance of the list, and his recent work provides an important comparative view of textual aspects of bureaucracies (1986).

7. Serjeant and Cahen 1957:23–33.

8. For other aspects of administrative change, see chapter 10 and Messick 1978.

9. This was actually a copy of a copy made by the same copyist three years earlier, commissioned in 1928 [A.H. 1346] by the Ibb governor Ismaʿil Basalama, from an original (known as *al-ʿabbasiyya*) that dates from 1764 [A.H. 1178] and which was kept in Sanʿaʾ. It contains a record of individual properties pertaining to the major endowments benefiting the Great Mosque of Ibb and other regional mosques. The copyist was named al-Majdhub, a former Endowments Office functionary whose son worked at the same office and helped me during my research.

The junior al-Majdhub also made decorated administrative (*idari*) calendars, including one prepared for me with lunar-Muslim, solar-Christian, fiscal, and star systems of reckoning. Wittfogel (1957:29) noted that "time keeping and calendar making are essential for the success of all hydraulic economies."

Daniel Varisco has important work in preparation on *Medieval Agriculture and Islamic Science: The Almanac of a Yemeni Sultan.* See also David King (1979) on mathematical astronomy.

10. See chapter 1, p. 29.

11. See examples in Salim 1982. The ones I photographed were sent to the Ottoman governor in Ibb from Sa'id Pasha at the Lahj front in World War I.

12. Photographs of documents dating from the early 1900s in my files.

13. Salim (1982:22) notes that these signatures got more complex over time, something that also occurred with seals. Niebuhr (1792, 2:261) remarked that Yemenis "sign their letters with a sort of cypher, to prevent the possibility of counterfeiting their signature; at least, the great and learned do so." Ibb governors of recent decades signed in an ink color no one else was allowed to use, such as the aquamarine of al-Qadi Ahmad al-Sayaghi in the 1950s. In general, contemporary Yemeni signatures have adapted to the discipline of horizontal lines, such as the signature space on a bank check.

14. Hobsbawm and Ranger 1983. Going further back into the history of Muslim seals and related coinage, it becomes clear that the use of writing and names on seals was not "original." Adoption of these calligraphic forms followed an earlier figural period (Grabar 1973:97–100, 135–36).

15. In a personal communication, Paul Dresch writes that the scholars of Huth in Upper Yemen refer to the spiral shape in such letters by the term *muhawsha* (from *hasha*), and indicate that the intention was decorative (*li-tajmil*). Among the imamic seal-bearing documents I photographed in Ibb are two letters (my numbers 578 and N173) from Imam Yahya to the local governor, Isma'il Basalama, and a document (N148) confirming the choice of a shaykh in nearby Ba'dan, all dated early in 1918, and also an attestation of 1928 for the just discussed foundation register (my number 9). Imam Yahya's seal also appears on an estate-division document I have from 1934. Two, slightly different seals used by Imam Ahmad appear above Appeal Court rulings on the backs of Yarim and Ibb shari'a court judgment documents dated 1950 and 1958. For other published examples of Imam Yahya's seal, see 'Afif 1982:256, 260, 270. A very different triangular seal was placed on envelopes containing such messages as an appointment for an audience (see Scott 1942:173).

16. E.g., an Ibb judgment scroll: "No objection to what the learned scholar Yahya bin Muhammad al-Iryani, may God protect him, wrote, on this date"; or after an appeal, "[May it be] affirmed what was decided by the Appeal Court on this date."

17. Coon 1935:225. In another traveler's summons to a private audience, the handwriting was "smeared with red ochre, a sign made by the Imam with his own fingers, as important as his seal" (Scott 1942:173).

18. It was often the case, however, that the imam would date the text at the end of the spiral before the applications of the seal and the *hamura* (see Salim 1982).

19. Lowick 1983:303–8, photo of coins p. 306.

20. Al-Thawr (1969:466, 468). The emblem (*shi'ar*) is said to be taken from that of the pre-Islamic Himyaritic state in Yemen (cf. M. al-Akwa' 1971:216).

21. For a description of such a section in Ottoman San'a', see Harris 1893 and Serjeant and Lewcock 1983.

22. J. Abu-Lughod 1980; Rabinow 1989.

23. See Mitchell 1988.

24. Weber 1978:957; cf. Goody 1986:105.

25. One of many Yemeni examples is the early-nineteenth-century visit by the imam, accompanied by al-Shawkani and others, to Lower Yemen (al-'Amri 1985:129).

BIBLIOGRAPHY

Abazah, Faruq 'Uthman. 1975. *Al-Hukm al-'Uthmani fi al-Yaman, 1872–1918.* Cairo: al-Maktabat al-'Arabiyya.

al-Abdin, al-Tayib Zein. 1975. "The Role of Islam in the State, Yemen Arab Republic (1940–1972)." Ph.D. diss., Cambridge University.

———. 1976. "The Yemeni Constitution and Its Religious Orientation." *Arabian Studies* 3 : 115–25.

———. 1979. "The Free Yemeni Movement (1940–48) and Its Ideas on 'Reform.'" *Middle Eastern Studies* 15 : 36–48.

Abu-Lughod, Ibrahim. 1963. *The Arab Rediscovery of Europe.* Princeton: Princeton University Press.

Abu-Lughod, Janet. 1980. *Urban Apartheid in Morocco.* Princeton: Princeton University Press.

Abu Shuja', Ahmad. 1859. Précis de Jurisprudence Musulmane. Arabic text and French trans. S. Keyzer [Keijzer]. Leiden: Brill.

———. 1894. (*matn* of Abu Shuja' embedded) al-Ghazzi, Ibn Qasim. 1894. *Fath al-Qarib.* Arabic text and French trans. L. W. C. Van Den Berg. Leiden: Brill.

Abu Zahra, M. 1948. *Al-Shafi'i.* Cairo: Dar al-Fikr al-'Arabi.

Adra, Najwa. 1982. "Qabyala: The Tribal Concept in the Central Highlands of the Yemen Arab Republic." Ph.D. diss., Temple University.

'Afif, Ahmad Jabir. 1982. *Al-Harakat al-wataniyya fi al-yaman.* Damascus: Dar al-Fikr.

al-Akwa', Isma'il b. 'Ali. 1968. *Al-Amthal al-yamaniyya.* Cairo.

———. 1980. *Al-Madaris al-islamiyya fi al-yaman.* Damascus: Dar al-Fikr.

al-Akwa' al-Hiwali, Muhammad b. 'Ali. 1971. *Al-Yaman al-khadra' mahd al-hadara.* Cairo: Matba'at al-Sa'ada.

———. 1987. *Hayat 'alim wa amir.* San'a' : Maktabat al-Jayl al-Jadid.

———. n.d. *Safha min ta'rikh al-yaman al-ijtima'i wa qissat hiyati.* Damascus: Matba'at al-Katib al-'Arabi.

al-'Alimi, Rashad Muhammad. 1989. *Al-Taqlidiyya wa al-hadatha fi nizam al-qanuni al-yamani*. San'a': Dar al-Kalima.

Amedroz, H. 1910. "The Office of Kadi in the Ahkam Sultaniyya of Mawardi." *Journal of the Royal Asiatic Society*, July, 761–96.

al-'Amri, Husayn b. 'Abd Allah. 1984. *Mi'at 'am min ta'rikh al-yaman al-hadith, A.H. 1161–1264 | A.D. 1748–1848*. Damascus: Dar al-Fikr.

————. 1985. *The Yemen in the 18th & 19th Centuries*. London: Ithaca.

Anderson, Benedict. 1983. *Imagined Communities*. London: Verso.

Anderson, J. N. D. 1959. *Islamic Law in the Modern World*. New York: New York University Press.

————. 1970. *Islamic Law in Africa*. London: Frank Cass. (Orig. 1955.)

————. 1976. *Law Reform in the Muslim World*. London: Athlone Press.

Arberry, Arthur J., trans. 1964. *The Koran Interpreted*. London: Oxford.

Arnold, T. W. 1965. *The Caliphate*. London: Routledge and Kegan Paul.

Asad, Talal. 1986. *The Idea of an Anthropology of Islam*. Washington: Center for Contemporary Arab Studies, Georgetown University.

al-'Azm, Nazih al-Mu'ayyad. 1937. *Rihla fi bilad al-'arabiyya al-sa'ida*. Cairo: Matba'at al-Halabi.

al-Azmeh, Aziz. 1986. *Arabic Thought and Islamic Societies*. London: Croom Helm.

al-Bajuri, Ibrahim b. Muhammad. 1974. *Hashiya 'ala sharh Ibn Qasim al-Ghazzi*. 2 vols. Beirut: Dar al-Ma'arifa.

Bakhtin, M. M. 1981. *The Dialogic Imagination: Four Essays*. Translated by C. Emerson and M. Holquist. Austin: University of Texas Press.

Beeston, A. F. L. 1983. "Background Topics," *Arabic Literature to the End of The Umayyad Period*. Cambridge University Press.

Benjamin, Walter. 1968. *Illuminations*. New York: Schocken Books.

Bennoune, M. 1976. "The Origin of the Algerian Proletariat." *Dialectical Anthropology* 1 : 201–24.

Benveniste, Emile. 1968. *Problems in General Linguistics*. Coral Gables: University of Miami Press.

Berkes, Niyazi. 1964. *Development of Secularism in Turkey*. Montreal: McGill University Press.

Bernal, Martin. 1987. *Black Athena*. New Brunswick: Rutgers University Press.

Black, Henry C. 1968. *Black's Law Dictionary*. 4th ed. St. Paul: West Publishing.

Bourdieu, Pierre. 1977. *Outline of a Theory of Practice*. Translated by R. Nice. Cambridge: Cambridge University Press.

————. 1984. *Distinction: A Social Critique of the Judgment of Taste*. Translated by R. Nice. Cambridge: Harvard University Press.

Bousquet, G.-H., trans. 1935–36. "Abrégé de la loi musulmane selon le rite de l'imam El-Chafi'i par Abou Chodja'." *Revue Algerienne, Tunisienne, et Marocaine de Legislation et de Jurisprudence* 51 : 193–207; 52 : 1–16.

————. 1949. "Avertissement," *Kitab et-Tanbih*. Translated by G.-H. Bousquet. Algiers: La Maison des Livres. Pp. 5–8.

Brockelmann, Carl. 1943. *Geschichte der Arabischen Litteratur*. Leiden: Brill.

Brunschvig, Robert. 1976. "Le Système de la Preuve en Droit Musulman." In Brunschvig, *Etudes d'Islamologie*, vol. 2, pp. 201–18. Paris: G.-P. Maisonneuve et Larose.

Bujra, Abdalla S. 1971. *The Politics of Stratification*. Oxford: Clarendon.

al-Burayhi, 'Abd al-Wahhab ibn 'Abd al-Rahman. 1983. *Tabaqat al-sulaha'* (*Ta'rikh al-Burayhi*). Edited by 'Abd Allah al-Hibshi. San'a': Markaz.

Burman, S. B., and B. E. Harrel-Bond. 1979. *The Imposition of Law*. New York: Academic.

Burrowes, Robert D. 1987. *The Yemen Arab Republic: The Politics of Development, 1962–1986*. Boulder: Westview Press.

Burton, Sir Richard. 1893. *Personal Narrative of a Pilgrimage to al-Madinah and Meccah*. 2 vols. London: Tylston and Edwards.

Bury, G. Wyman. 1915. *Arabia Infelix, Or the Turks in Yemen*. London: Macmillan.

Calder, Norman. 1990. "The Ummi in Early Islamic Juristic Literature." *Der Islam* 67(1): 111–23.

Cassirer, Ernst. 1955. *The Philosophy of Symbolic Forms*. Vol. 2. New Haven: Yale University Press.

Caton, Steven C. 1990. *"Peaks of Yemen I Summon": Poetry as Cultural Practice in a North Yemeni Tribe*. Berkeley and Los Angeles: University of California Press.

Chelhod, Joseph. 1975. "La Société Yemenite et le Droit." *L'Homme* 15(2): 67–86.

Clanchy, M. T. 1979. *From Memory to Written Record*. Cambridge: Harvard University Press.

Coon, Carleton. 1935. *Measuring Ethiopia and Flight Into Yemen*. Boston: Little, Brown.

Coulson, N. J. 1956. "Doctrine and Practice in Islamic Law: One Aspect of the Problem." *Bulletin of the School of Oriental and African Studies* 18:211–26.

———. 1964. *History of Islamic Law*. Edinburgh: Edinburgh University Press.

———. 1969. *Conflicts and Tensions in Islamic Law*. Chicago: University of Chicago Press.

Crone, Patricia. 1987. *Roman, Provincial, and Islamic Law*. New York: Cambridge University Press.

De Certeau, M. 1979. "Des outils pour écrire le corps." *Travers* 14(5).

Derrida, Jacques. 1974. *Of Grammatology*. Translated by G. C. Spivak. Baltimore: Johns Hopkins University Press.

Dorsky, Susan. 1986. *Women of 'Amran*. Salt Lake City: University of Utah Press.

Douglas, J. Leigh. 1987. *The Free Yemeni Movement 1935–1962*. Beirut: American University of Beirut Press.

Dresh, Paul. 1984. "Tribal Relations and Political History in Upper Yemen." In *Contemporary Yemen*, edited by B. R. Pridham. London: Croom Helm.
———. 1989. *Tribes, Government, and History in Yemen*. Oxford: Clarendon Press.
———. 1990. "Guaranty of the Market at Huth." *Arabian Studies*, University of Cambridge Oriental Publications, no. 42, pp. 63–91.
Durkheim, Emile. 1933. *The Division of Labor in Society*. Translated by G. Simpson, New York: Free Press.
Eickelman, Dale F. 1978. "The Art of Memory, Islamic Education and Its Social Reproduction." *Comparative Studies in Society and History* 20(4): 485–516.
———. 1985. *Knowledge and Power in Morocco*. Princeton: Princeton University Press.
Eickelman, Dale F., and James Piscatori, eds. 1990. *Muslim Travellers: Pilgrimage, Migration, and the Religious Imagination*. Berkeley and Los Angeles: University of California Press.
Encyclopedia of Islam. 1st and 2nd editions. Leiden: Brill.
Engels, Friedrich. 1972. *The Origin of the Family, Private Property and the State*. New York: International Publishers.
Fabian, Johannes. 1983. *Time and the Other*. New York: Columbia University Press.
Fahd, Toufic. 1966. *La Divination Arabe*. Leiden: Brill.
Fayein, C. 1955. *A French Doctor in Yemen*. London: Hale.
Fernandez, James. 1985. "Exploded Worlds—Text as Metaphor for Ethnography (and Vice Versa)." *Dialectical Anthropology* 10:15–26.
Fihrist Kutub al-Khizana al-Mutawakkiliyya. n.d. San'a': Ministry of Ma'arif Press. Catalogue of books in the Mutawakkiliyya Library, Great Mosque, San'a' (circa 1943).
Fischer, Michael M. J. 1980. *Iran: From Religious Dispute to Revolution*. Cambridge: Harvard University Press.
Fischer, Michael M. J., and Mehdi Abedi. 1990a. "Qur'anic Dialogues: Islamic Poetics and Politics for Muslims and for Us." In *The Interpretation of Dialogue*, edited by Tullio Maranhao. Chicago: University of Chicago Press.
———. 1990b. *Debating Muslims: Cultural Dialogues in Postmodernity and Tradition*. Madison: University of Wisconsin Press.
Fish, Stanley. 1989. *Doing What Comes Naturally*. Durham: Duke University Press.
Foucault, Michel. 1970. *The Order of Things*. New York: Vintage.
———. 1972. *Power/Knowledge*. Edited by C. Gordon. New York: Pantheon.
———. 1977. *Discipline and Punish*. New York: Vintage.
Frantz-Murphy, Gladys. 1985. "Arabic Papyrology and Middle Eastern Studies." *Middle East Studies Association Bulletin* 19(1): 34–48.
Furnival, J. S. 1948. *Colonial Policy and Practice*. Cambridge: Cambridge University Press.

Gavin, R. J. 1975. *Aden Under British Rule 1839–1967*. New York: Barnes and Noble.

Geertz, Clifford. 1973. *The Interpretation of Cultures*. New York: Basic Books.

———. 1979. "Suq: the Bazaar Economy in Sefrou." In *Meaning and Order in a Moroccan Society*, by C. Geertz, H. Geertz, and L. Rosen. Cambridge: Cambridge University Press.

———. 1980. *Negara: The Theater State in Nineteenth Century Bali*. Princeton: Princeton University Press.

———. 1983a. "Local Knowledge." In *Local Knowledge*, by Clifford Geertz. New York: Basic Books.

———. 1983b. "Centers, Kings, and Charisma: Reflections on the Symbolics of Power." In *Local Knowledge*, by C. Geertz, pp. 121–46. New York: Basic Books.

———. 1983c. "Common Sense as a Cultural System." In *Local Knowledge*, by C. Geertz. New York: Basic Books.

Gerholm, Tomas. 1977. *Market, Mosque and Mafraj*. Stockholm: University of Stockholm Press.

al-Ghazzali. 1964. *Counsel for Kings*. Translated by F. R. C. Bagley. London: Oxford University Press.

al-Ghazzi, Ibn al-Qasim. 1894. *Fath al-Qarib*. Arabic text and French translation by L. W. C. Van Den Berg. Leiden: Brill.

Gibb, H. A. R. 1962. "Tarikh." In *Studies on the Civilization of Islam*, by H. A. R. Gibb, pp. 108–37. Boston: Beacon Press.

Gibb, H. A. R., and H. Bowen. 1950 and 1957. *Islamic Society and the West*. Vol. 1, Parts I and II. Oxford: Oxford University Press.

Giffen, Lois. 1971. *The Theory of Profane Love Among the Arabs*. New York: New York University Press.

Gochenour, D. Thomas. 1984. "Towards a Sociology of the Islamisation of Yemen." In *Contemporary Yemen*, edited by B. R. Pridham. London: Croom Helm.

Goitein, S. D. 1968. "The Intermediate Civilization: The Hellenic Heritage in Islam." In *Studies in Islamic History and Institutions*, pp. 54–70. Leiden: Brill.

———. 1971. *A Mediterranean Society*. Vol. 2. Berkeley and Los Angeles: University of California Press.

Goldziher, I. 1981. *An Introduction to Islamic Law*. Translated by A. and R. Hamouri. Princeton: Princeton University Press.

Goody, Jack, ed. 1968. *Literacy in Traditional Societies*. Cambridge: Cambridge University Press.

———. 1977. *The Domestication of the Savage Mind*. Cambridge: Cambridge University Press.

———. 1986. *The Logic of Writing and the Organization of Society*. Cambridge: Cambridge University Press.

———. 1987. *The Interface Between the Written and the Oral*. Cambridge: Cambridge University Press.

Gottheil, R. 1908. "The Cadi: the History of the Institution." *Revue des études ethnographiques et sociologiques* 1:385–93.

Grabar, Oleg. 1973. *The Formation of Islamic Art*. New Haven: Yale University Press.

Graham, William. 1985. "Qur'an as Spoken Word: An Islamic Contribution to the Understanding of Scripture." In *Approaches to Islam in Religious Studies*, edited by R. Martin, pp. 23–40. Tuscon: University of Arizona Press.

———. 1987. *Beyond the Written Word: Oral Aspects of Scripture in the History of Religion*. New York: Cambridge University Press.

al-Haddad, Muhammad b. Yahya. 1976. *Ta'rikh al-yaman al-siyasi*. 3rd ed. Cairo: Dar al-Huna.

———. 1986. *Al-Ta'rikh al-'amm li-l-yaman*. 5 vols. Beirut: Dar al-Tanwir.

al-Hakim, Tawfik. 1989. *The Maze of Justice*. Translated by Abba Eban. Austin: University of Texas Press.

Hallaq, Wael B. 1984. "Was the Gate of Ijtihad Closed?" *International Journal of Middle East Studies* 16:3–41.

———. 1986. "On the Authoritativeness of Sunni Consensus." *International Journal of Middle East Studies* 18:427–54.

———. 1989. "Non-Analogical Arguments in Sunni Juridical Qiyas." *Arabica* 36:286–306.

———. 1990. "Logic, Formal Arguments and Formalization of Arguments in Sunni Jurispridence." *Arabica* 37:315–58.

Hamilton, Sir Charles, trans. 1870 [1st ed. 1791]. *The Hedaya*. Edited by S. G. Grady. London: W. H. Allen.

Harris, Walter B. 1893. *A Journey Through the Yemen*. Edinburgh: Blackwood.

Hart, H. L. A. 1961. *The Concept of Law*. Oxford: Clarendon Press.

Havelock, E. A. 1963. *Preface to Plato*. Cambridge: Harvard University Press.

Heidborn, A. 1912. *Droit Publique et Administratif de l'Empire Ottoman*. Vol. 2. Vienna.

Henry, Jean-Robert, and François Balique. 1979. *La Doctrine Coloniale du Droit Musulman Algerien*. Paris: C.N.R.S.

al-Hibshi, 'Abd Allah b. Muhammad. 1972. *Maraji' ta'rikh al-yaman*. Damascus.

———. 1976. *Al-Sufiyya wa al-fuqaha' fi al-yaman*. San'a': Maktabat al-Jayl al-Jadid.

———. 1979. Mu'allafat hukkam al-yaman. Edited by Elke Neiwohner Eberhard. Weisbaden.

———, ed. 1980. *Hawaliyyat yamaniyya*. San'a': Ministry of Information and Culture.

———. 1983. *Masadir al-fikr al-'arabi al-islami fi al-yaman*. San'a': Markaz al-Dirasat al-Yamaniyya.

Hobsbawm, Eric, and Terrance Ranger, eds. 1983. *The Invention of Tradition*. Cambridge: Cambridge University Press.

Hodgson, Marshall. 1974. *The Venture of Islam*. 3 vols. Chicago: University of Chicago Press.

Hubaishi, Husain. 1988. *Legal System and Basic Law in Yemen*. London: Sphinx.

Hunter, Capt. F. M. 1968. *An Account of the British Settlement of Aden in Arabia*. London: Frank Cass. (Orig. 1877.)

Hurgronje, C. Snouck. 1931. *Mekka*. Leiden: Brill. (Vol. 2 of orig. German 1888–89.)

———. 1957. *Selected Works of C. Snouck Hurgronje*. Edited by J. Schacht and G.-H. Bousquet. Leiden: Brill.

Husayn, Taha. 1981. *An Egyptian Childhood*. Translated by E. H. Paxton. Washington: Three Continents Press.

al-Husayn b. al-Qasim. 1926. *Adab al-ʿalim wa al-mutaʾallim*. Sanʿaʾ.

Ibn al-Amir, Muhammad bin Ismaʿil. 1971. *Subul al-Salam*. 5th ed. Beirut.

Ibn Hajar al-Haythami, Ahmad bin Muhammad. 1897. *Tuhfat al-muhtaj bi sharh al-minhaj*. Cairo.

Ibn Khaldun. 1958. *The Muqaddimah*. Translated by F. Rosenthal. 3 vols. New York: Pantheon.

———. 1981. *Al-Muqaddima*. Beirut: Dar al-Qalam.

Ibn Miftah, ʿAbd Allah b. Qasim. A.H. 1357. *Sharh al-Azhar*. 4 vols. Cairo.

Ibn Samura al-Jaʿadi, U. 1957. *Tabaqat al-fuqahaʾ al-yaman*. Edited by Fuʾad Sayyid. Cairo.

al-Jarida al-Rasmiyya (Official Gazette). Yemen Arab Republic.

al-Jirafi, ʿAbd Allah b. ʿAbd al-Karim. 1951. *Al-Muqtataf min taʾrikh al-yaman*. Cairo: ʿIsa al-Babi al-Halabi.

———. A.H. 1365. *Tuhfat al-ikhwan*. Cairo: al-Matbaʿat al-Salafiyya.

Johsen, Albert R. 1987. "Casuistry." In *The Encyclopedia of Religion*, edited by M. Eliade, vol. 3, pp. 112–14. New York: Macmillan.

Jourdain, John. 1905. *The Journal of John Jourdain, 1608–1617*. Edited by W. Foster. Cambridge: Hakluyt Society.

al-Juwayni, A. Imam al-Haramayn. n.d. "Al-Waraqat." In *Majmuʿ mutun al-usuliyya*, edited by J. al-Qasimi, pp. 27–39. Damascus: Maktabat al-Hashmiyya. (Cf. al-Mahalli.)

———. 1930. "Le 'Kitab al-Waraqat' (trans. L. Bercher)," *Revue Tunisienne*, pp. 93–105, 185–214.

Juynboll, G. H. A. 1969. *The Authenticity of the Traditions Literature*. Leiden: Brill.

———. 1983. *Muslim Traditions*. Cambridge: Cambridge University Press.

Kazi, K. A. 1962. "Notes on the Development of Zaidi Law." *Abr-Nahrain* 2:36–40.

Kennedy, John G. 1987. *The Flower of Paradise*. Dordrecht: D. Reidel.

Kerr, Malcolm. 1966. *Islamic Reform*. Berkeley: University of California Press.

Keyzer (Keijzer), S. 1859. "Introduction." In *Précis de Jurisprudence Musulmane par Abou Chodjaʿ*, translated by S. Keijzer. Leiden: Brill.

Khadduri, Majid, and Herbert Liebesny, eds. 1955. *Law in the Middle East*. Washington: Middle East Institute.

al-Khatib, Muhibb al-Din. 1972. "Muhibb al-Din fi al-Yaman." *Al-Thaqafa* (Algeria) 2(11): 97–103.

al-Khatibi, Abdelkebir. 1974. *La Blessure du Nom Propre*. Paris: Denoël.

al-Khazraji, A. 1911 and 1914. *Al-'Uqud al-lu'lu'iyya*. 2 vols. Cairo: E. J. W. Gibb Memorial Series.

King, David A. 1979. "Mathematical Astronomy in Medieval Yemen." *Arabian Studies* 5:61–65.

Knox-Mawer, R. 1956. "Islamic Domestic Law in the Colony of Aden." *International and Comparative Law Quarterly* 5:511–18.

Lévi-Strauss, Claude. 1966. *The Savage Mind*. Chicago: University of Chicago Press.

Lewis, Bernard. 1968. *The Emergence of Modern Turkey*. Oxford: Oxford University Press.

Liebesny, Herbert J. 1975. *The Law of the Near and Middle East*. Albany: State University of New York Press.

Lowick, Nicholas. 1983. "The Mint of San'a': A Historical Outline." In *San'a'*, edited by R. B. Serjeant and R. Lewcock. London: World of Islam Festival Trust.

Luqman, Ali Muhammad. 1972. "Education and the Press in South Arabia." In *The Arabian Peninsula*, edited by D. Hopwood, pp. 255–68. Totowa, N.J.: Rowman and Littlefield.

al-Mahalli, Jalal al-Din Muhammad. n.d. *Sharh al-waraqat*. Cairo: Matba'at al-Madani.

al-Mahmassani, S. 1961. *The Philosophy of Jurisprudence in Islam*. Translated by F. Ziadeh. Leiden: Brill.

Maine, Sir Henry. 1917. *Ancient Law*. London: J. M. Dent. (Orig. 1861.)

Al-Majalla. 1888 [A.H. 1305]. Arabic translation, third printing. Istanbul: Matba'at al-Jawa'ib.

Makdisi, George. 1981. *The Rise of Colleges*. Edinburgh: Edinburgh University Press.

———. 1986. "The Diary in Islamic Historiography: Some Reflections." *History and Theory* 25(2): 173–85.

Makhlouf, Carla. 1979. *Changing Veils*. Austin: University of Texas Press.

Maktari, A. M. A. 1971. *Water Rights and Irrigation Practices in Lahj*. Cambridge: Cambridge University Press.

Mandaville, Jon. 1969. "The Muslim Judiciary of Damascus in the Late Mamluk Period." Ph.D. diss., Princeton University.

———. 1984. "Memduh Pasha and Aziz Bey: Ottoman Experience in Yemen." In *Contemporary Yemen*, edited by B. R. Pridham. London: Croom Helm.

al-Maqbali, Husayn b. Muhammad. 1986. *Mudhakkirat al-Maqbali*. Damascus: Dar al-Fikr.

Mauss, Marcel. 1967. *The Gift*. New York: Norton.

al-Mawardi. 1915. *Al-Ahkam al-Sultaniyah*. Translated by E. Fagnan. Les statuts gouvernementaux. Algiers.

Meeker, Michael L. 1979. *Literature and Violence in North Arabia.* Cambridge: Cambridge University Press.

Messick, Brinkley. 1978. "Transactions in Ibb: Economy and Society in a Yemeni Highland Town." Ph.D. diss., Princeton University. Ann Arbor: University Microfilms.

———. 1983a. "Legal Documents and the Concept of 'Restricted Literacy.'" *International Journal of the Sociology of Language* 4 : 41–52.

———. 1983b. "Prosecution in Yemen: the Introduction of the Niyaba." *International Journal of Middle East Studies* 15 : 507–18.

———. 1986. "The Mufti, the Text and the World: Legal Interpretation in Yemen." *Man,* n.s., 21 : 102–19.

———. 1988. "Kissing Hands and Knees: Hegemony and Hierarchy in Shari'a Discourse." *Law and Society Review* 22 (4): 637–59.

———. 1989. "Just Writing: Paradox and Political Economy in Yemeni Legal Documents." *Cultural Anthropology* 4 (1): 26–50.

———. 1990. "Literacy and the Law: Documents and Document Specialists in Yemen." In *Law and Islam in the Middle East,* edited by Daisy H. Dwyer, pp. 75–90. New York: Bergin and Garvey.

Metcalf, Barbara Daly, ed. 1984. *Moral Conduct and Authority: The Place of* Adab *in South Asian Islam.* Berkeley and Los Angeles: University of California Press.

Mitchell, Timothy. 1988. *Colonizing Egypt.* Cambridge: Cambridge University Press.

Mottahedeh, Roy. 1980. *Loyalty and Leadership in an Early Islamic Society.* Princeton: Princeton University Press.

———. 1985. *The Mantle of the Prophet.* New York: Simon and Schuster.

El Moudden, Aberrahman. 1983. "État et Société Rurale à Travers la Harka au Maroc du XIXième Siècle." *Maghreb Review* 8 (5–6): 141–45.

Mourad, Youssef. 1939. *La Physiognomonie Arabe et le Kitab al-firasa de Fakhr al-Din al-Razi.* Paris: Geuthner.

Mundy, Martha. 1983. "San'a' Dress, 1920–1975." In *San'a',* edited by R. B. Serjeant and R. Lewcock. London: World of Islam Festival Trust.

———. 1988. "The Family, Inheritance, and Islam: A Re-Examination of the Sociology of Fara'id Law." In *Islamic Law: Social and Historical Contexts,* edited by Aziz al-Azmeh, pp. 1–123. London: Routledge.

al-Murtada, Imam al-Mahdi Ahmad b. Yahya. 1973. *Kitab al-Azhar fi fiqh al-a'imma al-athar.* Beirut: Dar Maktabat al-Hayat.

al-Muwafiq, 'Abd Allah. 1970. *Al-Shi'a fi al-Yaman.* Cairo Matba'at al-Salafiyya.

al-Muzaffar, al-Malik Yusuf ibn 'Umar. A.H. 1395. *Al-Mu'tamad fi al-adwiya al-mufrada.* Beirut: Dar al-Ma'rifa.

Myntti, C. 1979. *Women and Development in the Yemen Arab Republic.* Eschborn, W. Germany: GTZ.

al-Nawawi, Muhyi al-Din Abu Zakariyya. n.d. *Minhaj al-talibin.* Cairo: Dar Ihya' al-kutub al-'arabiyya.

————. 1882. 1883. 1884. *Minhadj at-talibin*. Arabic text and French trans. L. W. C. Van Den Berg. 3 vols. Batavia: Imprimerie du Gouvernement.

————. 1914. *Minhaj al-talibin*. English translation from the French. E. C. Howard. Lahore: Law Publishing Co. Reprint 1977.

————. 1927. *Tahdhib al-asma' wa al-lughat*. Cairo.

————. 1929. *Sharh Sahih Muslim*. 18 vols. Cairo.

Niebuhr, Carsten. 1792. *Travels Through Arabia*. Translated by Robert Heron. Edinburgh: Morison.

Nizam al-Mulk. 1960. *The Book of Government, or Rules for Kings*. Translated by Hubert Darke. London: Routledge and Kegan Paul.

Obermeyer, Gerald J. 1981. "*Al-Iman* and al-Imam: Ideology and State in the Yemen, 1900–1948." In *Intellectual Life in the Arab East, 1890–1939*, edited by Marwan R. Buheiry. Beirut: American University of Beirut.

Onar, S. S. 1955. "The Majalla." In *Law in the Middle East*, edited by M. Khadduri and H. Liebesny, pp. 292–308. Washington: Middle East Institute.

Ong, Walter J. 1982. *Orality and Literacy*. London: Methuen.

Pashukanis, Evgeny B. 1978. *Law and Marxism*. London: Pluto Press.

Pederson, Johannes. 1984. *The Arabic Book*. Translated by Geoffrey French. Princeton: Princeton University Press.

Peters, Frank. 1968. *Aristotle and the Arabs: The Aristotelian Tradition in Islam*. New York: New York University Press.

————. 1972. "Islam as a Western Civilization." *Arab World* 18(3): 13–19.

Peterson, J. E. 1982. *Yemen: The Search for a Modern State*. Baltimore: Johns Hopkins University Press.

Pickthall, Marmaduke, trans. 1976. *The Glorious Koran*. Albany: State University of New York Press.

Plato. 1952. *Phaedrus*. Translated by R. Hackforth. Cambridge: Cambridge University Press.

Playfair, R. L. 1859. *A History of Arabia Felix, or Yemen*. Reprint 1970. London: Gregg International.

Powers, David S. 1986. *Studies in Qur'an and Hadith: The Formation of the Islamic Law of Inheritance*. Berkeley and Los Angeles: University of California Press.

al-Qarafi, Ahmad. 1967. *Al-Ihkam fi tamyiz al-fatawa 'an al-ahkam*. Aleppo: Maktab al-Matbu'at al-Islamiyya.

————. A.H. 1344. *Al-Furuq*. Vol. 1. Mecca: Dar Ihya' al-Kutub al-'Arabiyya.

Rabinow, Paul. 1989. *French Modern: Norms and Forms of the Social Environment*. Cambridge: MIT Press.

Rahman, Fazlur. 1968. *Islam*. Garden City, N.Y.: Anchor.

al-Rahumi, Ahmad, et al., eds. 1978. *Asrar wa watha'iq al-thawra al-yamaniyya*. San'a': Dar al-Kalima.

al-Ramli, Muhammad b. Abi al-'Abbas. 1967. *Nihayat al-muhtaj*. Cairo: Mustafa al-Babi.

Redfield, Robert. 1967 [1955]. "The Social Organization of Tradition." In *Peasant Society*, edited by J. Potter, G. Foster, and M. Diaz. Boston: Little, Brown.

Renaud, Etienne. 1980–82. "Elements de Bibliographie sur le Zaydisme." *IBLA* 146:309–21.

Ricoeur, Paul. 1971. "The Model of the Text: Meaningful Action Considered as a Text." *Social Research* 38:529–62.

Rihani, Ameen. 1930. *Arabian Peak and Desert*. London: Constable.

al-Rihani, Amin. 1951. *Muluk al-'Arab*. 2 vols. Beirut: Matabi' Sadir al-Rihani.

Rosen, Lawrence. 1979. "Social Identity and Points of Attachment: Approaches to Social Organization." In *Meaning and Order in Moroccan Society*, edited by C. Geertz, H. Geertz, and L. Rosen, pp. 19–111. Cambridge: Cambridge University Press.

———. 1980–81. "Equity and Discretion in a Modern Islamic Legal System." *Law & Society Review* 15(2): 217–45.

———. 1984. *Bargaining for Reality*. Chicago: University of Chicago.

———. 1985. "Intentionality and the Concept of the Person." In *Criminal Justice: Nomos XXVII*, edited by J. R. Pennock and J. W. Chapman, pp. 52–77. New York: New York University Press.

———. 1989. *The Anthropology of Justice: Law as Culture in Islamic Society*. Cambridge: Cambridge University Press.

Rosenthal, Franz. 1947. *The Technique and Approach of Muslim Scholarship*. Rome: Pontificium Institutum Biblicum.

———. 1958. Introduction. *Ibn Khaldun, The Muqaddimah*. Vol. 1. New York: Pantheon.

———. 1970. *Knowledge Triumphant*. Leiden: Brill.

Rossi, Ettore. 1938. "La Stampa nel Yemen." *Oriente Moderno* 18:568–80.

Sabat, Khalil. 1966. *Ta'rikh al-tiba'a fi-l-sharq al-'arabi*. Cairo: Dar al-Ma'arif.

Sachau, Eduard. 1897. *Muhammedanisches Recht nach Schafiitischer Lehre*. Stuttgart and Berlin: W. Spemann.

Said, Edward. 1979. *Orientalism*. New York: Vintage.

———. 1983. *The World, the Text, and the Critic*. Cambridge: Harvard University Press.

as-Said, Labib. 1975. *The Recited Koran*. Princeton: Princeton University Press.

Salim, Sayyid Mustafa. 1971. *Takwin al-yaman al-hadith*. 2nd ed. Cairo: 'Ain Shams University.

———. 1982. *Watha'iq yamaniyya*. Cairo: al-Matba'at al-Fanniyya.

Salim, Sayyid Mustafa, and 'Ali Abu Rijal. 1976. *Majallat al-hikma al-yamaniyya wa harakat al-islah fi al-yaman: 1938–1941*. San'a': Markaz al-Dirasat al-Yamaniyya.

Salname (Yearbook for the Ottoman Province of Yemen). 1886. San'a': Government Press. [School of Oriental and African Studies library call no. E. Per 280670.]

al-Sayaghi, Husayn b. Ahmad, ed. 1964. "Qanun San'a'." *Majallat al-makhtutat* 10:273–307.

———, ed. 1978. *Safahat majhula min ta'rikh al-yaman.* San'a': Markaz al-Dirasat al-Yamaniyya.

Sayyid, Ayman Fu'ad. 1974. *Masadir ta'rikh al-yaman fi al-'asr al-islami.* Cairo: Institut Français d'Archéologie Orientale.

Schacht, Joseph. 1948. "Revue de E. Tyan, Le Notariat," *Orientalia,* n.s., 17:519–22.

———. 1959. *The Origins of Muhammadan Jurisprudence.* Oxford: Clarendon Press.

———. 1964. *Introduction to Islamic Law.* Oxford: Clarendon Press.

Schimmel, Annemarie. 1984. *Calligraphy and Islamic Culture.* New York: New York University Press.

Schopen, A. 1978. *Das Qat.* Weisbaden: Franz Steiner.

Schuman, L. O. 1962. *Political History of the Yemen at the Beginning of the Sixteenth Century.* Groningen.

Scott, Hugh. 1942. *In the High Yemen.* London: John Murray.

Serjeant, Robert B. 1951. *Prose and Poetry from Hadramawt.* London: Taylor's Foreign Press.

———. 1955. "Forms of Plea, A Shafi'i Manual from al-Shihr." *Rivista degli Studi Orientali* 30(1–2): 1–15.

———. 1957. *The Saiyids of Hadramawt.* London.

———. 1969. "The Zaidis." In *Religion in the Middle East,* edited by A. J. Arberry, vol. 2, pp. 285–301. London: Cambridge University Press.

———. 1977. "South Arabia." In *Commoners, Climbers and Notables,* edited by C. A. O. van Nieuwenhuijze. Leiden: Brill.

———. 1979. "The Yemeni Poet al-Zubayri and His Polemic Against the Zaydi Imams." *Arabian Studies* 5:87–130.

———. 1984. "The Caliph 'Umar's Letters to Abu Musa al-Ash'ari and Mu'awiya." *Journal of Semitic Studies* 29(1): 65–79.

Serjeant, Robert B., and C. Cahen. 1957. "A Fiscal Survey of the Medieval Yemen." *Arabica* 4:23–33.

Serjeant, Robert B., and Ronald Lewcock, eds. 1983. *San'a'.* London: World of Islam Festival Trust.

al-Shafi'i, Muhammad. 1940. *Al-Risala.* Edited by A. M. Shakir. Cairo: Mustafa al-Babi al-Halabi.

———. 1961. *Islamic Jurisprudence: Shafi'i's Risalah.* Translated by Majid Khadduri. Baltimore: Johns Hopkins University Press.

al-Shamahi, 'Abd Allah. 1937 [A.H. 1356]. *Sirat al-'arifin ila idrak ikhtiyarat amir al-mu'minin.* San'a': Matba'at al-Ma'arif.

———. 1972. *Al-Yaman.* Cairo: Dar al-Huna.

al-Shami, Ahmad Muhammad. 1975. "Yemeni Literature in Hajjah Prisons, 1367/1948–1374/1955." *Arabian Studies* 2:43–60.

Sharaf al-Din, Ahmad Husayn. 1963. *Al-Yaman 'abr al-ta'rikh*. Cairo: Matba'at al-Sunnat al-Muhammadiyya.
———. 1968. *Ta'rikh al-fikr al-islami fi al-yaman*. Cairo: Matba'at al-Kaylani.
al-Sharji, Ahmad. n.d. *Tabaqat al-khawass*. Cairo: Matba'at al-Yamaniyya.
Shaw, Stanford J. 1978. "The Ottoman Census and Population, 1831–1914." *International Journal of Middle East Studies* 9 : 325–38.
Shaw, Stanford J., and Ezel K. Shaw. 1977. *History of the Ottoman Empire and Modern Turkey*. Vol. 2. Cambridge: Cambridge University Press.
al-Shawkani, Muhammad b. 'Ali. A.H. 1348. *Al-Badr al-tali'*. 2 vols. Edited and with an appendix by Muhammad Zabara. Cairo: al-Sa'ada.
———. A.H. 1349. *Irshad al-fuhul*. Cairo: Muhammad Ali Sabih.
———. A.H. 1390. *Al-Sayl al-jarrar*. Cairo.
———. A.H. 1394. *Qawl al-mufid fi adillat al-ijtihad wa al-taqlid*. Cairo: Salafiyya.
———. A.H. 1396. *Umana' al-shari'a*. Cairo: Dar al-Nahda al-'Arabiyya.
———. 1969. *Rasa'il*. Madina: Maktabat al-Salafiyya.
———. 1979. *Adab al-talab*. Edited by 'Abd Allah al-Hibshi. San'a': Markaz al-Dirasat wa al-Buhuth al-Yamaniyya.
Shorter Encyclopedia of Islam. 1965. Leiden: Brill.
Shuman, L. O. 1961. *Political History of the Yemen at the Beginning of the Sixteenth Century*. Groningen.
Starr, June. 1978. *Dispute and Settlement in Rural Turkey*. Leiden: Brill.
———. 1989. "The Role of Turkish Secular Law in Changing the Lives of Rural Muslim Women, 1950–1970." *Law and Society Review* 23 (3): 497–523.
Starr, June, and Jonathan Poole. 1974. "The Impact of a Legal Revolution in Rural Turkey." *Law and Society Review* 8 (4): 533–60.
Stevenson, Thomas B. 1985. *Social Change in a Yemeni Highlands Town*. Salt Lake City: University of Utah Press.
Stookey, Robert W. 1978. *Yemen*. Boulder: Westview Press.
Strothman, R. 1912. *Das Staatsrecht der Zaiditen*. Strasbourg.
al-Tashri'at. Vol. 4 (January 1976–June 1977). Yemen Arab Republic.
al-Thawr, 'Abd Allah b. Ahmad. 1969. *Hadhihi hiya al-yaman*. Cairo: Matba'at al-Madani.
al-Thawra (newspaper). San'a'.
Todorov, Tzvetan. 1981. *Introduction to Poetics*. Translated by R. Howard. Minneapolis: University of Minnesota Press.
Turner, Brian. 1974. *Weber and Islam*. Routledge and Kegan Paul.
Tutwiler, Richard, and Sheila Carapico. 1981. *Yemeni Agriculture and Economic Change*. San'a': American Institute for Yemeni Studies.
Tyan, Emile. 1954. 1956. *Institutions du Droit Publique Musulman*. 2 vols. Paris: Receuil Sirey.
———. 1959. *Le Notariat*. 2nd ed. Harrisa, Lebanon: St. Paul.
———. 1960. *Histoire de l'organisation judiciaire en pays d'Islam*. 2nd ed. Leiden: Brill.

Udovitch, Abraham L. 1970. *Partnership and Profit in Medieval Islam*. Princeton: Princeton University Press.

———. 1985. "Islamic Law and the Social Context of Exchange in the Medieval Middle East." *History and Anthropology* 1 : 445–65.

V.V. 1938. "Nomina di un Comitato per la storia del Yemen." *Oriente Moderno* 18:91.

Vajda, Georges. 1983. "De la Transmission Orale du Savoir Dans l'Islam Traditionnel." In *La Transmission du Savoir en Islam*, by G. Vajda, pp. 1–9. London: Variorum.

Van Arendonk, C. 1960. *Les Débuts de l'Imamat Zaidite au Yemen*. Translated by J. Ryckmans. Leiden: Brill.

Van Den Berg. 1882. "Preface." In *Minhadj at-Talibin*, by al-Nawawi, trans. Van Den Berg, pp. v–xiii. Batavia: Imprimerie du Gouvernement.

———. 1894. "Preface." In *Fath al-Qarib*, by al-Ghazzi, trans. Van Den Berg, pp. v–xii. Leiden: Brill.

Varisco, Daniel M. 1985. "The Production of Sorghum (*Dhurah*) in Highland Yemen." *Arabian Studies* 7 : 53–88.

———. 1986. "On the Meaning of Chewing, the Significance of Qat (*Catha edulis*) in the Yemen Arab Republic." *International Journal of Middle East Studies* 18 : 1–13.

Vesey-Fitzgerald, S. G. 1951. "The Alleged Debt of Islamic Law to Roman Law." *Law Quarterly Review*.

———. 1955. "Nature and Sources of the Shari'a." In *Law in the Middle East*, edited by M. Khadduri and H. Liebesny, pp. 85–112. Washington: Middle East Institute.

Wakin, Jeanette. 1972. *The Function of Documents in Islamic Law*. Albany: State University of New York Press.

al-Wasi'i, 'Abd al-Wasi' b. Yahya. 1928 [A.H. 1346]. *Tarikh al-yaman*. Cairo: al-Matba'at al-Salafiyya.

al-Waysi, Husayn b. 'Ali. 1962. *Al-Yaman al-kubra*. Cairo: Matba'at al-Nahda al-'Arabiyya.

Weber, Max. 1978. *Economy and Society*. 2 vols. Edited by G. Roth and C. Wittich. Berkeley and Los Angeles: University of California Press.

Weir, Shelagh. 1985. *Qat in Yemen*. London: British Museum.

Weiss, Bernard. 1985. "Knowledge of the Past: The Theory of Tawatur According to al-Ghazzali." *Studia Islamica* 61 : 81–105.

Wenner, Manfred W. 1967. *Modern Yemen, 1918–1966*. Baltimore: Johns Hopkins University Press.

Wensinck, A. J. 1922. "The Refused Dignity." In *E. G. Browne Memorial Volume*, edited by T. W. Arnold and R. A. Nicholson. Cambridge: University of Cambridge Press.

———. 1971. *A Handbook of Early Muhammadan Traditions*. Leiden: Brill.

Wittfogel, Karl. 1957. *Oriental Despotism*. New Haven: Yale University Press.

Yemen Arab Republic. 1971. "Permanent Constitution of the Yemen Arab Republic." *Middle East Journal* 25(3): 389–401.

Young, G. 1905. *Corps de Droit Ottoman.* Vol. 2. Oxford: Oxford University Press.

Zabara, Muhammad b. Muhammad. 1929 and 1931 [A.H. 1348 and 1350]. *Nayl al-watar.* Vols. 1 and 2. Cairo: Matbaʿat al-Salafiyya.

———. 1952 [A.H. 1372]. *Aʾimmat al-yaman.* Taʿizz: Matbaʿat al-Nasr.

———. 1956 [1376]. *Aʾimmat al-yaman.* 3 vols. Cairo: Matbaʿat al-Salafiyya.

———. 1941 [1360]. *Nashr al-ʿarf.* Vol. 1. Cairo: Matbaʿat al-Saʿada.

———. 1958 [1377]. *Nashr al-ʿarf.* Vol 2. Cairo: Matbaʿat al-Salafiyya.

———. 1979. *Nuzhat al-nazar.* (Forward by al-Jirafi.) Sanʿaʾ: Markaz.

Ziadeh, Farhat J. 1957. "Equality in the Muslim Law of Marriage." *American Journal of Comparative Law* 5(4): 503–17.

———. 1968. *Lawyers, the Rule of Law and Liberalism in Modern Egypt.* Stanford: Hoover Institution.

Zysow, Aron. 1984. "The Economy of Uncertainty: An Introduction to the Typology of Islamic Legal Theory." Ph.D. diss., Harvard University.

INDEX

References to illustrations are printed in italic type.

al-'Abbas Ibn al-Imam, 194, 309n32
'Abd Allah b . Miftah, 40
'Abd al-Qadir bin Abd Allah, 93, 307n20
al-'Abdin, 'Ali Zain, 50
'Abduh, Muhammad, 150
Abu Bakr, 48, 272n28, 276n40
Abu Da'ud, 45
Abu Hanifa, 18, 143, 299n9
Abu Shuja'. See *Al-Mukhtasar*
Aden, 21, 41; British in, 8, 47, 59, 65, 66,
   101, 110, 224, 254; education in, 112–
   13; nationalism in, 52, 111–12, 119;
   newspapers in, 293n23; and trade, 9, 12,
   47, 111–12, 241
'Afif, Ahmad Jabir, 9
Ahmadiyya school (Ta'izz), 114, 116, 130
al-Akwa', 'Ali b. Husayn, 110, 114
al-Akwa', Isma'il b. 'Ali, 5, 40, 110, 125, 141,
   173, 185, 193, 269n36, 287n43; historical
   writing of, 128, 130; and printing press,
   119, 127; in prison, 111; on schools, 87,
   89–90, 94, 156
al-Akwa', Muhammad b. 'Ali, 5, 47, 97, 125,
   127, 130, 282n1, 291n45, 296n62; jailing
   of, 110, 111; *A Page From the Social History
   of Yemen and the Story of My Life*, 128; on
   Quranic schools, 75–77, 81, 82, 85, 89, 94
Algeria, 62, 65
Amedroz, H., 143
al-Amir, Muhammad Isma'il, 140, 141,
   272n31
al-'Amri, al-Qadi 'Abd Allah, 242

al-'Amri, Husayn b. 'Abd Allah, 267n28,
   271n21, 272nn22, 32, 273n33, 285nn28,
   31, 299n15
al-'Amri, Husayn b. 'Ali, 128, 190, 193, 307n20
Anderson, Benedict, 2, 117
Anderson, J. N. D., 60, 63, 65
al-'Ansi, Salih, 45, 46
al-'Ansi family, 102, 189
Arabic Government School (Aden), 112
Asad, Talal, 2–3, 279n19
al-'Awdi, Muhammad Zain, 114, 197
al-Azhar. See *Kitab al-Azhar*
al-Azhar mosque-university, 20
al-'Azm, Nazih al-Mu'ayyad, 52, 170, 192, 231

Ba'dan, 110, 111
al-Badr, Muhammad, 114
Baghdad, 15, 16, 19, 107, 129, 265n2
Bakhtin, M. M., 166, 265n4, 269n39
Basalama, Isma'il, 47–48, 50, 52, 53, 112, 170,
   192, 193, 194, *232*, 286n39, 309n30, 313n9,
   314n15
al-Basir, Ahmad, 103, 130, 225, 275n38,
   276nn39, 40
Basra, 20
Beirut, 116, 129, 231
Benjamin, Walter, 240
Berkes, Niyazi, 101, 275n38
Bookkeeping, 8, 231, 237–41, 248; inter-
   national (*duwali*) method of, 239
Bourdieu, Pierre, 5, 107, 249, 250, 266n7
Bousquet, G.-H., 66, 67, 281n42

LaVergne, TN USA
05 January 2010
168924LV00004B/36/A